THE
FOOD
BIBLE

THE
FOOD
BIBLE

JEAN CONIL

SUNBURST BOOKS

ACKNOWLEDGEMENTS

To my editor Hilaire Walden
and publisher Suneel Jaitly.

This edition published 1996 by
Sunburst Books
Kiln House, 210 New Kings Road
London SW6 4NZ

Copyright
Text © Jean Conil 1995
Layout and Design © Promotional Reprint Company Ltd 1996

ISBN 1 85778 190 2

Printed and bound in Great Britain

INTRODUCTION

We eat and drink in order to live but, of course, we get pleasure from doing so. Some people take this too far — living to eat, with all the consequent danger of obesity and heart disease. Over-eating is as bad as eating the wrong foods, or malnutrition.

To get the balance right, to buy wisely and eat healthy, safe food, it is necessary to have a knowledge of nutrition, and how to store and cook food correctly. Only then can food be enjoyed sensibly and appreciated in all its subtleties.

Food scientists are responsible for bringing the abundant and varied selection of foods that are found in markets and grocers today. Yet the term food science is but vaguely understood by the majority of people. They have the wrong conceptions of the food scientists' work, and they mistrust additives and many of the practises of the food industry — take for example the scares on irradiation of food for preservation.

Food science today requires many skills and areas of knowledge, such as mathematics, chemistry, physics, rheology, nutrition and microbiology.

Food scientists work closely with engineers to build the equipment to process food, packaging technologists, oceanographers and farmers who are specialists in all the different fields of agriculture.

Food scientists work on projects for poorer countries to help them increase the yields from their crops, and improve diets and financial viability.

The food industry is in a dynamic state of change with more efficient methods of producing higher and better quality goods for the convenience of a more demanding public. But at the end of the day, it is the taste of food that matters most.

This is where chefs come in. They are employed not only in expensive restaurants but also in the food industry to guide the scientists and technologists in producing food that will be acceptable to the consumer.

I have been a chef for many years and it is this experience I've drawn on to produce in this book a blend of all the subjects necessary to prepare tasty, healthy food — recipes, explanations of terminology, ingredients and, I hope, a little of the joy of cooking.

A

AALSUPPE A famous Dutch soup prepared with eels, leeks, cabbage, carrots, turnips, parsley and apples or pears, which are cooked in beer and eaten with buttered rye bread.

AARGAU CARROT CAKE A light sponge cake made with 10 percent grated carrots and 10 percent mixed nuts. It is a Swiss speciality from the town of Aargau, which is famed for using carrots as a sweetener – although some sugar is also used in this recipe.

After baking the cake is traditionally decorated with almond paste shaped into imitation carrots; an optional extra is to wrap the cake in green almond paste.

½ cup/2oz/50g each ground
  almonds, toasted hazelnuts
  and dry brown breadcrumbs
½ cup/2oz/50g all-purpose (plain)
  flour

1 tsp baking powder
1 tsp ground allspice or cinnamon
¾ cup/6oz/175g superfine (caster)
  sugar
7 eggs, separated
2 small carrots, grated
1 tsp grated fresh ginger root

Filling

⅔ cup/5oz/150g cream cheese
⅔ cup/5oz/150g sugar
3 tbsp confectioners' (icing) sugar
1 tbsp lime juice
  or the juice of 1 lemon

Decoration

confectioners' (icing) sugar
or
⅔ cup/5oz/150g cream cheese
8oz/225g almond paste, colored
  pale pink
a few strips of angelica

Optional

8 oz/225g pale green almond paste
  (use 3 drops green coloring)
⅓ cup/4oz/100g apricot jam

Mix together the nuts, breadcrumbs, flour, baking powder and allspice or cinnamon. Beat together the egg yolks and sugar until fluffy. Fold in the mixed dry ingredients, grated carrots and ginger.

Beat the egg whites in a clean bowl and fold them gently into the mixture. Fill a greased and base-lined 7in/18cm springform cake pan (tin) almost to the top.

Bake at 350°F/180°C/gas mark 4 for 45-50 minutes. Cool on a wire rack. Split the cake horizontally into two layers.

To make the filling, beat together the cream cheese, sugar and lemon or lime juice. Use this to sandwich the two cake layers together.

Dust the top with confectioners' (icing) sugar, or spread more cream cheese on top.

For the decoration, shape the almond paste into eight balls and roll them into the shape of carrots. Place them on the cake with little strips of angelica as the carrot leaves.

To cover the cake with pale green almond paste, brush it with the strained melted apricot jam, and cover with a thin circle of almond paste.

ABALONE, ORMER (Fr. ORMEAU) A univalve gastropod mollusk found mainly in the Mediterranean, South Pacific, and on the North and South American coasts. The edible portion is the broad foot of muscle by which the abalone clings to the rocks. The meat is tough and must be tenderized with a meat bat. It can be quick-fried for 30 seconds or cooked slowly for longer.

Abalone can be bought fresh, canned or dried and salted. Like all fresh shellfish, abalone should be alive when purchased and should have a sweet, not fishy, smell. Choose those that are relatively small. The iridescent shell is a source of mother-of-pearl.

ABATTOIR A slaughterhouse where animals are killed and the meat inspected to see if it is suitable for human consumption. If it is, the carcass is stamped.

ABBACCHIO Italian for baby lamb that has been killed between 30 and 60 days old. It is a great speciality of Rome, where it is cooked in several different ways, such as roasting, alla cacciatora, or pot-roasted then mixed with a piquant anchovy and oregano sauce before serving.

ABGAUCHTE A refreshing Iranian chilled soup made up of yogurt, cucumber, dill and lemon juice then garnished with seedless white grapes or raisins.

ABIGNADES A black pudding made from goose in the French Landes region.

A

ABLEMANU An African term for roasted ground corn.

ABOLOO A cornmeal and whole wheat (wholemeal) dumpling, popular in Ghana for use in stews.

ABOUKIR A yeast cake I created. It is baked in a charlotte mold and sliced horizontally in two layers, filled with chestnut and chocolate cream, coated with a coffee fondant and decorated with pistachios.

ACACIA GUM All the gum-yielding acacia trees have the same appearance, differing only in their gum-exuding properties. The gum harvest lasts for two weeks in the November of each year.

There are many kinds of acacia gum found in commercial use, including Kordofan gum, which comes from Egypt and Sudan; Senegal gum, which may either be a good substitute for the above or inferior in quality; Mogadore gum from Morocco and Indian gum, a sweeter gum.

The chemical constituents of acacia gum are arabin, calcium, magnesium and potassium. It is used as a stabilizer in pickles, bottled sauces and confectionery. It is usually mixed with tragacanth gum for a better product.

ACAR CAMPUR A stir-fried Indonesian vegetarian dish of mixed bell peppers, cucumber, beans, root vegetables and macadamia nuts. It is highly flavored with chili peppers.

ACETIC ACID A colorless liquid with a pungent smell. It is prepared from wood and lime heated together, which makes calcium carbide. This, slaked, makes acetylene gas, which in turn is converted to acetic acid. Pure acetic acid looks like a mixture of ice and water, which gives it its name of glacial acetic acid.

Acetic acid is the main ingredient of vinegar. Commercial vinegars contain between three and six percent acetic acid.

Weak acetic acid can be used in place of vinegar, and is less expensive, which is why it is used for commercial bottled sauces, chutneys and pickles. For pickles and chutneys to keep they must contain one percent acetic acid.

Acetic acid is antibacterial and at five percent concentration may be bactericidal. Strong acetic acid is a very caustic and irritant poison. Acetic acid is commercially available in crystal form that can be diluted in water in various amounts depending on the strength of acid required — to a maximum of 10 percent.

ACETOMEL   A sweet-and-sour syrup made up of vinegar and honey and used to preserve fruits such as pears, quince, apricots, peaches, and plums.

ACHAR   An eastern Indian bamboo-shoot pickle. Modern recipes include a mixture of bell peppers, melons, pumpkins, gherkins and mangoes.

ACHIOTE OIL   A cooking oil flavored with annatto seeds. *See Annatto.*

ACHIRA   A species of the canna lily. The roots yield a starch similar to arrowroot which is used as a thickener and stabilizer.

ACID   An acid is any substance that tastes sour in solution with water and changes the color of indicators, turning blue litmus paper red. An acid reacts with some metals, such as iron, to liberate hydrogen and neutralize bases.

Organic acids are found in all fruits and vegetables, in animal flesh, milk and eggs and in all fatty substances. They reinforce the taste of bland products, thus modifying and improving the flavor.

Each acid has a specific name and function. Amino acids are the component parts of protein, just as fatty acids are the substance of fats and oils. Citric acid is found in all citrus fruits, malic acid in apples and pears, lactic acid in milk and meat, and tartaric acid in grapes.

Medically, some weak acids are given to cure dyspepsia, usually after meals, to stimulate digestion in the stomach. Hydrochloric acid (the acid naturally present in gastric juice) or nitro-hydrochloric acid are mainly used.

For excess acid intake, cream of magnesia and baking soda (bicarbonate of soda) are given, with a large amount of water as well.

The degree of a substance's acidity is measured in terms of its hydrogen potential, which is discovered by using an electrical apparatus. The symbol pH is used to denote the degree of acidity, which varies from 0 (very acidic) to 14 (very alkaline). A pH value of 7 is thus the middle of the scale, being the pH of pure water, which is neutral. Any soda solution is alkaline.

ACID DROP   A candy (sweet) made from boiled sugar that has been colored and flavored, and cooked to the hard-crack stage.

ACIDULATED WATER   Acid ingredients such as vinegar or lemon juice are

A

added to the water in which fruits such as avocados, apples, pears, peaches and nectarines, and vegetables such as artichokes, potatoes and celery root (celeriac) are soaked to prevent their discoloration. This is caused by oxidation when these fruits and vegetables are peeled or cut.

ACINI DI PEPPE An Italian pasta the size of a peppercorn, used in soups and consommés.

ACKEE A red fruit from a tree that grows in many Caribbean islands and Jamaica. It bursts open when ripe and is only edible when cooked. It is available in cans and is used in Caribbean cookery in stir-fried vegetables and salt cod mixtures.

ACORDA A Portuguese garlic soup with poached eggs and bread and flavored with fresh coriander.

ACORN (Fr. GLAND DE CHÊNE) Acorns are the nuts of the oak tree. Some species are edible. Acorns can be ground and used as a substitute for coffee or mixed with flour and made into a type of bread.

ACRA An Hispanic salt fish cake dipped in batter and shallow-fried in olive oil. All kinds of salted fish may be used for acra. The fish should be soaked in cold water, cooked, mashed and mixed with the other ingredients such as yams, bananas, breadfruit, nuts, eggplants (aubergines), palm hearts, Caribbean cabbage, pumpkin and onions.

ADDITIVES Substances added to food intentionally to improve its color, texture, aroma or storage life, and to maintain and improve nutritional quality whenever possible.

All additives must be approved by law, and laws protect the consumer on all matters relating to health and product deception. This encompasses matters such as product safety, hygiene and purity.

In all western nations, industry and government are in constant contact over the regulation of permitted additives and their usage, and to improve the acceptance and presentation of food.

No highly-developed society could exist today without using preservatives in food. Without these additives, many foods deteriorate quickly and their nutritional value is consequently depleted. Without them food would be scarcer and therefore considerably more expensive.

The reasons for the use of additives in food include:

ANTI-CAKING AGENTS prevent the lumping of powder mixtures.

ANTIOXIDANTS prevent rancidity in oils, fats and fatty products.

ARTIFICIAL COLORS AND FLAVORS improve the taste and appearance.

DOUGH CONDITIONERS improve the maturing process, speeding up production.

EMULSIFIERS produce better homogeneity, and keep consistency, stability and texture up to established and acceptable standards.

HUMECTANTS maintain and retain an even level of moisture.

NUTRIENTS enrich or replace vitamins and minerals lost in the processing stages.

PH CONTROL AGENTS modify, improve or maintain the desired level of acidity or alkalinity.

PRESERVATIVES prevent food spoilage from bacteria, molds, fungi and yeasts.

THICKENING INGREDIENTS give a satisfying texture to sauces and soups.

LEAVENING AGENTS give products a lighter texture and more volume.

Additives are also used for anti-drying, anti-foaming, anti-hardening, anti-spattering, bleaching, buffering, chill-proofing, clarifying, dispersing, dissolving, drying, emulsifying, enhancing, enriching, firming, foaming, glazing, lining food containers, pressure dispensing, refining, replacing air in food packages, sequestering, stabilizing, sweetening, texturizing, waterproofing and water-retaining.

About 2,800 substances can be added to foods for one or more of these purposes. Nearly all of them would be accepted by good cooks to make their foods better in quality. Baking powder, acetic and ascorbic acids are useful food complements and are not considered as additives by many cooks (although legally they are listed as such), in line with sugar, salt, mustard, syrups and natural vegetable colors.

ADOBO A Philippine dish of chicken and pork marinated in vinegar, garlic, bay leaves and seasoning, then braised.

ADULTERATION OF FOOD The proce-

A

dure for the inspection of food is laid down by law so it is very rare for any food to be adulterated. Some of the adulterations that have occurred in the past are coloring matter, water, dried or condensed milk, liquids constituted from skimmed or separated milk, preservatives and thickening ingredients in milk.

In sausages, there has been too much fat or rusk in relation to lean meat; arrowroot has been adulterated with potato starch, rice or wheat flour; ground ginger has contained pepper; mustard has been sold mixed with cornstarch (cornflour) to keep the mustard grains separate and prevent it from caking.

ADZUKI A small, dried, red bean with a sweet flavor. It is popular in Japanese cookery and in confectionery, in the form of a paste.

AEBLEKAGE A Dutch apple pudding with fried breadcrumbs, shaped in a charlotte mold and served with crème fraîche.

AFRICAN GASTRONOMY The various African cuisines are beginning to become well-known on an international basis as a result of the gradual development of their tourist industry;

because Africans from different countries are now more frequently trained in Western kitchens and also because their native products are beginning to be sold more widely in supermarkets.

The character of African vegetation is largely determined by the distribution of heat and water, coupled with the enormous range in altitude. Where there is water, there is also food in abundance.

The staple foods of the African communities are similar to those in other tropical countries, principally consisting of corn (sweetcorn), cassava, yams, taro and sorghum or millet. Gourds and roots are made into stews with green leaves, peanuts, okra and chili peppers. Plantains are cooked in the same ways as potatoes and used with whatever fish or meat is available.

The meat of wild animals has been consumed for generations, particularly in areas suffering from recession or famine, with buffalo, camel, elephant, monkey, hippopotamus and even lion, crocodile and snake being eaten.

The most common meat dishes are in the form of hotpots and ragouts.

The northern and southern countries have a very sophisticated cookery used by talented African cooks working in internationally-famous hotels and gradually creating a new ethnic gastronomy that is well-worth being incorporated into the professional chef's repertoire.

AFRICAN LARD A vegetable fat obtained from the nut of the largest variety of coconut tree that is native to the coast of Guinea and the Seychelles. The fat is extracted from the nuts and hardened by refrigeration. It has a high content of saturated fatty acids, mainly palmitic acid, so is not a fat recommended for a healthy diet. *See also Coconut.*

AFTERNOON TEA CAKES These include almost anything from a small piece of plain cake to a petit four. These petits gateaux can be made very attractive with piped decorations and fillings. They can be made with a combination of sweet pie dough (pastry), angel cake or Genoese or Victoria sponge baked in small paper cases and served plain, or cut into various shapes and layered with cream or jam. They can be glazed with fondant, royal icing or chocolate, coated with buttercream or simply dusted with confectioners' (icing) sugar.

Typical dishes: Aidas, apfelmohn, apricot slices, banana marshmallow slices, Batavian fancies, Bordeaux croquets, Caen sablés, caramel tartlets, cheesecakes, cherry barquettes, chocolate and coffee éclairs, chocolate nougat cakes, choux à la crème, coconut macaroons, Danish pastries, dobos torte, Florentines, Helvetia cakes, lemon curd tartlets, madeleines, rum babas, pomponettes, marignan with pineapple, mille-feuille with cream and jam, palmiers, Neapolitan slices, gâteaux Pont-Neuf, puits d'amour, Sachertorte, sacristain, sand cookies, Swedish rings, Viennese macaroons, Victoria piped cakes, and wine biscuits.

AGAR, AGAR-AGAR A gelatin-like material that can be used by vegetarians in place of gelatin (agar makes stronger jellies). It can also be used as a stabilizer in canned soups and broths, jellies, ice creams, jams and syrups, and in confectionery.

Agar is extracted from a seaweed that is brownish-white in color with thorny projections on its branches. It is dried in the sun then boiled and crystallized into a powder. It is also marketed in blocks or strands. *See also Lava, Carrageen.*

AGARICUS (Fr. PSALLIOTE) A family of field and woodland mushrooms, typically with a white cap, pink then brownish gills, and a stalk bearing a

A

single or double ring. The cultivated mushroom is a member of the family.

AGAVE A member of the aloe family that grows in the southern states of North America, Mexico and Central America. Though it is poisonous when raw, agave has a sweet taste when cooked so it is very useful for the making of syrups.

AGEING The process of maturing meat under controlled conditions to tenderize it. The best temperature for this process is 34-38°F/1-3°C. Cheese is also matured by controlling its storage conditions.

AGI A variety of small chili pepper grown in Peru, from which a spicy bottled sauce is produced.

AGIDI A Nigerian cornstarch porridge which is served with spinach soup.

AGNOLOTTI An Italian crescent-shaped pasta made in various sizes, stuffed with meat, cheese or spinach. They are cooked by a similar method to that of ravioli and served with rich meaty or tomato sauces.

AIGO SAU D'OIU A thick French-Basque garlic-flavored fish soup that is served with slices of bread soaked in the soup. The name comes from the Latin *Deus*, meaning God.

AIGUILLETTE The under-fillet of birds; a long strip underneath the breast. It is also a thin piece of meat taken from the rump of beef, pork and veal.

AIÖLI Garlic mayonnaise that is a speciality of southern France and Spain. It is served with boiled salt cod or any poached smoked fish.

2 slices of white breaded crumb
3 garlic cloves, chopped
6 tbsp olive oil
1¼ cups/½ pint/300ml mayonnaise

Pound the bread, garlic and oil together to make a fine paste and blend in the mayonnaise.

Aiöli with pine nuts
½ cup/2oz/50g pine nuts
2 garlic cloves
2 tbsp water
1¼ cups/½ pint/300ml mayonnaise
salt, chili powder and spices

Pound the nuts and garlic with water to make a paste. Blend in the mayonnaise. Adjust the seasoning to suit your own taste using salt, chili powder and other spices.

AIR PUMP A confectioner's apparatus used to blow sugar into various shapes to imitate fruits or animals for decorative purposes. The pump is fitted with a slender tip (nozzle) operated by hand to squeeze air into the syrup after it has been cooked to the hard crack stage.

AJIACO A Colombian chicken soup-stew containing potatoes, watercress leaves, corn (corn on the cob), onions and coriander.

AJI-NO-MOTO *See Monosodium glutamate.*

AKBAB A Tunisian lamb casserole flavored with cumin, garlic, onions and tomatoes.

AKEBIA A sausage-shaped Asian fruit with black seeds and a pronounced flavor. It is an excellent dessert used with fresh cream or yogurt.

À L'ANCIENNE A term now used by cooks based on the principle that what is old is wise and good, such as rustic home-cooking. What most people really want is simple food which in the past was produced by mothers and grandmothers.

The term à l'ancienne gives our ancestral culinary tradition the reverence it deserves and so even in these days of modern creative cookery, chefs still use the term to describe Irish stew, scrumptious cakes or a traditional risotto.

ALBACORE (Fr. GERMON) A white-fleshed fish of the tuna family, esteemed for the quality and texture of the flesh. It is prized by the Japanese and used raw in sushi and sashimi.

ALBEDO The white inner spongy layer of citrus fruit skins. The colored outer part of the skin is called the flavedo and is used for its volatile oil, which is called terpene.

Albedo is a source of pectin, useful in setting marmalades, jellies and jams.

ALBERT SAUCE An accompaniment for boiled beef, made with horseradish mixed with a velouté sauce and named after Prince Albert, consort of British Queen Victoria.

ALBONDIGAS Spanish for meatballs. They are also very popular in Mexico.

ALBUFÉRA SAUCE A supreme sauce

A

colored pink by puréeing with red bell peppers, and flavored with chili pepper and saffron.

ALBUMENS, ALBUMINS A group of soluble proteins. Albumen is found in egg whites, and in milk in the form of lactalbumen.

Albumen water is used as a light form of nourishment for patients with a weak digestive system or suffering from diarrhoea.

An egg white is beaten with a little water, then left to stand for about one hour. Lemon juice can be added to give it some flavor.

ALCOHOL BURNER Tool used by confectioners when making pulled sugar.

ALEXANDER A biennial plant with a myrrh-like flavor. It is best eaten raw in salads. It can also be boiled and served as a vegetable.

ALFAJORE A round galette made with sweet flaky pastry, sandwiched with confectioner's custard or ground semolina cream blancmange.

ALFALFA Popularized by vegetarians, the seeds of this leguminous plant are sprouted for use in salads and with stir-fried vegetables.

ALGAE *See Seaweed.*

ALGAROBA BEANS *See Carob beans.*

ALGIN, SODIUM ALGINATE A gelatinous substance extracted from seaweed, used for puddings and soups.

ALIGOT A potato purée blended with its own weight of grated Cantal cheese, plus chopped garlic and olive oil. It can be eaten cold as a dip.

ALKALI A chemical base that can neutralize acids. Baking soda (bicarbonate of soda) is an alkali; it softens vegetables when added to the cooking liquid (however, it also destroys vitamins). With longer cooking the vegetables become mushy and disintegrate and when it is used with beans, they split on baking.

In a case of poisoning by an alkaline substance, the remedy is to drink plenty of water with a weak acid such as vinegar, lemon juice, or egg white in soda water, or plenty of milk.

ALLEMANDE A velouté sauce enriched with cream and egg yolks. It originated in Munich and the rich farming region of Bavaria, from where it spread all over Europe. It is used in rich veal and chicken dishes.

ALLERGY A somatic complaint arising from an unusual sensitivity to one or more substances in foods such as milk, cheeses, shellfish or strawberries.

ALLIGATOR The eggs and flesh of this reptile are sold as edible products. The flesh is cooked in similar ways to fish or veal.

ALLIGATOR PEAR *See Avocado.*

ALLONYA These starchy yam tubers are used in Caribbean cuisine instead of potatoes.

ALLSPICE, JAMAICA PEPPER, (Fr. PIMENT DE LA JAMAIQUE) From an evergreen tree, this spice smells like a mixture of cloves, juniper berries, cinnamon, pepper and nutmeg. It is used in pâtés and meat terrines, curries and mulled wines.

Allspice must not be confused with the mixture of spices which is sold under the name of 'mixed spice'.

ALLUMETTE 1) A name meaning 'cut into thin strips'. It is chiefly used for deep-fried potatoes.

2) The name is also applied to puff pastry rectangles which are cut after baking to a shape 1¼in/3cm wide and 2½in/6cm long. These strips are then sandwiched together with different pastes such as anchovy, shrimp (prawn), peanut, cheese or chicken, or pâté.

ALMENDRAS A Spanish caramel almond nougat, flavored with honey and cut into small squares.

ALMOND (Fr. AMANDE) There are two kinds of almond: sweet and bitter. Jordan and Alicante are considered to be the best sweet varieties. Almonds are available whole, split or chopped.

A strong extract is produced from a mixture of bitter and sweet almonds that are fermented and distilled. A synthetic almond extract is produced from benzaldehyde.

Almonds are used in almond paste, macaroons, cookies (biscuits), and Bakewell tarts.

Almond milk is obtained by warming two 2¼ cups/9oz/250g freshly ground almonds with 4⅓ cups/1¾ pints/1 liter water over low heat for 30 minutes. The mixture is liquidized, strained and used in the same way as cows' milk.

ALMOND CREAM A mixture of equal amounts of ground almonds, butter, sugar and eggs, beaten into a fluffy consistency.

A

ALMOND PASTE, MARZIPAN A mixture of two parts confectioners' (icing) sugar, one part ground almonds and half a part egg yolks. Boiled almond paste, also know as marzipan, is made by boiling one part ground almonds and two parts sugar together to make a paste.

ALSATIAN GASTRONOMY The region of Alsace may be politically and economically attached to France but is gastronomically and by language, truly Germanic. It has benefited greatly from both cultures and the food products are arguably the best in Europe. Much credit must be given to the Benedictine monks who promoted wine making and meat processing. The center of this wonderful food paradise is Strasbourg where the best restaurants and makers of the famous pâté de foie gras can be found.

Typical dishes: frog soups and stews, gefilte fish made with carp, hop shoots and kohlrabi in cream, kugelhoph, knepfles, plum tarts, red cabbage with chestnuts, spätzle, savarin, Strasbourg sausages, zewelewai.

ALUMINUM Considered to be one of the best all-round cooking materials, used for the making of pots and saucepan's of all sizes, although it is now suspected of being linked with Alzheimer's disease. Aluminum is also made into foil to wrap foods — but not acidic foods as the acid will react with the foil. Food wrapped in foil cannot be used for microwave cookery (use plastic containers) but it is a good conductor of heat in regular ovens.

ALVA An Indian quince paste.

AMARANTH There are about 50 varieties of this green leafy vegetable; most are annuals. Amaranth has a sweetish flavor. Both the leaves and seeds can be used.

AMARETTI A type of Italian macaroon traditionally made from both sweet and bitter almonds.

2¼ cups/9oz/250g ground almonds
1⅓ cups/11oz/325g sugar
5 egg whites
3 drops of almond extract
egg wash
nibbed or granulated sugar for sprinkling

Makes 48

Mix the ground almonds with the sugar and egg whites. Add the almond extract.

Fill a piping (pastry) bag fitted with a plain tube (nozzle). Pipe 1¾in/4cm amaretti onto rice paper or baking parchment on a baking tray. Brush with egg wash and sprinkle with sugar. Bake at 350°F/180°C/gas mark 4 for 20-30 minutes until golden.

AMBROSIA Mythically this was the food of the Gods, giving them immortality. The term is used to describe food with an exquisite sweet smoothness and flavor.

AMÉRICAINE, À LA A tomato and shellfish sauce or soup flavored with wine and tarragon. It is usually served with white fish, or in the classic dish homard à la Américaine, when the sauce is also enriched with brandy.

AMINO ACIDS The 'building blocks' of protein. Proteins are composed of 20 amino acids joined in long chains (polypeptides) which are combined in complex bundles. The type of protein is determined by the sequence of amino acids.

Of the 20 amino acids, eight must be provided by the daily diet (the rest can be manufactured in the body), so are know as essential amino acids; they are lysine, methionine, valine, tryptophan, threonine, isoleucine, leucine and phenylalanine. Children also need histidine as an additional supplement for growth; it is available from pharmacists.

Plants make amino acids from nitrogen salts in the soil.

During digestion, proteins are split into their constituent amino acids and absorbed into the blood stream.

AMMI SEEDS An aromatic spice extracted from an inferior relative of the cardamom. It is extensively used in Asiatic cookery.

AMMONIUM ALGINATE An extract from seaweed that is used as an emulsifier, stabilizer, diluent for coloring matter and as a thickener.

AMYL ACETATE A colorless liquid with a banana smell that is used as a flavoring for cakes and desserts.

AMYLASE A group of enzymes capable of splitting starch and glycogen into sugars. They are found in many plants and animals.

AMYLOPECTIN The principal component of most cereal starches. It is a polysaccharide with a branched structure built up of glucoside units. It is insoluble in water. *See also Amylose.*

A

AMYLOSE With amylopectin, the other polysaccharide component of cereal starches. It is water-soluble.

ANAEMIA The lack of the red pigment in blood, often found in pregnancy. Nutrients needed as remedies are iron, protein, Vitamin B1, folic acid, Vitamin B2, copper and Vitamin C.

ANALYSIS In laboratory work, this is the procedure of finding the composition of a substance. It can be done using for example colorimetry (determining the color intensity to find out the concentration of a substance), gravitation, calculation, spectrography and volumetry.

ANCHOÏADE Provençal paste made by pounding anchovy fillets with garlic, oil and herbs. It is used as a spread for bread and toast and as a dip for raw vegetables.

ANCHOVY (Fr. ANCHOIS) A fish of the herring family. It is usually filleted, salted and canned in oil. If the fillets are too salty, soak in milk for one hour then rinse, drain and pat dry. *See also Anchoïade.*

ANCHUSA ROOT A root used to color foods or drinks red.

ANDOUILLE A French sausage made from the stomach and intestines of the pig, to which may be added the flesh of the neck, heart and head of the animal. Andouille are highly seasoned with pepper. This gastronomic delight is manufactured all over France, particularly in Vire and Aire-sur-la-Lys, and it is well worth travelling to France just for a taste of it.

Andouilles are served cold, often as an hors d'oeuvre alongside other types of assorted charcuterie.

ANDOUILLETTE A smaller version of andouille. It is raw and has to be broiled (grilled) before eating.

ANELLINI Tiny pasta rings, used in soups or pasta salads.

ANGEL CAKE British angel cakes are a light sponge mixture made with whole eggs and fat. The version popular in the United States is more complicated. It is a light, airy cake made with a meringue and leavened (raised) with cream of tartar, which increases its acidity. If this is omitted, the cake will be more yellow in color.

The best proportions are 2¼ cups/ 9oz/250g finely sifted cake flour to 12 egg whites and 1⅓ cups/11oz/325g superfine (caster) sugar, but the amount of flour used may vary; the less flour used, the moister the finished product. Folding and handling should be as light as possible, since the lightness of the cake depends upon the amount of air beaten into the egg whites which is then maintained during the baking process.

Angel cakes can be flavored with chocolate or colored pink or yellow with appropriate flavorings.

ANGELICA (Fr. ANGÉLIQUE) A candied sweetmeat prepared from the stalks of the angelica plant. It is mostly used in cakes and Italian fruit ice creams.

Angelica is a traditional remedy for colds, coughs, colic and rheumatism. The juice is also used in the preparation of vermouth and Chartreuse liqueur. *See also Candy.*

ANGEL'S HAIR *See Capellini.*

ANGLERFISH *See Monkfish.*

ANGOLA PEA (Fr. POIS AMBREVADE) A pulse grown in India and Africa. Its color varies from green to dark red, with long pods of seeds. It is used in the same way as any other pulse, in soups, purées and as a thickening agent for curry sauces. A flour can be made from Angola peas and used for cakes, cookies (biscuits) and pancakes.

ANISEED (Fr. ANIS) The aromatic seeds are used for cakes, confectionery, liqueurs such as anisette, Chinese five-spice powder and French and Italian honey and gingerbreads. *See recipe page 188.*

Aniseed is a good remedy for colic in children, and as a mild expectorant.

ANNATO Annato seeds are used as a natural rusty-red food coloring agent for cheese and smoked fish, and also to flavor achiote oil. Annatto extract is a yellow food coloring.

ANRAITH NEANTOG A delicious Irish soup made of leeks, potatoes and young nettle leaves, enriched with buttermilk.

ANTACID A base or buffer that neutralizes acids. The term is used for a product such as magnesium hydroxide, that counteracts stomach acidity.

ANTHOCYANIN The pigment that gives a reddish color to berries, grapes, beets (beetroot), eggplants (aubergines) and cherries. The red color is accentuated with the use of acids, such as when beets are pickled and when the fruit is made into jam.

A

ANTIBIOTIC A chemical substance produced by micro-organisms such as molds, which can destroy bacteria or prevent their growth; eg Penicillin.

ANTICUCHOS A Peruvian dish of ox heart, cubed and marinaded in red wine, flavored with chili peppers, garlic and cumin, impaled on skewers and broiled (grilled). Serve with a sharp marinade sauce flavored with ground annatto seeds.

ANTIOXIDANT An antioxidant is used to prevent oxidation, a biological process which causes rancidity of fats and a darkening of fresh produce such as potatoes, artichokes and avocado pears when cut. Most antioxidants are only available for commercial use but citric and acetic acids, as found in some fruits and in vinegar respectively, are two antioxidants that are used in the kitchen to prevent the darkening of fresh products.

ANTIPASTI The Italian term for a collection of cold and hot hors d'oeuvre served before the pasta course.

The tingling challenges of Italian appetizers are so intense that, even when in a hurry, it only takes canned products to make a platter of these exquisite temptations. They include wonderful items such as black and green olives, anchovies, tuna fish, prosciutto, mortadella, asparagus, sweet and sour mushrooms, baby artichokes, and pickled peaches.

APPELLATION D'ORIGINE CONTRÔLLÉE (AOC) The French legal system of giving protection to the names of wines and foods which have achieved recognized standards of quality.

APPELLATIONS ON MENUS Currently, there is a reaction against the use of traditional names of dishes on menus, and instead chefs are using more personalized descriptions, citing the main ingredients of a dish. In a recent world-wide survey of menu nomenclature, French chefs working both in France and abroad observed that many old classical names have been discarded or ignored. In view of these results, in many cases I have omitted proper names such as those of famous people for special dishes as they are no longer relevant. The exceptions are where the dishes are so well-known — such as Béchamel, Condé, Impératrice, Soubise, Sabayon, Savarin, Victoria, Wellington. These are all part of the culinary repertoire, even if in some cases the names were originally from a known personality.

Many of the names that I have omitted are those from past aristocratic houses, artists, and writers, particularly those unconnected with the culinary or hotel professions, such as Agnes Sorel, Aiglon, Alphonse XIII, Aremberg, Bagration, Beauharnais, Bernhard, Brunswick, Buloz, Choiseul, Cussy, Dubarry, Joinville, Orloff, Sand, Sevigne, Talleyrand, Waleska.

Common names are retained where they are the names of regions, towns and countries or where they describe a style of national cuisine. These include Américaine, Artoise, Bordelaise, Bourguignonne, Bretonne, Chinoise, Danoise, Ecossaise, Espagnole, Indienne, Italienne, Japonaise, Lyonnaise, Normande, Polonaise, Provençale, Russe.

APPENZELLER CHEESE A whole-milk cheese made in the eastern Swiss canton. It has a golden yellow rind and a firm, strawberry-colored curd with tiny holes. It owes its flavor to the wine and cider wash it receives during its maturation.

APPETIZERS A modern term for hors d'oeuvre and savory canapés.

APPLE (Fr. POMME) There are over 1,545 varieties of apples grown in the world. They are high in pectin so combine them with berries for jams and jellies and fruit pie mixtures.

Soak peeled or cut apples in acidulated water to stop them from browning. When ripening other fruits like peaches or pears, place a single apple in a bag with them to help the process.

Apples are the main ingredients in many cakes, tarts, puddings, charlottes, fritters, mousses, sauces, fruit salads, cocktail cups, jams with berries and stone fruits, or as an apple sauce to accompany pork, duck, goose and oily fish. They are also served with cheese. *See also Apple butter, Apple cake, Apple pie, Apple tarts, Jellies.*

Apples are a laxative providing the skin is eaten. They contain Vitamin C but not in significant quantities unless four apples a day are eaten.

Typical dishes: Beignets de pommes, crêpes flambées Bénédictine, charlotte de pommes, mousse de pommes aux framboise, soufflé de pommes bonne femme, tarte Normande.

APPLE BUTTER The flavor and color of this fruit butter can be concentrated by adding strawberry and blackberry syrup after boiling.

APPLE CAKE A plain cake mixture

A

mixed with a quarter of its weight of sliced apples. After baking and cooling the top is dusted with confectioners' (icing) sugar mixed with cinnamon.

APPLE PIE Use quartered apples, packed into an individual pie dish and covered with sweet pie dough (shortcrust pastry). Serve hot with custard or cream.

APPLE STRUDEL Either use special strudel paste, which is similar to filo paste (filo pastry), or puff paste. Stretch it thinly across a floured cotton sheet on a large table. Sprinkle with sliced apples and golden raisins (sultanas). Roll up the strudel and bake it in a hot oven.

If you use strudel or filo paste, sprinkle melted butter over it before adding the fruit. The apples can be flavored with ground cloves and cinnamon.

APPLE TART There are three main types of open apple tart, usually made with thinly-sliced tart apples.

1) Alsatian tart is filled with creamy egg custard and baked until set.

2) Normandy tart is made with sliced apples over an almond cream mixture, then brushed with apricot jam after baking. Sweet short pie dough (shortcrust pastry) is used.

3) Parisian tart is usually made with puff paste topped with thinly-sliced apples which are slightly sugared so they caramelize. Brush with apricot glaze after baking.

APRICOT (Fr. ABRICOT) Apricots are available fresh, dried, candied and canned in syrup, or in jams or pastes. The kernel can be used in the same way as almonds to make a type of marzipan paste.

Apricots are used in tarts, pies, desserts, jam sauces, glazes, syrups, and confectionery pastes for petits fours.

Typical dishes: Abricot condé, charlotte d'abricots, tarte abricotine, savarin aux abricots.

APRICOT GLAZE Mix together equal amounts of apricot jam, confectioners' (icing) sugar and water. Boil for 5 minutes, then strain. Thicken with a little arrowroot, boil again for 5 minutes and strain. Use while it is warm. The color can be adjusted with yellow coloring or saffron.

Red glaze can be made with plums or redcurrants. A glaze can be flavored with any liqueur.

ARABINGALACTAN A gum used to stabilize and texturize syrups.

ARACHIDE OIL An alternative name for peanut oil. *See Peanut.*

ARAME An edible brown sea vegetable that has wavy strips or fronds and is grown along Pacific coasts and used in Japanese cookery. It is sold dried. To use, soak it in hot water for 20 minutes then boil in fresh water until tender, about 15-20 minutes.

ARAN SPIOSRAI A spicy Irish soda fruit cake with butter and honey.

ARBORIO Originating in Italy, this is the round, medium-grain rice that is used for making risotto. The rice grains absorb five times their volume during cooking and their starch is released to give a creamy texture.

AREPA Colombian and Venezuelan cornmeal flattened bun that is baked or cooked on an oiled griddle.

ARGININE An amino acid that is not essential to man, but it may be essential to children.

AROMATIC An ingredient with an odor and/or flavor which is strong and characteristic, but also sweet and pleasant, such as onions, garlic, leeks, herbs and spices, and root vegetables which are rich in sugar and so give a distinctive flavor when cooked until caramelized.

Many aromatic compounds are esters, such as amyl acetate which is found in pears. The odor of pineapple is caused by its methyl butyrate content and isoamyl isovalerate is the aromatic ester found in apples.

All plants and fruits contain volatile oil. Particularly aromatic extracts are distilled from the volatile oils of lemon, peppermint, cinnamon, cloves and lavender.

Tannin imparts an astringent, bitter flavor to some foods.

It is possible to produce a wide range of interesting flavors by combining several constituents which give a natural tart taste and so help to flavor foods: for example, sugar, mineral salts, volatile oils and organic acids.

AROMATIC SAUCES To add extra flavor to any savory sauce, add 10 percent of a herby wine such as vermouth, or a richer wine like dry Madeira, white Port or dry Sherry.

For a more specific aroma, make a sauce from one particular herb. Examples include parsley, dill, garlic, scallion (spring onion), chive, mint and basil. Add 1 tablespoon of the flavoring per 2½ cups/1 pint/600ml of the

A

base sauce and boil for 5 minutes. Strain.

Sauce Antiboise

3 garlic cloves, chopped
3 anchovy fillets, chopped
1¼ cups/½ pint/300ml velouté
  sauce
1 tbsp aniseed liqueur such as
  Pernod
3 black olives, pitted, for garnish
1 tbsp basil, chopped for garnish

Boil all the ingredients together, except the basil and olives, for 5 minutes. Pour into a blender or food processor and mix to a purée. Thin down with milk if required. Serve garnished with black olives and basil.

ARRACACHA A starchy tuberous plant similar to potatoes, much used in South American countries, particularly in its native Colombia. It can be ground to produce a starch flour similar to cassava.

ARRAP A Caribbean meat pastry, wrapped in cornmeal dough and deep-fried.

ARROWROOT A starch that is used like cornstarch (cornflour) as a thickening ingredient for milk puddings, sauces, soups and blancmanges, made with ground almonds or coconut milk. It is also used in cookies (biscuits).

ARTICHOKE *See Globe artichoke, Jerusalem artichoke.*

ARTISTRY That cooks needs inspiration from the artist is very true. Cookery should be manipulated in the interest of art.

To train cooks to be artists is like hitching the star to the wagon. The great problem of art teaching is that art will ever remain in a state of fluidity and growth. Fashions and trends in food are as fickle as in the clothing industry. For example, nouvelle cuisine brought with it the encouragement to present food in a style never before put in so many uses.

Food presentation today has become such an advanced procedure that food designers are constantly at work in magazines to show cooks how color, texture and shape can be harmonized.

In the teaching of art, it must first be realized that the artistic sense cannot be taught; it can only be awakened and fostered. An art teacher's value depends on the power to recognize artistic talent where it exists, and the wish to respect it as a rare phenomenon. Real talent, once it is awakened, will always find the means, where adequate training facilities are available, of making up deficiencies in past instruction. A gifted person in such circumstances feels a natural urge towards knowledge, which makes study a necessity and not a burden.

Artistry is not only the ability of being a good craftsman, but also understanding why certain things are done and for what purpose. It calls for the proficiency gained by constant practice. For example, all cooks should be able to decorate a simple birthday cake, without necessarily learning the higher art of confectionery and food design.

Cake decoration demands manual skill, a sense of form and color and a grasp of what is meant by good taste when applied to the decoration of any food. A simple canapé or a sweet petit fours should be as artistically designed as a huge wedding cake.

Before attempting to blend colorful ingredients, its a good idea to review the primary colors used by artists. These are red, blue and yellow, from which all other colors can be made.

The secondary colors are formed by mixing two primary colors:

RED + YELLOW = ORANGE
YELLOW + BLUE = GREEN
BLUE + RED = MAUVE

Tertiary colors are made by mixing two secondary colors. Coffee color is made with green and orange in equal amounts. A chocolate color is made by mixing mauve and green.

By studying a color circle, it can be seen that there are six complementary colors that are immediately opposite to each other. If these are placed side by side the colors are intensified.

SHAPES AND CONTOURS: foods can be round, rectangular, triangular, oval, square, crescent or half-moon. Designs — as befits our streamlined age — should be simple but interesting. A simple division can be in two, created indirectly by the placing of the decoration, or directly by a line, which may be straight or curved.

Templates are a ready means of establishing simple basic designs. An eight-point star is made by folding a circle of paper into eight. Cut the sides to form a pattern. When unfolded it resembles lace.

TEXTURES: The surface texture of decorative materials depends on the material used. Royal icing has a mat surface, whilst fondant and chocolate are shiny. Gelatins are more translucent, reflecting light. Various textures can be created by altering the reflective surface of

A

the material. A comb scraper or a palette knife used on the surface will break up the reflection into patterns of light and shade according to how they are used. Sugars used for decoration provide different textures, according to the type of sugar and how it is applied.

DECORATION: By learning to decorate a simple sponge cake, the student can move from sweet items to savory, applying the same decorative rules and techniques. It is amazing what can be done with a pastry (piping) bag and a tube (nozzle) to write letters on a cake saying *'Happy Birthday'*.

With various star tubes (nozzles), many scrolls can be made to create attractive patterns. Use mashed potatoes for a practice run to avoid wastage. Decorations made of pulled or blown sugar, or fondant can used to make a cake into a piece of art.

Most people should learn by observation – there are many colorful illustrations in modern cookery magazines which clearly show that each cook can have his own individual style. First copy an artist before you can become one yourself. There are certain artistic principles which will become apparent as your artistic sensibilities are awok-

en. For example, you need only a little red item when the decoration is full of greenery. If the main item is round then all garnishes and decorations must have rounded shapes. Above all, whatever the garnish or decoration, remember food must also always taste as good as it looks.

Artistry in cooking is the fundamental seed of creativity, from which technical methods can be learned to perfect and enhance it.

ARUGULA, RUGULA, ROCKET A leafy salad plant with a bitter, aromatic, peppery flavor. It is usually used in combination with other salad leaves.

ASAFOETIDA A strong, fetid-smelling spice that has a garlic smell and bitter taste. It is used in Indian curries.

ASCORBIC ACID, VITAMIN C A crystalline substance extracted from various fruits and vegetables or synthetically prepared. The main sources are citrus fruits, blackcurrants, pawpaws, guavas, endive (chicory), raw broccoli, tomatoes, and, in Western diets, potatoes. Ascorbic acid is lost in cooking, which is why it is important to include raw fruit and vegetables in the diet.

Ascorbic acid may be used as an antioxidant to prevent vegetables and fruits from discoloring. It is also used in making bread to tighten the dough. Vitamin C is available from pharmacists in tablet form.

ASEPTIC This term means 'free from bacteria'. It is an essential factor in food preservation.

ASH The leaves of ash trees are used for a hot drink. When young, they can be preserved in vinegar and used instead of capers.

ASH GOURD One of the gourd family, prepared in the same way as vegetable marrow and zucchini (courgette).

ASIATIC PEAR, NASHI PEAR There are over 100 varieties of this fruit, which originates from Japan and is cultivated in Italy, Chile and New Zealand. Apple-shaped and colored from pale yellow to russet, the Asiatic pear remains firm even when ripe. Its flesh is crunchy, very juicy and refreshing. It is used in compotes, and as a garnish for pork and duck dishes.

ASPARAGUS (Fr. ASPERGE) A perennial plant producing an edible stalk or spear. It is available fresh, frozen or canned in various sizes and colors.

Asparagus is used in appetizers, salads, soups, sauces, mousses and tarts. It can be served with French dressing, melted butter or hollandaise sauce.

Typical dishes: Soupe d'asperges, pointes d'asperges Parmesan, quiche aux asperges, mousseline d'asperges au fromage.

ASPARAGUS PEA *See Winged bean.*

ASPARTAME An artificial sweetener that is 180 times sweeter than sucrose. It is synthesized from two amino acids (L-aspartic acid and L-phenylalanine). It can be used in cold desserts but must not be heated as it will break down.

ASPIC JELLY This is used to glaze cold meat, poultry and vegetables or to fill the gap that occurs in meat pies after baking between the pastry and filling. A good jelly should be clear with a light amber hue and a meaty taste similar to beef or chicken consommé. Shank (shin) meat and calves' feet (trotters) boiled in water will produce a jelly on cooling. Leaf or powder gelatin can be used when a firmer texture is required.

*1lb/450g bones, cut into small
  pieces
1lb/450g shank (shin) of beef,
  boned*

A

2 calves or sheep's feet (trotters),
  blanched and boned
8 chickens' wings
1 of each — large carrot, large leek,
  medium onion, stick of celery,
  sprig of thyme, sprig of fennel
8⅔ cups/3½ pints/2 liters water

Put the bones in a roasting pan (tin) and cook in a medium oven at 400°F/200°C/gas mark 6 for 30 minutes. Drain off the fat and place the bones in a stockpot with the beef, calves' or sheep's feet (trotters), vegetables, herbs and water. Boil gently for 3 hours. Remove the scum and fat as they float to the surface.

Remove the meat. Let meat and jelly cool.

Dice the meat and use for a beef salad with chopped dill pickle or cucumber. Alternatively, use the meat for forcemeat or a terrine.

ASPIC OF SEAFOOD Assorted fish and shellfish in a trembling jelly flavored with dill or basil, make an ideal and attractive appetizer.

Fish stock is made in the normal way, then cooled and mixed with raw ground (minced) fish and chopped root vegetables, reheated gently until a crust forms, then strained through a cloth to obtain a clear broth, as when making a consommé. The fish is poached in fish stock until just cooked, removed, then served embedded in the delicious, tasty fish aspic, in a glass bowl.

ASPIC POWDER A mixture of gelatin and flavored hydrolyside proteins that is similar in taste to bouillon (stock) cubes. It is used for meat-flavored jellies.

ATEMOYA One of the custard apple family, this fruit is a hybrid between the cherimoya and the sugar apple.

ATOLE A Mexican drink made with milk and/or water and masa harina boiled to make a type of porridge that is drunk for breakfast. It is sweetened with sugar or honey and sometimes flavored with fruit juice.

ATTEREAUX Attereaux are served as a snack or for a light meal. Typical ingredients could be chicken liver, mushrooms, onion and meat balls. These ingredients are then carefully threaded on skewers, coated with a thick sauce and shallow-fried until thoroughly cooked.

AU BLEU The poaching of live fish, usually trout, in acidulated water.

AUBERGINE (Am. EGGPLANT) The eggplant got its name because of its smooth skin and ovoid shape. It is a native of Asia. It belongs to the same family as potatoes and tomatoes. When cooked together, these ingredients complement each other well.

Eggplants (aubergines) develop their best flavor when fried in olive oil as fritters. A dip made from the flesh emulsified with sesame seeds is also popular, particularly in the Middle East. Others include dips, a snack with cheese, pâtés. *See also Eggplant.*

AUTOCLAVE A thick-walled vessel with a tight fitting lid, in which foods are cooked under pressure at above boiling point. *See Pressure cooking.*

AUXIN A plant hormone which promotes the elongation and growth of plant cells and stimulates rooting.

AVGOLÉMONO A Greek lemon and chicken soup or sauce, which is much favored by both tourists and locals in Greece. Both the lemon juice and grated rind are used.

AVOCADO, ALLIGATOR PEAR Grown in all tropical and sub-tropical countries and the Middle East, the two most frequently-marketed avocado varieties are the pebbly-textured, almost black, Hass and the green, smooth and thin-skinned Fuerte.

When buying avocados choose ones that yield slightly to gentle pressure, although they will mature at kitchen temperature quite quickly.

To retard the browning of avocados, brush any cut surface with lemon juice, or leave the stone in one half, wrap the avocado well in a plastic bag and refrigerate.

Raw avocado has quite a high content of Vitamins A and C, so mash the pulp for fresh dips, with lemon juice and banana purée, serve as a garnish for crab or salmon or make into chilled pâtés and mousses. In chicken-based soups and sauces and fish stock, avocado purée gives an unctuous, creamy texture and also adds flavor when acidulated with lime juice.

AWVAM A Lebanese doughnut fried in oil and soaked in lemon and rose water syrup.

AXOA A Basque veal stew with red bell peppers, tomatoes and onions, simmered in local wine.

AYRAN A Lebanese drink made by mixing iced water with yogurt, fresh chopped mint and salt or sugar.

B

BABA A yeast cake studded with seedless dry currants that is often served as a dessert. It is baked in a small metal tumbler mold, soaked in rum syrup, filled with whipped cream through a slit in the side, and sometimes decorated with crystallized violets.

BABA GANOUSH An Egyptian dip made with baked eggplant (aubergine) flesh, tahini, lemon juice and garlic. It is traditionally served as part of a mezze table and is now served at many vegetarian parties.

BABOVKA A Czechoslovakian marble cake made with two layers of chocolate and vanilla sponge cake with hazelnuts.

BACALHAU, BACALAO *See Salt cod.*

BACON Bacon is available in roasts (joints) and in slices. It is made from the side, or side minus the leg, of the pig. It is cured by pickling in brine or dry-salting.

The signs of quality are that the fat should be firm, the skin thin and the bones small in roasts (joints). These are indications that the bacon has been produced from a young animal.

North American bacon is categorized as lean, leanest and prime. The weight of a side varies between 22½lb/25kg and 31½lb/30kg.

In Europe smoked bacon is available and is regarded by many cooks to have a superior flavor.

BACTERIA Small micro-organisms of a simple, primitive form. They exist everywhere; some are useful, such as those found in the production of cheeses and yogurt, while others are harmful.

Bacteria are the cause of many diseases and cases of food poisoning, so hygienic precautions must always be taken when handling raw ingredients and food. Fortunately, most bacteria-caused diseases can now be treated by antibiotics and bacteria can be destroyed by heat or by bactericides.

In the natural world bacteria perform an indispensable function by causing the break-down and decay of plant and animal debris.

BADIAN, BADIANE *See Star anise.*

BAEKENOFFA An Alsatian casserole of cubed mixed meats such as lamb, pork and beef, which are cooked very slowly in Alsace wine with potatoes, onions and garlic.

BAEL *See Ugli fruit.*

BAGATELLE Individual rounds of sponge cake filled with whipped cream that has added gelatin to give a marshmallow texture. The cake is decorated with strawberries flavored with kirsch.

A large cake can also be made, in which case it is often covered with a layer of green almond paste.

BAGNA CAUDA A hot dip from Piedmont, Italy, of garlic, anchovy fillets and oil into which are dipped raw vegetables such as cardoons, artichokes, bell peppers and celery.

BAIN-MARIE *See Water bath.*

BAKE BLIND To bake a pie shell (pastry case) while empty. To prevent the sides collapsing and the pie dough (pastry) rising, the shell (case) is lined with baking parchment (greaseproof paper) and filled with dry navy (haricot) beans. The beans and paper are removed after the shell has been baked. The beans can be used many times over.

BAKED ALASKA A celebration dessert made with ice cream put on a sponge soaked in a liqueur or fruit juice, then coated with meringue. It is baked quickly to color and set the meringue. It can be served with cherry jubilee, which consists of sour (morello) cherries reheated with the thickened juice and flamed in kirsch at the table.

BAKEWELL TART This may be a light spongy pudding enriched with ground almonds or a pastry tart filled with the same ground almond mixture over strawberry or raspberry jam.

This recipe was created in Dickens' day as a result of a mistake by a cook. It produces individual tarts rather than the usual large tart.

1lb/450g sweet pie dough (short crust pastry) or puff paste (see recipes page 274)
⅓ cup/5oz/50g raspberry jam

Almond filling
⅔ cup/5oz/150g soft sweet (unsalted) butter
⅓ cup/3oz/75g sugar

B

2 eggs
¾ cup/3oz/75g cake flour
⅓ cup/1½ oz/40g ground almonds
⅓ cup/1½ oz/40g unsweetened
  shredded (desiccated) coconut
2 drops vanilla extract
1 drop almond extract
boiling water
¾ cup/3oz/75g confectioners' (icing)
  sugar

Roll the pie dough (shortcrust pastry) or puff paste to ¼in/5mm thick. Using a fluted cutter, cut into rounds to fit 16 x 2¼in/6cm well-greased tartlet molds. Line the molds neatly with the dough and fill each one with 2 teaspoons raspberry jam.

To make the filling, beat the butter and sugar together in a bowl. Mix the flour, ground almonds, coconut and the two extracts. Stir this mixture into the butter to produce a semi-pouring batter. Fill the tartlets with 2 tablespoons of the filling and bake at 375°F/190°C/gas mark 5 for about 25 minutes.

Add a few drops of boiling water to the confectioners' (icing) sugar to produce a semi-liquid consistency. Coat the cold tarts.

BAKING Cooking in an oven by convected heat. The skill of baking requires a knowledge of the oven's capacity and its capabilities in terms of temperature and heat distribution. It also requires a knowledge of the correct temperature and exact timing needed by the size and nature of the foods being baked.

There are three main methods of baking:

WATER BATH or bain-marie.

WITH STEAM to obtain a gloss on Viennese and French breads and rolls. The steam is actually spread onto the surface of the food.

DRY-BAKING. This method cooks food without using liquid or fats. It is most suitable for baking potatoes or beets (beetroot) in their skin, pastries, cakes and some desserts. Certain types of unskinned oily fish such as salmon are also baked in dry heat.

• Make sure the oven is pre-heated to the right temperature.

• Rest pie doughs (pastry) before baking to prevent shrinking.

• Grease baking trays before placing bread rolls or choux buns on them, but for good puff pastry splash a little water on the trays.

• Glaze baked goods such as pastries

and breads with egg wash to improve their color.

Typical dishes: baked Alaska, baked bass in fennel, baked potatoes or baked beets, beef Wellington, bread, chicken and ham pie, Danish pastries, duck and game pies, fruit pies, macaroons, meringues, moussaka, salmon coulibiac, sausage rolls, savory and sweet soufflés, steak and kidney pie, stuffed eggplant.

BAKING POWDER A combination of an edible alkali and an edible acid. It is used to aerate (raise) cakes, cookies (biscuits) and puddings. Commercial baking powders often have a minute amount of starch added to keep them free flowing.

The usual recipe for home-made baking powder is four parts cream of tartar and two parts baking soda (bicarbonate of soda). The amounts used vary between recipes.

BAKING SODA (BICARBONATE OF SODA) This alkaline powder can be used to tenderize tough vegetable leaves; however it destroys their Vitamin C content. It is an ingredient in home-made baking powder, and can be used to leaven (raise) cake batters and honey and ginger cakes that contain an acid ingredient.

In kitchen emergencies, baking soda (bicarbonate of soda) can be applied to burns to prevent blisters.

BAKLAVA A dessert made with buttered sheets of filo pastry layered with a filling of pistachio nuts. It is baked and scored into lozenges, then soaked in rose-scented syrup.

The Turks claim to have invented this sweet pastry, which was integrated into the Middle East and North Africa when the Ottoman empire was at its peak, and it is now extremely popular in both Greek and Egyptian pastry shops.

BALACHONG A salty paste made up of pounded shrimp that is similar to anchovy paste.

BALANCED DIET A diet that prevents deficiency diseases and is the optimum one to sustain a healthy and vigorous life without increasing the weight of the person.

A balanced diet must contain all the essential amino acids, fresh fruit and vegetables, and a fair amount of tubers, roots and pulses and at least 2½ cups/ 1 pint/600ml fresh water per day.

BALLOTINE A parcel-like roast (joint) of meat or a bird which is boned,

B

stuffed, rolled and wrapped in cheese-cloth, then boiled, braised or poached in a rich stock with gelatinous bones. It is subsequently cooled — still immersed in the stock — then unwrapped and garnished and glazed with aspic. It is sliced and served in the same way as a meat loaf.

A galantine follows a similar procedure and resembles a ballotine — in fact, some cooks do not draw any distinction between them. However, strictly speaking, a galantine is composed of diced meat as the prime ingredient and the secondary mixture is a forcemeat of ground (minced) meat, egg, brandy and condiments.

Typical dishes: Ballottines d'agneau (using shoulder of lamb), ballottines de faisan (using the whole tough pheasant), ballottines de volaille.

BALOLO *See Sea cucumber.*

BALSAMIC VINEGAR Balsamic vinegar is one of the oldest vintage vinegars. It is produced in Modena, Italy, from grape must and aged in a succession of small barrels made of different woods. It is sweet yet sharp, and very costly. It can be used instead of wine to deglaze the frying pan after shallow-frying steaks, chops, kidneys or meat strips, and so produce a sharp sauce.

BALUSHAHI A northern Indian sweet pastry fritter or doughnut, cooked in ghee then coated in rose water syrup.

BAMBOO A giant grass which grows in tropical countries. The shoots are edible and are available in cans. They are popular in Chinese cookery.

BAMIA *See Okra.*

BANANA (Fr. BANANE) A native of the West Indies, it can also be grown commercially within 1,500 miles of the equator — in Costa Rica, Honduras, Jamaica, Guatemala, Nicaragua, Colombia, the Canary Islands and Africa.

The fruit when green is very starchy but when ripe the flesh should be yellow or yellow-brown and creamy in texture. Bananas can be cut up and eaten fresh in fruit salads. They can also be cooked in butter or syrup and used in many cakes and desserts, such as banana split.

Dried bananas are sold as banana chips or flakes, for use in breakfast cereals. In their native lands bananas are dried in the sun and sold to be eaten as snacks, in much the same way as figs. A flour is also made, to be used for porridge or cake batters. *See also Plantain.*

BANBURY CAKE A small oval pastry filled with mixed dried fruits, candied peel and spices.

BANH TRANG Vietnamese rice-paper wrappers. Used for wrapping Vietnamese spring rolls.

BANNOCK CAKE A thick, flat cake made of oatmeal that is cooked on a griddle.

BANON CHEESE A French goat's milk cheese that is matured in chestnut leaves and sometimes washed in Marc de Cognac. It has a soft to semi-soft texture and a mild lemony flavor. It is best eaten anytime from the spring until the end of fall (autumn).

BARA BRITH A rich Welsh yeast bread with currants, golden raisins (sultanas), candied peel and spices. The dough is sometimes made in two stages using a fermented sponge to start the fermentation process.

BARAQUILLE A haute cuisine dish which consists of a triangular flaky pastry shell filled with a stew of fresh goose liver, truffle, breast of pheasant, calves' sweetbreads and mushrooms mixed with a little Allemande sauce flavored with Madeira wine.

BARBADINE *See Star fruit.*

BARBECUE An outdoor grill heated with charcoal. The brazier can range anywhere from a simple firebowl that uses charcoal to an elaborate electric barbecue. The grilled foods are served with highly-seasoned sauces and salads. Potatoes may also be cooked on a charcoal fire, wrapped in foil.

Fish should be grilled in a well-oiled specially designed double-wire basket.

Barbecue sauce
This piquant sauce can be used as a marinade or brushed on fish, meat or poultry before and during cooking.

1 tbsp yeast extract (optional)
⅓ cup/3fl oz/75ml olive oil
1¼ cups/½ pint/300ml wine vinegar
⅔ cup/5oz/150g brown sugar
⅔ cup/5fl oz/150ml Port wine
½ tsp mixed spice
½ tsp black peppercorns, ground
1 tsp tomato paste (purée)
¼ tsp chili powder
¼ tsp mustard powder
1 clove garlic
¼ tsp ground ginger
1 tsp salt

Combine all the ingredients in a blender. Pour into a saucepan and boil

B

for 5 minutes. Pour into a screw-top bottle or jar. Set aside for a week. Shake before using.

BARBERRY *See Prickly pear.*

BARBOUILLE A jugged rabbit stewed in red wine, with the blood added to thicken the sauce.

BARCELONA NUT The best variety of hazelnut, used in nougat and other confectionery.

BARDATTE Braised cabbage stuffed with forcemeat made of rabbit and pork sausage meats, or game, with herbs and garlic.

BARFI An Indian dessert with the consistency of fudge, made with reduced milk, pistachio and sugar, flavored with rose water and almond extract.

BARLEY Barley is one of the most ancient of the cultivated foods. Hulled barley, with the husks removed, is used in soups or gruel. Pearl barley is used in puddings, stews and soups.

Barley sugar is a confectionery stick flavored with various citrus juices.

Barley water is a beverage made by simmering pearl barley in water for 2 hours, then adding sugar and lemon or orange juice to flavor, and straining.

Barley is also converted into malt to flavor some baked goods and American milk shakes, as well as in brewing some beers and as a prime ingredient of Scotch whisky.

BARON A roast (joint) made up of two legs including the saddle, usually from lamb and occasionally from beef.

BARRIGA DE FREIRA A Portuguese dessert made of sugar, breadcrumbs, eggs, nuts and candied fruits. It is baked in the same way as a bread pudding, but the result is richer and sweeter. It is cut into squares when cold.

BARTLETT PEAR Originally known as the Williams' pear and in French as Poire bon chrétien. It is usually used for canning in syrup.

BASBOUSA A sweet Egyptian semolina cake. It is brushed with butter and baked until golden, after which it is soaked with lemon and rose water syrup. It is decorated with almonds and cut into diamond shapes.

BASIL (Fr. BASILIC) Basil is a highly aromatic herb widely used in Mediterranean cookery. It is also used in fish cookery, but modern cooks now mix it in salads and in many nouvelle cuisine dishes. Basil is the main aromatic flavor of pesto and pistou soup. Basil can be preserved in oil.

BASELLA A tropical climbing plant known as vine spinach which is used as a green vegetable. In the West Indies, basella is prepared in much the same way as bredes.

BASLE LECKERLI This famous Swiss honey cookie (biscuit) is made using the same amount of flour as honey, with anise seeds, almonds and candied peel, and sometimes kirsch.

The leckerli is brushed with an almond glaze while still hot. It is cut into rectangular pieces.

BASS A collective name for many spiny-finned river and sea fish. The most common variety is the sea bass (Fr. loup de mer), a silver-scaled fish of the grouper family.

It is best broiled (grilled) or stuffed with dry fennel sprigs and baked.

BASTELLA A Corsican filled pastry bearing different names according to the type of filling: with a mixture of cottage cheese and spinach it is known as inarbittate, with zucchini (courgettes) and ground (minced) lamb as inzuchatte, and with cheese and onions it is known as incivulate.

BASTING Moistening the main ingredients usually during roasting, baking, grilling (barbecuing) and broiling (grilling).

BATAVIA CAKE An individual three-layer, round Genoese cake coated with apricot jam and rum-flavored buttercream, and topped with a ring-shaped cookie (biscuit) coated with almond fondant.

BATH BUN A rich yeast bun flavored with lemon and sprinkled with sugar crystals.

BATTENBURG An oblong cake made of alternating colors of sponge strips that are sandwiched with apricot jam. The cake is wrapped in almond paste and sprinkled with superfine (caster) sugar or decorated with piped icing.

BATTER There are many ways of preparing batters for frying foods depending on the texture required and the cost.

Yeast batter
This batter can be used for any kind of fritter.

B

1 tbsp active dry (dried) yeast
pinch of confectioners' (icing) sugar
½ cup/100ml/4fl oz milk, lukewarm
1 cup/8fl oz/225ml water, lukewarm
⅔ cup/5oz/150g bread (strong)
  flour, sifted
½ tsp salt

Dissolve the yeast and confectioners' (icing) sugar in the milk.

Add the water. Beat in the flour to obtain a smooth paste which will coat the spoon.

Cover with a cloth and let ferment for 1 hour. Add the salt.

Egg batter

2 cups/8oz/225g flour
pinch of salt
1 egg, beaten
1¼ cups/½ pint/300ml milk
1¼ cups/½ pint/300ml water
1 egg white

Mix together the flour and salt and sift them into a bowl.

Mix in the egg and stir in the milk and water. Beat until smooth and strain if there are any lumps. Rest for 1 hour.

Egg white batter

2 cups/8oz/225g flour
pinch of salt
1 egg, beaten
1¼ cups/½ pint/300ml milk
1¼ cups/½ pint/300ml water
1 egg white, beaten

This follows the same method as egg batter but fold in the egg white at the last minute to make the batter lighter.

Pancake batter

generous 1 cup/4½oz/125g flour
1 tbsp confectioners' (icing) sugar
1 whole egg
1 egg yolk
1 tbsp oil
⅔ cup/5fl oz/150ml water
⅔ cup/5fl oz/150ml milk

Sift the flour with the confectioners' (icing) sugar and stir in the egg, egg yolk, oil, water and milk. Beat the mixture to a smooth batter. Strain to remove lumps. Rest for 1 hour.

BAUMKÜCHEN A traditional German Christmas cake. It is a very light almond sponge baked on a revolving spit. At regular intervals batter is brushed or trickled onto the revolving cake; up to 14 layers can be added.

The last layer is made up of the same mixture, thinned down so it forms a crust. When cooled, the Baumküchen is coated with fondant.

BAVARIAN CREAM (Fr. BAVAROISE) A custard enriched with whipped cream and meringue and set with gelatin. It can be flavored with chocolate, coffee or fruit syrup. It is usually set in molds. To serve it is unmolded onto plates or flat dishes and accompanied by a sauce or fruit.

Bavarian cream can be transformed into a variety of frozen desserts provided the sugar content is increased to 50 percent of the total weight.

BAVETTINE Italian pasta shaped like minature cats' tongues. These are used for soups such as minestrone, and in consommés.

BAY LEAF Used frequently in meat, poultry and fish dishes and in stocks and stews.

Bay leaves are also packed with dried figs, and are an important ingredient of bouquet garnis, along with parsley, celery and thyme.

BEAN CURD, TOFU Ground (minced) soya beans, boiled with water, then strained and coagulated with sea water or an acid.

BEANS *See individual varieties.*

BÉARNAISE SAUCE A French emulsified egg yolk and butter sauce flavored with mixed fresh herbs and shallots.

Béarnaise sauce is usually served with broiled (grilled) fish, poultry or meat.

BÉCHAMEL A milky sauce thickened with a roux. It can be made from various stocks such as veal, fish or chicken for flavor, or with milk only, but flavored with an onion.

1 onion, studded with 3 cloves
4⅓ cups/1¾ pints/1 liter milk
3 tbsp white roux
salt and pepper
4 tbsp cream (optional)

Add the onion to the milk and heat to a boil. Whisk in the roux and simmer for 30 minutes.

Remove the onion and season to taste. If you wish, add cream for a better texture and taste.

BÊCHE DE MER *See Sea cucumber.*

BEEF (Fr. BOEUF) The meat of cattle which have been bred as domestic animals. The lean meat should be bright red in color and the fat should be white rather than yellow.

Bull's beef is darker in color, with a coarser grain and a marked aroma.

A variety of canned and pickled beef

B

products are available in various sizes, such as tongue.

Beef kebabs with rice

Kebabs are usually served with rice, although they are equally delicious served with baked or fried potatoes, broiled (grilled) bell peppers, eggplants, tomatoes, mushrooms, onions, salads and spicy sauces.

> 1½ lb/700g beef fillet, *cut into 1in/2.5cm cubes*
> 2 small eggplants (aubergines), cut into thick slices
> 8 small tomatoes
> 4 onions, quartered
> 1 red and 1 green bell pepper, seeded and cubed
> 4 tbsp oil for broiling (grilling)

Marinade

> 2 tbsp soy sauce
> 1 clove garlic
> ⅔ cup/5fl oz/150ml tomato juice
> 1 small green chili pepper
> salt
> 2 tbsp oil

Garnish

> 1 cup/8oz/225g long-grain rice, boiled, or baked potatoes
> salad of assorted salad leaves or 4 fresh tomatoes

Combine all the ingredients for the marinade in a blender and soak the meat cubes in it for one hour.

Remove the meat from the marinade and thread the cubes onto long kebab skewers, alternating the meat with eggplants (aubergines), onion, bell peppers and tomatoes. Season the kebabs with salt and brush with oil.

Broil (grill) the kebabs for 10-12 minutes, according to taste. Serve with boiled rice or baked potatoes and garnish with a green or tomato salad.

Boil the marinade and serve it separately in a jug.

Beef hotpot

This is a delicious one-pot meal. All of the vegetables are added to the gently simmering meat and the flavors combine to produce a wonderfully aromatic dish.

The vegetables that are served with the hotpot should be a uniform size, neatly trimmed and cut, if too large. Remember that root vegetables are usually more attractive.

Herb and onion dumplings made from whole wheat (wholemeal) flour and poached in beef stock would increase the calorific value of the dish and could be served instead of potatoes, if preferred. However many cooks serve both!

1lb/450g brisket, salted
1lb/450g thin flank or blade
1lb/450g shank (shin) beef or
knuckle
5 quarts/4.5 liters/1 gallon water or
beef bone stock

Vegetables for broth

1 carrot
1 leek
1 onion, studded with cloves
bouquet garni
1 celery stick
1 sprig of thyme and 1 bay leaf
2 cloves garlic
1 tsp anise seeds (optional)

Seasoning

2 tsp salt
6 peppercorns, crushed
4 cloves garlic
1 tsp brown sugar

To serve: 1lb/450g each of boiled small potatoes, celery, carrots, turnips and leeks, formed into small barrel shapes or sticks.

Bone the meat and chop some of the bones. Extract the bone marrow and keep it in cold salted water.

Place the meat and bones in a large stock pot and cover with the water or stock. Bring to a boil slowly and simmer for 2½ hours. Skim frequently to remove surplus fat floating on top.

After two hours, add the vegetables, bouquet garni, garlic and anise seeds for the broth, and the seasoning. At the end of the cooking time the liquid should be a rich amber color.

For a more pronounced color to the broth, you can include a peeled beet (beetroot) with the vegetables, or shallow-fry and caramelize 1 onion and include this in the pot.

Slice the reserved marrow and poach in water or stock for five minutes. Put three slices of meat, a little stock and an assortment of vegetables on each plate. Serve the marrow with the meat.

Beef fondue

This is always a popular dish and an excellent way of cooking fillet of beef. Guests poach the meat at the table in a strong stock and help themselves to a variety of garnishes, pickles, chutneys and sauces.

The pickled plum chutney can be made in advance.

4 x 4oz/100g fillet steaks, trimmed
4⅓ cups/1¼ pints/1 liter beef stock

Pickled plum chutney
½lb/225g large plums, pitted
½ cup/100ml/4fl oz red wine
½ cup/4fl oz/10 ml wine vinegar

generous 1 cup/8oz/225g sugar
½ tsp mixed ground spice
½ tsp ground black pepper
1 pinch chili pepper

Sauce

⅔ cup/5fl oz/150ml strong beef
*   stock*
½ cup/4oz/100g horseradish cream
1 tsp cornstarch (cornflour)
3 tbsp cream
1 tsp prepared mustard
salt and pepper

Bring the stock to a boil and poach the steaks for 8-10 minutes.

To make the plum chutney, bring all the ingredients to a boil and simmer for 8 minutes. Cool and serve cold.

To make the sauce, boil the stock and stir in the horseradish cream. Stir the cornstarch (cornflour) and cream together in a cup. Stir into the stock to thicken it. Cook for 4 minutes. Season to taste.

Remove from the heat, add the mustard and 2 tablespoons of plum chutney. Strain. Serve chutney and sauce separately to accompany the meat.

Variation

Filet de boeuf à la ficelle: poach the beef in the stock for 20 minutes and serve with vegetables.

BEEF À LA MODE Beef topside or silverside braised with wine and calves' feet to make a good sauce, using a mirepoix and bouquet garnie for flavor. Cook with a lid on for 2½ hours at 350°F/180°C/gas mark 4.

BEEF STROGANOFF Strips of beef fillet stir-fried with mushrooms and flamed in brandy. The sauce is finished with cream and tomato catsup (ketchup) and served with rice.

BEEF WELLINGTON Fillet of beef that is half-roasted, cooled, covered with a mixture of good liver pâté and duxelle mushrooms, wrapped in puff pastry and baked. It can also be made in individual portions.

BEETS (BEETROOT) (Fr. BETTERAVE) There are two main types of beets (beetroot) of culinary interest, the white-fleshed beet which is grown for its sugar, and the red beet, which is eaten as a root vegetable. The latter is eaten fresh in the summer.

If served as a vegetable, beets should be peeled and soaked in red wine rather than vinegar, but vinegar should be used if the beets are to be used for salads with celery and lamb's lettuce.

When fresh beets are boiled in water, the color of the broth will turn bright yellow, but beets pickled in vinegar will turn the liquid reddish. Therefore, fresh beets can be added to broths to give them a good yellow color; pickled beets for a rich reddish color.

Large beets are best baked in the skin for 45 minutes. Beets can also be pickled in vinegar and used in salads or for borscht.

The leaves are edible as a substitute for spinach, and called beet leaves (Fr. poirée à carde).

The mangel wurzel is a widely grown crop which is a variety of beet that is too coarse to be used a vegetable but is excellent cattle food.

Beet and red cabbage relish
This relish is ideal to be served with broiled (grilled) fish.

8oz/225g boiled beets (beetroot), grated
8oz/225g red cabbage, finely shredded
1 red chili pepper, chopped
1 apple, cored, peeled and diced
1 onion, chopped
2 garlic cloves, chopped
1 small piece of fresh ginger root, grated
1 tsp salt
⅓ cup/3fl oz/75ml distilled vinegar
⅔ cup/5fl oz/150ml water
⅓ cup/2oz/50g brown sugar

Place all the solid ingredients in a non-reactive mixing bowl. Boil the vinegar, water and sugar. Stir into the cabbage mixture.

Cool and put in jars with non-reactive lids. Keep in the refrigerator for up to 1 year.

BEETROOT (BEETS) *See Beets.*

BEIGNET A sweet or savory fritter.

Finnan haddie beignets
1lb/450g finnan haddie (smoked haddock fillets)
1¼ cups/½pint/300ml milk
1 cup/2oz/50g breadcrumbs
½ cup/2oz/50g Cheddar cheese, grated
salt and pepper
oil for deep-frying

Choux paste
¼ cup/2oz/50g butter
1 cup/4oz/100g bread (strong) flour
4 eggs, beaten
salt and pepper
oil for deep-frying

Poach the fish in the milk for 10 minutes. Drain the milk and reserve for the choux pastry. Skin and flake the fish and measure ¾ cup/5oz/150g. Make the choux paste.

Beat the fish, breadcrumbs, cheese and seasoning into the choux paste to bind it to a paste thick enough to be spooned into dumplings.

Fry in oil heated to 350°F/180°C/gas mark 4 for 3 to 4 minutes.

BEIJOS DE ANJO (ANGEL KISSES) Light individual sponge cakes soaked in syrup flavored with rum.

BEL PAESE A semi-soft Italian cheese not unlike French Port Salut but without a rind. It can be sliced or grated onto toast and then toasted.

BELGIAN ENDIVE (Eng. CHICORY, Fr. CHICORÉE, ENDIVE) A winter vegetable popularized by Belgian growers who call it witloof, meaning 'white leaves'. Endive is kept in the dark to prevent it from growing green. It has a bitter taste like all the plants of the same family but it becomes palatable with the addition of lemon juice.

It is served as a salad and can be boiled, drained of its moisture by pressure and reheated in butter

Chicory coffee is prepared from the white milky roots of the plant. In France Belgian endive (chicory) is used with coffee beans to give the drink a more distinctive taste.

BELILA A Middle Eastern wheat or barley milk pudding sweetened with a rose or orange flower water syrup, and decorated with nuts.

BELL PEPPER, CAPSICUM A comparatively hardy plant, but the fruit is very bland. It can be eaten raw in salads or cooked in pilaffs or stuffed with fish, meat or chicken.

They are available in several colors according to the stage of maturity, and variety: green, yellow, red, violet or black. Hungarian paprika peppers have a stronger, fiercer flavor.

BELLE VUE Elaborately displayed dishes on a buffet table.

Items such as whole salmon, crawfish, turkey and ham can be coated with chaudfroid sauce and garnished with truffles, or imitation roses made from tomato skins with imitation leaves made from asparagus fern, pineapple leaves or fresh tarragon.

BÉNÉDICTINE A holy name for a famous type of quenelle which is made from egg and salt cod and served with truffle — well worth an ecclesiastic blessing!

BENGAL GRAM A wrinkled, brownish garbanzo bean (chickpea) that is related to channa dal. *See also Dal.*

BENGAL GRAM FLOUR *See Besan.*

BENZOIC ACID An organic acid obtained from benzoin, a balsamic resin extruded from a tree in the Dutch West Indies. The acid is also found in cranberries. It has antiseptic and preservative properties.

BERCY SAUCE A classic veloute sauce flavored with white wine, shallots and mixed fresh herbs; sweet (unsalted) butter is added at the end. Bercy sauce is ideal for any kind of white fish.

BERGAMOT 1) A citrus fruit with a thick aromatic skin which is candied for cakes and from which the volatile oil thymol is extracted for use as a food flavoring.

The fruit was originally made into marmalade.

2) An ornamental herb used in desserts and herbal teas.

BERI-BERI A nutritional disease caused by a diet lacking in thiamin (Vitamin B1).

BERLIN DOUGHNUT A ball-shaped doughnut filled with jam and coated with sugar after deep-frying. Known as a jelly doughnut in the US.

BERLINGOT A pulled sugar candy (sweet) that is flavored with mint and pulled into a rope, then cut into small candies. Berlingots may be made by twisting two colors together.

BERNY A fried cork-shaped potato croquette that is coated in chopped almonds instead of breadcrumbs.

BERZA An Andalusian stew of pork cooked with garbanzo beans (chickpeas), cannellini beans, garlic, onion, bell peppers, green beans and black pudding.

It is one of the many stews with a high protein content.

BESAN, BENGAL GRAM FLOUR Ground garbanzo beans (chickpeas) used as a thickening for sauces and stews. It provides additional protein to the diet.

BETA CAROTENE Used as red and yellow coloring agent.

BETTELMAN An Alsatian bread and egg pudding with candied peel and pitted cherries. It is sometimes flavored with kirsch.

B

A bettelman can be baked in a pie dish or in individual ramekin dishes.

BEURRE BLANC A shallot-flavored emulsified sauce made from a white wine vinegar and wine reduction with soft butter whisked in.

BEURRE MANIÉ A paste of butter and flour used for thickening sauces.

BEURRE NOIR Butter is heated until it reaches the brown stage before adding vinegar and parsley. This sauce is used for skate with black butter and brains with capers.

BEURRE NOISETTE Butter which has been heated to the nutty stage after foaming; used for meunière dishes.

BEVERAGE Vital for food metabolism and the replacement of water lost through perspiration and urination. Beverages include natural and artificial mineral waters, fruit and vegetable juices, lemonades, hot or cold tea, coffee and chocolate, milk shakes, milky hot drinks and herbal teas.

BIBER YOGUTLU A Balkan appetizer of broiled (grilled) skinned bell peppers, cut into strips and tossed in yogurt with chopped garlic.

BICARBONATE OF SODA (Am. BAKING SODA) This alkaline powder can be used to tenderize tough vegetable leaves; however it also destroys their Vitamin C content.

Bicarbonate of soda is part of the baking powder mixture. It can also be used to leaven (raise) rich honey and ginger cakes. In kitchen emergencies, it can be applied to burns, to prevent blisters.

BIGOS A Polish hotpot of sauerkraut, bacon, garlic sausage, and other meats.

BILTONG South African sun-dried ox or wild buck.

BINDING AGENT (Fr. PANADE) A binding agent is used to hold forcemeats and stuffings together. It is made with flour or bread, with eggs as a coagulating protein.

Bread panade
Combine an equal amount of white breadcrumbs with boiled milk. Season to taste.

Flour panade
4⅓ cups/1¾ pints/1 liter milk
1 cup/8oz/225g butter
3¼ cups/1½lb/700g all-purpose (plain) flour

Bring the milk and butter to a boil. Stir in the flour to make a thick paste.

Frangipane panade

8 egg yolks
⅔ cup/5oz/150g melted butter or margarine
2¼ cups/18fl oz/500ml boiling milk.
salt, white pepper and grated nutmeg

Beat together the egg yolks and butter or margarine.

Stir in the boiling milk to make a smooth thick paste. Season with salt, white pepper and grated nutmeg.

Reheat the mixture for 5 minutes in the same way as choux paste. Remove and use for terrines or pâtés.

BIOFLAVONOIDS, FLAVONOIDS These widely-distributed plant pigments are derived from flavone, and include citrin and rutin. Citrin is found in citrus fruits and rutin in most cereals.

BIOLOGY The science of life. Food is the fuel of life and basic knowledge of related sciences should be familiar to all food technicians, epicures, dietitians and chefs.

BIOTIN, VITAMIN H A member of the B group of vitamins, it is essential to man who synthesizes it in his intestines.

BIRD'S NEST SOUP This is made from the nest of a member of the swallow family. It is a great and costly Chinese delicacy.

BIRDS Wild birds of many types, small and big, are called game in gastronomy. There are, however, many birds which are protected — in fact all those smaller than thrushes are free to fly. During the Second World War, crows and seagulls were eaten but the flesh was either tough or bitter.

The best game birds are grouse, partridge and pheasant.

Game birds are usually roasted at 400°F/200°F/gas mark 6 but smaller birds can be cooked at 425°F/220°C/gas mark 7 for 8-15 minutes. A 2¼lb/1kg bird will take about 30-40 minutes. Birds that are to be plain-roasted need not be marinated first, but those which are to be pot-roasted should be marinated in wine to improve their flavor and texture.

BIREWECK An Alsatian loaf filled with a mixture of dried fruits such as apricots, seedless raisins and prunes, and nuts. It is baked and served with fresh cream.

B

BIRTHDAY CAKE Celebration cake, often made with a sponge base, split and coated with jam, covered with almond paste and iced with fondant. It is usually decorated with an appropriate birthday greeting and sometimes the name of the person.

A birthday cake can also be made with a fruit cake base, again covered with almond paste and coated with royal icing. Such cakes are produced in different sizes and shapes and are sometimes also decorated with the appropriate number of candles according to the age of the person for whom the cake is baked.

BISCOTTE French cookie (biscuit) made by baking slices of bread, brioche or bun in an oven until golden and crisp.

The anise-flavored Italian biscotti is a sweet cookie with anise seeds and almonds, self-rising (self-raising) flour, eggs, sugar and very little butter. The dough is made in the same way as regular sweet pie dough (pastry), rolled until ¼in/5mm thick and cut into small ovals or rounds and baked until crisp.

BISCUIT 1) American cookie.
2) Biscuit (scone). Small buns leavened (raised) with baking powder and served with cream and jam. Often they contain golden raisins (sultanas). Some varieties are cooked on a griddle and made with buttermilk or sour (soured) cream.

BISQUE A creamy shellfish soup made from crawfish, crayfish, crab, lobster or shrimp (prawns). It is often flavored with brandy. The shell of the shellfish contributes to the characteristic flavor of the soup.

The flesh is mostly used as a garnish and need not even be used. Ground rice is the main thickening ingredient. Originally the soup was thickened with cookie (biscuit) crumbs, hence the name 'bisque'.

A lobster sauce à l'Américaine can be transformed into a delicious bisque by adding cream thickened with rice flour.

Bisques are available canned, frozen and in powder form, although these products cannot compare with the fresh variety.

Typical dishes: Bisque d'homard, bisque de crevettes à la Normande.

Shrimp (prawn) bisque

This soup can be frozen in 4⅓ cup/1¾ pint/1 liter plastic containers and used when required. It can also be made with crayfish, crawfish, crab, large shrimp (prawns) or lobster.

2tbsp sunflower oil

8oz/225g shrimp (prawns) in
  the shell

1 onion, chopped

1 carrot, chopped

1 fennel bulb, chopped

1 tbsp tomato paste (purée)

1¼ cups/½ pint/300ml water or fish
  stock

⅔ cup/5fl oz/150ml white wine or
  dry sherry

1 garlic clove

3 basil leaves

1 sprig thyme

½ tsp Chinese five-spice powder or
  1 small package of saffron

salt, black pepper and ground chili
  pepper

2 tsp ground rice or cornstarch (corn
  flour)

⅔ cup/5fl oz/150ml light (single)
  cream

In a sauté pan, heat the oil and stir-fry the shrimp and vegetables for 10 minutes. Add the tomato paste (purée), fish stock, white wine or Sherry, garlic, basil, thyme and five-spice powder or saffron and boil for 30 minutes.

Process the soup in a blender and pour it through a strainer. Reheat and season to taste.

Blend the cornstarch (cornflour) with the cream in a small bowl.

Gradually stir in ½ cup/4oz/100ml of the bisque. Stir the cream mixture into the boiling bisque. Simmer gently for 5 minutes.

Variation

Flavor the bisque more highly and serve any kind of white fish, quenelle, mousseline or timbale.

BITOKE A ground (minced) beef steak molded into a flat, oval or round shape. Introduced into French and German cuisine by Russian émigrés in the 1920s.

The German hamburger version took over and so dominated that the name became known world-wide and bitokes became burgers.

BITTER ORANGE Used for marmalades. Popular varieties include Seville, Malaga sours and Palermo bitters. The peel is used to flavor sauces, syrups and liqueurs.

BITTERS Bitters such as gentian, quassia, quinine and aloes are among the oldest prescribed drugs. They are alcoholic extracts of herbs which stimulate the appetite.

Bitters can be used as flavorings for tonics and other remedies or apéritifs — eg Pink Gins.

B

BLACKBERRY (Fr. MÛRE) Blackberries are in season in September and the first part of October. They are used for pies, jams and syrups.

BLACKCURRANT (Fr. CASSIS) This small, dark fruit is used in sauces, jams, jellies, puddings and cakes.

BLACK FOREST CHERRY CAKE A three-layer chocolate sponge soaked in kirsch and filled with cream. The top is decorated with cherries.

BLACK PEPPER *See Pepper.*

BLACK PUDDING Every region of France, Germany, Italy, Spain, the British Isles and Ireland has their own special black pudding.

Some black puddings are made with onions, others with chestnuts, many are flavored with rum, brandy or gin, but all have a mixture of spices that make this special sausage worth serving as a meal for breakfast or supper.

The famous Belgian, northern French and German boudin noir served with a purée of potato and apple is a gastronomic attraction. Many restaurants list it on their menus as 'Heaven and Hell'.

BLACK TREACLE (Am. MOLASSES) This consists of the clear, reddish-brown syrup made by filtering diluted molasses through cloth and charcoal, and concentrated to the required consistency of thick syrups.

BLANCH Originally, to whiten by boiling, such as boiling sweetbreads or brains to remove all traces of blood, or to boil almonds so the brown skins could be easily removed.

Nowadays the term is commonly used to mean parboiling, as in blanching vegetables prior to freezing, or precooking them so that they only have to be reheated, or, in the case of French fries, dipped in very hot fat, before serving.

A flour and water paste may be added to the water that is used for cooking artichokes, calves' heads or salsify, to prevent them browning.

BLANCMANGE Traditional blancmange is made by thickening almond milk with gelatin. This is then molded, cooled and served with fruit such as raspberries.

1 cup/4oz/100g blanched almonds
2¼ cups/500ml/18fl oz water
⅓ cup/3oz/75g sugar
1 tbsp gelatin dissolved in 4 tbsp
  water

raspberry coulis to serve
raspberries to decorate

Process the almonds and water in a blender until smooth. Boil and strain the liquid and sweeten it with the sugar. Reboil it and make it up to 2¼ cups/18fl oz/500ml with water.

Stir the dissolved gelatin into the boiling almond 'milk'. Cook for 5 minutes until thick.

Pour the almond milk into small oiled ramekin dishes and chill.

Turn out onto plates and serve with raspberry coulis. Decorate with whole raspberries.

BLAND DIET *See Dyspepsia.*

BLANQUETTE A white poultry or meat stew using white stock thickened with a roux, and enriched with milk or cream at the end of cooking. A blanquette is usually made from veal, but kid, lamb and chicken can also be used.

BLENDER AND FOOD PROCESSOR A blender is useful for making soups, sauces such as mayonnaise and hollandaise, and fruit and vegetable juices.

The speed with which a blender works means that air is incorporated into the food, which in turn lightens the color of the food; the color can be restored simply by stirring the food to expel the air.

A food processor can be used for making forcemeats, mousses and purees (soups and sauces can be thickened with the resulting purée, thus saving the task of thickening them with starch or a roux).

BLINI A small Russian yeast pancake made with a mixture of buckwheat and wheat flour. It is usually served with caviar or other fish roe, and sour (soured) cream.

BLOATER A washed ungutted herring that is cold smoked. Yarmouth on the English east coast is particularly celebrated for its bloaters.

BLOATER PASTE This savory fish paste should be made from plump, well-smoked fillets of bloater or herring. They are blended with butter, spices and crushed cereals.

BLOOD ORANGE Blood oranges come mainly from Malta, Israel, Sicily and Spain, and are remarkable for the blood-red or mottled crimson color of their flesh, skin and juice.

Seedless varieties of blood orange are now available.

B

BLOSSOM (FLOWER) Many edible blossoms are used in modern cookery for flavor and garnishing and decorating dishes.

Nasturtium, marigold, dandelion and zucchini (courgette) flowers are used for salads, while crystallized violets and roses, apple blossom, borage flowers, camomile, lavender, geraniums and jasmine are used for sweet dishes. Larger blossoms such as those of zucchini can be filled with a stuffing and deep-fried.

BLOWN SUGAR Sugar cooked to the hard-crack stage is blown with a special tube fitted with air-blowing apparatus, in the same way as glass is blown, to make fruits, animals, birds or other decorative items.

Blowing sugar requires a long period of experimentation and practice with sugar confectionery.

BLUEBERRY (Fr. MYRTILLE) A relative of the cranberry native to the USA. It is also related to the European bilberry and whortleberry. Blueberries are used in tarts, pies, bavarois, syrups and toppings for cheesecakes.

BOAR A male pig. Wild boar are classified as game and are still hunted in parts of Europe. Wild boar is cooked in a similar way to venison. To tenderize wild boar, marinate it in a mixture of wine and vinegar, with root vegetables and onions before cooking.

BOBOTIE A South African ground (minced) meat casserole flavored with curry powder, lemon, sugar and almonds and thickened with eggs.

BOILED CANDIES (SWEETS) Candies (sweets) made from sugar boiled to the hard crack stage

BOILING When the maximum vapour pressure of a liquid is equal to the external pressure to which the liquid is subjected, and the liquid is freely converted to vapour.

Boiling is a wet method of cookery (*See also Poaching*). Food is cooked in a liquid (usually water) at a temperature of 212°F/100°C. A slower bubbling movement — with the bubbles just breaking the surface — is known as simmering, and is used for making stocks, soups and sauces.

Short boiling or 'scalding' is used for poultry or meat to seal them. Long boiling is mostly used for root vegetables to break down the fibers and make them more digestible.

Salted meat should be soaked in cold water overnight before being boiled.

B

To preserve their natural flavor, fresh meat and poultry should be immersed in boiling liquid to seal the flesh and keep their juices inside. Any scum floating on top should be removed as it rises.

All root vegetables and raw bones for stocks should be started in cold water.

All food must be completely immersed in the liquid at boiling point. Most vegetables should not be covered with a lid to allow unpleasant smells to escape and so not impregnate the item. Any liquid losses should be replaced regularly to keep the level constant.

Fish should not be boiled because it is too delicate, instead it should be poached. *See also Glaze.*

BOK CHOY, PAK CHOI, Chinese celery cabbage. A leafy vegetable that can be eaten as a salad when young, and cooked in stir-fried dishes with strips of chicken breast when older.

BOLETUS *See Cep.*

BOLLITO MISTO An Italian hotpot with various kinds of meat, such as bacon, beef, veal and garlic sausage, plus vegetables. It is served with salsa verde.

BOLOGNA SAUSAGE A large Italian cooked sausage. It is cut thinly and served as an hors d'oeuvre or sandwich filling.

BOLOGNESE The style of Italian cuisine specific to the town and region of Bologna, using local ingredients, namely olive oil, tomatoes, Parmesan cheese and meat.

Bolognese sauce is made with ground (minced) beef, tomatoes, tomato paste (purée), chopped celery, onion, garlic and oregano cooked until tender. It is used with pasta.

BOMBAY DUCK The name is a misnomer since it refers to the dried, smoked and salted bombil or bommaloe fish. It is grated and used as a condiment in Asian countries, particularly India where its strong fishy taste is used to add flavor and extra protein to vegetable curries.

BOMBE An ice cream mixture shaped like an oval bomb. It can be decorated with whipped cream, candied fruits and flowers.

The mixture is composed of a sugar syrup boiled for four minutes beaten into egg yolks, using 1 generous cup/9fl oz/250ml syrup to eight egg yolks. The mixture is cooked in a

55

B

water bath in the same way as a custard. Whipped cream and flavorings are added to the cooked mixture.

A combination of different mixtures may be used to create a more interesting effect. For instance, a tangerine ice cream may be used to line the mold and the inside filled with a vanilla mix.

BONE This is composed of cartilage and calcium salts. When they are boiled, bones yield gelatin and flavor to the liquid, which is used for stocks.

Leg bones also contain marrow, a fatty substance that can be used as a garnish for some meat and vegetable dishes and for savories.

The best bones to use for stocks come from the shank (shin) and the breastbones of young animals such as calves.

BONING The removal of bones from meat.

BONITO A relative of tuna and mackerel. Bonito has 20 percent fat and firm, closely grained flesh. It is best broiled (grilled) or baked and served with fruit sauces such as gooseberry or apple. It may may also be cooked in wine or vinegar-flavored stock.

BORAGE (Fr. BOURRACHE) A perennial plant with bright blue flowers and a cucumber-like smell. It is used to flavor soups, stews, herbal teas, drinks and cocktail cups. Dip the blossoms in thin batter and then deep-fry them.

BORDEAUX SAUCE (Fr. SAUCE BORDELAISE) This sauce is made in the same way as Burgundy sauce, using claret instead of Burgundy wine, plus three tablespoons of brandy for each 4⅓ cups/1¼ pints/1 liter of sauce.

BOREK A savory Turkish filo pastry formed into triangular or cigar shapes, and baked. One of the most popular fillings is cheese and spinach.

BORSCHT A reddish-colored soup based on beets (beetroot). The other ingredients can vary.

There are vegetarian versions which use many vegetables such as fennel, carrots and onions with mushroom stock or vegetable bouillon (stock) cubes as a base.

Some borscht include meat, sausages, chicken or duck while others contain a mixture of cheaper varieties of fish, and mixed vegetables.

Dumplings are sometimes added to borsch, and strips of cooked beets used for a garnish. Sour (soured) cream is served as an accompaniment.

BOSANSKI KALJA OD KAPUSA A Bosnian stew of mutton, cabbage, garlic and tomatoes.

BOSTON CAKE Popularly known as Boston cream pie, this is a two-layer sponge cake filled with whipped cream or confectioners' custard, and sometimes fruit such as sliced bananas, and then coated with chocolate icing.

BOTARGO, BOUTARGUE, POUTARGUE Grey mullet (or tuna) roe that has been salted and pressed. It is served as a special hors d'oeuvre.

BOTTLED SAUCE Branded bottled sauces are the most convenient and reliable sauces, since they are created by food technologists and creative chefs from the United States of America and Britain and quality-controlled so that we can expect standards of perfection. A large selection of sauces to suit every gourmet taste is available: catsup (ketchup), soy and bean sauces, chili sauce, barbecue sauce and many more.

The spices and fruitiness, the color and the texture are all important factors to these products, which are always so popular with teenagers and children.

Many bottled sauces are also very useful for marinating fish and meat for barbecues.

Some bottled sauces, such as catsup can be made at home (*See page 87*).

Never use an iron or copper pan for the making of an acid sauce. A funnel and screw-top bottles are needed in addition to the usual kitchen equipment for pickle and jam making.

BOTTOM CUTS These are the cheaper cuts of meat from the lower part of the animal: the shank (shin), the feet (trotters), the breast and part of the neck. They are used for slow cooking in stews, casseroles and stocks.

BOTVINYA A Russian sweet-and-sour soup made with beet (beetroot) leaves, spinach and sorrel and garnished with pieces of cucumber. Small pieces of poached fish such as sturgeon or salmon, or shellfish are added to the soup or served separately.

BOUCHÉE A puff-paste (pastry) shell (case) about 1in/2.5cm in diameter. It is filled with a savory mixture such as mushrooms or shrimp (prawns) in cream sauce, and served as an appetizer or buffet snack.

BOUILLABAISSE A famous Provençal seafood dish which can be described either as a stew or a soup. It may include up to 10 varieties of typical Mediterranean fish such as scorpion, gurnard, rascasse, red mullet (goatfish) whiting, hake, mussels and lobster. It is highly flavored with garlic and saffron and served with the famous 'hot' garlic mayonnaise rouille.

The modern version of bouillabaisse, which is less messy to eat, makes a broth of the small fish and bones in which fish fillets and shellfish without their shells are poached.

BOUILLON A broth or clear soup made from meat, vegetables or fish.

BOUILLON CUBE (Eng. STOCK CUBE) Numerous types of bouillon (stock) cubes are available. They are mainly made from seasoning and soluble hydrolyzed protein derived from soya, meat or fish. Herbs, leek, onion and celery may be added to improve their rather bland taste.

BOUQUET GARNI An aromatic bunch of herbs and flavorings such as parsley, thyme, celery and bay leaf. It is used in soups, stews, stocks and hotpots.

BOURGUIGNON For boeuf bourguignon beef is marinated in Burgundy wine before braising, and the cooked dish garnished with button mushrooms, onions and herbs.

BOURRIDE A Provençal strained fish soup that is thickened with garlic mayonnaise. It is garnished with diced fish which has been poached separately in the fish stock at the early stage of the soup preparation.

BOUTARGUE *See Botargo.*

BOUZOURATE A refreshing drink made from the puréed seeds and flesh of water melon. The drink is strained and served with ice cubes. Popular in Africa and the French colonies.

BRAIN (Fr. CERVELLE) This consists largely of a fatty substance containing cholesterol and lecithin, the latter being rich in phosphorus. Brains are highly digestible and considered to be a great delicacy by gourmets. The best brains are obtained from lamb and veal. Poach and then coat them with foaming butter. They can also be served hot with French dressing.

BRAISING The long, slow cooking of food in a sealed container with liquid equal to half the volume of the main ingredient.

When the cooking is complete, the

liquid can made into a sauce to be served with the main ingredient. However before braising begins, the meat must be seared over high heat to brown the outside.

BRAN The outer husk of wheat, a good source of fiber with a high vitamin B and phosphorus content. Bran is added to many breakfast cereals. It can be bought separately.

BRANDADE A smooth mixture of cooked salt cod, olive oil and puréed potatoes flavored with garlic. It is served with fried bread and can be garnished with truffles.

BRANDY BUTTER Sweetened beaten butter flavored with five percent brandy. In Britain it is traditionally served as an accompaniment to Christmas pudding.

BRANDY-SNAP A thin, brittle caramel cookie (biscuit) shaped into a cornet or cylinder. It can be filled with brandy-flavored whipped cream.

BRAT PAN A modern multi-purpose cooking utensil that is ideal for large-scale catering. It can be used for shallow-frying large amounts of food and for braising or pot-roasting. It is pedestal-mounted and can be gas or electrically operated.

BRAWN (Fr. FROMAGE DE TÊTE) A jellied terrine made from pickled pig's head meat, including the tongue, embedded in strong aspic.

BRAZIL NUT Imported from the Amazon regions and mainly used in confectionery.

BREAD One of the cheapest sources of nourishment. There are about 400 varieties of bread made with all types of flour, from all-purpose (plain) white flour to whole wheat (wholemeal) and shaped in many different styles. However, when the term 'bread' is used without any qualifying description, it usually refers to leavened yeast bread.

Bread has been an important food in European and Middle Eastern diets for thousands of years. It is one of the cheapest sources of energy and can be a good source of protein, vitamins and minerals; furthermore, some breads also provide fiber.

In the West in the last century the consumption of bread was much higher; the decline in bread consumption has been associated with an increase in the consumption of meat, fat and

B

sugar, with a corresponding increase in the number of people dying from heart disease.

Whether it is a baguette or a brioche give people bread if they are hungry, for this is the best way to satisfy hunger. Although whole wheat (wholemeal) bread is widely recommended by health experts because it contains the highest content of fiber, minerals and B Vitamins, eating different types is the epicurean way to enjoy bread. Furthermore it is better to enjoy this diversity than to eat more meat than bread.

In India, nann and chapatis are eaten at every meal to mop up rich sauces. Pita bread in the Middle East is used with hummus or tahina with green salad and tomato. In France, Italy and Spain many soups have bread to thicken the broth; cheese soup, onion soup and pumpkin soup with croûtons are examples. Greeks soak their bread in olive oil with garlic, and in England bread, cheese and pickle was the traditional ploughman's lunch.

Bread making, in common with other crafts that depend on fermentation, is not an art but a technical process that can be learned quickly; for many centuries, housewives made bread daily as a matter of routine.

Leavening bread by the sourdough method is as ancient as the Babylonians, and the method is still used today for some non-yeast breads.

Hard wheat flour makes better bread than soft flour, which has to be enriched with eggs to make it more acceptable. The best breads are made from flour that contains at least 12 percent gluten. Bread is usually made from wheat flour, but in many countries rye or mixtures of wheat and rye are used. If possible, use fresh yeast rather than dry (dried); double the amount of fresh to dry is needed. Bread can be enriched with fat, eggs, milk, sugar and honey and a variety of nuts and dried fruits.

Today bread making should be carried out in a scientifically controlled manner to be successful. Home-bakers should try to have a complete knowledge of the raw materials. They should know the characteristics of wheats used by the local miller. The properties of yeast must also be known and understood. Scientific control involves the study of temperature during the whole process from dough making to bread baking.

When faults occur, look at the complete bread making method to trace where the fault originated.

The contributory factors when things go wrong may be:

B

- A faulty or unsuitable ingredient.
- Using the wrong proportions of ingredients, such as too little or too much water or yeast or the lack of salt.
- Using the wrong recipe.
- Incorrect dough temperatures during fermentation.
- Incorrect handling of the dough at any given stage.
- Incorrect handling after baking.

The correct control of fermentation during the resting periods of the dough is the way to obtain quality in bread. The qualities needed in most types of bread — texture, color, flavor, crumb softness, good crust, palatability, and retention of moisture for perfect freshness — are governed by the way in which fermentation occurs.

Wrapped bread can be frozen and kept for several months.

Traditional breads: Abruzzi bread, banana bread, French breads — baguette, ficelle, pain boulot, pain couronne, pain Viennoise, brioche, pain au lait and briochin, Irish potato bread, focaccia, lepinja, lichki, panettone, pogaca, cornbread and rye bread plus many more.

Bread rolls

1 tbsp active dried (dried) yeast
2 tsp sugar
scant 1¼ cups/9fl oz/250ml lukewarm water
⅔ cup/5fl oz/150ml lukewarm milk
1½ tsp salt
1 tbsp/½oz/15g butter
4 cups/1lb/450g bread (strong) flour
milk for brushing

Makes 12

Dissolve the yeast and sugar in 4 tablespoons of the water. Dissolve the salt in the remaining water. Cut the butter into the flour. Mix all the ingredients together into a smooth elastic dough, knead for at least 8 minutes. Cover and let stand on the board for 35 minutes.

Knock back by punching the dough, then divide into 12 evenly-shaped rolls. Place on an oiled baking sheet. Brush the rolls with milk and let rise again for 35 minutes.

Bake at 450°F/230°C/gas mark 8 for 12-15 minutes.

Variation

For a large loaf use the same dough and shape into one loaf shape or bake it in a greased loaf pan (tin) at 400°F/200°C/gas mark 6 for 35 minutes.

Country bread (pain de campagne)

4 cups/1lb/450g whole wheat

(wholemeal) flour
½ cup/2oz/50g rye flakes
2 tbsp caraway seeds
¼ cup/1oz/25g milk solids (powder)
2 tsp salt
2 tbsp butter
1½ tbsp active dry (dried) yeast
2 tsp sugar
4 tbsp lukewarm water
2⅔ cups/21fl oz/625ml milk plus
   extra for brushing
                      Makes 1 or 2 loaves

Mix the flour, rye, caraway seeds, milk solids (powder) and salt. Cut in the butter. Dissolve the yeast and sugar in the water; add the yeast liquid and the milk to the flour mixture and mix. Knead the dough for 6 minutes.

Divide in half. Mold into one or two round shapes. Place on a greased baking sheet and score down the middle with a sharp knife. Then cut on the slant either side of the middle line to give a leaf-like design on the top.

Brush the top with milk. Let rise for 45 minutes. Bake at 450°F/230°C /gas mark 8 for 35 minutes.

BREAD AND BUTTER PUDDING The perfect bread and butter pudding is made by using only two layers of buttered crustless slices of bread, with dried fruits sprinkled over the first layer (these should not be put on top otherwise they would shrivel and burn on baking) and brown sugar sprinkled on top.

Two eggs beaten into 2¼ cups/18fl oz/500ml of milk are poured onto the bread and left to stand for 30 minutes before baking.

Bread and butter pudding is an ideal way to use up stale bread. Bread and butter pudding can also be made in individual pie dishes.

BREADFRUIT A tropical fruit that is a staple part of the diet of West Indians. It can be as large as a melon and has a thick, green, inedible skin. It is boiled, baked or fried in the same way as potatoes.

BREAM (Fr. BRÊME) There are many species of freshwater and sea water bream. The red bream is particularly renowned for its fine flavor. It is not to be confused with the red mullet (goatfish), the redfish, the red gurnard, or the pandora. It can be baked in a casserole or broiled (grilled).

BREDES A dish made with plant leaves and bacon and served with rice. The tastiest bredes are made with watercress, dandelion, bacon, tomatoes and garlic, cooked in a frying pan in the same way as the Irish colcannon.

BRESOLLES A hot meat loaf made by layering raw ground (minced) beef blended with onions and eggs with sliced veal, ham and mushrooms. The dish is cooked in a casserole or pie dish. It is served with a wine sauce and garnished with boiled chestnuts.

BRETONNE (À LA) In the style of Brittany, with white navy (haricot) beans, especially with lamb.

BRETON SAUCE (Fr. SAUCE BRETONNE) A sauce for fish made with onions, Muscadet wine, mushrooms and leeks. It is thickened with a roux and finished with thick (double) cream.

BREWING The infusion of herbs, tea or coffee, or the fermentation of beer from hops. The infusion of tea or other plants is achieved by saturating the dried leaves in boiling water or other liquid, leaving the infusion to stand for a short time, and then drunk immediately with milk, sugar or pieces of lemon.

BRIDGE ROLL Made from a bread dough that contains milk and 1 beaten egg per 1¼lb/500g dough. They are finger-shaped with pointed ends and glazed with egg wash. They are baked for 15 minutes and used mainly for special afternoon functions.

BRIE CHEESE A fermented soft cheese made in the French region of Brie. It is matured for six weeks. Made in large rounds but often cut into wedges that are packed in triangular boxes.

There are several kinds of Brie cheese. The best are:

• Brie de Meaux, which is about 14in/35cm in diameter. The best comes from Grand Morin.

• Brie de Melun, which is about 11in/28cm in diameter and molded by hand.

• Brie de Montereau, which is about 7in/18cm in diameter and has a lower fat content.

• Brie de Coulommiers is 10in/25cm in diameter and matured for 1 month.

Brie should be served when just ripe and a golden color.

BRIK A North African triangular filo pastry containing a number of different savory fillings. Briks are fried and served as a snack or part of a mezze table.

BRILL (Fr. BARBUE) A large flat fish similar to turbot with a pale brown spotted skin. It is usually poached as

B

steaks on the bone and served with Hollandaise sauce.

BRINE A brine is a salt solution used for the preservation of meat and vegetables. It should have 10 percent salt, one percent curing salt (saltpeter) and three percent sugar for preserving meat. 10 percent salt is the right proportion for vegetables.

The solution is sterilized by boiling. For flavor, peppercorns or herbs can also be used.

Coarse-grained sea salt is the best for brines. Table salt contains chemicals that form a scum on top of brine.

The proportion of coarse salt to be used per 11½ cups/8¾ pints/5 liters of water to 4⅓ cups/2¼lb/1kg, plus 3tbsp/2oz/50g sodium nitrate (saltpeter), if available and ¼ cup/2oz/50g of sugar.

BRIOCHE A traditional French yeast mixture containing eggs and butter to produce a light, sweet bun.

Brioche are shaped into round loaves with a small knob on top. They are brushed with egg wash and baked in small or large fluted well-greased pans (tins) in the same way as bread rolls, but at the lower heat of 350°F/180°C/gas mark 4.

Brioche dough can also be baked in oblong or tube (ring) pans or moulded and braided (plaited) into crowns.

The brioche are then glazed with an apricot glaze after baking to give an attractive sheen and decorated with candied fruits and nuts.

Parisian brioches

1½ tbsp active dry (dried) yeast
1tbsp superfine (caster) sugar
1¼ cups/½ pint/300ml lukewarm water
generous 1 cup/4¼ oz/115g bread (strong) flour.

Egg dough

10 eggs
2tbsp superfine (caster) sugar
7g /¼oz salt
2½ cups/1lb 3oz/ 570g bread (strong) flour
2¼ cups/500ml/18fl oz milk
1¼ cups/9oz/250g butter

Makes 32 small brioches

Dissolve the yeast and two teaspoons of the sugar in the water. Add the flour and mix well. Leave to ferment in a warm room for 30 minutes.

To make the dough beat the eggs, sugar and salt. Warm them slightly over a double saucepan at a maximum of 83°F/27°C.

Place the flour on a cold counter

(work top) and make a well in the center. Pour in the eggs and milk and form into a dough. Knead well.

Combine with the first dough. When well-kneaded, cut the butter into cubes and place on top of the dough.

Cover with a cloth and let rise for 40 minutes until doubled in size.

Knead the dough well again to incorporate the butter and make a smooth dough. Divide some of the dough into small buns to fit inside well-oiled or buttered fluted pans (tins).

Shape the remaining dough into pear shapes with pointed ends. Make a hole in the center of each bun in the pan (tin) and push the small pear-shaped buns to fit into the bigger buns.

Brush thoroughly with egg wash. Bake at 350°F/180°C/gas mark 4 for about 15 minutes.

Variation

For a larger loaf bake for 20-25 minutes at 425°F/220°C/ gas mark 7.

Brioche filled with taramasalata
Serve as an appetizer.

2 freshly baked individual, small
  brioches

Filling
4 tbsp taramasalata
2 tsp grated cheese

Serves 2

Remove the brioche tops. Scoop a cavity for the filling in the brioches. Beat the taramasalata and cheese together and spoon into the brioches. Chill for two hours.

BRIOLI A rich French porridge made from chestnut purée with cream and egg yolks. It is usually sweetened but sometimes may be sprinkled with grated cheese.

BRIOUAT A filled Moroccan filo pastry. Briouts can be shaped into cylinders or triangles, then filled with a number of different fillings and either baked or fried.

BRISKET The breast of beef. It is often pickled and boiled and served cold, or used for a hot dish like a beef hotpot. *(See recipe page 42-43).*

BRISLING A small oily fish from the North Sea with a delicate pink flesh. It is available canned in oil or brine.

BRIX A scale that measures the density of a sugar syrup.

B

BROAD BEAN (Am. FAVA BEAN) There are many different varieties; young beans can be cooked and eaten straight from the pod, but some varieties and older, tougher, beans can be improved by peeling the outer skin after cooking. The pod is too tough to be edible but the tops of the young plants can be cooked in the ways as spinach.

BROCCOLI White, green and purple broccoli are closely related to cauliflower. The fresh spears are boiled quickly in salted water for 8 minutes at the most and 5 minutes more for the stalks. Broccoli is best served with either melted butter, hollandaise or mornay sauce.

BROCHETTE The French word for a metal or wooden skewer used for kebabs. Meats to be broiled (grilled) on skewers are best marinated in wine or fresh pineapple juice and lemon for a better texture and taste.

BROMELIN The enzyme of fresh pineapple that is used for tenderizing meat; Chinese cooks used fresh pineapple juice to marinate ducks and pork for that reason.

Heat inactivates the enzyme, so always use the fresh juice straight from the pineapple not the canned juice.

BROTH The liquid resulting from boiling vegetables, meats and bones. It has a stronger flavor than stock.

BROUFADO A Provençale beef stew containing gherkins, herbs, capers and anchovy fillets.

The best way to prepare this stew is to boil the meat in white wine and stock until tender, then the sauce can be made in a similar way to a French vinaigrette with capers, garlic, fresh herbs and diced pickled gherkins.

BROWN SAUCE (Fr. SAUCE ESPAGNOLE) This basic brown sauce owes its origin to the Spanish cookery which dominated Europe in the 16th century. Brown sauce can be made into brown chaudfroid sauce by adding 3 tbsp/ 25g/1oz powdered gelatin or about 4 sheets of leaf gelatin to the hot sauce; this is used to coat meat or poultry for buffets.

Brown sauce can be boiled until reduced by half to make demi-glace.

½ cup/4oz/100g mirepoix
2 tbsp oil
1¼ tbsp tomato paste (purée)
4⅓ cups/1¾ pints/1 liter brown
  stock
2 tbsp/25g/1oz flour
2 tbsp butter

*½ cup/4fl oz/100ml medium
Madeira or dry sherry
1 tsp salt
¼ tsp black pepper*
Makes 4⅓ cups/1¾ pints/1 liter

Brown the mirepoix in the oil for few minutes then add the tomato paste (purée) and stock. Boil for 30 minutes. Make a roux with flour and butter.

Whisk the roux into the stock. Simmer for 1 hour.

Add the Madeira or Sherry and the seasoning. Strain the sauce.

BROWNIE Small, chewy chocolate and nut cakes with a dense, fudge texture. They are considered to be typically American.

The batter is cut into thick squares after baking.

*⅔ cup/4oz/100g chocolate, chopped
½ cup/4oz/100g sweet (unsalted)
  butter
2 large eggs, beaten
1⅓ cup/10oz/300g sugar
1 cup/4oz/100g all-purpose (plain)
  flour
1 cup/4oz/100g chopped walnuts or
  pecan nuts
1 tsp vanilla extract
1 tbsp rum*
Makes 24

Melt the chocolate and butter in a bowl over a saucepan of hot water.

Remove the bowl containing the chocolate. Gradually add the eggs to the melted chocolate mixture.

Stir in the sugar and flour in three batches. Add the nuts. Flavor with vanilla extract and rum.

Pour the batter into a greased 7in/17.5cm square by 1in/2.5cm deep baking pan. Bake at 350°F/180°C/gas mark 4 for about 30 minutes.

Let cool on a wire rack and cut into squares.

BRULÉ(E) Literally meaning 'burnt', the term is used to refer to a dish with a crisp coating, usually of caramelized sugar.

For example, a sweet omelet which is dusted with confectioners' (icing) sugar and burned on the outside with a red-hot skewer that caramelizes the sugar and marks the omelet with distinctive black criss-cross lines.

BRÛLOT Alcohol that is flamed before being drunk, as when making hot punches or mulled wine.

BRUNOISE Vegetables which are cut into very small cubes and used as a garnish for consommés and sauces, and for stuffing.

B

BRUSSELS SPROUTS (Fr. CHOUX DE BRUXELLES) These could be described as round, miniature cabbages growing on a large stalk. The smaller they are the better.

They are delicious when cooked and served with chestnuts or tossed in butter after they have been boiled for a short while.

BSTILA A Moroccan pie made with a type of filo pastry and filled with diced, cooked pigeon meat, eggs, mixed dried fruits and spices.

BUCATINI Italian pasta similar to spaghetti but with hollow strands.

BUCCELATO An Italian ring-shaped sweet bread containing dried figs, seedless raisins and nuts. It is traditionally given to children for their confirmation by their godparents.

BUCKWHEAT Although not a grain or cereal but a relative of rhubarb and sorrel, buckwheat is for making dark breads and blinis.

The seeds resemble beechnuts.

BUDINO DI RISO TURINO An Italian rice pudding with eggs and candied peel baked in a shallow dish. The rice is cooked first, then mixed with the other ingredients before being baked until set.

BUFFALO Zebu cattle are found extensively on most of the continents of the world. They are characterized by a prominent hump above the shoulders, pendulous skin under the throat, on the dewlap, navel and the sheath of the males. The rump is drooping, the head is long and narrow and the ears are long and drooping.

The horns differ widely according to sex and strain; the color also varies from shades of grey to black. The size and form of the cattle are influenced by the climate, soil and feed that is available. The Santa Gertrudis, which have loose skin, are well-adapted to semi-tropical conditions.

Cross-breeding between British and Brahman breeds has produced animals with a better tolerance to both heat and tick-borne diseases.

Buffaloes were originally introduced into Australia from Indonesia in 1800 and there are now 30,000 domesticated buffaloes living in disease-free areas of the country. A substantial buffalo meat export industry has developed with Europe, since the meat from the Australian breeds is leaner than meat from the European animals.

The Indian buffalo is larger than the

ox. It is employed in farm work, but the cow's milk has a peculiar flavor. Wild buffaloes are among the most dangerous of the big game animals, although when they are domesticated they can become quite docile.

In the United States buffalo meat has traditionally been a staple part of the diet of the native Americans. Today the meat is cured, smoked and dried.

BUFFET FOOD There are a huge variety of dishes that are suitable to serve for a buffet: a vast range of cooked and smoked meats and poultry, and many ready-prepared pies and terrines as well as sausages.

Carving cold roast beef, ham, pork, turkey and chicken in front of guests can be unnecessarily laborious, so simply serve the meat already sliced on large platters.

Terrines, pâtés, pies and other pastry dishes should be cut into portions. Mousses and dips should, whenever possible, be made and served in individual molds. To ensure that the food looks fresh, leave the final touches including glazing, decorating and garnishing, until a few hours before the buffet is to be eaten.

Every item should have its own distinct taste, flavor, color and texture. Even aspic jelly should have the same flavor as a rich consommé. Remember that the food should look fresh and be attractively prepared.

Many different sauces can be made quickly and easily from mayonnaise. Add, for example, tomato catsup (ketchup), mixed fresh herbs, cream, yogurt, fruit purée or spices.

The aim should be to serve only a small selection of well-made dishes. Remember that it is not expensive items like fois gras, caviar or smoked luxuries that will impress your guests, but the attractiveness of the selection of dishes and the way in which the foods complement each other. Keep it simple. Make it look appetizing, attractive, fresh and tasty and it will be a success.

The appearance of a buffet table is always vitally important. Use a selection of garnishes, salads and sauces to make the meal as attractive as possible and do not forget the many mayonnaise dressings, aspics, dips, mousses and crudités that can be served to enhance the main dishes.

BUGNE A Burgundian pastry fritter sometimes flavored with rum and orange flower water. The dough is cut into strips 4in/10cm long and ¾in/2cm wide. A slit is made in the center and an end is threaded through it to form a

B

knot. The bugnes are deep-fried in oil and well drained, then served dusted with confectioners' (icing) sugar.

BULGHUR A type of cracked wheat. It is boiled and dried before being cracked, and then reboiled for 10 minutes. It is widely used in the Middle East and by vegetarians. It is sold alongside other cracked cereals such as barley, rye and buckwheat.

BULLACE A very acidic fruit, so it is rarely used for jams, but it can be made into syrups.

BUN Yeast rolls made with a small amount of fat and egg and a little sugar and spice. They are available plain or studded with fruits.

Fruit buns

¼ cup/2oz/50g butter
5 cups/1lb 4oz/500g bread (strong) white flour
½ tsp salt
1 package/½oz/15g dry (dried) yeast
2 tsp superfine (caster) sugar
⅔ cup/5fl oz/150ml lukewarm milk
⅔ cup/5fl oz/150ml lukewarm water
1½ cups/225g/8oz mixed dried fruits such currants, golden raisins (sultanas), candied peel or seedless raisins
1 tsp vanilla extract

Glaze
½ cup/4oz/100g sugar
3 tbsp water

Makes 16

Cut the butter into the flour and salt. Dissolve the yeast and sugar in the milk and water. Add the yeast liquid, vanilla extract and dried fruits to the flour; mix to a smooth dough. Set aside for 1 hour to double in volume.

Divide the dough into 16 pieces and shape into balls. Place the buns on an oiled baking sheet, spaced well apart. Let them rise again for 40 minutes. Bake at 450°F/230°C/gas mark 8 for 15 minutes.

To make the glaze, dissolve the sugar in the water. Brush over the buns while they are still hot.

BUÑUELO A Mexican or Spanish fritter that is served hot, sometimes sprinkled with sugar and cinnamon.

BURDOCK (Fr. BARDANE) A large herbaceous plant that grows wild in Europe but is cultivated in Japan. The roots can be cooked in the same way as salsify and the young shoots and leaves can be boiled and served with egg sauces or used for soups.

BURGUNDY SAUCE (Fr. SAUCE BOURGIGNON) A brown sauce enriched with red Burgundy wine, shallots and mushrooms. It is one of the classic brown sauces.

1¼ cups/½ pint/300ml red
  Burgundy wine
4 chopped shallots
1 sprig of thyme
2 mushrooms, sliced
8¾ cups/ 3½ pints/2 liters brown
  sauce

Boil the wine, shallots, thyme and mushrooms for 5 minutes. Add the brown sauce and boil again for 15 minutes. Strain the sauce.

BUSECCA A delicious Italian soup made with calves' tripe, small beans, sorrel and spinach.

BUTCHERY The skill of dissecting meat and poultry into roasts (joints) and portions. There are many different styles of butchery and many countries have their own ways of dividing a carcass; methods can even vary between regions. French, American and British cuts have been referred to in this book.

French butchers have their own patron saint, Saint Anthony.

BUTTER Butter is made out of the fat from milk. It is available salted and unsalted. Sweet cream (unsalted) butter is made with fresh cream. It is especially appropriate for delicate pastries, special cakes and frostings (icing).

Salted butter is made from fresh or sour (soured) cream and has 1.5 percent salt added as a preservative. Most European butter is unsalted and made from ripened cream but the reverse is the case in America and Britain.

Butter can be colored pale yellow with annatto but some natural butter is made without coloring as the fat has its own pale color depending on the type of feed given to the cow. The juices of carrots or buttercups are used as natural food coloring.

Butter is rich in Vitamin A. It also contains cholesterol and is consequently often replaced by polyunsaturated margarine.

Tips
• Chilled grated butter is easiest to mix into dough when making Danish and puff pastries.
• Sweetened butter keeps even better than salted butter in pastries.
• Sizzling butter will not spit if salt is

B

added to the frying pan before frying.

• Butter can be added to the top of custards and sauces to prevent a skin forming.

• Butter is the best fat to use for soufflés, egg cookery, omelets, choux pastries, béchamel sauce, fudges, chocolate nougat and butterscotch.

• Butter is essential for emulsions such as hollandaise sauce, butter sauce, beurre meunière and beurre manié (butter and flour paste).

• Butter is important for making shortbread and butter cookies (biscuits), croissants and Danish pastries and brioches.

Butter sauce (sauce beurre blanc)

This sauce is an emulsion of butter and concentrated stock. Water cannot be used in place of the fumet because the sauce would then not emulsify and remain stable. Butter sauce is usually served with bland white fish such as cod or hake. It can also be used to flavor boiled vegetables such as cauliflower, asparagus or chicory.

⅔ cup/5fl oz/150ml fish fumet
1 tsp lime juice
1 tbsp shallots, chopped
1 cup/8oz/225g sweet (unsalted)
  butter, chopped
salt and pepper

Boil the fish fumet with the lime juice and shallots until soft, about five minutes. Gradually add the butter pieces while whisking the sauce to obtain a smooth emulsion.

Serve immediately.

BUTTERCREAM A frosting (icing) made from sweet (unsalted) butter and an equal amount of confectioners' (icing) sugar. It can be flavored with extracts or liqueurs and colored accordingly. Buttercream is used with gâteaux and tortes. A little confectioners' custard can be mixed with it to produce a better texture and a less greasy taste.

BUTTERMILK Traditionally, the liquid that is left after the cream has been removed when making butter.

Commercial buttermilk on sale today in cartons is made from skimmed milk that is cultured in the same way as yogurt, and tastes similar to it. Buttermilk is used for cakes and breads, as well as drinking.

BUTTERNUT 1) A type of squash.

2) A member of the same family as walnut. It has a soft oily flesh, which resembles avocado pulp.

BUTTERSCOTCH A caramel candy

(sweet) made with a quarter of butter to the sugar used, cooked to the hard crack stage.

BUTYLATE HYDROXYANISOLE, BHA An antioxidant that is not destroyed by heat so is useful in baked goods.

BUTYLATE HYDROXYTOLUENE, BHT A commercial antioxidant that is added to margarine and fatty foods to prevent rancidity.

BUTYRIC ACID A fatty acid extracted from butter and used in the form of its esters to impart a butter flavor to manufactured products.

CABBAGE (Fr. CHOU) Cabbage comes in many forms and colors — green, white, red, round, oblong, crisp and tender. Cabbage is rich in Vitamins C and A as well as mineral salts.

Select green or red cabbage with firmly packed. fresh, crisp-looking leaves. The head should be heavy and compact for its size. Store cabbage wrapped in a plastic bag — if left outside in the kitchen heat, it will wilt in no time.

Cabbage should be cored and the leaves finely shredded to shorten the cooking time. To maintain the best color it is best to blanch green cabbage for five minutes, then reboil it in the minimum amount of water in order to retain the vitamins and minerals.

Cabbages should be boiled uncovered because of their high sulphur content. White cabbage is best cooked with a little lemon juice and dry white

C

wine added to the water. After boiling, the cabbage can be mixed with butter, cream, or bacon fat, or served plain. Do not discard the liquor but use it in puréed soups.

In Central European countries caraway seeds and juniper berries are used to enhance the flavor.

Red cabbage should be cooked with a little red wine, apples and beets (beetroot) to improve the flavor and color, it takes from one to one and a half hours to braise. All other cabbages can be cooked in 6-12 minutes.

For the preparation of coleslaw, make sure the cabbage is finely shredded, not grated, then soaked in iced water for one hour. Drain and refrigerate it in a plastic bag until ready to use.

There are many dishes cooked or served with cabbage: boiled bacon, garlic sausage, duck, goose and beef hotpot. Cabbage soups are also popular in many countries.

Eating cabbage can cause flatulence; this can be relieved by a carminative.

Broccoli, cauliflower, Brussels sprouts, kohlrabi and kale belong to the same family as cabbage.

Traditional dishes: Berlin sauerkraut soup, caldo verde (green cabbage soup), chartreuse de perdreau, choux farcis, chou polonnais, colcannon.

See also Sauerkraut.

CABINET PUDDING 1) A classic French custard-based dessert made with leftover cake or brioche and candied fruits, and a custard set with gelatin. It is unmolded and served with thin custard or cold with a fruit coulis.

2) A traditional hot British pudding of bread or cake crumbs soaked in sweetened egg and milk, with candied fruits, and baked in a water bath or steamed.

CABRILLION A small French cheese made in the Auvergne from goat's milk.

CACAO A tropical evergreen tree. It is a native of Central America but is now also grown in African countries to satisfy the huge world demand for chocolate which is derived from the fruit of the cacao. *See also Cocoa.*

CACCIATORE (Fr. CHASSEUR) One of the classic Franco-Italian chicken casseroles made with field or wild mushrooms, wine and tomatoes.

CACHOU Far Eastern aromatic candies (sweets) intended for sweetening the breath.

CACIOCAVALLO An Italian cheese made from cows' milk in Calabria and

Romano, which is molded into the shape of a gourd. It can be eaten fresh or be matured for up to six months, by which time it will be quite strongly flavored and hard, so it is usually grated and used on pasta.

CAERPHILLY CHEESE One of the finest cheeses made in Wales. It has a moist, semi-firm texture, and is made in cylindrical shapes or in blocks.

CAESAR'S MUSHROOM (Fr. ORONGE) One of the most tasty large mushrooms. It has an orange-yellow cap. A delicious soup can be made with this mushroom, combined with toasted hazelnuts, onion and celery.

CAFFEINE An alkaloid present in coffee, tea, cocoa and cola, which possesses highly-stimulating qualities.

Medicinally, its main uses are as a cerebral and cardiac stimulant, and as a diuretic. In mild doses, it decreases reaction time and increases mental alertness, the heart rate and the flow of urine. It is also of value in some cases of asthma. Granular effervescent citrate of caffeine forms a useful, non-intoxicating stimulant in headaches caused by fatigue.

However, caffeine is toxic in high doses and can cause sleeplessness, palpitations, tremors and depression. It should also be avoided by pregnant women.

CAILLETTE A flat dumpling made with pork and beet (beetroot) leaves, spinach, dandelion and nettles leaves, which are wrapped in a pig's caul in the same way as a faggot and fried. Cailletes are best served cold with potato salad.

CAJASSE A rum-flavored pastry from Sarlat, in south-western France.

CAJUN Cajun cookery is derived from the 1,600 French Arcadians expelled from their lands by the British in 1785. The Arcadians brought with them a distinctive style of gastronomy with the use of chili peppers, bell peppers and other local products with a characteristic flavor.

This cuisine is redolent of rustic French preparations where pork fat, roux and other thick sauces are still in evidence.

Cajun cookery is based on barbecue grilling. The fish, meat or poultry is marinated and highly seasoned with mixed chili powder and cooked quickly. A ready-mixed Cajun powder is available from food stores, made of ground chili peppers, black and white

C

peppercorns, cumin, celery seeds and marjoram.

Cajun cooking cannot be compared to New Orleans' Creole cookery. rather, it is a combination of French and southern American cuisines, is robust, country-style and uses a roux to thicken sauces. Creole cooking places an emphasis on butter and cream and uses more tomatoes and chili peppers. Both styles make good use of filé powder, bell peppers, onions and celery

CAKE MAKING Cakes are made from recipes that have been developed over years of trial and error. A balanced recipe will produce a cake with a perfect texture, taste, color and flavor. It can be baked in small paper cases, or made in deep round, oblong or square metal cake pans (tins).

There are hundreds of cakes made in many different styles. Some are plain while others are filled and decorated with a frosting (icing).

Cakes may be classified either according to their texture, which reflects their method of preparation, or by their ingredients.

The three main classes of cake according to how they are made are:

BUTTER CAKES Pound cakes such as Madeira are butter cakes made by the creaming method, with the use of baking powder in the cheaper variations. The fat and sugar are beaten together until fluffy. The eggs are beaten in one at a time then the flour and any flavorings are folded in.

The classic proportions for a good creamed cake are equal weights of fat, flour, sugar and eggs. Any alterations or reductions in quantity of these items must be made up by substituting equivalents: for example, baking powder to replace some of the eggs, milk to compensate for loss of moisture or reduction in fat.

SPONGE, ANGEL AND GENOESE CAKES are known as foam cakes because they are produced by whipping eggs for lightness. Special cake flours which are low in gluten and allow the maximum absorption of fat, eggs and sugar are used.

YEAST CAKES such as kugelhopf panettone, Sally Lunn and savarin.

It is possible to vary the flavor of basic cake batters by using extracts. spices, chocolate, coffee, nuts, dried fruits and candied peel. Line all cake pans with baking parchment (greaseproof paper).

Typical traditional cakes: Almond cake, Battenburg cake, Black Forest cherry cake, chocolate cake, Christmas cake, coconut cake, Dundee cake, farmhouse fruit cake, layer cake, lemon cake, Madeira cake, quatre-quart, Simnel cake, strawberry angel cake, torta d'arancio, Victoria sandwich, wedding cake, Windsor cake.

Victoria sandwich

⅓ cup/3½oz (85g) superfine (caster) sugar
⅓ cup/3½oz/85g butter or margarine
2 eggs, beaten
1 tbsp milk
scant 1¼ cups/4¾oz/135g self-rising (raising) flour
jam for spreading
confectioners' (icing) sugar for sifting

Beat the sugar and butter or margarine until fluffy. Gradually beat in the eggs to avoid curdling. Lightly stir in the milk and flour.

Divide the mixture between two greased 6in/15cm layer (sponge) cake pans (tins). Level the top. Bake in an oven at 375°F/190°C/gas mark 5 until golden, about 20 minutes.

When cool, sandwich the 2 layers with jam. Dust the top with sifted confectioners' (icing) sugar.

CAKE MIX A dry mixture of powdered cake ingredients which can be made into a batter by the addition of water or milk and eggs.

CALABASH Round or elongated gourd. It is a watery vegetable when young and should be boiled or stir-fried in olive oil in the same way as zucchini (courgettes), pumpkin or vegetable marrow.

CALALOO (CALLALOO, CALLILU) A West Indian soup and the name of the leaves that are the soup's main ingredients. Calaloo leaves come from various yams, notably those known as dasheen and yautia. The leaves of amaranth are also used.

There are many versions of calaloo but typically it contains salted meat or bacon, crabmeat, coconut milk, garlic, chili peppers and okra. Traditionally, the soup is served with a dish called foofoo, which is a thick purée of potatoes and taro root or plantain.

CALAMARES *See Squid.*

CALCIUM A mineral supplied in milk, cheese, the bones of small fish such as

C

whitebait, and the bones of canned salmon and sardines. Calcium is essential for bone formation.

CALCIUM CHLORIDE Added to tomatoes to keep them firm during canning, and to pickled onions to keep them crisp.

CALCIUM PHOSPHATE Used as a leavening (raising) agent.

CALCIUM PROPIONATE A preservative used in dairy and baked products.

CALDO VERDE The national soup of Portugal made with potatoes, onions and, most importantly, shredded green cabbage.

CALLA ROOT A tuber of the calla lily. A speciality of Florida, these delicate tubers are cooked in the same way as potatoes.

CALORIE A unit of heat; the amount of heat needed to raise the temperature of 1g of water by 1°C. Calories are used for nutritional measurement as well.

CALZONE A Neapolitan yeast turnover filled with meat, mozzarella cheese, spinach and garlic. It can be fried or baked.

CAMBRIDGE SAUCE An English version of hollandaise sauce, flavored with anchovy essence and mustard.

CAMBRIDGE SAUSAGE Pork sausage made to a standard recipe for a good wholesome breakfast meal.

CAMEMBERT A soft fermented cheese made mainly in Normandy and Picardy. Maturing can be stopped by freezing.
To ripen the cheese leave it at room temperature. A wedge of Camembert coated in breadcrumbs and shallow-fried is delicious.

CAMOMILE, CHAMOMILE The flowers are used to make a hot herbal drink, which is recommended for people suffering from dyspepsia and insomnia. When sweetened with honey the drink is a wonderful night-cap.

CANAPÉ Small appetizer served for parties. They are made from toasted or fried bread cut into small oblongs, rounds or triangles and coated with various pastes, mousses, vegetables, cheeses, fish, meat, poultry or game.
Traditionally cold canapés are coated with aspic. Nowadays, hot spicy Indian and south-east Asian canapés are popular.

CANDIED FRUITS Use firmly-textured fruits, stems or peels. They should be ripe enough for the flavor to be developed, but not too mature as they will then be too soft.

Puncture hard-skinned fruits such as plums, peaches, kumquats and ginger by pricking them with a needle. Cherries should be pitted and pears should be peeled, cored and halved or quartered.

Poach the fruit at a low heat so that it cooks gently. Soft fruits may only need 3 minutes, but quince and pears may need 15-30 minutes. The syrup should be made from the liquid in which the fruit has been poached. The starting amount of sugar for this process is 2⅔ cups/12oz/300g sugar per 2½ cups/1 pint/600ml water.

Candied fruits can be diced and used in cakes, ice cream gâteaux and nougat confections.

Candied peel

1½ lb/700g equal amounts of
orange, lemon and lime
1⅓ cups/300g/10oz sugar, plus
3½ cups/1¾lb/800g for soaking fruits
1 cup/5oz/150g powdered glucose
5 cups/2 pints/1.2 liters water

Cut the citrus fruits into wedges or quarters. Remove the segments which can be squeezed to obtain juice. This can be added to the water to make 5 cups/2 pints/1.2 liters.

Remove some but not too much of the albedo or white pith from the peel. Wash the peel and rinse.

Simmer the peel in the water until tender, about 20 minutes.

Dissolve the sugar and glucose in the water, and orange juice if using, and boil for 5 minutes.

Pour into a bowl and set aside to soak overnight.

Next day, strain off the syrup into a saucepan, add ¾ cup/4oz/100g sugar, bring to a boil and simmer for 5 minutes. Pour onto the peel and soak for 8 days, repeating the process each day Soak the peel for 4 more days in this thick syrup.

Drain, put the fruits on a wire rack and set aside in a warm, draught-free place until they are coated with a thick, firm glaze.

Variation

Candied kumquats: prick the skin of each kumquat all over, but leave the fruit intact. Follow the recipe above.

Candied angelica

8⅔ cups/2 liters/3½ pints water
2 tsp salt
1½lb/700g angelica stems

C

4⅓ cups/1¾ pints/1 liter boiling
   stock syrup
2⅓ cups/1lb/450g sugar, plus 4⅔
   cups/1¾lb/800g over 8 days
6 drops of green coloring

Bring half the water and the salt to a boil. Remove from the heat and soak the angelica stems for 10 minutes. Drain the angelica and then boil it in the remaining (unsalted) water for 5 minutes. Drain and scrap the stems to remove the outer skins.

Place the stems in a bowl and pour over the boiling stock syrup. Then proceed as for candied peel, but adding the green coloring on the third day.

Variations
a) Use celery stalks instead of angelica.
b) Use sliced fennel bulb, instead of angelica.

Candied ginger
When buying fresh ginger, look for roots that are roundish with almost kidney-shaped nobbles. The skin should be a light reddish-brown color. Choose samples that are up to 4in/10cm long and up to 1in/2.5cm thick.

1lb/450g fresh ginger root
2½ cups/1 pint/600ml water
1⅓ cups/12oz/350g sugar

scant 1 cup/4oz/100g powdered
   glucose
2⅓ cups/1lb/450g of sugar added
   in amounts of ½ cup/4oz/100g
   each day
3 tbsp lemon juice

Peel the ginger with a potato peeler. Cut into equal pieces as big as a small plum. Boil the ginger pieces in the water for 15 minutes. Add the sugar, glucose and lemon juice and heat, stirring until the sugar and glucose have dissolved.

Transfer to a bowl. Let it soak for 24 hours. The liquid density should be 16 degrees on the Baumé scale.

Repeat as for candied peel above.

Variations
1) To make ginger in syrup, pour the ginger and syrup into sterilized jars after it has been soaked for 4 days.
2) Use small pieces of carrot instead of ginger.
3) Use instead Jerusalem artichokes or pumpkin.
4) Use melon or pawpaw (papaya).

CANDY 1) A candy (sweet) is a sugar confection of a number of different types, such fudge, marshmallow, taffy (toffee), soft centers, nut, nougat and chocolate.

Typical candies: almond dragées, barley sugar, berlingots, caramels (hard and soft), chocolate truffles (*See page 105*), fudge, marshmallows, nougat, sherbet lemons, taffy, Turkish delight.

2) To preserve fruit, fruit peels, vegetables and aromatic roots and stems such as ginger and angelica, in a sugar syrup which increases in degree of concentration over a number of days.

The syrup penetrates the food by osmosis (the diffusion of two miscible solutions through a permeable membrane until their concentrations are equalized), which is paramount in preserving the texture of fruits and vegetables. Dissolved sugar can only go through the cell walls very gradually, hence, the system of saturating the food slowly.

Each day more sugar is added to the syrup and it is boiled to increase its concentration by just under 2 degrees Baumé. The syrup should measure 16 degrees Baumé on the first day and at the end of 8 days it should be 32 degrees. At this stage the fruit is set aside to dry in a warm, dry, draught-free place. *See also Marrons glacé recipe page 97.*

CANDY FLOSS A solution of sugar and glucose boiled to the hard crack stage and spun to a floss. The most usual colors are yellow, pink and green. It may be used as a decoration for ice cream desserts. For occasions such as banquets, a machine is available for large-scale production.

CANDY SUGAR These brown, brittle sugar crystals are used in fruit compotes and salads because they do not dissolve rapidly. Some people prefer candy sugar in their coffee.

CANNARONI, ZITONI Wide Italian pasta tubes.

CANNED FOOD It is difficult to imagine the modern civilized world without canned foods. A prejudice against canned food still exists as it is often felt that fresh ingredients are better.

However, all fresh foods cannot always be found in the stores. Canned foods can also save preparation time and some are cheaper than the fresh equivalents. Useful canned foods include tomato paste (purée), beans, artichokes, truffles, palm hearts and fruits out of season such as cherries, pineapples, guavas and quinces.

Soups of all types can be made very quickly, so canned soups are really not needed unless they are of the more unusual, expensive or time consuming

C

kind to prepare, such as game soups or shellfish bisques.

Canned sardines, tuna, pilchards and salmon can quickly be puréed and made into mousses or seafood pâtés.

CANELLING The technique of making grooves with a small knife, known as a cannelling knife, on the caps of raw mushrooms and in the rind of citrus fruits and melon to make them look more attractive.

CANNELLONI Filled rolls of Italian pasta. Cannelloni can be made from pre-shaped tubes, which can be difficult to fill, or squares of pasta that are rolled around the filling.

The pasta is boiled before filling to soften it, but it must not be allowed to become too soft. The filled cannelloni are usually placed in a buttered baking dish, covered with a sauce and sprinkled with grated cheese and browned in the oven or under the broiler (grill).

Plain pancakes can also be used for cannelloni wrappings, as can Chinese spring roll wrappers.

CANNING Packing food in metal containers, or special jars, and heating for long enough to kill bacteria or spores and sterilize the food. The containers are processed under pressure at a high-er temperature than boiling water.

Canning times vary considerably according to the type of food, its acidity and texture, and the size of the container, ranging from 20 minutes to 1½ hours at 240°F/115°C. Acidic products take less time to process than alkaline products.

CANOLA OIL *See Rapeseed oil.*

CANTALOUPE *See Melon.*

CANTHAXANTHIN A widely-used natural red coloring extracted from a number of foods such as mushrooms.

CAPE GOOSEBERRY, PHYSALIS A golden, ball-shaped fruit encased in a papery envelope. The fruit is juicy and tart and contains edible seeds.

Cape gooseberries are used to make jam or served fresh dipped in fondant for petit fours.

CAPELLINI, ANGEL'S HAIR Long, extremely fine pasta strands.

CAPER (Fr. CAPRE) The pickled flower-bud of the caper plant, which is very common around the Mediterranean coast. The plant is a relation of the garden nasturtium.

Capers are used in tartare sauce and

tapenade as well as tossed into green salads, however they are classically served with skate cooked in butter.

CAPONATA A sweet-sour Sicilian dish of eggplants (aubergine), celery, olives, tomatoes, onions and capers. It is cooked gently and flavored with wine vinegar and sugar. It is usually served cold as an appetizer.

Caponata alla marinara is bread dressed with olive oil, with anchovy fillets, garlic and olives.

CAPPELLETTI Italian pasta fashioned in the shape of small hats. They are usually stuffed and cooked like ravioli.

CARAMBOLA *See Star fruit.*

CARAMEL Sugar, when boiled to 320°F/160°C, turns rich golden brown and has a full, intense flavor. When making caramel, use a sugar thermometer for accuracy — caramel very quickly over-cooks.

Caramel can be turned into taffies (toffees) by beating in butter or cream. Nuts and candied fruits can also be added.

Caramel sauce is made by diluting hard caramel crystals in hot stock syrup. It is then used for flavor and color.

CARAWAY (Fr. CARVI) A seed used in confectionery, stews, cabbage dishes and rye bread.

CARBOHYDRATE A member of the large group of organic compounds composed of carbon, hydrogen, and oxygen. Carbohydrates include starches, sugars and cellulose.

Chemically, they are classified as mono-, di-, and polysaccharides. Fruits, vegetables, pulses and grains such as rice and flour, are composed mainly of carbohydrates.

Carbohydrates play an essential part in the metabolism of all living organisms and provide the energy.

CARBON DIOXIDE A colorless gas with a faint tingling smell and taste. It occurs in the atmosphere as a result of the oxidation of carbon and carbon compounds. Atmospheric carbon dioxide is the source of carbon for plants and photosynthesis.

Carbon dioxide is solid at 170°F/78.5°C at atmospheric pressure, and is known as dry ice. This is used for the preservation of frozen food and ice cream. Carbon dioxide gas is heavier than air and does not support combustion, so it is used in fire extinguishers. It is also used to carbonate drinks and beers.

C

Carbon dioxide when produced by yeast during the fermentation process acts as a leavening (raising) agent in bread making.

CARBON(N)ADE Belgian and northern French speciality of beef and onions braised in dark beer or stout.

CARBONARA An Italian cream, egg, bacon and cheese sauce for spaghetti.

CARDAMOM (Fr. CARDAMOME) A member of the ginger family and native of India, where it has been used for thousands of years. The pods can be either green or white when sold.

Cardamom has a pungent, spicy flavor and is used in sweet and savory Indian and Middle Eastern dishes. It is one of the three most expensive spices after saffron and vanilla.

CARDOON (Fr. CARDON) A prickly plant, closely related to the thistle and globe artichoke but cooked in the same way as celery.

The stalks must be grated or lightly shaved with a sharp knife or peeled with a potato knife. A cup of flour-and-water batter is mixed into the cooking liquid to prevent discoloration through oxidation, by forming a crust on top of the liquid.

CARIBBEAN CABBAGE (Fr. CHOU CARAIBE) The edible root of a plant cultivated in the West Indies as a vegetable. The peeled root is cooked like a turnip and can be grated and used in the mixture for fish fritters.

CARMINATIVE Preparation to relieve flatulence. The essential constituent is an aromatic volatile oil, usually of vegetable extraction.

The best-known carminatives are caraway, cardamom, camomile, cinnamon, cloves, dill, ginger, nutmeg and peppermint.

To relieve flatulence, especially after eating beans, eat carminatives in salads with French dressing.

CAROB, LOCUST BEAN A member of the pea family. The carob fruit looks like a rough fava (broad) bean. It was known as St John's bread because John the Baptist lived on carob beans when he was in the wilderness.

The dried pods are rather sweet and can be eaten in the same way as confectionery. They are ground and used as a substitute for cocoa, particularly by people who are allergic to cocoa. Carob can be made into cakes and desserts or drinks.

CAROB GUM A natural exudation of

the carob tree that is used to add texture to bottled sauces and thicken chutneys. It is also used in sugar confectionery for making sugar gums.

CAROLINE Savory éclairs made of choux pastry and filled with cold liver mousse or hot salmon purée.

CAROTENE A natural orange pigment present in carrots, dark green vegetables, apricots and butter. It is converted into Vitamin A in the body.

Carotene acts as a photosynthetic pigment in plant cells that lack chlorophyll. There are no losses in cooking because it does not dissolve in water and is heat stable.

CARP (Fr. CARPE) A round fish found in lakes. Before cooking, carp should be soaked in water with a little vinegar and rinsed several times. It is often ground (minced) and shaped into a sort of dumpling.

Carp can be poached or made into fish cakes. In Jewish cuisine carp is used for gefilte fish or baked in casseroles.

Typical dishes: Carpe à la Chambord, Carpe Solomon.

CARPACCIO An Italian dish of thinly sliced raw beef fillet dressed with olive oil and lemon juice, and sometimes topped with shaved Parmesan cheese.

CARPETBAG STEAK An Australian fillet steak stuffed with raw oysters before broiling (grilling), then pan-fried with crushed black peppercorns.

CARRAGEEN, IRISH MOSS A seaweed from which a gelatinous substance is extracted to make desserts and jellies. Carrageen is also used in fish soups.

CARROT (Fr. CARROTTE) Of all vegetables, these are next in importance to cabbage and potatoes. More than 500 species are grown all over the world.

Carrots are best cooked with water, honey and a little butter until the water evaporates, giving a glossy appetizing finish to the vegetable. Carrots are used in salads, sauces, soups, or mixed purées with potatoes.

Desserts and sweet products are also made with carrots, such as tarts, jams and preserves in ginger syrup.

CARTILAGE The hard but pliant substance which forms part of the skeleton of animals and fish. When boiled for a long time it yields gelatin.

CARVING As a general rule, meat is carved thinly and perpendicularly to

C

the direction of the muscle fibers; the slices should be as large as possible and evenly sized.

There are two knives for carving; both are about 11in/28cm long, one is plain and one serrated. They are made from stainless steel.

CASEIN The protein of milk and the main substance of cheese.

CASHEW (Fr. CACHOU) A kidney-shaped nut used as a cocktail snack, in fruit cakes, confectionery, stews and Indian curries.

CASSATA A colorful Italian ice cream gâteau made of two or three different flavors, one of which is mixed with candied fruits and pistachio nuts.

CASSAVA, MANIOC The starchy root from which tapioca is produced.

CASSIA Inner bark of a tree that is used as a spice similar to cinnamon.

CASSIS The French name for blackcurrant. It is often made into a cordial.

CASSOLETTE This takes its name from a dish which resembles a small pan with handles. It is just large enough for one portion.

The contents can be a stew of pigeon legs or grouse, or asparagus tips and lobsters. It is a luxurious and expensive item.

CASSOULET A famous French casserole of goose and lamb with navy (haricot) beans and sausages. The meat and beans are layered in an earthenware casserole and baked.

CASTAGNACI Thick Corsican fritters made with chestnut flour, eggs and milk.

CATECHU A reddish extract which is very astringent and rich in tannin. It is made into tablets with cinnamon and nutmeg as a remedy for diarrhoea, and is useful in relaxing sore throats.

CATERING Arranging, cooking and serving meals for a family or for a group of people.

Commercial catering and hospitality is a huge, diverse industry. It includes hotels, restaurants, sports camps, cafés, railroads, airplanes, cruise ships, schools, colleges and universities, nursing homes, hospitals and military catering.

Such establishments encompass all standards of catering and cooking and many styles of gastronomy are offered which cover classic, ethnic and modern dishes and snacks.

CATFISH (Fr. ROUSETTE) A large family of mainly freshwater fish, although some tropical varieties also inhabit salt water. Varieties include the tiger fish and the dog fish.

Catfish can be broiled (grilled), fried, poached, smoked or stewed. It is used in ethnic as well as French restaurants where it is often served in a meunière, shallot, red wine or tomato sauce.

Typical dishes: Roussette au beurre blanc, smoked catfish with green salad and lemon.

CATSUP (KETCHUP) A thick fruit sauce made with one or two main ingredients, it is less spicy than most other fruit sauces.

Catsup is usually bottled and kept refrigerated, but if processed in a water bath it can be kept for longer.

Tomato catsup

8oz/225g tomatoes, seeded, skinned
  and chopped
2 tbsp sugar
1 tbsp cider or wine vinegar
1 tbsp tomato paste (purée)
2 tsp cornstarch (cornflour)
4 tbsp water
salt and pepper

Boil the tomatoes, sugar, vinegar and tomato paste (purée) for 15 minutes. Process in a blender.

Stir the cornstarch (cornflour) and water together. Stir into the tomato purée and bring to a boil, stirring until thickened. Season.

Pour into sterilized bottles and cover with non-reactive lids. Process in a water bath for 25 minutes. Let cool. Store in a cool, dark, dry place.

Red plum catsup

8oz/225g red plums, pitted
1 shallot, chopped
⅓ cup/3oz/75g chopped dried dates
1 tbsp vinegar
1 tsp cornstarch (cornflour)
2 tbsp water

Boil the plums, shallot, dates and vinegar until soft. Process in a blender.

Stir the cornstarch and water together. Stir into the plum purée and bring to a boil, stirring. Boil for 10 minutes.

Pour into sterilized bottles, cover with non-reactive lids. Process in a water bath for 25 minutes.

Let cool. Store in a cool, dark place.

CATTLE The term 'cattle' is applied to different animals in different countries: buffalo in Africa and India; yak in Tibet and China; gayal and batin

C

cattle in India; zebu in Africa; and our domesticated cattle bred all over the Western world.

Cattle are sold as males, or bulls; if sterilized they become steers. Young females are known as heifers, but once they have produced a calf they become cows. Castration is practiced on animals to improve the fattening process.

Good meat can only come from healthy, well-reared livestock. It is interesting to note that animal feeds constitute 85 percent of the cost of producing cattle. Pastures which provide a mixture of grasses and legumes are best for all cattle. In winter, root crops, hay and straw are needed to supplement the diet.

CAUL A strong, nearly transparent membrane with islands of fat which give it a lacy appearance. It is used to cover products such as faggots and gayettes to prevent them drying out during cooking.

CAULIFLOWER (Fr. CHOU-FLEUR) Some of the green leaves and core are edible. Either cook the whole cauliflower or separate it into sprigs. The modern way to cook cauliflower is to boil it gently for only 10 minutes, to a crunchy texture.

Cauliflower can be served au gratin, made into soups, soufflés, quiches and served in salads with French dressing.

Typical dishes: chou-fleur Dubarry, chou-fleur mornay, chou-fleur polonnais, cauliflower cheese.

CAVATAPPI An Italian short, narrow, ripple-edged pasta shaped like a shell.

CAVIAR The salted roe of sturgeon. The main supply comes from the Black and Caspian Seas. The fish are caught during spawning in winter and spring when they swim up the rivers.

There are three types of caviar classified according to size, color and species of sturgeon.

BELUGA This comes from the Beluga or great sturgeon. The eggs are more or less dark grey, firm, heavy, large and well separated.

OSIETRA This comes from a large sturgeon weighing up 88lb/40kg. The eggs are smaller than Beluga but evenly-sized, gold-yellow to dark brown and quite oily. It is considered to be the best variety.

SEVRUGA This caviar comes from the stellate sturgeon, a smaller fish; the grains are lighter. It is the cheapest of the three.

C

Pressed caviar is made with the broken eggs and is almost like a paste.

Caviar should be served cold in small containers. Blinis and sour (soured) cream and chopped hard-cooked (hard-boiled) eggs are the usual accompaniment. It can also be served on small canapés or in small pastry tartlets.

Caviar should be stored at 32°F/1-2°C.

CAYENNE A red chili pepper that is dried and ground to a peppery powder for use in the kitchen. It originates in Cayenne in Guyana and is grown all over the West Indies and South America. It is used in curries, Mexican dishes and chili pepper sauces.

CELERIAC (CELERY ROOT, Fr. CELERI RAVE) This root resembles a rutabaga (swede) and has a flavor similar to that of celery It can be eaten raw in mustard mayonnaise or cooked lightly with a white sauce.

Celery root (celeriac) tends to darken when peeled, so immerse it immediately in cold water with some vinegar to prevent oxidation.

CELERY (Fr. CELERI) Celery grows wild in many countries. It is now cultivated and can be green or white.

The best way to cook celery when young is to slice it diagonally and parboil it for 5 minutes only. It can then be stir-fried with onion and carrots in the best Chinese style with a pinch of ground aniseed. It can also be used in sauces, hotpots or stews for its flavor.

Celery seeds can be used as a tangy condiment.

CELL The unit of life. Many micro-organisms such as bacteria, yeasts and protozoa consist of one cell, whereas a human being is made of several million cells.

CELLULOSE A polysaccharide that forms the supporting cell structure of plants, and provides fiber in the human diet. The best way to insure a good intake of fiber is to eat fruit with the skin on; it is much cheaper and healthier than buying bran products.

Liquid cellulose is used by bakers to spray bread rolls to give them a more glossy appearance.

CELSIUS A system of measuring temperature in which the freezing point of water is 32°F/0°C and the boiling point is 212°F/100°C.

CENTERPIECE A table decoration which can be made of a flower

C

arrangement, nuts and fruits or imitation fruits in pulled and blown sugar. They are presented in sugar baskets or other ornamentation such as nougat, caramel or chocolate or sculptures carved out of ice blocks, or sculpted in butter. This is all part of the artistic work of specialist chefs.

CEP (Fr. CÈPE) A flavorsome wild mushroom with a brown cap. It is usually fried with garlic and herbs and used in Provençal stews.

CEREAL A family of foods that includes wheat, sorghum, oats, barley, rye, buckwheat, maize, rice, millet, tapioca and arrowroot.

Cereals are an excellent source of energy, and indeed can be regarded as the mainstay of civilization. However, they must be supplemented with protein and fat as found in eggs and milk to provide a balanced diet.

Cereals can be ground to produce flour for use in cooking.

Some cereals are made into popular breakfast cereals to be served with milk. These include corn flakes, porridge and puffed corn.

CEVICHE, SEVICHE Raw fish marinated in lime juice, served throughout Central and Southern America.

CEYLON MOSS Native of the Indian Ocean and used for jellied desserts.

CHAFFING The removal of the husk of grains such as wheat and oats.

CHAMPIGNON Cultivated white mushroom graded in various sizes. Small or button mushrooms can be tossed with cream, a dash of brandy and nutmeg and served on toast, or cooked à la Greque.

Mushrooms à la Greque
Use as an appetizer or hors d'oeuvres.

8oz/225g small mushrooms
8oz/225g very small onions
1¼ cups/½ pint/300ml dry white
  wine.
juice of 1 lime
2¼ tbsp olive oil

Seasoning
small handful of chopped fennel
1 bay leaf
1 garlic clove, crushed
6 crushed coriander seeds
salt and white peppercorns

Boil the mushrooms and onions with the wine and lime juice for 6 minutes. Add the seasonings. Let cool then chill for 2 hours.

Variations

Young root vegetables such as carrots and turnips can replace the mushrooms.

CHAMPVALLON A very old lamb or mutton dish created at the time of Louis XV in France and still popular for lunch. It consists of lamb or mutton cutlets, sliced onions and potatoes baked in the oven.

CHANFAINA A West Indian dish of sheep's liver braised with bell peppers, tomatoes and chili peppers.

CHANFANA A Portuguese casserole of slowly-cooked kid or lamb in red wine with onion, garlic and bacon.

CHANGES OCCURRING IN COOKING There are seven basic cooking methods — boiling, roasting, steaming, frying, broiling (grilling), braising and baking. During any type of cooking food undergoes changes which make it palatable, perhaps more presentable, and if the heating is long enough, sterile as well.

Chemical changes include coagulation, tenderizing and swelling. Starchy foods become digestible and less chewy; pectin and most minerals leach into the liquid.

Natural sugars caramelize, giving a better taste and color to food. The essential oils may evaporate but the fragrance has been absorbed by the food itself. Harmful bacteria and their spores can be destroyed, but unfortunately so can Vitamin C, thiamine and niacin.

Many foods change color, such as cakes and breads, meat, fish and poultry and vegetables. The color of green vegetables can be revived by plunging them into iced water.

CHANTERELLE (Fr. GIROLLE) A mushroom found in all kind of woodland but commonly under pine, beech and birch trees. Chanterelles appear in July until the frosts of winter. They have an egg-yolk yellow color and a taste not unlike apricots.

Chanterelles can be shallow-fried with diced bacon and herbs, used in omelets or served lightly cooked in mixed salads.

CHANTILLY *See Cream chantilly.*

CHAPATI An flat Indian bread made with whole wheat (wholemeal) flour.

1 ¼ cups/½ pint/300ml lukewarm water
1 tbsp sunflower oil

5½ cups/1lb 6oz/650g whole wheat
 (wholemeal) flour
1 tsp salt
oil for frying

Makes 20

Mix the water and oil together with the flour and the salt.

Knead well, cover with a damp cloth and refrigerate for 8 hours. When ready to cook, shape into 20 balls. Flatten them into ovals. Heat a little oil in a frying pan and fry them on both sides until lightly browned. Serve as an accompaniment to curry — as well as, or instead of, rice.

CHARCUTERIE The charcuterie trade is a major industry in France, competing with butchery and catering. So many dishes can be bought from a French charcuterie that it would be possible to eat a different dish every day for a month without repeating a single meal.

CHARD (Fr. CARDE) The leaves can be creamed or steamed in the same way as spinach. A quiche of chard with Emmenthal cheese is much appreciated at a buffet party.

CHARLOTTE A hot or cold molded dessert. For a hot charlotte the mold is lined with bread and filled with a thick fruit purée. For a cold charlotte the mold is lined with lady (sponge) fingers and filled with a bavarois cream.

A charlotte mold is a metal pan (tin) with sloping sides and a 2½ cup/1 pint/600ml capacity.

Typical dishes: Charlotte aux pommes, charlotte chocolatine, charlotte à la Muscovite.

CHARTREUSE A sweet or savory mousse encased in a solid decorative ingredient.

Chicken chartreuse with leeks
Leek ribbons line the base and sides of the mold. When the dish is unmolded the attractive stripped green lining can be seen, while the mousse is hidden inside the casing.

4 small leeks
¼ cup/2oz/50g soft butter
5oz/150g raw skinless chicken
 breast
1 cup/4oz/100g broccoli florets, par-
 boiled
2 eggs
4 sprigs of chervil
1¼ cups/½ pint/300ml milk
⅔ cup/5fl oz/150ml heavy (double)
 cream
salt

pinch of white pepper
pinch of ground mace

Sauce

¼ cup/2oz/50g sweet (unsalted)
  butter
1 carrot, sliced
1 stick celery, sliced
1 small leek, white part only,
  cleaned and sliced
1¼ cups/½ pint/300ml leek stock
  (reserved from cooking the 4
  leeks)
1¼ cups/½ pint/300ml boiling salted
  water
1 small sprig of thyme or fresh
  coriander, chopped
2 tbsp clear honey
juice of ½ lemon
4 tbsp heavy (double) cream
salt and pepper

Garnish

2 small carrots, cut in batons
2 sticks celery, cut into batons
16 small broccoli florets
bunch of chives, snipped

Cut the leeks into ½in/1.25cm x 3 in/7.5cm strips. Wash the leeks and cook them quickly in the boiling salted water for 1 minute.

Drain the leeks and set aside the cooking liquid.

Quickly refresh the leeks in ice water to revive the green color. Pat dry on a cloth and divide the leeks into green and white ribbons.

Coat the inside of eight ⅔ cup/5fl oz/150ml ramekin dishes with soft, but not melted butter. Line them with the leek ribbons, alternating the white and the green parts, radiating outward from the center and hanging the ends outside the ramekins so that they can be folded over the chicken mixture.

Purée the chicken, broccoli, eggs, chervil and thyme or coriander. Season to taste. Fill the lined ramekins to the brim with the chicken mixture. Fold the overlapping leek ribbons up and over the filling toward the center to cover the top.

Line a shallow baking pan (tin) dish with baking parchment (greased paper) and half-fill with warm water. Place the ramekins in the pan and bake at 350°F/180°C/gas mark 4 for 20-25 minutes. Remove from the oven and keep warm in the pan, while preparing the butter sauce.

To make the sauce, heat half the butter in a saucepan and stir-fry the vegetables for 4 minutes to allow the flavor to develop, but do not brown.

Add the reserved leek stock and boil for 12 minutes. Add the honey and lemon juice. Strain off the stock and

C

gently boil again for about 5 minutes. Whisk in the cream and cubes of the remaining butter to emulsify the sauce — it should have a smooth, glossy finish. Check the seasoning.

To make the garnish, boil the carrots, celery and broccoli for 4 minutes so that they remain crisp.

Pour a pool of sauce onto the plates and unmold the chicken chartreuse out into the center. Garnish with the blanched vegetables.

CHÂTEAUBRIAND A cut of beef steak from the center of the fillet. It is usually large enough for two portions.

Châteaubriand is served with Béarnaise sauce, château potatoes and watercress, making a dish that was created in honor of the famous French writer Châteaubriand. It is often only served for two in restaurants.

CHAUDFROID A béchamel, brown or pink sauce which is set with gelatin and used for coating cold meat or poultry. The sauce must be used when still warm and before it sets to achieve an even coating.

CHAYOTE, CHRISTOPHENE, CUSTARD MARROW, (Fr. CHRISTOPHE) This pear-shaped member of the squash family can be stuffed and baked or used raw in salads. It is a good source of potassium.

CHEDDAR CHEESE This hard cheese takes its name from a village in the west of England. It is now also made in Canada, the United States, New Zealand, Australia, Holland and France.

Cheddar cheese is better than any other hard cheese for quiches, soups, vegetables and milk sauces.

CHEESE France alone is reputed to produce over 400 different cheeses, many named after the town or village where they are produced. If we add commercial brands to this, there must be over a thousand different cheeses in the world.

Cheeses can be made from milk, cream, skimmed milk, or a mixture of these.

Cheese is composed of the solids of milk which have been coagulated by being warmed and mixed with rennet or acid, separated from the whey, and sometimes wrapped in a cheesecloth and pressed in a strong vat, hoop or a mold until dry.

These cheeses are often left to mature or ripen for varying lengths of time in cool, dark places such as cellars. During this time, chemical and physical changes occur; it loses its tough, rubbery texture and becomes soft and mellow, and almost crumbly.

As much as 50 percent of the nitrogenous (casein) constituents may be converted to soluble forms, although the average for hard cheese is 30 percent.

Volatile and other acids, which play an important role in the distinctive flavor and aroma of cheeses, develop. Lipolysis (the splitting of fats into glycerol and fatty acids) occurs to a greater extent in semi-hard cheeses, especially blue-veined ones such as Roquefort and Dolcelatte, than in hard cheeses.

Unpressed fresh soft cheeses are especially popular in the summer, eaten with berries or made into dips with herbs.

Pressed and ripened or matured cheeses have more flavor and are eaten with fruits, nuts, crackers (biscuits) and bread, as a snack or as a meal.

BLUE CHEESES These get their characteristic blue veining by injection with penicillin mold. Examples include Stilton, Roquefort, Danish blue and Gorgonzola.

EWES' MILK CHEESES include Broccio, Venaco and Pecorino.

FRESH SOFT CHEESES which may be salted. Some are made with cream, or are blended with cream.

GOATS' CHEESES with a downy rind, include Saint-Marcellin, Cabecou, Chabichou and Chevreton amongst the many French varieties.

PRESSED AND COOKED CHEESES include the smooth and rather rubbery Beaufort, Gruyère, and Emmenthal.

PRESSED CHEESES are curdled by rennet and the draining is accelerated by cutting and stirring. They include Cantal, Reblochon, Saint-Nectaire, Tômes, Cheddar.

PROCESSED OR COOKED CHEESES sold under brand names, such as Kraft.

SHAPED-CURD CHEESES are mainly Italian and include of spun-paste cheeses such as Mozzarella, Provolone and Caciocavallo.

SOFT CHEESES WITH A DOWNY RIND which are molded and washed with a salt solution during ripening. For example Brie, Camembert and Neufchâtel.

SOFT CHEESES WITH A WASHED RIND

C

include Livarot, Munster, Époisses and Pont-l'Evêque.

VEGETARIAN CHEESES curdled with lemon juice or vinegar rather than rennet may be more acceptable to vegetarians, since rennet is an animal extract. For example Quark.

The more mature a cheese the better it will mix with other ingredients in dishes such as soufflés, fondues and sauces.

Cheese is enormously useful for improving the food value of vegetarian dishes.

Soft cheeses may be combined with eggs, cream and sugar, for cakes or other dishes.

Swiss cheese fondue
This fondue will freeze well.

½ cup/4fl oz/100ml dry white wine
2 cups/½ lb/225g hard cheese such
   as Cheddar or Gruyère, grated
6 egg yolks
½ cup/4fl oz/100ml heavy (double)
   cream
salt, pepper and grated nutmeg

Bring the wine to a boil then stir in the grated cheese. Simmer until the cheese is melted.

In a bowl combine the egg yolks and the cream and gradually stir this mixture into the melted cheese. Season.

Variations
Many kinds of cheese can be cooked together with wine, beer, cider or milk to produce similar fondues.

CHEESECAKE   There are two main types of cheesecake: those that are baked and those that are set with gelatin and usually lightened with whisked egg whites. A fruit topping can be added to both types either after baking or setting.

CHELSEA BUN This is made from yeast dough which is rolled into a rectangle, spread with butter and sprinkled with mixed dried fruits, candied peel and spices.

The dough is rolled up like a jelly roll (Swiss roll) and cut into slices. These are placed flat in a buttered baking pan (tin), set to rest for 35 minutes then baked in a hot oven.

They are glazed with syrup while still hot.

CHERRY (Fr. CERISE) There are many species and over 150 varieties of cherry, but they may all be brought into two groups:

SOUR CHERRIES which are red or black, round or oblate, with acidic juice; a well-known variety is morello.

SWEET CHERRIES which can be black, white or red, and nearly heart-shaped.

The best French cherries come from Montmorency, hence the well-known decoration for tarts and cakes.

A small gadget to pit cherries is readily available and quite useful.

Typical dishes: Berlin cherry torte, Black Forest cherry cake, canard aux cerises, cherry jubilee, clafoutis, gâteau Montmorency.

CHESTNUT (Fr. CHÂTAIGNE, MARRON)
To peel chestnuts the hard skin must be slit and the nuts either roasted in a hot oven or broiled (grilled) until the skins crack. Peel off the hard skin and boil the chestnuts for 10 minutes. Drain and remove the inner soft brown skin, exposing the creamy nut.

Chestnuts can be boiled and used as with Brussels sprouts, or ground to a paste and mixed with chocolate for a delicious dessert or ice cream.

Marrons glacés
2¼ lb/1kg peeled chestnuts
2 cups/10oz/300g powdered
    glucose
2 ⅓ cups/1lb/450g sugar
4⅓ cups/1¾ pints/1 liter water
600g/1lb 7oz sugar, added ½ cup/
    4oz/100g amounts daily over 6
    days

Make a slit through the hard skin of each chestnut and bake them at 400°F/200°C/gas mark 6 until the skins crack open. Remove the skins. Boil the chestnuts in water for 10 minutes. Drain and remove the thin brown second skin.

Dissolve the glucose and the 2 cups/1lb/450g sugar in the water. Add the chestnuts and boil for 5 minutes. Let soak for 24 hours. Drain the syrup the next day, add ½ cup/4oz/100g sugar, boil for 5 minutes and soak the chestnuts again for 24 hours. Repeat daily for a total of 6 days, adding the same amount of sugar until it has been used. The syrup by then will show 34 degrees Baumé.

Drain the chestnuts. Dry in a warm oven. Pack in attractive boxes and store in a cool, dark, dry place.

CHICKEN (Fr. POULET) The young bird of a domestic fowl.

A chicken should have tender flesh that is elastic to the touch and not flabby. The breast bone should be soft and flexible. The bird should have a well-rounded breast, fleshy thighs, and well-distributed fat. The legs may be white or black, according to the race, but they should never be yellow. They should be soft and pliable.

The skin must be smooth and white. The parson's nose should be white, or slightly pink, with a small mass of fat covering the back.

If a fresh chicken is to be kept for a few days before it is to be cooked, it should be washed under running water, inside and out, or soaked in salted water with a little vinegar. After washing or soaking, pat the chicken dry and place it on waxed paper on a clean tray in the coldest part of your refrigerator. Cover it with a plastic wrap (cling film) to prevent it contaminating any cooked food.

Never refreeze poultry once it has been partially, or completely thawed. Refreezing will not spoil the meat, but thawing the meat to room temperature will have allowed the dormant bacteria to be reactivated. Freezing does not, as many people imagine, kill bacteria, it simply prevents it multiplying.

Hygiene precautions
• All chicken should be thoroughly washed before it is cooked.
• All tools should be sterilized in hot water with detergent.

• Personal cleanliness demands that you wash your hands before and after handling chicken.
• Cutting boards must also be washed with soap and bleach.
• To avoid cross-contamination avoid storing raw chicken with cooked food.

Boned chicken with Parmesan stuffing
Boned, stuffed and rolled chickens are most suitable for a buffet as they can be carved in the same way as a terrine.

The Italian-style stuffing has a robust garlicky taste. Have your butcher bone the chicken. The cooked and cooled chicken can be coated with chaudfroid sauce and aspic, or garnished to suit your taste.

A tomato salad would be an ideal accompaniment for this excellent summer dish.

5lb/2.5kg chicken, boned

Forcemeat
1 cup/8oz/225g pork sausagemeat
1 small onion, chopped
3 garlic cloves, chopped
½ cup/2oz/50g Parmesan cheese, grated
1 egg
1 cup/2oz/50g field mushrooms, chopped

1 cup/2oz/50g fresh whole wheat
(wholemeal) breadcrumbs
3 basil leaves
1 tbsp parsley, chopped
½ cup/2oz/50g pine nuts, chopped
2 tomatoes, skinned, seeded and
chopped
¼ red bell pepper, diced
1 tsp salt
good pinch of black pepper, nutmeg
and celery salt

Serves 6-8

1 red bell pepper, seeded and cut
into cubes
1 onion, chopped
2 tbsp seasoned flour
1 tsp tomato paste (purée)
1 tsp vinegar
2tsp sugar
2/3 cup/5fl oz/150ml chicken
stock
1 tsp ground ginger
1 small green chili pepper, seeded
and chopped
8 ripe apricots, whole or halved
according to size
salt

In a large bowl combine all the ingredients for the forcemeat. Place the forcemeat inside the boned chicken, and sew the bird up with string.

Wrap in cheesecloth and poach in gently simmering water for 1½ hours. Let cool in the stock. Chill in the fridge overnight.

Chicken in sweet and sour sauce

It is now considered healthier to cook chicken without the skin to reduce fat intake. This popular recipe is easy to prepare. The inclusion of apricots and bell peppers give the dish a unique piquant flavor. Serve with Chinese noodles, bell peppers and zucchini (courgettes) cut into strips.

2 tbsp oil
1lb/450g chicken breast, diced

Heat the oil in a frying pan and stir-fry the chicken for 5 minutes. Add the bell pepper and onion and fry for 2 minutes. Sprinkle in the flour and mix well.

Stir in the tomato paste (purée), vinegar, sugar, stock, ginger and chili pepper. Simmer for 10 minutes.

Add the apricots and cook for 5 minutes more. Season with salt.

CHICKPEA (Am. GARBANZO BEAN, Fr. POIS CHICHES) This pulse is a rich source of vegetable protein so is a useful addition to vegetarian diets.

It can be made into a delicious dip with garlic, olive oil and coriander seeds, or stewed or in a casserole.

C

Garbanzo beans must be soaked in water for at least 2 hours before being boiled gently for up to 2 hours. Canned garbanzo beans in brine are readily available in the shops.

CHICORY (Am. BELGIAN ENDIVE, Fr. CHICORÉE, ENDIVE) A winter vegetable popularized by Belgian growers who call it witloof, meaning 'white leaves'. This plant is blanched by being kept in the dark to prevent it from growing green. It has a bitter taste like all the plants of the same family but it can be made palatable with lemon juice to counteract the bitter flavor.

It is served as a salad and can be boiled, drained of its moisture by pressure and reheated in butter.

Chicory coffee is prepared from the white milky roots of the plant. In France Belgian endive (chicory) is used with coffee beans to give a more distinctive taste.

CHIFFONADE Leaves such as lettuce or spinach, cut into ribbon-like strips.

CHILAQUILES Mexican fried tortilla chips served with a sauce.

CHILI CON CARNE A Mexican-style dish originating in America. It consists of ground (minced) beef simmered with chili peppers, spices, herbs and tomatoes, with pre-cooked or canned red kidney beans added a short while before serving.

CHILI RELLENOS Mexican stuffed bell pepper filled with ground (minced) pork or beef, flavored with herbs, garlic, nuts and spices and braised in a rich tomato sauce. There is also a Spanish version.

CHILL (Fr. FRAPPER) To cool food in the refrigerator, or in the freezer for a short time.

CHILL-COOKERY A seven-stage process of food preparation and short-term food preservation. It is based on rapid chilling techniques, vacuum packing, and precise temperature-controlled refrigeration for between one and five days.

CHIMICHANGA A Mexican tortilla wrapped around a filling which may contain a mixture of ground (minced) meat, beans, or chicken before frying.

CHINESE COOKING Chinese cooking is an ancient art where food is regarded as the cornerstone of life, around which all the philosophic concepts have been explored to the point that cooking and eating are almost a religious ritual.

Steaming and stir-frying are the two principal cooking methods, used for the preparation of a very wide range of dishes.

In the past, this eclectic catalogue of fare has included snakes, swallow's nests, shark fins, bear's legs, carp's lips, rhinoceros, a pig's bones, sea slugs and the use of soya milk to produce a curd.

Peking duck, jumbo shrimp (king prawns) and crab soup might be their pièce de resistance but the Chinese have wider talents and skills than most Western chefs. They have produced even more basic creations than India and the Middle East.

The combined cuisines of China have often been compared to French and Italian cuisines as having made the greatest contribution to the world of food.

There are five Chinese styles of cookery:

CANTONESE specializing in meat broils (grills) and shark soups.

FUKIEN on the east coast featuring fish stews, soups and all types of shellfish.

HUNAN featuring sweet-and-sour and stir-fried dishes.

PEKING leading the way in the cooking of ducks and poultry and generally regarded as the main style of Chinese haute cuisine.

SZECHUAN famous for its hot spicy foods.

A meal can start or end with soup. The many dishes may be brought together on top of a rotating table for the guests to move around so that they can help themselves to a large selection of fish, meat, poultry, stir-fried vegetables and rice dishes.

Chinese emperor chowder

This is one of the grand dishes of old China, still very popular in Shanghai.

1 tbsp sunflower oil
1 shallot, chopped
8oz/225g mushrooms, sliced
5oz/150g scallops, sliced
1⅓ cups/8oz/225g canned
   bamboo shoots, sliced in strips
1 tbsp grated fresh ginger root
scant 1 cup/5oz/150g crab meat
1 bunch of scallions (spring onions),
   thinly sliced diagonally
1 tbsp soy sauce
2 tbsp sake wine
8¼ cups/3¾ pints/2.1 liters fish
   stock

C

salt and pepper
2 pancakes, cooked and cut into thin
    shreds, to garnish

Heat the oil in a large pan. With rapid movements stir-fry the shallot and mushrooms for 2 minutes. Add the scallop meat and cook for 3 more minutes. Stir in the remaining ingredients. Season to taste and gently simmer for 12 minutes.

Serve in individual bowls with hot shredded pancakes.

CHINESE LEAF *See Chinese cabbage.*

CHIPOLATAS Small sausages which can be made of beef, pork or chicken and are broiled (grilled) or shallow-fried and served with roast turkey, or for cocktail parties.

CHIPS (Am. FRENCH FRIES, Fr. POMMES FRITES) These are potatoes cut into strips ⅜in/1cm through and 3in/7.5cm long and deep-fried. For really good French fries (chips) they should be cooked in a two-stage process *See Deep-frying. See also Pont-neuf, Allumette.*

CHLOROPHYLL The green pigment in plants plays an important role in their synthesis of carbohydrates.

The cells of the mesophyll of the leaf contain chloroplast or chlorophyll-corpuscules, the nucleus, and the cell liquid with its dissolved materials. The chloroplast contains four pigments: two green ones — chlorophyll (a) and chlorophyll (b), and two yellow ones — carotene and xanthophyll. The structure of chlorophyll is similar to that of haemin from haemoglobin, which indicates a close relationship between these two vital pigments.

Chlorophyll is not soluble in water. It is, however, soluble in acetone, ether, and benzene.

Chlorophyll reacts with alkaline solutions such as baking soda (bicarbonate of soda) to produce an olive green color but it softens the cellulose too much and destroys Vitamin C so should not be used.

Acids such as lemon juice added to cooked spinach will intensify the taste and the color.

CHOCOLATE A confectionery manufactured from cocoa powder, cocoa butter and sugar.

Chocolate contains mainly fat, with some protein, tannin, ash, acid, caffeine and theobromine, an alkaloid related to caffeine which is responsible for the mildly stimulating properties of cocoa and chocolate.

The type of chocolate produced depends upon the amount of sugar, lecithin and vanilla added.

For cakes and desserts, choose chocolate with a high cocoa content and also some cocoa powder.

BITTER-SWEET CHOCOLATE must contain 32-35 percent chocolate liquor.

COUVERTURE is a special chocolate for culinary purposes. It has a higher cocoa butter content than ordinary chocolate, and is used for dipping, molding and for making candies with both soft and hard centers.

MILK CHOCOLATE has 10-12 percent milk in powder form added and is unsuitable for cooking.

SEMI-SWEET OR SWEET CHOCOLATE contains 15-35 percent cocoa solids.

WHITE CHOCOLATE is a mixture of sugar, cocoa butter, milk solids, lecithin and vanilla,used for sauces or mousses and marquises but not petits fours and other small sweetmeats.

• Store the chocolate in a cool, dry place. The temperature should be 20 to 25°C/60°F to 70°F. Dark chocolate can last for years when stored properly. Otherwise, it will develop a pale grey 'bloom' (surface streaks and blotches) when the cocoa butter rises to the surface. It can also form sugar crystals. If this happens the chocolate can only be used for drinks, puddings or sauces.

• Chocolate should be heated in a water bath. Avoid getting water in the chocolate as it will turn to an unsightly mass and be ruined.

• For piping scrolls, add a little glycerine to melted chocolate, then pipe onto paper with a pencil design for accuracy of shapes and contours.

• For small candies (sweets), do not flavor the chocolate itself but flavor the centers and fillings. For professional results use dark chocolate couverture — the more bitter, the richer the flavor of the end product.

• A white bloom appearing on the surface of chocolate is a result of dampness and the sugar dissolving and re-crystallizing.

Typical dishes: Bavaroise, brazilians, bûche de Noël, chocolate éclairs, florentines, Sacher torte, marquise, pot de chocolat, truffles.

See also Chocolate confectionery.

Chocolate marquise

5 squares/5oz/150g dark chocolate
5 tbsp egg yolk (about 3 egg yolks)

C

5 tbsp heavy (double) cream
3½ tbsp rum or orange liqueur
3 egg whites

Melt the chocolate in a bowl over a saucepan of hot water. Add the egg yolks and cream. Stir well until smooth. Flavor with the rum or orange liqueur.

Beat the egg whites until soft peaks form then fold gently into the mixture.

Line a 2¼ cup/18fl oz/500ml plastic tray with baking parchment (grease-proof paper), making sure it fits well. Pour the chocolate mixture in and chill. Serve in thick slices with lady (sponge) fingers or poached pears.

Chocolate cake frosting (icing)
The base cake can be Victoria sandwich mixture *(See recipe page 77)*, Genoese sponge or a meringue flavored with cocoa powder.

Coat the cake with hot apricot jam before the frosting is spread.

4½ squares/4½ oz/125g dark
  chocolate
1 cup/4oz/100g confectioners'
  (icing) sugar, sifted
⅓ cup/3oz/75g unsalted (sweet)
  butter
3 tbsp cold water
2 tbsp rum or orange liqueur

Melt the chocolate in a bowl placed over a saucepan of hot water. Add the confectioners' sugar, then the butter, water and rum or orange liqueur.

Cover the base cake while the frosting is still warm enough to work.

Chocolate sauce
Serve the sauce warm with profiteroles, poached pears or bananas and ice cream.

4½ squares/4½ oz/125g dark
  chocolate
⅔ cup/5fl oz/150ml thick (double)
  cream
½ cup/2oz/50g confectioners' (icing)
  sugar
¼ cup/2oz/50g sweet (unsalted)
  butter

Melt the chocolate with the cream, sugar and butter. Bring to a boil while stirring. Remove from the heat and serve.

CHOCOLATE CONFECTIONERY A wide range of confectionery is produced by chocolate-coating various centers of different flavors and colors.

There are more than a 100 soft and hard centered chocolates, such as ganache (with cream), almond paste, caramel, nougat, Turkish delight, soft fondant and fruits. Belgian chocolates are a particular delicacy.

The chocolate should be bright and glossy, which is why dark chocolate is more suitable.

Line small foil candy (sweet) cases with melted chocolate, cool it then fill up with the chosen filling.

Chocolates are an essential part of a petits fours selection which could include: Andalousians, Arabellas, Brazilians, caramel sticks, Chambéry truffles, chocolate nuts, coffee centers, chocolate nougat, croquant nougat, ginger triangles, honey nougat, kirsch fondant, liqueur chocolates, Maraschino centers, almond paste centers, marquisettes, moccatines and truffles made from flavored ganache.

Chambéry truffles
9 squares/9oz/250g dark chocolate,
9½oz/275g fondant
scant 1 cup/7oz/200g butter
grated chocolate or unsweetened
  cocoa powder for sprinkling

Praline
⅔ cup/5oz/150g sugar
juice of ½ lemon
¾ cup/3oz/75g hazelnuts
¼ cup/1oz/25g almonds
                    Makes about 45

To make the praline, cook the sugar with the lemon juice until it turns almost to caramel, 340°F/170°C. Add the hazelnuts and almonds. Turn onto an oiled cold surface and let cool. When hard, crush to a grainy powder with a pastry (rolling) pin.

Mix the praline with the chocolate, fondant and butter. Let cool. Divide the mixture into about 45 small balls. Roll the balls in grated chocolate or unsweetened cocoa powder.

Place each one in a small foil or paper candy (sweet) case. Store in an airtight container in a cool, dry place.

Variations
1) Roll the truffle mixture into balls and coat in extra melted chocolate.

2) Add a scant 1 cup/3½ oz/100g chopped almonds to the truffles.

Basic chocolate fudge
5oz/150g fondant
1¼ cups/5oz/150g confectioners'
  (icing) sugar, sifted
I tbsp evaporated milk or cream
50g/2oz plain dark chocolate
⅓ cup/3oz/75g butter

Soften the fondant by stirring it in a bowl placed over a saucepan of hot water. Mix in the confectioners' sugar, evaporated milk or cream and the

C

chocolate. Add the butter last and mix well but do not beat. Boil the chocolate mixture to 234-240° F/112-115°C, then take it off the heat.

Continue to stir the mixture until smooth. Pour into a 6in/15cm square baking pan (tin) lined with buttered foil. Let cool.

When the fudge is cold cut into 1in/2.5cm squares. Place in candy (sweet) cases and store in an airtight container in a dry cool place.

Variations

1) The fudge mixture can be made into a filling by adding a little heavy (double) cream and beating it to aerate it to a fluffy mixture.

2) A coating can be made of fudge by warming the mixture and pouring it over a cake which has been glazed with hot apricot jam to insulate and form a layer between the cake and the fudge glaze.

Chocolate amandine
Serve as almond petit fours.

9 squares/9oz/250g dark chocolate
cup/2oz/50g candied peel
¾ cup/3oz/75g chopped almonds
2 tbsp seedless raisins

Melt the dark chocolate in a bowl over a saucepan of hot water. Stir well and add the candied peel, almonds and raisins.

Drop spoonfuls of the mixture onto a tray lined with baking parchment (greaseproof paper); space them at ¾in/2cm intervals as they will spread.

Chill. When cold serve with ice cream decorated with raspberries.

CHOCOLATE TEMPERING Tempering determines the texture and color of chocolate. To master the process of tempering, it must be understood that cocoa butter is a complex mixture of fats, each having a different melting and setting point. It is the presence of these different fats that makes it so important that couverture chocolate is correctly tempered.

Cut the chocolate into small pieces, put it in a dry bowl and place it over a saucepan half-filled with hot water. Make sure that no drops of water enter the chocolate, otherwise it will thicken and be useless for coating. Also make sure the chocolate does not get into contact with direct heat.

Stir with a wooden spoon (not metal because it will cool the chocolate too much) as the chocolate starts melting, which will be at 115-118°F/46-47° C for dark chocolate and 110°F/43°C° for milk couverture.

It is very important to use a thermometer to measure the temperature. Remove the bowl from the heat and wipe the bottom. Pour the chocolate onto a clean cold surface, preferably marble, and spread it with a palette knife. This will cool the chocolate and set it again.

Return the chocolate to the bowl and very carefully heat it over the same saucepan of hot water. The temperature must not exceed 88°F/31°C for dark chocolate and 84°F/29°C for milk chocolate couverture.

If tempering is done correctly, the chocolate will set quickly and molded figures can be removed easily. For molding chocolate, the mold beforehand must be thoroughly clean and polished with cotton wool.

CHOLESTEROL A sterol which is one of a class of solid alcohols; these are waxy materials derived from animal tissues. It is the source from which bile acids are manufactured.

The rising incidence of arterial disease in western countries in recent years has drawn attention to the relationship between high levels of cholesterol in the blood and hardening of the arteries. For this reason animal fats should be avoided and only olive, walnut, corn and sunflower oils used.

CHOLLENT A Jewish meat casserole originating from Poland. The recipe varies, but usually consists of forequarter meat such as chuck or shank (shin) with beans, barley and aromatic ingredients.

Chollent is cooked slowly on a low heat on the Friday for the Sabbath on Saturday, since Jews do not cook on their day of rest.

CHOP SUEY A Chinese dish popularized by Chinese immigrants during the Gold Rush in America.

It is a stir-fried meat dish with bean shoots, strips of bell peppers, carrots, celery, ginger and onions, and flavored with soy sauce and garlic.

CHORBA, TCHORBA A North African dish which is thick and rich enough to be described as a stew rather than a soup.

Chorba contains meat or fish with garbanzo beans (chickpeas) and sometimes beans and vermicelli.

CHORIZO A highly-peppered Spanish pork sausage which can be eaten cooked or raw.

CHORON SAUCE A variation of the béarnaise sauce flavored and colored with tomato paste (purée).

C

CHOUX PASTRY (Fr. PÂTE À CHOUX)
This is made for éclairs and other cream-filled buns.

> *1¼ cups/½ pint/300ml water*
> *¾ cup/6oz/175g butter or margarine*
> *1¾ cups/7oz/200g bread (strong)*
>   *flour*
> *5 large eggs*
> *egg wash for brushing*
>   Makes 1lb/450g choux paste

Boil the water and butter until the butter has completely melted. Remove from heat. Beat in the flour then beat in the egg a little at a time. Return the pan to a low heat and beat until the mixture comes away from the sides of the pan.

To make choux buns or éclairs, use a pastry (piping) bag fitted with a large, plain tip (nozzle), pipe small buns or finger shapes onto a tray greased and dusted with flour, then brush each bun or finger-shape with egg wash.

Bake in a hot oven at 400°F/200°C/gas mark 6 for about 30 minutes — do not let them burn.

Cool on wire racks and fill with cream. The tops can be coated with melted chocolate.

Typical dishes: Choux à la crème, choux fritters, churros, croquembouche, éclairs, gâteau St. Honoré, gâteau Paris-Best, pommes de terre dauphine, profiteroles, gâteau religieuse.

CHRISTMAS CAKE The traditional British Christmas cake is a rich fruit cake made from a creamed cake batter with seedless raisins, golden raisins (sultanas), currants, candied cherries and peel, chopped dates, mixed spice, vanilla and almond extracts and lemon juice. It is baked in a low oven for a long time.

The cake pan (tin) is lined with two or more layers of baking parchment (greaseproof paper) according to size, and paper is tied around the outside of the pan to prevent the cake from becoming too brown on the outside before the center is cooked.

The cake is coated in reduced apricot jam and covered with a thin layer of almond paste and then fondant or royal icing.

Christmas decorations are usually put on top after a piped decoration with a Christmas greeting such as 'Merry Christmas' has been inscribed in red icing.

Christmas cakes can also be made from jelly (Swiss) rolls coated with piped chocolate buttercream, like the French bûche de Noël.

Rich fruit wedding cakes are made in

a similar manner to Christmas cake and coated with almond paste and royal icing to a specified size, depending on the size of the wedding party.

CHRISTMAS PUDDING For a traditional British Christmas pudding the mixture is similar to Christmas cake except that the fat can be beef suet. It is steamed for between 2-6 hours depending on the size of pudding to develop the color and flavor, then stored for at least 2 months.

Christmas pudding is traditionally served with brandy butter and a pouring egg custard.

CHRISTOPHENE *See Chayote.*

CHUPES A Venezuelian conger eel stew with sweet potatoes and onions.

CHUTNEY A sweet-sour condiment which can be made with many kinds of fruit and vegetables, and flavored with spices.

Mango chutney
1 shallot, chopped
2 large mangoes, peeled and chopped
1 large tart apple, cored, peeled and quartered
½ cup/2oz/50g brown sugar
¼ cup/2fl oz/50ml cider vinegar
⅔ cup/5fl oz/150ml water
1 tsp salt
1 small green chili pepper, chopped
1 tsp mixed spices

Boil all the ingredients together for 20 minutes until the mixture becomes as thick as jam.

Heat sterilized jars in the oven for 10 minutes and fill them with the mango mixture. Cover with sterilized non-reactive lids, giving them a half twist only. Let cool inverted. When cold tighten the lids. The chutney can then be stored for up to one year.

CIAMBELLA An Italian ring-shaped pound cake that may be flavored with raisins and lemon or rum.

CINNAMON (Fr. CANNELLE) A spice produced from the bark of a tree grown in many tropical regions. Cinnamon leaves are used for the production of eugenol for the manufacture of vanillin, an artificial vanilla extract.

Cinnamon is used in mulled wines, fruit compotes, curries and numerous poultry and meat terrines.

CIOPINO A chowder made of shrimp (prawns), mussels, clams, fish, garlic,

C

tomatoes and wine. It is a great speciality of San Francisco.

CITRIC ACID The acid found in all citrus fruits, tomatoes and some vegetables. It is used to acidify sauces, desserts, drinks and candies (sweets).

Citric acid can allay thirst by stimulating the flow of saliva, and can create a feeling of coolness.

CITRIC ACID CYCLE A complex cycle of enzyme-controlled biochemical reactions which occur within the living cells, as a result of which pyruvic acid is broken down into carbon dioxide and energy. It is also involved in the synthesis of amino acids.

CITRON (Fr. CITRUS) A large member of the citrus family. The green skin is used for oil and for candied peel.

CITRONELLA A colorless liquid aldehyde existing in several isometric forms, used in the manufacture of lemon flavorings.

CITROUILLAT A pumpkin tart from the south of France.

CIVET A rich wine stew of venison or hare thickened with the animal's blood.

CLAFOUTIS A dessert that originated in the Limousin region of France. It is a custard dessert made from a rich egg batter containing cherries or plums. It is baked in a shallow dish. In many respects, it is similar to far Breton, which is made with prunes.

Limousin cherry clafoutis
A few drops of maraschino or kirsch may be sprinkled over the dessert before serving.

1lb/450g pitted sour red cherries
¼ cup/2oz/50g superfine (caster) sugar
¼ cup/2oz/50g unsalted butter for the dish

Batter
generous 1 cup/4½ oz/125g strong bread (strong) flour
large pinch of salt
¼ cup /2oz/50g superfine (caster) sugar
3 eggs, beaten
1¼ cups/½ pint/300ml milk
confectioners' (icing) sugar, to serve

Sprinkle the cherries with sugar and let stand for 45 minutes. Coat the inside of a baking dish with butter.

To make the batter, combine the flour, salt, sugar, eggs and milk and beat for 5 minutes. Strain it if there are any lumps.

Place the cherries and their juice in the buttered dish. Pour the batter over the fruit and bake at 350°F/180°C/gas mark 4 for 40 minutes until golden. Sift over confectioners' sugar to serve.

CLAM (Fr. PALOURDE) Clams are not as popular in Britain as in the United States, Australia and France, where many cafés serve them raw in the same way as oysters. There are also many recipes for clams using different sauces. Most of the small types can be prepared in the same ways as mussels or scallops.

The two main varieties of clams are hard-shell and soft-shell.

The smallest hard-shell clams are littleneck clams, which are less than 1½in/3.75cm diameter.

Next come the medium-sized cherrystone clams, which are about 2in/5cm in diameter.

Finally come the largest of all called quahogs, these have a fluted shell and are particularly good in chowders.

The soft clams include the steamer and the long finger type known as the razor clam.

The geoduck clam is a conical 4¾in/12cm long clam with a neck that can reach up to about 16 in/40cm long.

Broiled (grilled) clams Brittany style
Garlic and herb flavors impart a characteristic taste to these easily-prepared clams. The recipe is similar to snails with garlic butter, but this dish may be more acceptable to many people, since some do not fancy snails.

24 clams, opened in the same way as oysters (See page 266), with the flesh adhering to the bottom shell

Garlic butter
1 cup/8oz/225g soft butter
3 garlic cloves, chopped
2 canned anchovy fillets, chopped
2 tbsp fresh parsley, chopped
juice of ½ lemon
pinch of chili pepper or cayenne pepper

Place the clams in metal snail plates with special cavities, or put crumbled foil in a shallow baking dish. Make sure the flesh of the clams has been loosened underneath.

To make the garlic butter, beat the butter and mix in the garlic, anchovies, parsley, lemon juice and chili pepper or cayenne pepper.

Coat each clam with the flavored butter and put on the snail plates or in the foil so they are upright. Chill until the butter hardens.

C

When required, cook under a broiler (grill) until the butter is frothy.

CLARIFYING Removing particles in suspension to clear stock, syrup or butter. Simple straining may not be enough.

Clarification can be done with charcoal for syrup and with raw egg whites or ground (minced) fish or meat for savory stock.

Butter is clarified by melting it and letting the solids drop to the bottom. Carefully pour off the clear liquid through cheesecloth, leaving the sediment behind. The sediment contains the protein, casein, so it is nutritious and can be mixed into potato purées or used in thick soups.

CLARY SAGE A kind of sage used to flavor dull wines in the 17th century. It is used in the flavoring of vermouth.

CLEMENTINE A hybrid of a tangerine and Seville orange. It is more acidic and juicy than a tangerine. It is used in sherbets (sorbets) and the segments and rind can be soaked in syrup and crystallized.

CLINGSTONE FRUITS Varieties of peaches or large plums in which the pit (stone) grows embedded in the flesh.

Freestone, on the other hand, are fruits where the pits (stones) come off easily.

CLOD (Fr. JUMEAU) The neck muscle of the neck of beef. It is suitable for making beef hotpot (*See page 42*).

CLOTTED CREAM This thick traditional west of England cream is made by heating milk very slowly until the cream has risen to a thick layer on top. The cream is then removed and cooled. Clotted cream has a a unique slightly cooked flavor and a minimum fat content of about 55 percent.

CLOTTING The formation of solid deposits or clots in liquids, often caused by the coagulation of soluble proteins dissolved in liquids such as blood and milk.

CLOUDBERRY This berry grows in cold climates and is usually considered to be superior to the bilberry and cranberry.

CLOVE (Fr. GIROFLE) The highly spiced, aromatic fragrance of the dried unopened flower buds of the clove tree. Their essential oil has antiseptic properties and can be applied to the gums to reduce toothache.

Cloves can be studded into an onion

and added to stews or hotpots, spiked into baked ham or studded in baked or poached pears and apples.

COBBLER A savory dish or dessert usually baked in a shallow oblong baking dish.

The filling can be fish, meat, chicken or fruits. Rounds of biscuit (scone) dough are put on top of the filling so that when baked the rounds join together.

COBNUT A type of hazelnut that is used in nougat confectionery.

COCADA AMARELA A Mozambique coconut custard dessert flavored with ground cinnamon and cloves and served cold.

COCHINEAL A red color obtained from the pulverized dried insect.

COCK-A-LEEKIE One of the most exciting hotpot soups in Scotland. It is made with chicken, leeks and barley and is traditionally served with prunes filled with chicken liver stuffing.

COCKLE (Fr. BUCARDE) A bivalve mollusk which requires soaking in running water for 2 hours to remove the sand before cooking.

COCKTAIL Fruit and vegetable juice cocktails are in line with healthy eating and are part of the sensible diet.

Classic combinations are pineapple and mango; grenadine, carrot and honey, and orange and ginger. *See also Composite food cocktails.*

COCOA A powder which is produced from the 'beans' inside the fat pods of the cacoa tree.

A cacao tree produces 50-100 pods a year. Each pod contains 20-30 beans or seeds. These seeds are sun-dried until the outer skin is hard and crisp, and can easily be removed.

The dried hulled beans are roasted and ground into cocoa powder. This is separated from the fat, which is known as cocoa butter and used in the preparation of chocolate.

The percentage of the cocoa butter used determines the quality and texture of the chocolate — the higher the percentage, the better the quality.

The principal varieties of cocoa are arriba, balao, machala and caraquez. From Venezuela come the celebrated Caracas cocoa and maracaibo. Baia and para come from Brazil.

The bulk of the world's supplies are the forastero variety, which although often regarded as inferior to criollo has a better flavor and is not so bitter.

C

Cocoa powder is used in Mexican sauces and as a flavoring in many desserts and cakes.

COCONUT The tree of life for people where this source of food and drink grows easily on tropical islands.

The fresh liquid from coconuts is a very refreshing drink. The flesh is used to make canned coconut milk and cream, blocks of creamed coconut, and unsweetened shredded (desiccated) coconut, which are all widely available in supermarkets.

Coconut is also grated and dried for many confectionery products. The milk is used in curries and sweets. The sap is extracted to produce sugar. The fibrous husks are made into rope and door mats.

Typical dishes: Coconut macaroons, coconut rice, coconut salad, Indian lamb curry with coconut milk.

COD (Fr. CABILLAUD) A large fish with fine-flavored firm flesh that flakes easily when cooked.

Traditional dishes: Cabillaud boulonnaise, cabillaud Dieppoise, English cod and chips.

COD-LIVER OIL The purified oil obtained from pressed fresh cods' liver. It has a high Vitamin D content so is often used in the prevention and treatment of rickets.

COFFEE There are many types of coffee widely available on the market providing a huge range of strength and consistency:

BRAZIL 60-70 percent of the world's coffee comes from Brazil, and 45-50 percent from the São Paulo district. It is specially smooth, acid and pungent.

COSTA RICA A rich bodied coffee.

JAVA A very fine, light colored coffee

KENYA Mild coffee with a full body.

MOCHA This has a heavy, smooth body and is aromatic.

MYSORE Broad term for Indian beans.

SUMATRA The finest coffee the world can produce. Smooth, heavy body, almost syrupy.

There are many aromatic substances present in coffee which give it its characteristic flavors.

To prepare coffee, the beans must first be roasted to various degrees, depending on the requirement.

C

Coffee is used as a flavoring in custards and ice creams, and in icing and frostings for cakes. It is often blended into chocolate to add to the flavor.

Decaffeinated coffees are available.

Typical drinks: café Viennois, café cognac, café au lait, Irish coffee.

COLCANNON A traditional Irish dish made of a mixture of mashed potatoes and chopped white cabbage or kale that is shaped into cakes and fried.

COLLAGEN An insoluble protein in skin, tendons, connective tissue and bone that forms gelatin on contact with moist heat.

COLLARED MEAT Boneless meat roast (joint) braised slowly until tender.

COLLOIDAL SOLUTION A solution in which the solute is present in the form of starch, albumen and colloidal metals. The solvent is known as the dispersion medium and the dissolved substance as the disperse phase.

COLOCASIA A white, starchy vegetable similar to yam. It is available canned from specialist stores.

COLOMBINE A case made of cooked rice mixed with eggs and formed into tartlet or boat shapes. Colombine can be filled with all kinds of meat or poultry in sauce and sprinkled with Parmesan cheese. They are baked to crust the top.

COLOR One of the most attractive aspects of food can be its color. So much so that it often takes precedence to taste in modern cuisine.

First impressions are lasting impressions, and there is much to be said for the statement 'we also eat with our eyes'.

Foods acquire their color from various sources, such as natural plant and animal pigments. Green coloring from chlorophyll is found in leaves like spinach, for instance, and can be used to make sauces and soups greener.

Carotene gives the orange color to carrots and corn; lycopene contributes to the red of tomatoes and watermelon; anthocyanins contribute to red beets (beetroot) and blueberries; and haemoglobin gives the red color to cured meats when it is combined with saltpeter (sodium nitrate).

Natural pigments are highly susceptible to chemical changes, as when fruits ripen and meat matures. They are also sensitive to chemical and physical effects during food preparation. Chopping and grinding generally

C

change food colors. This is because many of the plant and animal pigments are in cell tissues and pigment bodies, such as the chloroplasts which contain green chlorophyll. When these cells are partially broken by grinding and chopping the pigments leach out and are partially destroyed on contact with air.

Some foods darken when they are cut or exposed to air for long periods. This is due to chemical interactions between sugars and protein — it is known as the Mallard reaction.

In this case an amino acid group from a protein combines with an aldehyde or ketone group of a reducing sugar to produce a brown color. One example is the darkening of dried milk solids in long storage. By a similar process, chopped or sliced apples, artichokes, celery root (celeriac) and potatoes turn brown when left in contact with air.

High heat can denature all pigments. Heat also causes sugar to caramelize, which is why foods containing sugar or starch turn brown when cooked.

Cooks pickle beets (beetroot) and red onions in vinegar to fix the red color. When beets are cooked in a liquid without acid they color the liquid a deeper golden-yellow.

Food scientists have produced a for-midable collection of artificial colors to improve the appearance of foods, while food technologists have created countless colorful products using the colormetric chart. For example, fresh red shades such as those of tomato paste (purée) or raspberry coulis can be improved by using lemon juice, as in jam-making. However, to try the same effect on some other dishes such as tomato soup, requires a great degree of artistic talent.

COLZA *See Rapeseed.*

COMB SCRAPER   A plastic serrated square used to scrape cream or batter, or to make designs and patterns on gâteaux and torten.

COMFREY   A perennial herb. The leaves can be cooked like spinach. while the stalks can be cooked in the same way as asparagus and the roots can be used as a coffee substitute.

COMPOSITE BUTTER PASTE   Flavored butter used as a flavoring for broiled (grilled) fish, steaks or poultry, or for stuffing fish and snails in their shells.

The butter paste is rolled into a cylindrical shape and chilled until firm. The resulting sticks can be cut into slices as required.

Montpellier butter

1 cup/8oz/225g salted butter
2 chopped or minced anchovy fillets
1 tbsp fresh mixed herbs such as
   tarragon, parsley and basil

Beat together the butter, anchovy fillets and herbs. Roll into a cylinder and wrap in paper.

Chill and cut into ¼in/5mm thick slices.

Variations

Snail butter: Follow the above but add three finely chopped garlic cloves.

Shrimp butter: The same as before, but use 1 cup/8oz/225g shelled cooked shrimp finely pounded to a paste, instead of anchovy. Flavor with a little paprika.

COMPOSITE FOOD COCKTAIL Shrimps (prawns) in tomato-flavored sauce served on shredded lettuce has been the most popular composite food cocktail for a long time. However, there are other combinations such as mixtures of fish and shellfish.

Fruit and vegetable cocktails in yogurt are also featured in unlimited permutations, using ingredients such as asparagus, avocados, grapefruit, melon and exotic fruits.

COMPOTE Fresh or dried fruits gently poached in syrup. The syrup can be made with wine or tea. A stick of cinnamon and a few cloves are used to give a spicy flavor or, alternatively, for a sharper edge, slices of lemon and orange are added.

Typical dishes: Apple and plum compote, apricots in China tea, syrup and honey, fresh fig compote, pears in red wine, peaches in Port wine.

CONCHIGLIE Italian pasta in the shape of a shell.

CONDENSED MILK Condensed milk is made by the evaporation of some of the water from sweetened pasteurized milk under reduced pressure so that the resulting condensed milk contains 40-45 percent sugar, no less than 28 percent total milk solids and no less than 8 percent milk fat.

CONDIMENT Today the term condiment includes spices, seasonings, sauces, pickles, mustard and dressings. Condiments can be raw or cooked.

CONDUCTION The method of heating in which the heat moves from one particle to another by contact; this occurs in straight lines. *See also Convection, Radiation.*

C

CONES Coarsely ground rice used by bakers when molding bread or dough to prevent sticking onto the pastry board.

CONFECTIONERS' CUSTARD (Fr. CRÈME ANGLAISE) Some of the eggs used in a custard sauce are replaced by cornstarch (cornflour). Confectioners' custard can be flavored with liqueur, chocolate, strawberries or pistachios, and used as a filling for éclairs, gâteaux, or Danish pastries.

> 2½ cups/1pint/600ml milk
> generous ½ cup/4½ oz/125g (caster)
>   sugar
> 4 egg yolks
> ⅓ cup/1¼ oz/40g flour or corn
>   starch (cornflour) mixed with
>   3 tbsp cream
> 1 tbsp rum (optional)
> 3 drops vanilla extract or other
>   flavoring
> 2 tbsp/1oz/25g sweet (unsalted)
>   butter

Heat the milk to boiling point. Beat the sugar and egg yolks and sugar for 4 minutes until thick then stir in the flour or cornstarch (cornflour) and cream.

Slowly pour the hot milk onto the eggs while beating. Return to the heat and cook, stirring until the sauce thickens.

Remove the sauce from the heat and add the rum, vanilla extract or other flavoring, and the butter to prevent a skin forming.

CONFECTIONERY 1) Flour confectionery, which may also use sugar, such as cakes, pastries and creams.

2) Sugar confectionery, which includes almond pastes, nougat, butterscotch, fudge, Turkish delight, marshmallow, fondant and crystallized fruits and items using chocolate and syrups. Sugar confectionery is a profession in its own right which requires as much artistic talent as craftsmanship and knowledge.

The modern professional confectioner producing confectionery on a large scale usually prepares his products in batches using a continuous process. A number of specialized machines may be used to extrude, divide, cover and otherwise process these confections.

In the preparation of thin mints, the supersaturated, partially-crystallized sugar mixture is flavored with mint (menthol) and cooled from boiling point to about 160°F/72°C. At this temperature it is semi-liquid and can easily be dropped as small dabs onto a

118

moving belt. The mints quickly solidify on further cooking.

Firmer chewy centers are usually extruded by being pressed through molds. The candy (sweet) pieces are then cut off with a wire. They may then travel on a moving belt to be covered with molten chocolate.

Some candies such as jellies and marshmallows are formed from a very thin liquid mixture. They are shaped by molding before they harden. This may be done in a starch molding machine. In this case, trays of powdered cornstarch are continuously imprinted with concave impressions.

The hot liquid is filled into the impressions as the trays are conveyed under a hopper. Quick cooling solidifies the candies, which are automatically tipped together with the cornstarch from the trays, over a screen which separates the candies from the starch. The starch is then removed by a brush.

Candies such as nougat and marshmallows are aerated with egg whites and gelatin to give them a lighter texture. A chocolate coating can also be applied and gum Arabic may be sprayed on to give a glaze.

For liqueur-filled chocolates, the syrup must be supersaturated to be firm enough to form a hard fondant, then it can be coated with chocolate. The liqueur fondant later becomes liquid again, but by now safely inside the hard chocolate coating.

The fondant is also treated with an invertase enzyme. This inversion only takes place during the normal storage of the candy. Invert sugar is more soluble than sucrose in the moisture of the fondant, and so it melts under the chocolate layer and converts the firm center to a creamy liquid with a strong liqueur flavor.

Typical confectionery includes such varied candies as: Almond nougat, berlingots, butterscotch, candied peel, caramel (soft and hard), cherry fondant, coconut kisses, candied fruits, marrons glacés, fudges, liqueur chocolates, marshmallow, marzipan dates, almond paste prunes, sugared almonds, minted fondant, pulled sugar baskets and flowers, cotignac, taffies, truffles, Turkish delight, white nougat and many, many more.

CONFIT 1) Duck or goose cooked slowly in its own fat and then preserved by being completely covered by the fat.

The duck or goose is reheated with cooked dried beans as a stew, or reheated and served with tomato or brown sauce.

C

Duck confit

5½lb/2.5kg duck, boned and
quartered and fat reserved
4 tbsp coarse salt

Place the duck in a deep dish and
thoroughly sprinkle with salt. Refrigerate for 24 hours, turning the pieces
over three times during this time.

Remove the duck to a heavy casserole with 2¼lb/1kg of its own fat.
Cook slowly without boiling for two
hours. While the fat is still hot, strain it
into a sterilized dish or large jar. Pack
the duck pieces in the fat so that they
are completely covered. Cover the
dish or pot and refrigerate.

2) A dragée glazed with a coating of
sugar syrup.

CONIGLIO ALLA CÁDIZ A southern
Spanish rabbit casserole bathed in
medium Sherry, with tomatoes, garlic,
cumin, chili pepper, onions and bacon.

CONSOMMÉ A clarified strong stock
which can be made with fish, meat,
poultry or game. A consommé should
be clear and will set on cooling. To
give the consomme a golden color add
a raw beet (beetroot), to produce a red
color use a cooked beet pickled in red
wine, and to get a pink color use tomato paste (purée). It can be served hot or
cold and be flavored with Madeira,
Sherry, Port wine or vegetable bouillon (stock) cubes. A good strong consommé is an ideal appetizer.

Consommés may be garnished using
any one of the 150 suitable garnishes.
The simplest are a julienne or brunoise
of vegetables, cooked separately in
butter.

Others garnishes can include cooked
small pasta, rice, pearl barley or savory
custard cut into shapes, small pieces of
fish, meat or poultry, miniature
quenelles or very small profiteroles,
cheese straws, small sprigs of aromatic
herbs, asparagus tips, finely diced
tomato, root vegetables scooped into
tiny balls, mushrooms, truffles and
quails' eggs.

Some classic French consommé garnishes are: Colbert, florette, Monté
Carlo and princesse.

A good strong consommé is an ideal
appetizer before a substantial dinner.

Beef consommé

8¾ cups/3½ pints/2.1 liters of beef
stock

Clarification

1 cup/8oz/225g ground (minced)
beef shin
2 egg whites

*1½ cups/8oz/225g mixed chopped
celery, onion, leek, carrot and raw
beets (beetroot)
1 tsp salt
¼ tsp pepper
½ tsp brown sugar*

Combine the clarification ingredients in a bowl.

Place the cold stock in a large saucepan, fitted with a tap if possible.

Stir the clarification ingredients into the liquid. Bring gently to a boil. The solids will gradually solidify on top and form a crust. Do not disturb this crust. Let it simmer for 1 hour.

If you have a saucepan with a tap, the liquid can be poured out without disturbing the crust. Otherwise gently make a hole in the crust and ladle the liquid through it into another pan over which is placed a conical strainer lined with cheesecloth, to keep the consommé absolutely clear.

CONVECTION A method of heating which involves movement of the air.

CONVENIENCE FOODS Ready-prepared meals sold in packets, canned, chilled or frozen and only requiring reheating.

Pre-cooked items such as pies, pizzas, quiches, salads and delicatessen products are convenience foods, as are cakes, pies and pastries.

COOKIE (BISCUIT) Originally, cookies were a type of hard, dry bread eaten by sailors on long voyages; they were soaked in water until soft enough to be eaten. Most cookies are made with soft flour. The best-flavored cookies are those made with butter. There are many different types.

DROP COOKIES made from a soft batter dropped from a spoon onto a baking sheets, such as gingersnaps, tuiles and florentines.

FLAPJACKS AND CHOCOLATE COOKIES Then there are the large selection of chocolate cookies and flapjacks made with oats and syrup.

PIPED COOKIES made from mixtures such as sponge batters and meringues piped in finger shapes onto baking sheets, such as sponge fingers and langue de chats.

ROLLED COOKIES made from a thick dough which is rolled out and cut into rounds, squares, oblongs or triangles.

The whole cookie repertoire would fill an encyclopedia, but just some of

C

the examples are: Almond drop cookies, almond scrolls, amaretti di Sarono, anisette cookies, Basler brown cookies, biscuits à la cuillère.

Bolkero cookies, butterscotch cookies, boudoir cookies, chocolate chip cookies, coconut cookies, craquelins, duchesse cookies, ginger nuts, petits beurres, sand cookies, sablés de Trouville, Zurich nuts.

COPPER PAN Copper pans are being replaced by stainless steel pans which do not require retinning and are easier to keep clean. Nevertheless, the copper pan is a better conductor of heat and this is a distinct advantage when sugar boiling for confectionery and in jam making.

Copper pans are very costly to buy at the outset, but those without a tin lining are necessary for high temperature confections.

CORALLI Tiny tube-shaped Italian pasta which is used in soups.

CORIANDER (Fr. CORIANDRE) A member of the carrot family. The fresh green leaves are used as a herb in similar ways to parsley. The seeds are used in pickles and marinades and to flavor Greek vegetable dishes and mushrooms for hors d'oeuvres.

CORN, MAIZE Corn on the cob, or sweet corn as it is known in Britain, is used as a vegetable. It can be boiled and served with butter. Corn kernels can be mixed with a macédoine of vegetables and served as a salad.

Ground corn, known as cornmeal or polenta is used to make Italian gnocchi, breads and cakes.

Some varieties of corn are used as animal feed.

CORN SUGAR SYRUP *See Xanthan gum.*

CORN SYRUP A sweet syrup made commercially by heating cornstarch (cornflour) and water under pressure with a little hydrolic or sulphuric acid added to hydrolize the starch into sugar.

It can be used like golden syrup, or used like liquid glucose in sugar confectionery to prevent crystallization during the boiling of sugar to high temperatures.

CORNED BEEF In America corned beef is a piece of salted beef, but in England the name usually applies to a precooked tinned meat often used in sandwiches. The shredded cured meat is pressed into a can so that it forms a solid piece when cold and can be eaten without further cooking.

CORNFLOUR *See Cornstarch.*

CORNISH CAKE Saffron-flavored yeast cake with golden raisins (sultanas) and currants, baked in an oblong pan (tin).

CORNISH PASTY Individual boat-shaped savory pie that is filled with a mixture of raw beef, diced potatoes and carrots or rutabaga (swede), chopped onions, parsley, salt and black pepper. Then baked in the oven.

CORNMEAL, POLENTA Cornmeal is available in various grades of fineness for savory and sweet puddings, cakes, porridge and pancakes. It has a low protein content, which can be supplemented by mixing it with wheat flour and eggs or cheese.

CORN SALAD, LAMB'S LETTUCE (Fr. MÂCHE) A popular salad leaf, usually mixed with celery root (celeriac) and beets (beetroot) and served with a French dressing.

CORNSTARCH (CORNFLOUR) The starch extracted from maize. To thicken sauces it is made into a thin paste with water or milk and added to the liquid, which is then boiled until thickened.

Four teaspoons cornstarch (corn-flour) are used for 2¼ cups/18fl oz/500ml of liquid.

A sauce thickened with (cornflour) cannot be kept warm for longer than one hour in a water bath otherwise it will become thin.

COTIGNAC A French paste made of quinces and sugar. It can served with crème fraîche or thick yogurt and crisp cookies (biscuits) for dessert, or served as a petits fours with coffee. *See also Alva.*

COTRIADE A white fish stew with a creamy sauce.

COULIBIAC An oblong Russian pie containing fish — traditionally salmon — a cooked grain, onion, dill and parsley, and sometimes hard-cooked (hard-boiled) eggs all wrapped up in yeast pastry.

COULIS A smooth purée served as a sauce. Coulis can be made from cooked vegetables or fruits, or raw berries or tomatoes. Originally a coulis was any kind of sauce. *See also Tomato coulis.*

Coulis à la Provençale
This sauce is suitable for use with pasta and seafood.

C

1lb/450g sweet tomatoes, skinned,
seeded and chopped
1 tbsp sugar
2 garlic cloves, chopped
I small package of saffron
2 tbsp olive oil
2 basil leaves, chopped

Boil all the ingredients until soft, about 10 minutes.

Process the coulis in a blender or food processor, or pour through a non-reactive strainer.

COULOMMIERS A soft, fresh French cheese made from whole cows' milk.

COUPE A cup-shaped dish or container. A coupe may be made of glass or metal and may hold fish cocktails, ice cream desserts or fruit salads.

The number of popular classic desserts which can be served in coupes is very large. It includes peach melba, coupe Jacques, coupe dame blanche, coupe Veronica and coupe de melon au lait champagne.

COURT-BOUILLON An aromatic stock for poaching fish and shellfish. While vinegar and wine are used for fish, no acid should be used to boil shellfish; sea water is the best for all shellfish.

For oily fish a court-bouillon should

consist of carrot and onion, celery or fennel, parsley, bay leaf, crushed peppercorns and coriander seeds, salt, 2 tablespoons vinegar and ⅔ cup/5fl oz/150ml white wine per 4⅓ cups/1¾ pints/1 liter water.

A court-bouillon should be boiled for 15 minutes.

When poaching large fish, start them in cold court bouillon but put small fish and fish steaks into boiling court bouillon. Fish steaks require only 5 minutes poaching, whole salmon and turbot will take as much as 30 minutes. Shrimp (prawns) take 5 minutes and lobsters, crawfish and crab 15 minutes per 1lb/450g.

COUSCOUS Small particles of semolina that are used in north Africa to make a stew of the same name. Couscous (the grain) is available in supermarkets and instructions for cooking it are on the packaging. The semolina should be rubbed with a mixture of butter and olive oil to allow the grains to separate on steaming. However, it can also be cooked in a sauté pan, in which case it will only need a very small amount of liquid to get the texture of wet crumbs. Cooked by this method, the couscous can be ready in 10 minutes without lumps, as is likely to happen if the grains are steamed.

Couscous can be served with stews of fish, meat or poultry, but most usually mutton or lamb, plus vegetables and spices.

COUVERTURE *See Chocolate.*

COVENTRY PUFFS Triangular pastries filled with raspberry jam and dusted with superfine (castor) sugar.

COW-PEA This nourishing legume belongs to the bean family. There are several varieties of different sizes and colors — including principally red, black, purple and speckled.

After soaking in water overnight, cow-peas are better baked in a casserole rather than boiled on top of the stove.

COWSLIP An old-fashioned remedy was an infusion made from cowslips which was used as a soporific. It can be used to color confectioners' custard.

COZIDO A Portuguese term for any boiled dish. It may consist of meat, sausage and/or smoked ham, beans and vegetables. A cozido is usually served as three courses; first the broth, then the vegetables and beans and lastly the meats accompanied by boiled potatoes cooked separately.

CRAB (Fr. CRABE) The most common types of crab caught commercially are the common brown European crab and the spider crab, which can be great wanderers — moving tens if not hundreds of miles in a year from feeding to spawning grounds. Baited pots are used for capture, often far from shore.

Spider crabs only provide meat from their legs and are not so highly valued. Small soft crabs can be made into chowder. Velvet crabs can swim but are still caught in pots.

A fresh whole crab should be heavy for its size. Shake it — there should be no sound of water; the shell must not be holed or cracked. Break the top shell from the rest and spoon out the brown meat. Discard the feathery gills and small stomach sac. Break open the legs, crack the claws and extract the white meat.

Crab in its shell can be served with the claws cracked, to be eaten simply with brown bread and butter, dressed in its own shell, or with mayonnaise.

Crabmeat can also be bought canned or frozen.

Crab soup can be made in the same way as lobster bisque.

CRAB APPLE This wild fruit is ideal for making firm jams, jellies and pastes, because it is rich in pectin.

C

CRACKLING (Fr. BEURSADES) 1) The crispy rind of roast pork, cut into small squares or strips and served with the meat.

2) Crackling may also refer to the crisp skin of Chinese-style roast duck. The duck is first scalded in water for 3 minutes, dried for 1 hour, then roasted at a high temperature for the first 30 minutes of the cooking time.

CRAMIQUE A Belgian and northern French loaf containing raisins. It is eaten hot with butter.

CRANBERRY (Fr. CANNEBERGE) Tart-tasting red globular berry that is sweetened and served with turkey.

CRAQUELIN A crisp French cookie (biscuit).

CRAWFISH, SPINY LOBSTER, ROCK LOBSTER (Fr. LANGOUSTE) This crustacean has no claws and therefore cannot possibly be confused with lobster. It varies in color depending on its habitat, has five pairs of legs and can reach a large size, which may be enough to feed four people. The flesh is slightly firmer than lobster.

Some gourmets prefer lobsters boiled and served with mayonnaise. Others enjoy the many preparations in spicy tomato sauce, in cream and sherry sauce or in pilaffs and casseroles.

The unusual combination of fresh pineapple and crawfish is particularly flavorsome, and the fruit is especially useful for those people who find shellfish otherwise indigestible, since it contains a powerful tenderizing enzyme which aids the digestion of protein. The pineapple must be fresh, however, since cooking or canning destroys the precious enzyme.

Crawfish Tahiti

This refreshing and piquant dish is ideal for lunch, and can be varied by the addition of fish such as red mullet, tuna or cod to stretch the more expensive crawfish.

4 slices of fresh pineapple
1 tbsp kirsch
100g/4oz white mushrooms
2 tbsp pineapple juice
½lb/225g crawfish tail meat, cut
*   into cubes after boiling*

Sauce
½ cup/4fl oz/100ml heavy (double)
*   cream*
1 tsp Dijon mustard
1 small piece of fresh grated ginger
salt, pepper and chili powder
mixed salad leaves to serve

Cut the slices of fresh pineapple to your preferred thickness, trim the tough exterior and core them.

Place a slice on each serving plate and sprinkle a little kirsch onto them. Leave for 30 minutes.

Reserve two tablespoons of the juice that comes from the crawfish.

Place the mushrooms in a bowl to marinade in reserved juice. In a bowl, mix the crawfish, cream, mustard and ginger. Season to taste.

Serve the crawfish on top of a pineapple slice surrounded by a mixed salad leaves.

CRAYFISH (Fr. ÉCREVISSE) A small freshwater crustacean that looks like a lobster.

The Scandinavians simply make a feast of boiled crayfish flavored with dill. The dark thread along the back of crayfish must be removed.

CREAM The types of cream available in the USA are:
HALF-AND-HALF CREAM has a fat content of 10-18 percent.
HEAVY CREAM, with a fat content of 36-40 percent.
LIGHT CREAM, with a fat content of between 18-30 percent.
LIGHT WHIPPING CREAM has a fat content of 30-36 percent.

The creams available in the United Kingdom are:
CLOTTED CREAM: 55 percent fat
DOUBLE CREAM: 48 percent fat
HALF CREAM: 12 percent fat
SINGLE CREAM: 18 percent fat
SOURED CREAM: 18 percent fat
WHIPPING CREAM: 35 percent fat

UHT cream has been subjected to ultra-heat treatment and is completely sterilized; however, the taste is adversely affected.

Aerosol creams provide a quick way of decorating desserts but the cream collapses if left standing.

CREAM CARAMEL A classic custard dessert with a soft caramelized top.

2 egg yolks
3 whole eggs
2½ cups/1 pint/600ml milk
⅓ cup/3oz/ 75g sugar

Caramel
½ cup/4oz/100g sugar
¼ cup/2fl oz/50ml water

To make the caramel, heat the sugar in the water until melted then boil until copper-colored. Pour into the bottom of 4⅔ cup/5fl oz/150ml metal molds. Set aside to cool and set.

C

Mix together the egg yolks, whole eggs, milk and sugar. Pour into the molds and bake in a water bath in an oven at 325°F/170°C/gas mark 3 for 35 minutes. Let cool then unmold. It is best when eaten the following day.

CREAM CHANTILLY Sweetened chilled whipped cream flavored with a few drops of vanilla extract.

CREAM CHEESE Fresh cheese can be made at home very simply by using rennet and boiling milk, as for junket, then straining the milk.

Cream cheeset can also be made by adding yogurt or lemon juice to heated milk to obtain a fine curd. The curd can then be eaten while soft or pressed and dried.

Traditional dishes: Mousse au fromage blanc aux herbes, cheese fritters, sweet cherry cheesecake, lemon cream cheesecake, baked cheesecake.

CREAM OF TARTAR Potassium hydrogen tartrate used with sodium bicarbonate as baking powder because it acts more slowly than tartaric acid and gives more prolonged evolution of carbon dioxide.

Cream of Tartar is tartrate baking powder; phosphate baking powder contains calcium acid phosphate or sodium hydrogen pyrophosphate.

Cream of tartar is also used to invert sugar when making syrups.

CRÈME BRULÉE A custard made with one whole egg and four egg yolks per 2½ cups/1 pint/600ml light (single) cream. This dessert was reputedly created at Trinity College, Oxford, before the Second World War.

The word brulée literally means 'burnt', referring to the caramel crust on top of the custard. This is produced by sprinkling a thin layer of sugar on top of the set cold custard and then putting it under a very hot broiler (grill) until caramelized.

CRÈME FRAÎCHE The standard French cream. In France, crème fraîche is made from ripened, often unpasteurized, cream, which is curdled by the addition of bacteria. In other countries, different cultures are used with fresh, pasteurized cream.

Crème fraîche can be made by adding buttermilk or yogurt to heavy (double) cream, heating it to 90° F/35°C and letting stand at room temperature until thickened.

CRÊPE The French name for a thin savory or sweet pancake made with eggs or yeast and all-purpose (plain) flour or whole wheat (wholemeal) and rye flours.

Classic dishes: crêpettes farcies de volaille, crêpes Montmorency, crêpillon à la Normande, crêpes soufflées, crêpes Suzette.

Cheese soufflé pancakes

1¼ cups/½ pint/300ml pancake batter (See page 40)

Cheese soufflé filling

½ cup/4fl oz/100ml béchamel sauce
2 egg yolks
½ cup/2oz/50g grated Cheddar cheese, plus extra for sprinkling
1 pinch cayenne pepper
1 pinch salt
4 egg whites, beaten

Serves 6

Prepare and cook 6 pancakes. Lay them on a oiled baking sheet ready to be filled with the soufflé mixture.

To make the filling, combine the sauce, egg yolks, cheese, cayenne pepper and salt. Fold in the beaten egg whites. Spoon the mixture over half of each pancake. Fold over the pancakes in a half-moon shape. Sprinkle a little grated cheese on top and bake at 400°F/200°C/gas mark 6 for about 12 minutes.

CRÊPINETTES Little meat faggots wrapped in a pig's caul.

Crêpinettes can be made up of ground (minced) pork, beef, lamb or partridge or other game.

CRESS The most important cress for culinary use is watercress. Garden cress or pepper cress is a native of Iran.

Cress also is part of the mixture known as mustard and cress and is mainly used for garnishing food and in egg and cress sandwiches.

CRIMPING A technique for making designs around the edge of tarts, either by pinching the pie dough between forefinger and thumb, by pressing the prongs of a fork around it, or by carving a half circle with the end of a knife.

CROISSANT A Turkish pastry invented in 1686 and now an integral part of the light Continental breakfast which is served and enjoyed in hotels around the world.

The word is literally translated as crescent, although the French term is in common usage.

A croissant, as it is made today, consists of yeast dough layered with butter and folded four times to produce a flaky structure. It is cut in triangles, rolled up from the long side, brushed

C

with egg wash and baked after rising for 15 minutes.

Typical dishes: Almond paste croissant, savory croissant.

CROMESQUIS, KROMESKIES Ground (minced) meat or poultry mixed with a thick béchamel sauce, formed into shapes and shallow-fried in butter.

CROQUANT A confectionery of nuts embedded in caramel.

CROQUEMBOUCHE A conical cake made of caramel-coated choux buns filled with rum-flavored confectioners' custard and decorated with pulled sugar flowers. It is traditionally served as a wedding cake in France.

CROQUETTE A mixture of ground (minced) and diced ingredients mixed with eggs, or mashed starchy vegetable such as potatoes, that is coated in flour, eggs and breadcrumbs or nuts and deep- or shallow-fried.

CROSNE, JAPANESE ARTICHOKE A small tuber with a sweet taste. It can be cooked in the same way as the Jerusalem artichoke.

CRUMPET A yeast cake cooked on a hot plate or griddle inside a 2½in/6cm diameter ring. As the crumpet cooks, holes appear on top as air bubbles rise to the surface and break. To serve, crumpets are toasted and spread with butter.

CRUSTACEAN A fish that lives encased in a jointed, multi-hinged shell, for example shrimp (prawns), crayfish, crab, lobsters and crawfish.

The shells provide the unique flavor for bisques and sauces. All crustaceans should be alive before cooking to be as fresh as possible. Crustaceans which are bought ready cooked do not have the same flavor as those that are fresh.

CRYSTALLIZED FRUITS Candied fruits which are coated in thick syrup. Flowers such as primroses, roses and violets can also be crystallized and used for cake decorations.

CUCUMBER (Fr. CONCOMBRE) For the cook cucumbers are divided into two main categories, those for eating and those for pickling. Those for eating are usually dark green with tapering ends and pale flesh, although some are lemon-colored and round. American eating cucumbers are shorter and fatter than European eating cucumbers.

Pickling or Kirby cucumbers are smaller than eating varieties and are characterized by their small black or white spines. They can be bitter when raw. Most familiar are American dill, British gherkins and French cornichons; they give their name to the specific pickle in which they are used.The flavor of cucumber is in the skin, which is some people like to use it unpeeled for sandwiches or in salads.

A green cucumber pickle can be made and eaten within 24 hours. Simply cut the unpeeled cucumber into thick chunks. Sprinkle it with salt and soak it overnight in strong sweet vinegar.

Eat with pickled boiled tongue or corned (salt) beef and rye bread.

An Indian dressing is even more interesting: it consists of peeled sliced cucumber in yogurt flavored with garlic and chopped mint.

Typical dishes: Gazpacho, raita, tartare sauce.

Cucumber in dill and tarragon sauce
This pickle is ideal to be served fresh with hard-cooked (boiled) eggs.

1 cucumber, cut into thick chunks
¾ in/2cm thick
4 tsp salt
⅓ cup/3fl oz/75ml sour (soured) cream
⅓ cup/3fl oz/75ml thick yogurt
2 tsp each dill and tarragon
¼ tsp white pepper
1 tsp sugar
2 tsp salt

Sprinkle 2 teaspoons of the salt onto the cucumber pieces and chill for 30 minutes. Rinse and drain them. Place in a bowl.

Mix the sour (soured) cream and yogurt. Stir in the herbs, pepper, sugar and the remaining salt. Toss the cucumber in this dressing and serve.

Cucumber raita
Serve with salmon or trout.

1 ¼ cups/½ pint/300 ml thick yogurt
½ cucumber, peeled, seeded and sliced
2 tbsp fresh spearmint leaves, chopped
salt and pepper
1 tsp sugar

Combine all the ingredients together.

CUMIN The Germans use cumin to flavor their Munster cheese and the Norwegians add it to their fish pickles. It is also used in pickles, chutneys and curries.

CUMQUAT *See Kumquat.*

C

CURD 1) The coagulated part of the milk which separates from the whey when milk is curdled.

2) The name of a preserve of citrus fruit, usually lemon, sugar and eggs.

CURRANT, RED (Fr. GROSEILLE) This delicious fruit is used mainly for making jams and jellies, which may be served an accompaniment for roast lamb, or used as a glaze for open fruit tarts.

CURRY Curry is not just a sauce for a meat stew prepared from a powder such as Madras, but a complete system of preparing and cooking many vegetables, fish, eggs, meat and poultry in a combination of spices, nuts and sometimes fruits and serving them with an attractive and appetizing range of salads, chutneys and other accompaniments.

CURRY LEAVES The flavor of curry leaves is redolent of the overall and authentic taste of curry. It is from these leaves that the term curry originated. However, in spite of this connection, curry powder is not made from curry leaves.

CURRY POWDER A mixture of spices such as cardamom, cassia, cayenne, celery seed, cinnamon, cloves, coriander, cumin, fenugreek, ginger, mustard, nutmeg, and turmeric or saffron. The permutations of these can fill a book on curries.

The Indian cook is like a French chef; he makes his own mixture according to his mood and personal preferances, a bit of this and dash of that, and if the flavor is acceptable then it has made his day. However, he may not always be able to repeat the same formula or proportions.

CUSTARD A custard is an emulsion and coagulation of eggs with a liquid such as syrup, milk or wine. A custard may be a sauce or a set curd, depending on the proportion of eggs or starch, and the cooking method. For nutritional and economic reasons the amount of eggs can be reduced and replaced by starch, as in confectioner's custard.

All custards can be flavored with fruit purées, chocolate, coffee or liqueurs, using a minimum of ¼ cup/2oz/50g sugar per 1¼ cups/ ½ pint/300ml milk.

Custards are used for desserts, sauces and ice creams and iced desserts such as bombes and cassata. *See also cream caramel and crème brulée*

Typical dishes: Crème anglaise,

crème chiboust, crème mousseline.

Custard sauce

   4 large egg yolks
   ½ cup/4 oz/100 g sugar
   1 ¼ cups/½ pint/300 ml milk
   1 vanilla pod, split

Beat the egg yolks and sugar together in a bowl placed over a saucepan of hot water until very thick, about 8 minutes.

Boil the milk with the vanilla pod. Remove the vanilla pod. Pour the milk into the egg mixture while whisking.

Reheat the sauce, stirring constantly, until it thickens enough to coat the back of a spoon, this takes about 5 minutes.

Variations:

1) Use 2 egg yolks and 2 teaspoons cornstarch (cornflour) per 1¼ cups/½ pint/300ml of milk.

2) Omit the eggs and use 1 tablespoon cornstarch per 1¼ cups/½ pint/300ml milk. Mix the cornstarch with the sugar and pour on the boiling milk. Reheat, stirring continuously, until thickened.

3) Use 1 teaspoon of vanilla extract instead of the vanilla pod, but the flavor will not be as good.

CUSTARD APPLE *See Chayote.*

CUSTARD POWDER This was invented by a clever food technologist. Available in Britain, it is a simple mixture of cornstarch (cornflour), yellow coloring and vanilla flavoring, and sometimes sugar, which enables a type of custard to be made quickly and easily.

The custard powder is mixed with a little cold milk, boiling milk is stirred in then the mixture boiled until thickened. The most recently developed custard powders require only boiling water to be stirred onto them, with no further cooking.

CUTTLEFISH (Fr. SEICHE) A cellaphod related to squid. Squid and cuttlefish have an ink sac containing a liquid which can be added to the cooked fish after it has been cooked long enough to tenderize it; the ink would coagulate if added too soon.

The flesh has to be beaten with a hammer to make it soft. It can also be salted and roasted; this is sold commercially in India under the name 'Sarume'.

CYRNIKI A light Polish or Russian cheese dumpling. It is made with sour (soured) cream, grated cheese, eggs, flour or breadcrumbs, and herbs. The dough is rolled and cut into triangles and either fried or poached in stock, then fried in butter.

DAAL *See Dal.*

DAB (Fr. LIMANDE) The smallest of the flat fish found in the North Sea, English Channel and Atlantic Ocean. It is a lean fish which is best broiled (grilled) or pan-fried on the bone.

DACQUOISE A French hazelnut meringue gâteau. The same mixture can be made into smaller cakes 4¾in/12cm in diameter and filled with coffee buttercream.

DAIKON, MOULI A long, fat, white radish with a milder flavor than a red radishes. It is used in Japanese and Asian cooking, in salads and garnishes.

DAL, DAAL, DHAL The Hindu word for split lentils or other pulses. There are very many different varieties of dal, each of which has its own taste and texture. The most common dals are mung or mug bean, channa (garbanzo bean, chickpea), tur (pigeon pea) and urd (black garbanzo bean, chickpea). Dals do not need soaking.

Dals appear in many different guises in Indian cooking, such as in soups, sauces, side dishes and as thickening for casseroles; in the south, which is mainly vegetarian, they are a valuable source of protein.

DAMSON A small and tart-sweet fruit that is ideal for making jams, a thick paste which tastes as good as Turkish delight, and delicious pies, especially when mixed with apples. The only problem is that, because of their small size, the pits (stones) are difficult to remove.

DANDELION (Fr. PISSENLIT) A perennial herb tossed in salads with fried bacon and bread croûtons.

Larger leaves can be boiled like spinach. The roots are par-boiled and roasted like parsnips.

DANISH PASTRY A flaky pastry made with a yeast dough layered with half its weight of butter. It is made in the same way as puff paste but with only three half turns.

Danish pastries are made in a number of shapes such as stars and cornets,

and may be filled with cooked apples, almond cream or confectioners' custard and sprinkled with flaked almonds.

DARNE A fish steak on the bone. *See also Fish.*

DARPHIN POTATO Grated potato shallow-fried in a small omelet pan to resemble a flat cake.

DARTOIS A savory snack made of two layers of puff pastry stuffed with anchovies and olive, chicken or salmon, and then cut into fingers after baking.

Sweet dartois are filled with frangipane and candied fruit and coated with fondant.

DASHI A basic Japanese stock made with kelp and flavored with dried bonito and soya concentrate.

DATE One of the oldest fruits grown in the Middle East. Dates are rich in potassium and folic acid, and are a good source of iron so they should be used more frequently in dishes such as savory rice.

Fresh dates are delicious when eaten on their own. Dried dates are very sweet when dried in the sun. They can

D

be stuffed with almond paste and glazed in caramel, or they can be chopped and added to cake or pudding batters.

DAUBE Marinated meat, usually cubed beef, and vegetables braised slowly in a lidded casserole or daubière. The marinade is used for the cooking.

Typical dishes: Daube de boeuf à la Provençale, épaule de pork à la Normande.

DAUPHINE POTATO Deep-fried, egg-shaped balls of mashed potatoes and choux paste.

1 1¼ cups/14oz/400g mashed
  potatoes
2 egg yolks
⅔ cup/5oz/150g butter
oil for deep frying

Choux paste
¼ cup/2oz/50g butter
½ cup/4fl oz/100ml water
1 cup/4oz/100g bread (strong)
  flour
2 small eggs, beaten
salt and pepper

To make the choux paste, heat the butter in the water until the butter has melted, then bring to a boil. Add the flour. Stir until the mixture forms a stiff paste. Remove from the heat and leave until cold.

Beat the eggs into the paste. The mixture should now have a semi-pouring consistency. Season to taste.

Beat the mashed potato with the egg yolks and butter.

Mix together the choux paste and mashed potatoes. Mold the mixture into shapes using 2 tablespoons and place them on baking parchment (greased greaseproof paper).

Drop the molded mixture into deep hot oil at 350°F/180°C and fry until crisp and a golden brown, about 4 minutes. Drain and serve.

DECOCTION A liquid obtained by boiling an ingredient in water to extract its flavor.

DECORATION An edible sweet ingredient or ingredients added to sweet dishes, cakes and pastries in a way that enhances their appearance.

DEEP-FRYING The cooking of food by total immersion in preheated oil. It is done at 340°F- 375°F/160-190°C.

With the exception of potatoes, all foods that are deep-fried require a coating to protect the surface from intense heat, to prevent the escape of liquids and nutrients from the food and to control the speed of heat penetration.

The best oils for deep-frying are peanut, soybean, rapeseed and corn oil. *See also Fats and Oils.*

Tips

• When deep-frying keep the temperature of the oil correct:

— for blanching or par-frying especially of French fries (chips), 325°F/160°C.

— for frying medium pieces 350-375°F/175-190°C.

- for browning small fish and French fries (chips) 375°F/190°C.

• When several batches are being fried, allow the oil to reheat to the correct temperature in between batches.

• The filling for pastries that are deep-fried is usually cooked beforehand or needs no cooking.

• All oils must be strained after use and should never be heated above their smoking points; as a guide, for groundnut oil, which has one of the highest smoking points, this is 220°F/425°C.

• Never fill the fryer or saucepan more than half-full as the oil would overflow and set on fire, and do not cover the fryer or saucepan with a lid during frying.

• Use a basket for food coated in batter or breadcrumbs as they would stick.

• Use a basket for French fries.

• Use a slotted spoon for removing fried food.

• Fried foods are served with an acid sauce like tomato or tartare, or with vinegar or lemon wedges.

DEER (Fr. CERF) A ruminant animal which is marketed as venison.

Wild deer have been hunted throughout Europe and the Middle East from the earliest times until the present day. From the Middle Ages onwards, great country houses often had deer parks, and many still do. Today, however, most venison comes from farmed deer.

Deer farming has greatly increased in recent years to meet the steadily growing demand for this healthy meat. Deer are naturally gregarious animals. In the wild they live in large herds and when farmed they are kept in open fields, surrounded by high fences, in which they can graze in peace. Deer farmers provide shelter for their animals and supplement their diet with hay and root vegetables, but deer cannot be factory farmed.

Fallow, red and sika deer are the principal breeds which are farmed.

D

Apart from their size there is very little difference between them, so unless you buy venison direct from the farm you are unlikely to know from which breed it comes.

DEFICIENCY DIET A diet that lacks a particular nutrient or nutrients that are essential to the well-being of the body.

DEGLAZE To dissolve congealed cooking juices in a pan in which meat, poultry or game have been fried or roasted. This is achieved by adding liquid and scraping and stirring vigorously while bringing the liquid to a boil. This is then reduce to half its original volume. This concentrates the liquid into a glaze, hence the name 'deglaze'. The sauce is strained and seasoned.

DEHYDRATION OF FOODS The commercial drying by artificial heat under carefully controlled conditions. Eggs, milk, potatoes, coffee, fruit juices, soups and other convenience foods are commercially dehydrated.

Dehydration can be done by heating trays of the food in the oven. A drum may be used for milk, soups or eggs.

Other dehydration processes include atomization by a current of hot air and sublimation by freeze-drying. *See also Drying.*

DELICATESSEN A store which sells ready-prepared foods and unusual delicacies. They are sources of unusual condiments, spices, confections etc.

Also this term includes cold cuts (cooked meats), preserved sausage, pâtés, terrines, cheeses, pies, cooked dishes, dips and salads.

DELIQUESCENT A substance that can pick up moisture when exposed to the air to such an extent as to dissolve in it and become liquid.

DEMI-GLACE Brown sauce boiled until reduced by half.

DENDANG Indonesian clam.

DENSITY Relative density is also known as specific gravity. It is used in the milk, confectionery and oil industries. Relative density can be measured with a hydrometer, an instrument which floats in the liquid.

To calculate the densityof a liquid, divide the weight of an ingredient by its volume.

DESALTING Removing the salt from salted or pickled fish, meat or vegetables. It is done by running cold water over the salted item over two hours for small portions, or by soaking a large piece for several hours in cold water, changing the water two or three times.

DESICCATED COCONUT (SHREDDED DRIED COCONUT) The dry sliced and shredded flesh of the coconut. It is used in cakes and coconut meringues or it can be reconstituted in water to produce coconut milk for curries or ice creams.

DESSERT In traditional classical cooking the dessert is differentiated from the entremet, the former being something light that is served as the very last course, whereas the latter is a more substantial dish.

Nowadays, dessert refers to the sweet dishes served at the end of the meal, or in between the main dish and cheese if this is eaten last.

A dessert should complement the dishes that have been served before it. For example, spicy and more vigorous dishes should be followed by a dessert that is light and feathery, such as a strawberry soufflé.

DEVILLED A dish or sauce that is highly seasoned with a hot ingredient such as mustard.

Typical dish: Poulet grillé à la diable.

DEXTRIN A mixture of gummy poly-saccharides obtained by the partial hydrolysis of starch. This happens when bread is injected with steam during baking, producing a glossy appearance on the surface.

DEXTROSE *See Glucose.*

DIABETES A disease resulting from an insufficient or ineffective supply of the hormone insulin, which prevents sugars from being utilized as an energy source.

The remedy is a low carbohydrate diet, cutting out bread and any desserts or drinks. It is a tough diet to follow!

DIASTASE *See Amylase.*

DIET Dietetics are concerned with effective food combination in order to supply an optimum intake of nutrients for individuals or groups of people.

More than half of all deaths in western countries are believed to be associated with diseases aggravated by eating the wrong food and what we drink. Many people are affected by atherosclerosis, a furring of the arteries, as a result of a diet with an excess of sugar, alcohol and fat.

Our Western diet may not always cause ill-health or early death but

D

often brings about constant discomfort and pains: constipation, haemorrhoids, varicose veins, gallstones, diverticular disease, tooth and gum disease, peptic ulcers and obesity. A change in diet can delay or prevent these diseases occurring, or may sometimes even reverse them.

The consequences of a bad diet have inspired me to caution readers about the effects of the abuse of food. The simpler the food is the better, as long as it is fresh and free from contamination. A return to country cooking rather than manufactured convenience products might be a way of improving the diet. Eat lean meat (most people should also eat less of it), chicken and game and eat plenty of vegetables, salads and fruit and include the skins as often as possible because they provide fiber, which will help to avoid constipation. Eat coarse-grain breads and more fish, and do not drink milk but dilute yogurt with water as a thirst-quencher. Cereals and pulses are especially good for you, but eat less rich, sweet pastries.

Discipline yourself in your eating habits and follow the diet which will benefit you most at all times. Food is the fuel of life and life can be sustained with considerably less food than we normally eat.

Dietetic principles

Our body is comparable to an engine. It requires fuel to supply the muscles with energy for bodily activity, and it needs materials to repair muscles and tissues from wear and tear. For this, protein is needed, since it contains nitrogen. For energy, carbohydrates and fats are required.

In addition, water must be taken into the body in sufficient quantity to make up for loss through urine and sweat. Mineral salts are also very important to the body.

The number of calories we use up depends directly on our physical activity, metabolism, weight and body structure.

After the energizing power of a food has been ascertained, there remain several other factors which determine its suitability as part of the diet:

ABSORBABILITY is very important. Few substances are completely broken down and absorbed into the body. Some, such as vegetable proteins, may be rejected, or if taken in large amounts are passed by the bowels completely unchanged.

Thus a considerable bulk of food eaten each day, especially of the coarser kinds, actually remains unused and only partially digested.

DIGESTIBILITY The food has to be digestible to be acceptable. *See also Digestive system.*

ECONOMY Animal protein in terms of meat is relatively the most expensive source of protein. Among the cheapest protein sources we have are eggs, milk, cheese and fish. Fat has double the energy value of carbohydrate.

FRESHNESS This is probably the most important factor determining the suitability of food, but fresh foods are relatively expensive. Most convenience foods have a comparatively low vitamin content. For this reason the daily diet should include vegetables, fruit, milk, fish, poultry and meat, unsaturated margarine, and cheese. *See also Vegetarian diet.*

PREPARATION The reason for cooking food is to develop flavor and texture, and so make it more palatable and digestible, and to kill harmful organisms which may be present in food.

SATISFACTION is of great importance, and depends partly upon the amount of food and partly upon its preparation. Except in certain special circumstances, such as food for invalids, food should not be digested very rapidly.

Cooking foods with fat, which penetrates other foods, retards digestion and slows the process.

To a certain extent, the less digestible the food, the more satisfying to the appetite; this is one of the chief reasons why different foods as well as different methods of preparation and cooking suit persons of diverse physiques and digestive powers.

DIGESTIVE SYSTEM Food is softened and converted to a form which is soluble in the watery fluids of the body or, in the case of fat, into very minute globules.

Salivatory digestion
Saliva contains an enzyme, ptyalin, that changes the starch in carbohydrates such as bread and potatoes, into sugar.

Chewing food well is very important as it churns the food particles and mixes them thoroughly with pylalin. This process continues for over one hour while the food is in the stomach, then the stomach acid and gastric juices take over.

Gastric digestion
Gastric juice begins to be secreted before the food enters the stomach, at the sight and smell of food (this is

D

known as psychic secretion). Gastric juice contains an enzyme, pepsin, which breaks down proteins into smaller molecules. Free hydrochloric acid is also present. This aids the action of the pepsin and prevents the putrefaction of food. Acid salts such as phosphate of soda have a similar action.

The main function of the stomach is to break down the ingested food to make it soluble. This material, known as chyme, is then passed through the pylorus into the intestine.

Gastric digestion of a simple meal of tea, bread and butter and jam should take about one hour to complete. A meal containing milk and eggs requires three hours and a rich dinner with wine and beer can take as much as seven hours.

Intestinal digestion
When the chyme leaves the stomach and moves into the bowels, it is exposed to bile, pancreatic juices, intestinal juices and bacteria.

• Bile consists mainly of complex salts and pigments, which assist in digesting fats.

• Pancreatic juice contains four powerful enzymes: lipase breaks down fats into glycerol and fatty acids; amylase completes the digestion of starch; trypsin and chymotrypsin continue the breakdown of protein begun in the stomach.

• Intestinal juice contains small amounts of enzymes which complete the breakdown of proteins into amino-acids. They also act upon the disaccharides, maltose, sucrose and lactose, converting them into the monosaccharide glucose, and split fats into fatty acids and glycerol.

• Bacteria have first a fermentative action, and in later stages, a putrefactive one. In the former process they act upon carbohydrates to produce acetic, butyric, and lactic acids. In the latter, bacteria decompose as histamine, phenol, cresol, indole, skatole. The bacteria also play an important role in the manufacture of the B group of vitamins.

Absorption
Alcohol and water are the two substances which pass quickly from the stomach to the intestine in a few minutes. Fats are taken up by the lymph vessels known as lacteal, and ultimately reach the blood, while sugars, salts and amino acids pass directly into the small blood vessels of the intestines.

Further absorption is probably assisted by the leucocytes or white cells of the blood, which increase in numbers after a meal, and which are capable of taking food particles into themselves.

Food materials are absorbed almost exclusively by the small intestine. The larger intestine, or colon, absorbs water and salts. The waste is rejected from the body in the faeces.

2 quarts/3 pints/1.8 liters of water a day are needed to assist the body in doing its work properly.

DIGLYCERIDE A fatty acid.

DILL (Fr. ANETH) A herb used in the sauce served with Scandinavian gravlax.

DIM SUM Small Chinese noodle dough rolls, fritters, dumplings and steamed buns served between meals, or at ceremonies and parties.

DINNER Dinner is the main evening meal. The time it is eaten varies between countries. Dinners can be formal or informal, homely or gastronomic. The menu will obviously reflect the style of dinner, but basically the season of the year determines the content and number of dishes.

A three-course dinner may consist of a soup, poultry and hot dessert. In addition, there may be a fish dish.

In a French dinner a tray of seven to ten assorted cheeses may be served after the main dish but before the dessert.

DIP A dip is a light paste with a consistency of a mousse or thick mayonnaise or whipped cream, and solid enough to be spread on a cracker without breaking it.

There are three main types of dip:

• Thick mayonnaise mixed with smoked fish, fruit or vegetable purée and whipped cream.

• Seafood mousse mixtures lightened with whipped cream.

• Fruit dips, lightly set with gelatin, lightened with beaten egg whites and often well-flavored with spices.

Dipping ingredients can be a selection of finger-strips of vegetables, florets of cauliflower or broccoli, raw mushrooms, radishes, daikon, scallions (spring onions), dill pickles, wedges of pear or apple, crackers, Italian bread sticks, toast fingers, crisp French bread, fried langoustines, fish fingers or fried dumplings on wooden toothpicks (cocktail sticks), or fish sausages.

DISACCHARIDE A sugar composed of two monosaccharide molecules combined, with the elimination of a mole-

D

cule of water. Examples are glucose, lactose and maltose.

DISODIUM PHOSPHATE, SODIUM GUANYLATE A flavor enhancer.

DISTILLATION The convertion of a liquid into vapor, condensing this vapor, and collecting liquid or distillate.

DISTILLED WATER Water purified by boiling and distillation. Distilled water should be used to soak dried beans as hard water tends to coat the beans with insoluble minerals.

DITALINI Small thimble-shaped macaroni which is about ½in/1.2cm long.

DOBOS TORTE An Austrian layer cake filled with buttercream and coated with a caramel nut topping.

DODINE A sauce made from duck bones with ground (minced) liver and cream, strained and served with the meat of the roasted boned duck.

DOLCELATTE CHEESE A mild blue Italian cheese.

DOLICHO A genus of pulses of which several are cultivated in the Indian sub-continent as well as other tropical and sub-tropical regions of the world.

The most common is the mongette dolicho, which is widely cultivated in China, Louisiana and the south of France. It is smaller than a navy (haricot) bean. The young pods can be cooked in the same way as asparagus tips or snowpeas (mangetout).

DOLMA Greek stuffed vine leaf filled with cooked rice, and ground (minced) lamb, pine nuts and raisins. They may be served with a tomato or lemon sauce.

DORINE A small tartlet filled with confectioners' custard, decorated with marrons glacés, glazed with apricot and sprinkled with toasted almonds.

DOSA A crisp Indian pancake made from rice and ground dal.

DOUGH A mixture of flour and liquid that is soft, elastic and pliable enough to be rolled with a pastry (rolling) pin. Fat is often added. For example, a plain dough can be adapted for puff paste by layering it with butter.

Yeast can be added to a dough. Bread dough will contain as much as 60 percent water but yeast doughs enriched with eggs and fat will take considerably less. The combined fat and eggs of these doughs should be at least 50 percent of the flour used.

DOUGHNUT   A deep-fried rich yeast mixture coated in sugar after cooking; the sugar may be flavored with cinnamon. A doughnut may be ring-shaped, or a jam-filled ball, known as Berlin or jelly doughnuts in America.

⅓ cup/3oz/75g butter
5 cups/¼lb/500g flour
2 tbsp/1 oz/25g sugar
1 tsp salt
1 tbsp dry (dried) yeast
1 cup/8oz/225ml milk
2 eggs, beaten
grated rind of ½ lemon
oil for deep-frying

Makes 10

Cut the butter into the flour. Dissolve the sugar, salt and yeast in the milk. Stir into the flour mixture with the eggs and lemon rind to make a dough.

Knead the dough for 10 minutes. Roll into a ball. Cover and set aside for 30 minutes. Divide the mixture into 10 balls. Deep-fry the doughnuts in hot oil at 370°F/188°C for 4 minutes.

DRAGÉE   A candy (sweet), usually a sugar-coated almond. The process of making dragees is lengthy as a number of successive coats have to be applied.

DRESSING   *See Salad dressing.*

DRIED FOODS   For centuries foods have been dried in the sun to preserve them. Fruits such as apples, peaches, apricots, plums to make prunes, dates, figs, grapes for currants, raisins and golden raisins (sultanas), herbs, pulses, cereals, seeds, spices and some vegetables like tomatoes and chili peppers.

However, sun-drying can be unreliable, so nowadays commercial organizations use heated air for artificial drying under controlled conditions; many fruits dried commercially are treated with sulphur dioxide before drying to prevent browning.
See also Dehydrated foods.

DRIED HERBS   *See Herbs.*

DRUMSTICK   1) An Indian vegetable which is similar to a squash, but which has a long skinny shape. It is available fresh or canned.

2) The second from the top portion of the leg of birds such as chicken and turkey.

Drumsticks can be skinned and fried or barbecued.

DUBLIN BAY PRAWN   *See Langoustine.*

D

DUCHESSE 1) Creamy mashed potato with added eggs, which can be piped into rosettes and baked until golden.

2) A variety of pear.

3) Petits fours containing nuts and chocolate.

DUCK (Fr. CANARD, CANETON) In France, the word canard applies to the live bird but caneton is the usual word used on menus. Ducks have been domesticated in China for 2,000 years and are probably the most popular food of this great nation of gourmets.

Small, tender duck, or ducklings as younger birds are sometimes called, can be roasted on a spit but the larger ducks are best roasted or braised in the oven. They are very fatty birds, so take this into account when cooking.

Typical dishes: Caneton à l'orange, caneton à la presse de Rouen, caneton aux cerises, pâté d'Amiens en croûte, terrine de caneton aux marrons, civet de mallard au Chambertin.

Duck in orange sauce

Duck in orange sauce is a classic dish. The secret is to ensure that the caramelization is done perfectly: to do this rub 2 lumps of sugar over the rind of an orange and mix with 1 table-spoon of wine vinegar before the brown sauce is added with the orange juice. To enhance the orange flavour add a few chopped mint leaves.

Serve the duck with dressed lettuce leaves, boiled potatoes with chives and pitted tart red cherries.

5lb/2.25kg oven-ready duckling
¼ cup/2oz/50g seasoned flour
salt and pepper
pinch of cinnamon
butter or oil for coating
¼ cup/2oz/50g seasoned flour

Sauce

2 lumps of sugar
2 oranges
1 tbsp wine vinegar
1¼ cups/10fl oz/300ml brown sauce
1 tsp tomato paste (purée)
½ cup/4fl oz/100ml white Port wine
1 tbsp orange liqueur
4 mint leaves, chopped
8oz/225g pitted tart red cherries

Garnish

segments of 2 oranges
12 pitted red cherries
mint leaves

Season the duckling inside and out with salt, pepper and cinnamon. Coat with little butter or oil and dust with

D

seasoned flour. Roast at 425°F/220°C/ gas mark 7 for 25 minutes then at 350°F/180°C/ gas mark 4 for a further 20 minutes. Baste the duck frequently with the fat and turn it each time.

Remove the duck from the oven and drain the juice from the roasting pan (tin) for use in the sauce. Also drain away the excess fat from the pan.

To make the sauce, put the roasting pan over the heat. Rub the sugar lumps over the rind of 1 orange rind and place in the pan, moisten with wine vinegar and heat until caramelized.

Add the sauce, tomato paste (purée), Port wine, mint leaves and juice from the orange. Gently boil for 10 minutes. Strain the sauce into a smaller saucepan. Add the orange liqueur and season to taste.

Remove the rind from the remaining orange and cut into fine strips. Boil the strips in water for 10 minutes. Drain and add to the sauce with the cherries. Boil again for 2 minutes.

Cut the duckling into two halves. Chop away the backbone and discard the ribs of the two breasts.

Place the duck on a plate coated with the sauce. Garnish with orange segments, cherries and mint leaves.

DULSE A seaweed that can be eaten as a vegetable with fish. Dulse should be soaked in fresh water for at least six hours to desalinate, then tossed in butter and seasoned with black pepper. It can also be chopped and mixed with mashed potatoes then refried to make croquettes.

DUSTING Sprinkling a powder such as flour or confectioners' (icing) sugar in a light, controlled manner.

DUTCH CHEESE The main cheeses from Holland are edam and gouda.

DUXELLE A mixture of chopped mushrooms, onions, shallots and fresh herbs, fried in butter until the moisture has evaporated. It can be thickened with chopped eggs and breadcrumbs and flavored with garlic.

Duxelle is used as a stuffing for coulibiac, beef Wellington, courgettes, baked potatoes tomatoes, eggplants (aubergines) or pancakes.

Typical dishes: Omelette duxelle, côte de veau duxelle, pâté de champignons à la duxelle.

DYSPEPSIA, INDIGESTION A bland diet mainly of fish and milky foods such as light custards, is prescribed to patients suffering from dyspepsia.

EARTHENWARE CASSEROLE The most common earthenware vessels used in modern and traditional cookery are oven-glazed dishes, gratin dishes and casseroles. Such dishes are called daubière in Provence, guichon in Normandy and cassoulet in Toulouse.

ECCLES CAKE A puff or flaky pastry filled with dried currants, candied peel, butter and nuts. The currants should be washed and well drained to plump them up.

ÉCLAIR A popular finger-shaped dessert pastry of a choux paste filled with confectioners' custard or whipped cream and iced with chocolate or coffee fondant icing.

EDAM CHEESE A ball-shaped Dutch cheese with a red wax skin. It usually has 40 percent fat and can be used in any dish which requires grated cheese.

EDDOE A tuber related to colocasia. It is grown in Africa and the West Indies.

EEL (Fr. ANGUILLE) A river fish with a dense oily flesh that is enhanced by herbs when stewed or cooked in water or wine and eaten in its own jelly. Its young are called elvers and they are delicious shallow-fried in butter with garlic.

The conger eel is found in the sea and is the largest variety. It is very bony and can reach a terriffic length. It is best stewed in a casserole. The Dutch have a celebrated dish of eels with green herbs.

EGG Eggs are used in many ways in cooking and are very nutritious. One third of a chicken's egg is the yolk, which is 30 percent fat including lecithin and cholesterol, 16 percent protein, plus iron and Vitamins A, B, D and E. Egg white contains nine percent protein.

The extensive use of eggs in cookery is made possible by the protein content. The protein coagulates during heating, bringing about thickening as in custards, or binding foods together as in croquettes.

The elasticity of the egg protein is also important in products such as choux pastes, popovers and Yorkshire pudding; the protein stretches when the moisture in the mixture changes to steam and expands then as the temperature increases, the protein coagulates to aid in forming the framework of the product.

Coagulation of egg white starts at 145°F/62°C. The egg white changes from a clear, transparent mass to a white, opaque one. Coagulation of the yolk occurs at about 155°F/70°C. Salt and acid hasten the coagulation of both egg white and egg yolk.

The eggs of many birds can be eaten and used in cookery if freshly laid. Gull's eggs are a gourmet food and so are plover's and quail's eggs. For ordinary cooking purposes, however, fresh chicken's eggs are best. Fresh, high-quality eggs are particulalry important for poaching.

Egg yolks are used for mayonnaise, hollandaise sauce, custards and sabayons. Egg whites are used for meringues, macaroons, angel cakes, soufflés, mousses, and quenelles and for the clarification of stocks and consommés. Whole eggs are used in ice creams, many desserts, cakes, cookies (biscuits) and as a binding agent in forcemeats.

As a light lunch eggs are made into omelets, poached, fried, scrambled or hard-cooked (hard-boiled) and served with hot or cold sauces. *See also Yolk.*

Typical dishes: Oeufs bénédictine, oeufs à la Florentine, soufflé au fromage, oeufs en cocotte à la crème, omelette Norvégienne, omelette à la paysanne.

EGGNOG A drink made by beating 1 egg yolk with 1 tablespoon of superfine (caster) sugar for 4 minutes then mixing with brandy or rum, and milk. It can be drunk either hot or cold.

EGGPLANT (AUBERGINE) This vegetable can be baked and the flesh made into a dip or paste. Otherwise, it may be fried, toasted with cheese or used with tomatoes and bell peppers, as in ratatouille.

EGGWASH Egg yolks and water mixed together to be used as a shiny glaze for baked goods such as breads, buns and pastries.

ELDERBERRY The juice of the elderberry is made into a syrup (cordial) with flavorings such as cloves and cinnamon.

EMMENTHAL CHEESE A large wheel-shaped cheese made in Switzerland and which weighs 132-286lb/60-

E

130kg. The interior is pale yellow with many large holes. Emmenthal is used for fondue.

EMPANADA A savory South American and Spanish pie or turnover that is either baked or shallow-fried.

EMULSION A mixture of two liquids that are not mutually soluble. Hollandaise sauce and mayonnaise are typical examples.

An unstable emulsion, such as French dressing or reduced stock emulsified with butter, will break after a short time. To make an emulsion permanent there needs to be an emulsifying agent, such as eggs or mustard powder, which will absorb the oil.

ENCHILADA A Mexican corn pancake stuffed with chili pepper, ground (minced) meat or cheese and tomato salad.

ENDIVE (Fr. CHICORÉE) A winter salad leaf with pale yellow leaves, belonging to the chicory family.

ENSALADA The Spanish word for salad.

ENTRÉE In North America, the entrée is the main course; in Europe classically, it is a light course served between the first course and the fish and main courses.

ENZYME An enzyme is a biological catalyst that enables a wide variety of biochemical reactions to occur without changing themselve. They are the main agents that cause the breakdown of protein into amino acids and fats into fatty acids and glycerol. *See also Amylase, Pepsin, Lipase and Oxidase.*

ERINGOES These roots are roasted and eaten in their skins, and the leaves are used as spinach .

ESCABECHE A method of preservation by steeping food in vinegar. It is carried out in hot places such as Spain and Southern American. Fish are usually treated in this way, but meat, poultry and game are also sometimes used.

The food is cooked before being marinated in the vinegar. Oil, lemon or lime juice, chili peppers, onion, herbs such as dill and mint, and salt are also added.

ESCALOPE (Am. SCALLOP) A thin slice of meat taken either from the loin or from the thick part of the leg. Escalopes are beaten with a meat bat to a paper thin thickness for tenderness and presentation. They can be coated in breadcrumbs and shallow-fried in butter.

Typical dishes: Scaloppine Marsala, escalope Viennoise, paupiette de veau Liègoise.

ESPAGNOLE *See Brown sauce.*

ESSENCES *See Extracts.*

ESSENTIAL OILS *See Volatile oils.*

ESTOUFFADE Braising meat or vegetables in a casserole with a tightly fitting lid to retain the moisture, using the lowest possible heat. Traditionally the latter method was over the ashes of a dying fire for several hours.

The method is extensively used by Jews for cooking food for the Sabbath because they are not permitted to cook on that day.

ETHNIC FOOD The term cover foods from Asian countries including India, China and Japan, the Pacific islands, Africa and Central and South America; in short 80 percent of the world's population. Many people have at long last recognized that much of the best food in the world comes from these countries.

The greed of the Western world has led to a restriction of the agricultural potential of poorer countries that could given a chance feed themselves, instead of growing dangerous drugs.

The problems in the Western world were solved 1,700 years ago when a Roman emperor ordered the destruction of French vineyards because the soldiers were intoxicated by alcoholic drinks. We have the same problems today with far too much wine being produced at the expense of necessary cheaper foods.

Indo-Chinese countries have always had a flair for producing marvellous, simple tasty meals using grains, beans, vegetables and fruits. Cutting a vegetable in an unconventional way can make a humble carrot or daikon look like a natural flower.

The Arabic and Semitic peoples have been leaders in the field of ethnic gastronomy for centuries. They introduced a range of spices to the modern world and made food more respectable and hygienic than any other nations had done before the age of manufactured convenience foods.

The gastronomic standards and culinary talent in countries such as Malaysia, Thailand and Hong Kong are far superior to those in Europe at present. It is gratifying to note that most luxury hotels are now promoting

E

ethnic cooks to executive chef positions. So much has been published about ethnic foods that they are becoming part of our culinary repetoire, and enriching it.

EUCALYPTUS An Australian tree which produces a very aromatic volatile oil used by Australian cooks to flavor foods.

EXTRACT (ESSENCE) A flavoring that is produced chemically or from the volatile oils of plant materials, which are extracted by pressure or distillation. Extracts (essences) are used to give a distinctive aromatic taste to cakes, creams, custards and other desserts.

Chemists are able to imitate some natural flavorings, and these can sometimes be more effective than the natural products.

Pineapple extract consists of butyric ether dissolved in alcohol or byric acid treated with sulphuric acid. Pear extract is the product of amyl alcohol and potassium acetate.

Artificial strawberry extract consists of five parts acetic acid, three parts amyl-acetic ether, two parts amyl butyric, five parts butyric ether, one part formic ether, one part methyl salicylic ether, one part nitrous ether and two parts glycerine and enough alcohol to make 100 parts.

Other flavors that can be produced include raspberry, cherry and mango, almond, lemon, orange, peppermint, rum, Sherry and vanilla. Their purity and safety are not questioned and the standard is so great that distillers use them for producing well known liqueurs.

Continental chefs prefer to use the real aromatic from the fresh pods of vanilla for instance or from the range of some 200 liqueurs.

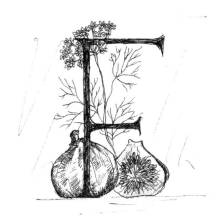

FAGGOT (Fr. CRÉPINETTE) A flat pork sausagemeat dumpling made with breadcrumbs, liver, onion and seasoning wrapped in pig's caul.

FAGIOLI The Italian word for beans. In old French the slang word for beans is fayot a derivative of the Latin name fayoli.

FAHRENHEIT A temperature scale in which 32 degrees represents freezing point and 212 degrees is boiling point. It can be converted to Celsius by subtracting 32 from the Fahrenheit reading, multiplying by five and dividing by nine.

FAJITAS A Mexican dish of strips of steak marinated in lime juice and oil with chili pepper. It is stir-fried and usually served as a filling for tacos.

FALAFEL An Israeli fritter of puréed cooked garbanzo beans (chickpeas) or dried lima (broad) beans. Falafel are an ideal meat substitute for vegetarians. Falafel are often served served as a filling for pitta bread, with salad leaves seasoned with a yogurt and tahini.

FALETTE Boned and rolled breast of mutton stuffed with a light herb-flavored panada and braised in the oven with carrots, onions and white wine.

FANCHONETTE A tart filled with confectioner's custard. After baking it is decorated with piped meringue and browned briefly in the oven.

FAR BRETON From Britany, western France, a thick baked custard containing pitted soaked prunes, similar in style to clafoutis. Some versions have a pie dough shell (pastry case), but that is not correct.

FARCI Pork forcemeat that is mixed with eggs and flavored with garlic and fresh herbs.
   Typical dishes: Farci du Poitou, tomates farcies, gâteau de Picardie, saucisse Dauphinoise.

FARÇON In Savoie, France, farçon is a mixture of mashed potatoes, herbs and eggs that is baked in a dish.

F

FARFALLE Butterfly-shaped Italian pasta. It is made in different sizes such as small farfallini and large farfallone.

FARINA In the USA farina is a granular, protein-rich meal made from any hard wheat other than durum, with the bran and most of the germ removed.

In Britain the name can be applied to any type of flour or meal from wheat, corn, nuts or starchy roots, but it usually refers to potato flour or starch.

FARINACEOUS Ingredients and products containing flour made from cereals, nuts or starchy roots such as potatoes and the legumes from which a flour is extracted, for example soya beans.

FARINADE DE CHATAIGNE A dumpling made of chestnut flour, fat and eggs poached in milk.

FARL A term used in Scotland, Ireland and Wales for a quarter of a round oatcake, or bannock, cooked on a griddle.

FASTING In the strict sense of the word, fasting is the abstention from food and drink, but it is commonly also applied to a severely restricted diet, either by the rejection of certain customary foods or by a reduction of the total quantity of food consumed.

Many religions have fasting laws, for example as a penance for committing sins. Hindus and Buddhists have a period of strict abstinence and the customary observance of fasting as a preparation for the worship of ancestral spirits.

Moslems, Jews and Christians restrict or prohibit the eating of foods such as pork, shellfish, or dairy products mixed with meat, or impose periods of fasting.

Fasting is recommended for your health's sake because it gives the digestive system a rest, and should be undertaken as a rest from eating too much rich food. However, isn't it more sensible to control our food intake, plus a little regular fasting?

FATS AND OILS There are many types of fats and oils used in cooking, such as butter, margarine and the wide range of oils produced from seeds, nuts and plants.

Fats and oils are lipids. The difference between them is that fats are solid at room temperature and oils are liquid, although some thicken when refrigerated. Oils have a higher smoking point than butter and margarine, which is why most cooks mix them with oil in equal proportions when shallow-frying.

BUTTER is used for its flavor, which cannot yet be imitated in spite of making use of butyric, one of its aromatic fatty acids.

COOKING FATS add flavor, color and texture, and hamper the development of gluten in rich yeast doughs.

LARD has been a favorite in the country for its taste and texture; those who have been fed on pork drippings will understand why pâté de foie de pork with quite a lot of pork fat has been so popular in the past.

MARGARINE is manufactured by many brands for making pastries and cakes. Some have the plasticity of butter and are recommended for making flaky, puff and Danish pastries; others are used for their creaming properties, while others are used because they are made with polyunsaturated oils.

MONO-UNSATURATED FATS have a hydrogen molecule count in between the other two types.

POLYUNSATURATED FATS have the lowest number of hydrogen compounds and are considered relatively healthy. They are found in vegetable and seed oils.

SATURATED FATS have the highest number of hydrogen molecules and are known to be a contributory factor in heart disease because they can lead to an increased level of cholesterol in the blood. They come primarily from animal sources such as butter, cheese, cream, meat and chicken fat. Hard margarines also contain saturated fats.

In France, food cooked 'au gras' means cooked with animal fats and cooked 'au maigre' indicates vegetable oil has been used for fish and vegetables. *See also Fatty acids.*

FATTY ACIDS Fats differ from carbohydrates and proteins in that they are not polymers of repeating molecular units. They do not form long chains and they do not contribute structural strength to plant and animal tissues. Fats are greasy substances which are insoluble in water.

Fats always have other substances associated with them in natural foods, such as the fat soluble Vitamins A, D, E and K, cholesterol in animal fats and ergosterol in vegetable fats, and phospholipids.

F

There are about 20 different fatty acids that may be connected to glycerol in natural fats. They differ in the lengths of their carbon chains. Formic acid, acetic acid, and propionic acid are the shortest of the fatty acids. Stearic acid is one of the longer common fatty acids, it is a saturated fat. Oleic acid is a polyunsaturated fat.

Short-chain fatty acids contain 2-6 carbon atoms, medium chain 8-10, and long chain 12-30. Fatty acids containing their full quota of hydrogen atoms are called saturated fatty acids.

Animal fats and hydrogenated fats such as hard margarines tend to contain more saturated fatty acids — lauric, myristic and palmitic acids — and have been found to raise the cholesterol level of humans.

Fatty acids with less than their full quota of hydrogen atoms are called unsaturated fatty acids. In this case the hydrogen is replaced by a double bond between the carbon atoms. Most plants and fish oils contain a greater proportion of unsaturated fatty acids than animal fats, thses are liquid at room temperature.

Fatty acids with only two hydrogen atoms missing and one double bond are called monounsaturated fatty acids. They have no effect on the blood cholesterol.

Oleic acid — a mono-unsaturated fatty acid with 18 carbon atoms — is the most common fatty acid; most fats and oils contain 30-65 percent of their fatty acid content as oleic.

Fatty acids with four or more hydrogen atoms missing and two or more double bonds are called polyunsaturated fatty acids or PUFA.

Polyunsaturated fatty acids have been found to lower the blood cholesterol, but they are less effective in lowering the blood cholesterol than saturated fats are in raising it.

Linoleic acid with 18 carbon atoms and two double bonds, is one of the most abundant fatty acids in plant oils — but it also occurs in small amounts in animal fats.

Fish oils tend to contain large amounts of other polyunsaturated fatty acids. Linoleic is the initiator of the family of essential fatty acids which are the polyunsaturated fatty acids with an arrangement of double bonds that cannot be imitated in the body. All other fatty acids can be synthesized by the body and are not essential nutrients.

FAVA BEAN (BROAD BEAN) There are several different varieties of fava bean, which can be improved by peeling of the outer skin after cooking. The pod is too tough to be edible but the tops of the young plants can be eaten in the same way as spinach.

FECULA This word is derived from the French word fécule, the starch of roots such as potatoes.

FEDELINI A thin Italian pasta that is used in soups.

FEET (Eng. TROTTER, Fr. PIED) The feet of pigs, calves, cows and sheep are boiled and served with sharp sauces and enjoyed by many gourmets. Feet are used in stocks for making meat jellies and sauces.

FEIJOA A small egg-shaped fruit which tastes like a mixture of quince, pineapple and eucalyptus. Feijoa are best eaten as a fruit on their own or combined with berries in fruit salads and ice cream.

FEIJOADA A Brazilian beef stew cooked with red or black haricot beans. It can be made up of feet (trotters), tails or bacon. It is very spicy and pungent with chili powder. It is served with rice and green cabbage cooked separately.

FEIJOES Portuguese for dried beans.

The same word is also used in Brazil.

FENNEL (Fr. FENOUIL) An aromatic biennial bulb with a spicy flavor. Fennel can be served like celery with a savory or tomato sauce, also used in fish soups, and salads with garlic and green beans. Fennel seeds are used in confectionery and in some ginger and honey cakes.

Fennel sauce
Serve with bass, red snapper, goatfish (red mullet) or broiled (grilled) trout.

1 tbsp olive oil
1 fennel bulb, chopped
1 tsp anise seeds
1¼ cups/10fl oz/300ml fish stock
1 tsp flour
1 tsp butter
salt and pepper

Heat the oil and fry the fennel for 3 minutes. Add the anise seeds and stock and boil for a further 10 minutes.
 Beat the flour and butter to a paste. Whisk into the sauce. Simmer for 10 minutes.
 Strain or purée the sauce.

FENUGREEK Fenugreek seeds are used in Indian cookery. The leaves can be used in salads.

F

FERMENT *See Enzyme.*

FERMENTATION The transformation or metabolization of compounds without the use of oxygen. The process is carried out by living organisms (molds, yeasts and bacteria) and their enzymes.

Fermentation is used in the production of vinegar, cheese, yogurt, sauerkraut, breads and soy sauce.

FERRITIN A protein found in the liver, spleen and bone marrow that contains iron.

FETA CHEESE A semi-soft white cheese traditionally made from ewes' milk but now it is also made from cows' milk. It is cut in slices or cubes and packed in brine. It is used in salad and Greek dishes.

FETTUCELE The same as fetuce but a little wider.

FETTUCINE Italian pasta cut in ¼in/5 mm wide strips.

FETUCE A flat egg noodle about ½in/1.2cm wide.

FEUILLETÉE Made from puff paste (puff pastry or pâte feuilletée), and often cut in diamond shapes.

Typical dish: Feuilletée de homard à l'Américaine.

FIADONE A sponge cake made of cream cheese, eggs, flour and lemon peel flavored with Corsican liqueur. It is reputed to have been a favorite cake of Napoleon.

FIBER In dietetics and nutrition, the cellulose of leaves, stems, roots, seeds and fruits that is not digested by enzymes produced in the human digestive system.

Fiber therefore increases the bulk of the diet and stimulates the movement of the bowel, helping to prevent constipation.

FICELLE 1) A long, thin French loaf.

2) A rolled pancake filled with ham, mushrooms and cheese, sprinkled with hard grated cheese and browned in the oven. Leeks may be included in the filling.

FIDDLEHEAD FERN Grown in Virginia in the USA and Canada, fiddlehead fern tastes like a cross between asparagus and green beans. It is slightly chewy.

Fiddlehead fern is usually boiled in salted water and eaten with melted butter or egg sauce.

FIDEO Spanish thin spaghetti.

FIG (Fr. FIGUE) The fig appears to be the oldest tree in cultivation. There are many varieties of figs but all have soft flesh and abundant tiny seeds. They range in color from purple-black to almost white and in shape from round to oval. Their nutritional value lies mainly in their mineral content.

Fresh figs can be eaten with pork and rabbit dishes and are particularly succulent with pheasant cooked in wine. They can also be served with an assortment of cheeses or cooked in a red wine syrup.

Dried figs can be used in puddings or in cakes. They may be eaten plain or stuffed with almond paste or walnuts.

Typical dishes: Figues à la mousse de framboise, tarte aux figues sur pâté d'amandes, figues fraîches au jambon crû, côtelettes d'agneau aux figues mieleuse.

FIGATELLI A pig's liver sausage from Corsica.

FILBERT Variety of English hazel nut.

FILÉ A substance that is extracted from the dried leaves of the sassafras tree and ground to a powder. It is used in Cajun and Creole cookery as a thickening and flavoring agent.

FILLER An ingredient added to a main ingredient to stretch it and make the product cheaper. For example, starch, flour and eggs can be added to a forcemeat to make it go further.

FILLET 1) The under, tender part of the sirloin or loin of beef, veal, pork, lamb, venison, rabbit and hare. It is a choice cut and cooks quickly.

The whole fillet can be roasted, and the small cuts can be broiled (grilled) or shallow-fried.

Fillet can also be cut in strips Chinese-style, and stir-fried with vegetable strips.

2) In poultry and game birds, the part below the breast.

3) Of fish. *See Fish.*

Typical dishes: Filet de boeuf à la Perigourdine, beef Wellington, filet mignon à la Bordelaise, beef Stroganoff.

FILLETING Removing the bone, usually of fish.

FILO, PHYLLO A very thin dough made with very little or no fat. It is used for baklava, strudel and many sweet Middle Eastern pastries.

F

FINANCIER A crunchy cake made with ground almonds and meringue.

FINES HERBES Mixture of finely chopped herbs, usually parsley, chervil, chives and tarragon.

FISH (Fr POISSON) Fish are classified as round or flat and white or oily.

Fresh white fish should be neat, white and translucent in color.

Sole and salmon will improve in flavor and texture if kept on ice for several days. Fresh fish can be kept in the refrigerator overnight if unwrapped, placed on a plate and covered losely.

Frozen fish should be frozen hard. They can be kept in a household freezer for several months provided there are no signs of partial thawing. Fish can be cooked from frozen. Do not thaw it in water as the fish will lose texture, flavor and nutrients. Do not refreeze fish that has been previously frozen.

Extremely versatile, fish can be made into a great variety of nourishing and tasty dishes. Try combining different fish with fresh herbs, spices and fruits to bring a new dimension to your diet. Combine fish with low-fat, fiber-rich starchy foods, such as potatoes, rice, pasta, cereals and pulses.

Eat salad with broiled (grilled) fish as a light lunch or dinner. Fish in mayonnaise is an excellent sandwich filling. Poached fish can be creamed to produce dips, fish cakes and soufflés. Try serving fish with Asian peanut or savory fruit sauces. Use oatmeal to coat fried fish.

Cold fish marinaded in sweet and sour dressings are delicious in the summer with green salads. Use fish to start a meal.

For snacks there is nothing better than a smoked fish and cheese on toast.

Learn to make more sophisticated dishes, and interesting chowders and soups for in winter a bowl of soup with crusty French bread.

How to scale a fish

• Wash the fish in cold water. If the scales are firmly attached to the fish, wash it in warm salted water.

• Wipe and dry it well. Place a cloth on the board or over the table.

• Place rounded fish such as herrings on their side on the cloth. Hold the fish by the tail and with the blade of a small knife, scrape off the scales, holding the knife slantwise and working quickly from tail to head with small, jerking backward and forward strokes. The knife may slide if placed the wrong way.

Remove all the scales from both sides of the fish. Wash the fish again and dry it thoroughly.

How to skin a fish

FLAT FISH

• Make a small cut on the skin across the center of the tail. Scrape the tail backwards and forward with the point of a knife, to loosen the skin from the flesh.

• Grab the skin with a cloth and pull it off towards the head of the fish in one swift movement.

ROUND FISH

• Lay the fish flat on its stomach.

• Make an incision ½in/1.2cm deep all along the vertebral bone from head to tail with the point of a knife.

• Insert the tips of the fingers of the left hand, and loosen the flesh.

• Scrape the point of the knife against the rib bones, without cutting the flesh, until the fillets are separated. Then remove the skin of the fillets in the same way as flat fish.

SKATE

• Cut the skate into six or eight pieces according to size, first cutting it through along the backbone from head to tail, then cut it in as many portions as required, depending on the size of the skate. Wash the pieces in water acidulated with vinegar.

• Place the pieces in a saucepan, cover with water and bring slowly to a boil. Remove from the heat and cool the skate in the liquid.

• Lay each portion of fish with the black skin upward and pull off the skin.

NOTE: Skate always smells, even when fresh. It is advisable to soak it in cold water, strongly acidulated with vinegar and to rinse it under running water afterwards.

How to bone plaice in two pieces

• Cut the head slantwise, remove the entrails.

• Extend the fins well.

• Make an incision near the fins on one side. Insert the blade of the knife flat against the bone. Scrape along one side of the bone until the flesh on one side of the top side is free.

Continue in the same manner on the other top side, until you reach the center bone.

• Pass the knife under the skin, without cutting it, until the top part of the fish with the two fillets adhering to the skin, has been completely removed from the bone.

• Turn the fish over and repeat the process.

F

How to open the top fillet of flat fish

All flat white fish such as sole, turbot, brill and halibut can be opened in this way. The bone is easily removed after cooking and the fish can be stuffed with savory butter or shelled shrimp (prawns). Alternatively, the bone can be removed from large fish before cooking and the fish filled with fish mousseline.

- Scrape the white skin and remove the black skin. Cut off the head slantwise and clean the fish.
- Insert the point of the knife in the middle of the fish and make a small incision from head to tail. Run the fingertips along the opening, to enlarge it. With a flexible filleting knife, separate the two top fillets without detaching them completely. When the bone is free cut it in two places with a pair of scissors, near the head and near the tail, taking care not to cut the flesh.
- Carefully fold the open fillet back into position.

How to bone a herring

- Remove the entrails through the gill slits and cut off the gills without cutting the fish.
- Lay the fish on its side.
- Make an incision along the back bone from head to tail.

- Hold the fish in the left hand and insert the tip of your finger along the incision to separate the fillet and loosen the flesh.
- Cut the bone across neatly close to head, then near the tail, using the point of a flexible knife or scissors. Then lift out the bones, pulling off the flesh with one hand and holding the fish with the other. The fish will then be free of its bone and will open out.

See also individual fish and cuts of fish.

FISH COOKERY
Fish can be poached, deep-fried, shallow-fried, stir-fried, broiled (grilled), barbecued and cooked 'au bleu'. Care must always be taken when cooking fish to make sure that it does not become over-cooked.

FISH SAUCE A fish sauce should be acidulated with wine, lemon or vinegar to balance the bland taste, the rather strong smell, and the richness of oily fish. The sauce is part of the overall flavoring of a dish and should not dazzle or swamp the fish.

Match the sauce to the fish. For example, fried fish requires a thick tartare sauce. Wines also play an important part in a great many of these fish recipes, using as much as 50 percent wine in well formulated sauces.

Mussels cooked in fish stocks flavored with white wine taste better than cooked in water. Use dry white wine such as chardonnay for fish sauces and avoid using sweet wines that give the sauce a grey color.

On the other hand, adding beer or hard cider to a sauce for oily fish will sharpen its taste.

Cream, butter and cheese are of course fundamental to the classic French sauces. In modern cookery, yoghurt, low-fat soft cheeses and crème fraîche are used more often.

Emulsified sauces such as mayonnaise, béarnaise and paloise are the best accompaniments for all fish.

Is there anything more sophisticated than poached turbot with hollandaise sauce or broiled salmon with green mint mayonnaise, or fried langoustines with tartare sauce?

Typical sauces: Américaine; anchovy, aurore , Bercy, caper, gooseberry, homard, Joinville, poulette, Nantua, Newburg.

FLAGEOLET Small, green bean from the finest green French beans. They are available dried and in cans. Flageolet can be mixed with green beans and served with roast lamb.

FLAMICHE A classic leek or onion and cheese tart from northern France.

FLAMRI A French baked semolina pudding served cold with puréed red fruit.

FLAMUSE A Burgundian apple batter pudding similar to clafoutis.

FLAN A sweet or savory open custard tart. The custard can be thickened with rice, semolina, or other starch. The pastry case should be baked blind. Fruit can be included for sweet flans. *See Quiches for savory flan fillings.*

Old French country flans include flaugnardes made in the Auvergne, Limousin and Pcrigord region.

Typical dishes : Blue cheese flan, flan de volaille Chavette, flan à la Florentine, shellfish flan, cheese and onion flan.

FLANK (SKIRT STEAK) A lean cut of beef that is taken from the abdomen and chest cavity. After trimming the meat is beaten with a meat bat to tenderize it and, providing it is broiled (grilled) or fried underdone, it will be tender enough.

FLAVONOIDS *See Bioflavonoids.*

FLEURON A small crescent of pastry

F

baked as a garnish, usually for seafood dishes in sauces.

FLOATING ISLAND (Fr. OEUF À LA NEIGE) A cold egg custard topped with spoonfuls of cooked meringue. Decorations include caramel and crystallized violets. It can be served with thin almonds cookies (biscuits).

FLORENTINE 1) Round cookie (biscuit) made of butter, honey and sugar sprinkled with candied fruits and peels. It is coated with chocolate after baking and cooling.

2) (à la) Dishes containing spinach. In Italy, the dishes named after the town of Florence do not actually contained spinach.

FLOUR The starch of cereals extracted for making flour confectionary goods.

Wheat flour is the type most usually used in the West. Different grades of wheat flour are available:

ALL-PURPOSE (PLAIN) FLOUR This flour contains a mixture of hard and soft wheat flours, but in general North American flours contain a higher proportion of hard wheat than European flours.

BREAD (STRONG) WHITE FLOUR This flour contains about 12 percent gluten and is suitable for making bread, puff paste, choux paste and roux for sauces.

CAKE FLOUR A low gluten content makes this flour suitable for cakes, pie doughs (shortcrust pastries), cookies (biscuits) and puddings. Five percent cornstarch (cornflour), or 3 tbsp/1oz/25g per 5 cups/1¼lb/500g all-purpose flour can added to make a substitute for cake flour, although the results will not be quite the same.

MALTED FLOUR This is made in Britain by adding soy flour and barley malt flour to wheat flour. Sugar is also added to some brands. Bread made with this flour has a nutty taste.

POTATO FLOUR Can be used without reducing the volume of bread providing it does not exceed five percent of the flour used. Ground nuts are also nutritious additives used to produce healthy modern vegetarian breads and savory goods.

SELF-RISING (SELF-RAISING) FLOUR The right amount of leavening (raising) agents are added to make this flour suitable for most cake-making.

WHEATGERM FLOUR In Britain wheatgerm and salt are added to whole wheat (wholemeal) flour to make a flour with a unique flavor.

Wheat flours can be mixed with other flours, cereals, root starches or nuts to produce different nutritious products such as pancakes, fritters and pasta.

WHOLE WHEAT (WHOLEMEAL) The whole grain is ground to a coarse or fine flour. The two milling methods used today are roller-milling and stone-grinding. Roller-milled flour tends to be finer than the stone-ground, which is done in much the same way as a thousand years ago in Egypt where bread was first made.

Whole wheat flour is high in fiber and retains the natural flavor and nutrients of the whole grain. Whole wheat flour absorbs more water than white flour — which must be remembered when using it for such recipes as doughs and batters.

All flours are hygroscopic so can absorb moisture from the air, and with differences in the humidity the moisture content of flour can vary considerably. Moisture affects the strength and keeping properties of flour. To keep flour completely dry, store it in airtight containers.

FLOWERS (Am. blossoms) Many edible blossoms are used in modern cookery for flavor as well as for garnishing and decorating. Nasturtium, marigold, dandelion and zucchini (courgette) blossoms are used for decorating and flavoring salads.

Crystallized violets and roses, apple blossom, borage blossom, chamomile, lavender, geraniums and jasmine are used for sweet dishes. Larger blossoms such as those of zucchini can be filled with a stuffing and deep-fried.

FLUMMERY A fruit purée thickened with potato starch and served with cream. *See also Kissel.*

FLUORIDATION The addition of minute quantities of fluorides to drinking water supplies to give protection against caries (decay) in the teeth, especially of growing children. One part per million of fluoride ion is usually added.

FLUTE A long French crusty bread stick. It is also a culinary operation consisting of crimping or making grooves, slashes or decorative marks on vegetables, mushrooms or pastries.

FOAM A colloidal suspension of a gas in a liquid. *See Meringue.*

F

FOCACCIA An Italian round-shaped bread, brushed with olive oil scented with rosemary.

FOIE GRAS The enlarged liver of a fattened goose or duck. It can be purchased raw or canned.

The best foie gras is produced in south eastern France in the region of Toulouse and Auch. Other sources are from Austria, Hungary the former Czechoslovakia, Luxembourg. and Israel.

To prepare foie gras for cooking in one piece, remove the veins and open the lobes. Season the foie gras with salt and white pepper. Close each lobe, wrap tightly in cheesecloth and refrigerate overnight.

It can then be put in a terrine, covered with Port wine aspic or goose fat and poached for 4 minutes per 4oz/100g. Cool and chill and serve after 24 hours.

Raw foie gras can be fried in butter, poached in white Port wine and served with a slightly acidic cream sauce, or made into a pâté by baking at a low temperature and flavoring with truffles and celery salt.

Typical dishes: Escalope de foie gras aux raisins, foie gras poché aux huîtres et écrevisses, foie gras au poivre, mousse de foie gras, foie gras en aspic, brioche de foie gras, pâté de foie gras en croûte.

FOLD To add flour or sugar gently to beaten egg whites or batters, in a waving rather than a beating action, so mixing the ingredients while keeping the maximum aeration in the mixture.

FONDANT 1) Small croquettes of purées of meat, poultry, vegetables or chestnuts.

2) A sugar paste used to decorate cakes, and as a filling for chocolates. Fondant should be snowy white and plastic enough to be velvety. It must not be dry and crumbly — the crystals must be imperceptible not gritty — on the palate. Fondant should melt in the mouth. Cream of tartar can be added to produce smaller crystals and so add smoothness to the fondant. Flavors and colors can also be added.

Commercially made fondant is readily available.

1 cup/8oz/225g sugar
⅓ cup/3fl oz/75ml liquid glucose
pinch of cream of tartar

Put the sugar, liquid glucose and cream of tartar in a saucepan and boil to the soft ball stage — about 6 minutes. Brush down the sugar particles that

F

form on the sides of the saucepan, and skim the syrup. Pour the syrup onto a marble slab and let cool.

Stir the fondant until the desired consistency is reached.

FONDUE 1) A dish cooked over an alcohol (spirit) burner at the table. Guests dip small pieces of food on long forks, into the fondue.

The best known fondue is the Swiss cheese fondue (*see recipe page 96*) in which Gruyère or Emmenthal cheese is melted with white wine and a little kirsch. However other cheeses can be used, such as Camembert. Brie or Cheddar. Beer can be used instead of wine with Cheddar cheese, and Worcestershire sauce or soy sauce added for flavor in place of kirsch.

Koreans and Japanese have fondues using fish or tender meat such as lamb cooked in a strong stock, with various accompanying vegetables and sauces.

In Burgundy the beef fondue (*see page 43*) has given birth to cooking fillet of beef attached to a string and plunged into boiling stock to make boeuf à la ficelle .

There is also a chocolate fondue into which guests can dip an assortment of fruits like banana, pears, apples and peaches. *See also Sukyaki.*

2) Vegetables cooked slowly in butter until they are reduced to a pulp. This method is followed when making French onion soup.

FONTINA VAL D'AOASTA CHEESE   A semi-firm Italian cheese.

FOOD FLAVORS Food flavors are more complex than coloring agents. In coffee over 200 constituents that contribute to the flavour and aroma have been found. The organic flavoring chemicals are highly sensitive to air, heat, and interaction with one another, the flavor and aroma of coffee, milk, cooked meats and most foods is in a constant state of change. Usually it becomes less desirable as the food is handled and stored. There are exceptions, of course, as in the improvement of flavor when cheese is ripened, or meat is hung.

Flavor is a mixture of many chemicals in minute amounts, recognised by taste and aroma. It is important in stimulating the appetite and identifying foods but the way in which flavor is perceived is only partly known. Zinc and perhaps Vitamin A are necessary for flavor perception. The taste buds on the surface of the tongue are sensitive to sweet, sour (acid), bitter and salt. The sense of smell is the primary detector of aromatic substances.

F

To have a nose for food is to have flair and a sense of gastronomic perception. It is an inborn talent which is not given to everyone.

About 1,500 flavoring agents are used by the food industry and each one can be permutated to produce an even larger number. The four main groups of flavoring agents are those (about 30) found in foods; those in herbs and spices (about 150); those (about 250) found in volatile oils, extracts and distillates; and those (about 1,000 specified chemicals) that are synthetic.

Salt, sweeteners and monosodium glutamate are also used to enhance other flavors.

All natural flavors can be imitated artificially and all aromatic substances can be identified by gas chromatography which records graphically the different smells — a most precious apparatus to identify the bouquets of wine for instance!

So flavors are not just produced with a pinch of salt or sugar or a bouquet garni but by an entire jungle of plants smelling like a perfume factory.

FOOD SCIENCE This is concerned with creating new sources of cheap, nutritious food for the ever increasing world population. For example, the production of protein from micro-organisms fed on petroleum waste, and the making of meat substitutes from soybeans. The storage life of fruits and vegetables has been extended by using refrigerated warehouses which have controlled atmosphere.

Food science is involved in the farming of seafood and sea plants, and the prevention of outbreaks of food poisoning through the judicious application of better food preservation methods. In the meat trade, food scientists have been able to inject animals before slaughtering with tenderizing hormones and they have found ways of producing meat with less fat.

Food scientists are now working on the production of flavors by specific enzyme systems acting on basic raw material substrates. The age of working with computers makes mass food production far more accurate.

It is by scientific applications and quality control at every stage of food development and production that standards can only be established and maintained.

FOOD SPOILAGE AND DETERIORATION
All animals and plants deteriorate after slaughtering, harvesting or processing. Food continues to deteriorate after it has reached a shopping basket; by the

time it has been cooked, food is still at risk of being spoiled and may sometimes be unfit to eat due to lack of hygiene or culinary skill.

Depending upon the ingredients, the deterioration may be very slow, as in the case of nuts and seeds, or it may be so rapid as to render the food virtually inedible within a day.

Everything alive needs nourishment. Bacteria, yeasts, molds, insects and rodents are continuously competing with humans for food.

Furthermore, the highly sensitive organic constituents of food, and the biochemical balance of these compounds are subject to destruction at nearly every change in the natural environment. Heat and cold, light, oxygen, moisture, dryness, the enzymes themselves, and time all contribute to food deterioration.

Shoppers suffer when cauliflowers, onions or fish packed ready for collection are not removed quickly and given proper storage and protection. All the work that went into their harvesting will have been wasted if they are not collected on time.

This is also the case for the majority of man's food. Animal flesh, fish and poultry can become worthless in one or two days at room temperature, as can highly perishable fruits and vegetables, milk and fresh dairy products such as yogurts.

At temperatures above 70°F/21°C food can become useless within a matter of hours. Unless the factors that cause deterioration are stringently controlled there will be no food for the population and no highly-advanced society will survive.

Major causes of food spoilage and Deterioration

The major causes of food spoilage are:
ACTIVITIES of natural enzymes.
AIR and more particularly oxygen.
GROWTH and activity of micro-organisms, principally bacteria and their spores, yeasts and molds.
INFESTATION of insects, parasites and rodents.
LIGHT.
MOISTURE and dryness.
TEMPERATURE, both heat and cold.
TIME.

Bacteria, yeasts and molds

There are a thousand species of micro-organisms. Not all cause food spoilage, some are useful in the production of foods and many are used in preserving foods, such as the lactic acid producing organisms of different cheeses, sauerkraut and even certain meat sausages.

F

Others are used for the fermentation of fruit juices in wine, beer and hard cider making, or enhancing the flavor of other foods. Bacteria and yeasts useful for food production are cultivated by selective inoculation, or by controlled conditions that help their growth over the breeding of less desirable varieties; micro-organism multiplication on or in foods is the major cause of food deterioration.

These harmful micro-organisms are found everywhere — in the soil, water and air, on the skins of cattle and the feathers of poultry, and within the intestines and all other cavities of an animal's body. They are active in the skins of vegetables and fruits, on the hulls of cereals and the shells of nuts. They are found on kitchen utensils and equipment which have not been sterilized, as well as on the hands, skin and clothing of people handling food, inclding in the home.

Bacteria, yeasts and molds will attack virtually all food constituents; some will ferment sugars and hydrolyze starches and cellulose, others will break down fats and produce rancidity, while others will digest proteins and produce putrid and ammonia-like smells. Some will produce acid and make the food sour, others will emit gas and make food foam, some will discolor foods, and a few will produce enough toxins to cause food poisoning and death. Together they can make simultaneous changes causing acidity, gas formation, putrefaction and discoloration.

Bacteria is the most important cause of food deterioration. They may not be found within healthy living tissue such as within the flesh of fit animals, or the flesh of plants but they can enter and penetrate the tissue below if the skin is broken or if it is weakened by disease or death.

Milk when secreted may be sterile but it can become contaminated when passing through the cow's teat or by dirt in the air and on dirty utensils. Egg shells are porous so eggs are particularly susceptible to contamination. Meat can be subjected to bacterial infection when the animal is slaughtered and butchered.

All bacteria are very minute. Many are mobile by virtue of whip-like flagella. Others produce spores which are seed-like and remarkably resistant to chemicals, heat and cold. Bacterial spores are the cause of more food poisoning than the bacteria themselves and the reason why lengthy heat sterilization is necessary.

Most bacteria multiply best at between 60°F/23°C and 212°F/100°C.

Some will survive freezing temperatures and some, called thermophillic, will grow at temperatures as high as 180°F/80°C.

Some spores can even survive prolonged exposure to boiling water and then multiply when the temperature is lowered.

Bacteria that need air to survive are called aerobic, those that can survive without air are called anaerobic.

Bacteria multiply by cell division, doubling all the time. Milk infected with 100,000 units can reach a bacterial count of 25 million in 24 hours at a certain temperature.

Yeast are larger than bacteria, and molds even bigger.

Air and oxygen

Oxidation of food can cause the loss of Vitamins A and C as well as changes in color, flavor and texture. It also activates the growth of molds and yeasts. During canning, bottling and sealing bags for chilled foods, air is excluded by drawing a vacuum in a container or by flushing it with an inert gas.

Enzymes

Enzymes are found in animals, plants and all micro-organisms. Each enzyme can only do one specific job without changing itself. They are responsible for growth. respiration and germination. Each one can only do one specific job without changing. Great use is made of enzymes in food processing.

Pepsin helps digest protein in the animal intestine but in a healthy animal it does not digest the intestine. However, when the animal is killed the enzyme attacks the tissues and starts the breaking down process. Unless these enzymes are inactivated by heat or chemicals they continue to catalyze reactions within foods.

Some of these enzyme reactions may be desirable — as in the ripening of a tomato or pear or the tenderizing of meat — although ripening beyond a certain point becomes food deterioration and decay. This can happen in the field, market or in the domestic refrigerator given sufficient time.

Insects, parasites, and rodents

Insects destroy more than 5-10 percent of the annual grain crop in the Western world and more than 20 percent is completely spoiled in third world countries where the insect population is greatest.

Insects also cause bacterial, yeast and mold contamination. Insects are usually controlled by fumigation with

F

chemicals such as methyl bromide, ethylene oxide and propylene oxide. The last two are prohibited for use with foods that contain a high moisture content.

The parasite found in some pigs was the original reason why kosher food law forbade Jews to eat pork. Modern farming and hygiene methods help to ensure the safety of pork products in many Western countries but it is still a good idea to cook pork meat thoroughly, as an extra precaution.

The problems with rodents are the same as for insects, the filth they leave behind can cause serious food poisoning, and they can carry and pass on food poisoning organisms.

Light

Exposure to sunlight can cause changes in the color of foods packed in glass containers, for instance, red fruit jams and jellies darken. Light also hastens the rancidity of oils. Light-sensitive foods may easily be protected from light by using impervious packaging.

Moisture and dryness

Surface moisture due to changes in the humidty is a main cause of lumping and caking of dry mixtures, as well as such surface defects as mottling, crystallization, and stickiness. The slightest amount of condensation on the surface causes bacterial contamination or the growth of undesirable molds.

Moisture can also be caused by the respiration and transpiration of raw or cooked foods. This moisture can be trapped in packaging, condense and promote bacterial growth.

Temperature

Between 50°F/23°C and 212°F/100°C for every 18 degree rise in temperature the rate of chemical reactions can be doubled. At high heat all enzymes and other mirco-organisms are inactivated, but excessive heat denatures proteins, breaks emulsions, dries out foods and destroys vitamins.

Uncontrolled cold will also destroy foods including milk. At 40°F/20°C some fruits and vegetables can begin decaying.

Time

After harvest, slaughter or food processing, there is a time where the food is at its best. But this is a question of timing. All deteriorative changes progress with time, so the longer a food is left the greater the changes will be. However, time is also beneficial for maturating products under controlled conditions, such as cheeses, pickles and chutneys.

But as a general rule time is an enemy and there is no substitute for freshness in food.

Preventing food spoilage
The best means of controlling bacteria, yeasts and molds and preserving food are heat (*See Cooking food*), cold (*See Refrigeration, Freezing*), drying, removal of oxygen (*See Sous-vide, Vacum packing*), use of acids (*See Vinegar*) as in pickling, saturation with sugar (*See Candy*) or salt, use of preservatives and irradiation.

FOOL   A dessert of chilled puréed fruits and whipped cream, served with short bread biscuits in Britain.

It can be made with ripe gooseberries, raspberries, strawberries, avocadoes and other fruits.

FORCEMEAT (Fr. FARCE) A mixture of meat, vegetables and eggs used as a stuffing, for pâtés or terrines.

FOUGASSE   A French yeast cake or bread originally baked in the hearth. A fougasse may be plain or flavored with candied fruits.

FOUR SPICES *See Quatre epices.*

FRANGIPANE   1) An almond paste made of ground almonds mixed with eggs or egg yolks, and sugar and sometimes flavored with an almond liqueur. It is used as a filling for tarts and Danish pastries.

2) A thick savory roux-based sauce used to bind delicate meat pâtés and forcemeats.

FRANKFURTER   A cooked sausage made of beef or pork bound with cereals. The frankfurter needs only to be reheated in boiling salted water for 8 minutes. It is served in a long, soft roll.

FRÉCHURE   A French stew of pig's liver, heart and lungs cooked in red wine with onions, carrots and garlic, and served with potatoes.

FREEZE-DRY   The removal of frozen water by volatilization at low pressure and temperature. It is used to dry vegetables and make coffee powder (instant coffee).

FREEZER BURN   A discolored patch on frozen food caused by a tear in the packaging, or inadequate packaging and has lost texture by evaporation.

FREEZING   When 1g of water changes from 32°F/0°C to ice at 32°F/0°C giving off 79.9 calories of heat.

F

FREEZING FOOD When done efficiently freezing preserves food without major changes in size, shape, texture, color, flavor or nutritional value.

At the present no other form of food preservation is as well suited to providing maximum convenience, allowing a safe and cheap method of storing a range of foods from meats to bread.

Effects and changes in freezing

Freezing can disrupt food texture unless it is controlled because, for example, it can break down emulsions and denature proteins.

For most foods to maintain quality in a frozen storage the food must be completely or very nearly frozen stiff. An unfrozen core or a partially frozen zone will deteriorate in texture, color and odor, and there may be microbe and enzyme activity.

The more salt, sugar, minerals or protein in a solution the lower its freezing point and the longer it will take to freeze. If water and fruit juice are placed separately in a freezer the water will freeze first. The same applies to soups, sauces and solid ingredients in liquids.

A given unit of food, whether it is a bottle of milk, a cut of lamb, or sliced apples in syrup will not freeze uniformly; that is, it will not suddenly change from liquid to solid. The top becomes frozen first, then the liquid part beneath it becomes frozen next.

For as long as free water is freezing and giving up latent heat of crystallization or fusion, the temperature of a pure water and ice mixture will not drop below 32°F/0°C.

Excessive levels of lactose may cause ice cream and sauces to develop a sandy texture. Solutes can cause protein denaturation, acidic solutions may coagulate protein; the balance of particles may be disturbed resulting in a loss of tissue rigidity on thawing.

Ice crystal damage can be caused to ice cream, meat, fish, fruits and vegetables by freezing them too slowly. Fast freezing is necessary for quality products as it produces small ice crystals.

A freezing rate equivalent of about ½in/1.2cm per hour is satisfactory for most products. This would mean that a flat package of food about 2in/5cm thick and frozen from both top and bottom should be frozen to 0°F/-18°C or below at its center in about 2 hours. Plate freezers easily do this in household freezers, and use of nitrogen in industrial freezing plants.

Food composition

Like metals and other materials, food constituents have different thermal conduction properties which change with temperature. The greater the conductivity the greater the cooling and freezing rate. In the cooling and freezing temperature range, the heat conductivities of water change little until there is a phase change of the water into ice.

Then the thermal conductivity of ice is far greater than that of water, and the conductivity of food increases rapidly as it passes from the unfrozen to the frozen state. Fat has a much lower thermal conductivity than water, and air has less conductivity than water and fat.

These factors influence the freezing rate of foods. For example, structural systems like cuts of meat should conduct heat at different rates depending upon whether the meat is in contact with a refrigerated surface in a direction parallel or perpendicular to the layers of fat, and to the direction of orientation of the muscle fibers.

Freezing Rate

When freezing food remember these factors increase the freezing rate: the greater the temperature differential between the food; the thinness of the packaging; the greater the velocity of refrigerated air; closer contact between the food and the refrigerant; the refrigerating effect or heat capacity of the refrigerant.

Methods of food freezing

The basic freezing methods in commercial use are blast freezing, freezing by indirect contact with a refrigerant, and freezing by direct immersion in a refrigerating medium. In the case of solid foods in containers this mostly involves providing a flat surface of refrigerated plates, which may be in contact with one or two surfaces of the food or package.

If contact freezing is done in the home, packages should be well-filled taking into account that food expands on freezing, to make good contact with the plates.

Solid, compact products such as meat or fish fillets freeze more rapidly than shrimp (prawns) or vegetables packed in individual pieces and separated from each other.

In loose-pack or open freezing, food is frozen before it is packed. This is usually done with items such as peas or raspberries so that they will not be one solid mass when frozen. It also avoids the formation of large crystals in foods with a high water. content

Freezer cabinets

In selecting a freezer the considera-

F

tions that must be taken into account are the size of your family, the number of meals you have to prepare each day, how often you plan to entertain visitors, and how much space is available. The capacity of a freezer is measured in cubic feet/liters. A 5.9cu ft/167 liter freezer will freeze 22lb/10kg of food in 24 hours.

Do not exceed more than one tenth of the total capacity of unfrozen food during a 24-hour period — enough for small batches of home-grown produce.

Equipment for freezing food

The usual kitchen equipment is needed, as well as a freezer thermometer, packaging materials and labels, and a large saucepan with a wire basket for blanching vegetables.

Packaging

If food is not sealed properly it will not keep in good condition. The surface will dehydrate and fruits will lose their color. All containers should be thoroughly cleaned and checked to ensure that they are airtight and completely moisture proof.

Plastic bags are useful as food can be reheated in boiling water. Foil can be used for odd shapes and bigger packages of food such as fish, meat and poultry; put the wrapped food in a plastic bag or overwrap with thick plastic for safety.

Foil containers are ideal for meals that are to be reheated in the oven, but they should not be put in a microwave oven. Foil should not be use for fruits either because of acidic reactions.

To wrap foods, place the food in the center of a sheet of freezer wrap and draw two sides of the sheet together. Fold the sides downward toward the food to produce a tight covering.

Fold the ends like a package as close to the food as possible and seal with special freezer tape. Overwrap again with a plastic bag for good measure, makig sure that you eliminate as much air as possible by pressure from all corners. Seal securely with wire or plastic ties or freezer tape.

Use plastic wrap between thin slices of smoked salmon, ham, pancakes, burgers and sliced breast of poultry.

Make sure to label clearly all foods with their name and date.

Thawing

When food thaws the smallest ice crystals melt first — thawing is only completed when all crystals have dissolved.

Food packed in plastic containers can be thawed more quickly in a microwave oven using the defrost setting. Be careful: if the thawing is done too quickly the food may start cooking on the outside.

Most vegetables and small items like langoustines, fish fillets, steaks and scallops (escalopes) be can be cooked in boiling water without thawing.

All poultry and game must be thawed completely before cooking. Once cooked they should be eaten as soon as possible. Poultry are best thawed at a cool room temperature of 65°F/16°C or in the refrigerator.

The freezer and microwave are both excellent modern aids for today's more hectic and busy lifestyles. Cooked and frozen food that is reheated by microwave often retain their color, texture and taste. Furthermore frozen meals can be served quickly and successfully. *See Microwave cooking.*

Foods not suitable for freezing
These include foods such as salad leaves, emulsified sauces like mayonnaise, dips, low-fat yogurt and fresh soft cheeses, milk, highly flavored dishes and those containing garlic, and watery vegetables and fruits such as cucumbers, melons and whole strawberries, plums and tomatoes.

Tips for food freezing
• All food used must be of the best quality and freshness; bulk-buying makes economic sense.

• Food must be cooked rapidly, cooled as quickly as possible and then frozen immediately to prevent contamination.

• All tools and packaging material must be scrupulously clean.

• All vegetables must be blanched before freezing.

• All cooked meals should be placed in bags or aluminium or on a plastic tray with a sauce or gravy to speed freezing.

• Sauces must be thickened with cornstarch (cornflour) not with wheat flour as this breaks down, thinning the sauce.

• All cooked foods must be cooled before freezing.

• Packaging materials must be moisture and vapor-proof and resistant to cross-contamination with other foods. Exposure to air and moisture will damage foods.

• Do not use glass containers.

• Use the freezer for long term preservation for fruit and vegetables, for medium term preservation of fish, meat and poultry, and for short term storage of ready meals.

• Fruit and vegetables should be frozen within six hours of picking to keep them as perfect as possible.

F

- All fresh fish and crustaceans should be frozen in small quantities within 24 hours of being caught.
- Leave a headspace of ¾in/2cm for purées of foods with liquid so there is room for expansion on freezing.
- Do not freeze left over cooked foods.
- Cooked meat or poultry should never be refrozen.
- Uncooked frozen food may be thawed, cooked, cooled quickly and refrozen.
- Vegetables are usually blanched and refreshed in iced water before freezing.
- Do not forget to transfer freshly frozen food to the main part of the freezer and do not forget to turn the fast-freeze switch off after newly frozen foods have been in the freezer for 24 hours.
- Label frozen foods with their names and dates.
- Use the food in rotation.
- Maintain a steady temperature at 0°F/18°C.
- Defrost the freezer regularly, especially around the door seal.
- Be alert to possible power break down.
- Insure the contents of the freezer in case of power failure as all the food inside could be ruined.

FREEZING MIXTURE Salt when it is dissolved in water or mixed with crushed ice, considerably lowers the freezing temperature.

FRENCH BEAN (Fr. HARICOT VERT) Slender, tender pod of a variety of bush-growing bean that has an intense flavor. It does not have any strings down the sides so only the ends need to be trimmed. They are are best blanched for 5 minutes and tossed in butter, or served hot with French dressing.

FRENCH FRIES (Fr. POMMES FRITES, Eng. CHIPS,) Potatoes cut into strips 3in/7.5cm through and 2¼in/8cm long and deep-fried. For really good French fries they should be cooked in a two-stage process. *See Deep-frying, Pont-neuf, Allumette.*

FRICADELLE Danish meatballs made of ground mixtures of veal, meat or pork and fried in butter. They are usually served with a sauce.

FRICANDEAU 1) Round (topside) of veal braised with vegetables such as endive (chicory).
2) Meat balls made of liver, pork and herbs wrapped in pig's caul and fried like a sausage.

FRICASSÉE A light white stew of chicken, veal, rabbit or vegetables, thickened with cream and egg yolks. The meat may first be seared in butter.

Typical dishes: Fricassée de poulet à la Berichonne, fricassée de lotte, fricassée d'agneau aux petits oignons, fricassée de legumes à la Périgourdine.

FRIJOLES Mexican boiled beans flavored with chili peppers. Frijoles refritos is made from refried mashed cooked beans.

FRITELLE A Corsican chestnut flour fritter eaten with cheese.

FRITTATA An Italian flat omelet cooked like a pancake with the filling or flavoring mixed with the eggs.

FRITTER (Fr. FRITOT) Food coated in batter or breadcrumbs and deep-fried. The ingredients used in fritters are always pre-cooked; they are mixed together, shaped and dipped in flour and batter before cooking.

A fritter can be made from, for example, a cauliflower sprig, a mushroom, or a fish cake. Serve as a snack. See also Beignet.

FROGS' LEGS Frogs' legs have delicate white meat that tastes like chicken. Eat only the hind legs and skin them before cooking. Fry them in butter with shallots or garlic.

FRUCTOSE, LEVULOSE A monosaccharide sugar found in the nectar of flowers, ripe fruits and honey. It is used as a sweetener.

FRUIT Botanically, fruits are the parts of plants which house seeds or nuts. Therefore, some foods considered as vegetables are in fact fruits, such as tomatoes, eggplants (aubergines), avocados and cucumbers.

However in everyday parlance, fruits are defined as having a sugar and acid content and are used in desserts and for sweet confectionery.

Fruits are classified according to their characteristics:

BERRIES with soft skins: currants, raspberries, strawberries, blueberries, gooseberries.

CITRUS FRUITS: kumquats, oranges, limes, grapefruit.

PIP FRUIT: apples, pears and quinces.

STONE FRUITS: apricots, peaches, cherries, plums, nectarines.

F

TROPICAL FRUITS: melons, bananas, dates, mangoes, guava, pawpaw, pineapples and figs.

Most fruits have a high water content, are low in protein and low in fat, except avocado. Fruits are important sources of minerals and vitamins.

Fruits play a more imporant part in our cookery and diets as complements to protein foods. They can be eaten raw and cooked and drunk as natural juices and fermented drinks.

FRUIT BUTTER A smooth, thick fruit paste of strained fruit pulp, and sugar. Apples, quinces, not-too-ripe pears, plums, nectarines, or a mixture of apples and gooseberries can be used. The juice of berries can be added for color and flavor.

The basic equipment is the same as for jam making, with the addition of a non-reactive strainer or a food processor.

• Clean and roughly chop hard fruits such as apples and quinces, discarding any bruised parts. Small fruits may be used whole.

• Place the fruit in a saucepan with the minimum of water and cook the fruit until tender.

• Rub the fruit mixture through a fine strainer to obtain a purée, or process in a food processor. Measure the purée and put it in a clean saucepan.

• Add 1½ cups/12oz/350g sugar for each 2½ cups/1pint/600ml fruit purée and cook again, stirring continuously, until creamy with no visible moisture.

• Brush warm, sterile ramekin dishes with glycerine or flavorless oil and fill them with the fruit butter. Cover and keep in a cold place.

FRUIT CRYSTALS Fruit crystals can be made by mixing together sugar, citric acid and appropriate flavorings. The crystals will dissolve in water and provide a pleasant drink.

FRUIT JELLIES *See Jellies.*

FRUIT PASTE A fruit paste has the consistency of marshmallow or Turkish delight, it can be made by using fruits rich in pectin and a gum such as agar.

Use 2lb/1kg fruit pulp and 2½lb/1.2kg sugar. It is cooked like fruit butter, then transfered to a pan (tin) and dried in a cool oven for 6-10 hours. The paste is cut into ¾in/2cm cubes or rectangles when cold. The pieces are coated with sugar and kept in an airtight container.

FRUIT SALAD Some combinations of

fruit are more harmonious than others. For example, oranges go well with strawberries, pineapples with raspberries, blackberries with pears, and bananas with star fruit.

Richer fruit salads may be made by flavoring the cut fruit with kirsh or an orange liqueur.

FRUMENTY A porridge prepared by steeping wheat grains in water before baking until the grains split and swell. The grain is then boiled in milk, sweetened to taste and flavored with spices, nuts and dried fruits.

Unsweetened frumenty was made in the Middle Ages in England.

FRYING Cooking in fat or oil in a pan on the heat. *See Shallow-frying, Stir-frying and Deep-frying.*

FUDGE A sugar confectionary made with evaporated milk or cream, butter and sugar boiled to the soft-ball stage and beaten until creamy. It is cut in small squares like soft taffes (toffees). Fudge should be kept in airtight containers. Serve as a candy (sweet).

FUMET A concentrated stock flavored with herbs and mushrooms. It can be made with fish, poultry, white or red meat or any kind of game.

Fish fumet
This flavored liquid is used for poaching fish fillets. To make:

4⅓ cups/1¾ pints/1 liter fish stock
⅔ cup/5fl oz/150ml dry white wine
bouquet garni

Boil the stock, wine and bouquet garni for 20 minutes until reduced by a quarter.

FUNGI Simple plants including molds, bacteria, yeasts and mushrooms, that contain no chlorophyll. They consist of one cell or of many cellular filaments. Although some fungi are edible there are others that cause disease in plants and animals.

FUNGICIDE A product used to destroy fungi.

FUSILLI A spiralled Italian pasta.

FUZZY MELON A long, hairy melon sold in Chinese vegetable markets.

Fuzzy melon has a firm flesh and a creamy color. Best eaten peeled and cut in small pieces and served like a fruit salad.

G

GALANTINE A mixture of ground (minced) pieces of fish, meat or poultry, blended with eggs then wrapped in cheesecloth and baking parchment and braised in the oven in a rich stock. A galantine is cooled in the cooking liquid, unwrapped then glazed with aspic and garnished. It is served cut in thick slices and accompanied by salad leaves or pickles as an appetizer.

GALETTE A traditional round flat cake or pancake which was probably the first attempt our ancestors made at making breads and cakes. In Brittany, a galette is a pancake but in the French pâtisserie, a galette is made of flaky or puff paste (pastry) like galette des rois that is served in France to celebrate Twelfth Night.

GAME (Fr. GIBIER) The name includes all wild birds and furred animals which are killed for food. The hunting and consumption of game are still matters of survival in many countries of the world where buffaloes, goats, bears, boars and deer still roam wild.

Guinea-hen (guinea fowl), pheasant, ptarmigan, mallard (wild duck), teal, widgeon are all considered to be two portion birds.

Snipe, woodcock, partridge and grouse serve one portion. *See also Birds, and individual game.*

GAMMON In Britain, the leg of a side of bacon which is cured while still attached to the whole side. It may be smoked.

Traditional dishes: Boiled gammon with cabbage, braised gammon in cider, broiled (grilled) gammon with pineapple.

GANACHE A mixture of equal quantites of melted chocolate and heavy (double) cream. Chopped nuts can be added. Ganache is used to cover or fill gateaux, or mixed with cake crumbs and rum and made into chocolate truffles (*see recipe on page 105*).

GARAM The Indian term for a mixture of spices. It can include more or less of the following: cinnamon, cloves, coriander, cumin, cardamon, chili peppers, fennel, mace, nutmeg, peppercorns, mustard. They can be mixed in any permutation of quantities producing several hundred types of masala.

This is why Indian cooks rarely reproduce twice the same flavor in their own standard recipes. The temptation to experiment and the lack of accurate measurement cause huge variation in the taste and pungency. Commercial brands of masalas have the advantage of being consistent.

GARBANZO BEANS (Eng. CHICKPEAS, Fr. POIS CHICHES) This pulse is a rich source of vegetable protein so is a useful addition to vegetarian diets. Dried garbanzo beans (chickpeas) must be soaked in water for at least 2 hours before being boiled gently for up to 2 hours. Canned garbanzo beans in brine are readily available.

Garbanzo beans can be made into a delicious dip with garlic, olive oil and coriander seeds (hummus), or stewed or casseroled.

GARBURE A thick soup that is a speciality of the Bearn region of France. The flavor depends on the vegetables and meat used. It must include navy (haricot) beans as the main pulse plus a piece of bacon. The meat is removed after cooking and the stock and vegetables are puréed.

GARGOUILLAU A pear pudding made like a clafoutis.

GARLIC (Fr. AIL) Garlic is a powerful antiseptic and is widely used in the cookery of southern Europe, the Middle East and Asia.

Garlic originated in the Kirhiz Desert in central Asia and has been cultivated in Mediterranean countries for centuries.

There are many varieties of garlic, some stronger than others. Garlic cloves can range from ½in/1.25cm to 1¼in/3cm in length. Elephant garlic grown in California can grow to the size of a grapefruit.

Garlic is peeled, chopped and used in a composite butter for broiled (grilled) fish and meat and on French bread, or it can be used in tomato sauces of Spanish and Italian origin. Garlic can also be blended with cream cheese and herbs, added to fish soups, or roasted unpeeled and served as a tasty spread on toast as an appetizer.

Typical dishes: Poulet à l'ail, aïoli, beurre d'escargots, pomme purée à l'ail, gigot d'agneau à la Provençal, cassoulet d'oie à l'ail.

GARLIC BREAD Split French bread brushed with garlic butter and reheated in the oven when needed.

G

GARLIC PRESS A kitchen gadget to extract the juice of garlic.

GARNISH In classic cooking, a garnish refers to one or more subsidiary ingredients served with the main ingredient of a dish to give it a particular character; so a garnish would include the vegetables and sauce that are an integral part of the dish.

However, a garnish now popularly means a small amount of an edible ingredient, such as a sprig of leaves or chopped herbs, that are added to a cooked savory dish to enhance its appearance.

Garnishes should be appealing and complimentary to the main item in flavor and taste.

In classic cuisine, over a period of 200 years, the cooks of the kings of France made it a point of honor to create harmonious combinations of complementary vegetables and other items to garnish their dishes, and names were given to them, often reflecting the name of the home of members of the aristocracy.

After the French Revolution, classifications were made of these accompaniments and recorded in many professional books. These became the standard of practice for top chefs. After Carême, chefs Escoffier and Montagne added numerous combinations of vegetables from many parts of the world.

During the early 1980s something dreadful happened with a sudden change of discipline which allowed chefs to make up their own garnishes each day as they went along. The result was perhaps a new presentation of food, but the harmony in taste and flavor went overboard.

It would be sacrilegious to abandon all the classical garnishes in one sweep but a compromise ought to be reached between the practical and the technical value of classification by names.

The names of garnishes may not be respected but the content must be. For the sake of practicality, some consistent means of identification must be made for the sake of customers and apprentice chefs alike.

It may not matter very much if a steak garnished with foie gras and truffle was once called Rossini, in honour of the composer, as long as another name is substituted to identify the garnish.

A dish should not need to have two or three sentences of explanation to describe its garnish.

Much is to be learned from the Japanese skill in presenting food and the Chinese numerical system of classifying dishes.

G

GAYETTE   A slightly flattened dumpling of ground (minced) pork with herbs, garlic. They are baked in oven and served hot or cold as an hors d'oeuvre at lunch time. A gayette is called a faggot in England.

GAZPACHO A chilled Spanish soup of cucumber, tomato, red bell pepper, bread, olive oil, garlic and vinegar.

Gazpacho is served with diced mixed bell peppers, diced cucumber and croûtons. It is very refreshing and makes an ideal appetizer for a summer dinner party.

GÂTEAU A French name that is widely used for decorated cakes.

GASTRIQUE   Caramelized sugar deglazed with vinegar and used in fruit-flavored savory sauces such as duck with orange (*see recipe on page 146*).

GASTRONOMY   Many erudite books have been written defining this Greek word meaning 'the law of the stomach'. The laws of gastronomy are regularly broken by over-eating due to a lack of discipline.

Brillat-Savarin, the celebrated French writer and gourmet, attempted to define gastronomy as the supreme formula for happy eating as he wrote 'Some dishes are of such indisputable excellence that their appearance alone is capable of arousing a level-headed man's tasting powers. All those who, when presented with such a dish, show neither the rush of desire, nor the radiance of ecstasy, may justly be deemed unworthy of the honors of the sitting, and its related delights'.

All food must be chewed slowly and thoroughly. Water or other drinks should not be taken with food because it encourages swallowing before food has been properly chewed. Drinks should be taken between or after meals, and strong coffee, tea and alcohol should not be drunk on an empty stomach.

Smoking should not be allowed before or between dishes.

Large fatty meals should be not taken. Small, frequent meals are best eaten at regular intervals as snacks. It is advisable to rest before and after meals.

The gastronomic diet should be low in carbohydrate, sugar and alcoholic drinks and high in fiber.

Gastronomy might be interpreted as the science of gourmet food and drinks, but there is a difference between testing and tasting, as there is between appreciating and assessing.

G

What people like is not necessary the same thing as what tastes good to eat, but what people are conditioned to enjoy by natural heritage and sheer traditional customs, parental environment and national pride. A dish of glutinous tripe and onions cooked in cider might be the apex of gastronomic delight to some Normans in Caen, in western France, but in the smart dining rooms of palatial hotels in the rest of the world it would not rate higher than a dog's dinner.

Gastronomy is loaded with snobbism, and false pride in national fare.

Gastronomy can be sustained by a simple diet.

The real epicure is the one who appreciates the natural taste of the food and fine bouquet of a rare wine but eats in moderation.

That's the key to the joy of eating. No intellectual discourse on the meaning of the word can be as logical as the Greek word where the stomach is the laboratory breaking down all our nutrients to simple substances as the life blood for our survival.

Gastronomy should make food be our best medicine as its basic law.

GAUDE A creamy Burgundian cornmeal porridge served with boiled bacon.

GEFILTE FISH Jewish fish dumplings made either of ground (minced) carp or pike mixed with onion, matzo and seasoning including a little sugar. It is shaped into balls and poached in a good fish stock. It is served in its own jellied stock accompanied by pickles.

GELATIN Gelatin is made from the gelatinous parts of animals and fish. It is sold completely deodorized. It is also part of aspic powder and is used for all cold buffet dishes needing a glaze.

Gelatin is available ground and in sheets. Different brands have different strengths so follow the directions on individual packages.

Gelatin should be soaked in cold water before using. Do not boil liquids containing gelatin as the gelatin would lose its strength.

Gelatin can be replaced by the same amount of agar for vegetarian dishes.

GELLING AGENT An additive used in industry to make products set. For example, liquid and powdered pectin, alginic acid and powder, agar, carrageen and modified starch.

GENOA (FR. PAIN DE GÊNES) An almond-flavored cake made by the creaming method. It can be served plain, filled and iced, or sprinkled with kirsch and served with a glass of sweet white wine.

Genoa cake with strawberries
 generous ½ cup/4½oz/125g sweet
  (unsalted) butter
 ½cup/4½oz/125g superfine (caster)
  sugar
 1 cup/4oz/100g ground almonds
 3 tbsp all-purpose (plain) flour
 pinch of salt
 3 drops almond extract or 2 tsp
  aniseed liqueur
 3 eggs
 confectioners' (icing) sugar for
  dusting
 strawberries and cream to serve

Line a cake pan (tin) with greaseproof paper (baking parchment), brush it with oil and sprinkle with flour; shake off the surplus.

Beat the butter and sugar until fluffy and light. Mix the ground almonds and flour together. Stir into the butter mixture. Flavor with salt and almond extract or aniseed liqueur. Beat in the eggs one at a time.

Pour the batter into the pan. Level the top and bake at 350°F/180°C/gas mark 4 for 40 minutes.

Turn onto a wire rack to cool. When cold dust with confectioners' sugar.

Serve with strawberries and cream.

GENOESE The most common of the classic whisked sponge cakes. It is moist and light and can be served alone or filled and iced. Butter can be added for richness.

 3 eggs
 1⅓ cup/3oz/75g sugar
 ¾ cup/3oz/75g flour
 3 tbsp/1½oz/40g sweet (unsalted)
  butter, melted and cooled
  (optional)
 ¾-1tsp vanilla extract (essence)

Beat the eggs and sugar together until thick enough to support a trail of the batter when the beater is lifted.

Sift the flour over the batter in three batches and fold in as lightly as possible. Add the butter, if used, with the last batch.

Pour the batter into a greased and floured 8in/20cm cake pan and bake at 350°F/180°C/gas mark 4 for 20-30 minutes.

Let cool in the pan for 2 to 3 minutes. Transfer to a wire rack.

GERMINY A soup made with sorrel cooked in butter then stock. It is thickened with egg yolks and cream before serving.

G

GHEE A type of clarified butter used in Indian cookery. It is available in Indian stores.

GHERKIN A small cucumber with a rougher skin mainly used for pickles. Pickled gherkins can be used in sharp, piquant sauces and as an accompaniment to cold cuts.

GIBASSIER A Provençal yeast cake in the shape of a crown flavored with orange, or aniseed and candied lemon.

GIBLETS Poultry variety meats (offal) used for soups, stocks and gravies.

GIGOT The hind leg of lamb. It can be studded with garlic cloves, roasted slightly pink and served with a mixture of cooked flageolet beans and kidney beans tossed in butter at the last minute.

GIMBLETTE A small ring cookie (biscuit) made of flour, eggs, almonds and candied peel. They are immersed in boiling water, dried and baked.

GINKGO NUT The nut of the maidenhair tree.

The skin must be removed by soaking the nuts in boiling water. On cooking, the nuts go from a buff color to green. They are popular in Japan where they are stir-fried into dishes with shrimp (prawns), chicken and mushrooms and served with rice.

GINGER (Fr. GINGEMBRE) A well know spice obtained from a knotty, fibrous rhizome native to China but cultivated in the West Indies, Latin America, most Asiatic countries and part of Africa. The best ginger is produced in Jamaica.

Ginger can be used fresh in Chinese cookery in most stir-fried dishes and sauces, or preserved in syrup and used in candies (sweets) and desserts. *See Candy.*

GINGER AND HONEY CAKE Spices and honey give this cake its characteristic flavor and texture. The leavening (raising) agent is baking soda (bicarbonate of soda).

Examples include cakes as Appenzeller honey cake, leckerli, buttersperkulatius, pain d'épice, German honigteig, lebkuchen and honey cake.

½ cup/4oz/100g butter
⅓ cup/4oz/100g honey
2 tbsp black treacle
scant 1 cup/7oz/200g plain (all-purpose) flour
1 tsp mixed spice

2 tsp grated fresh ginger root
¼ cup/2oz/50g brown sugar
scant ¾ cup/4½ floz/125g milk
1 tsp baking soda (bicarbonate of
   soda)
2 eggs, beaten

Heat the butter, honey and treacle together in a saucepan.

In a bowl, stir together the flour, mixed spice and ginger. Pour the treacle mixture into the flour and spices. Stir in the sugar.

Warm the milk and dissolve the baking soda (bicarbonate of soda). Stir into the main batter. Beat in the eggs.

Line a square 5 cup/2 pint/1.25 liter cake (pan) tin with baking parchment (greaseproof paper) and dust it with flour. Shake off the surplus.

Pour the cake batter into the tin and bake at 325°F/170°C/gas mark 3 for 1-1½ hours.

GINGERSNAP Thin, brittle cookie (biscuit) made with light molasses (golden syrup), ginger, butter and flour.

GINSENG A sweet liquorice root used in soups and teas.

GIRROLE See Chanterelle.

GJETOST A strong-tasting Norwegian cheese made of cows' and goats' milk, molded into brick shapes of various sizes.

GLACIAL ACETIC ACID Pure acetic acid.

GLASSWORT See Samphire.

GLAZE 1) A coating of reduced meat extract brushed over roasts or poultry.

2) Exposing food to radiated heat to produce a coating, as in custard or cheese-coated dishes à la mornay.

3) A syrup or icing brushed over yeast or pastry products like buns or brioches to make them glossy.

4) Reduced jam to coat fruit tarts.

GLOBE ARTICHOKE (Fr. ARTICHAUT) The fresh leaves are used as a vegetable. The fleshy part known as the heart (Fr. fond) can used as a garnish or eaten in its own right as an appetizer or accompaniment, and in salads. The hearts are available canned in brine.

Typical dishes: artichaut à la barigoule, artichaut aux champignons, artichaut à l'Italienne, gratin d'artichaut et pommes au fromage.

GLOUCESTER CHEESE A hard but mild cheese similar to Cheddar.

G

GLUCOSE, DEXTROSE Glucose is found in honey and plant tissues. It can be manufactured from the starch of Indian corn by heating it in water with hydrochloric acid to convert it into glucose. It is filtered and sold in syrup or powder form for making candies (sweets) and fondant.

GLUTAMIC ACID A non-essential amino acid. Monosodium glutamate is made from glutamic acid extracted from sugar beet and wheat gluten.

GLUTEN The protein of flour, espcially wheat flour, which is developed when a dough is kneaded, making it elastic, giving the product structure and shape, like a frame work.

GLUTINOUS RICE, STICKY RICE Round, pearl-like grains that become sticky on cooking, used by Thais and Japanese to make sushi and rice cakes.

GLYCERINE, GLYCEROL A thick syrup obtained by the saponification of fat. It is used in confectionery and cake batters to produce and retain moisture in the finished product.

GLYCINE The simplest amino acid, which is sometimes used mixed with saccharin to make an arificial sweetener. It is one of the essential amino acids. Glycine is used to make new body nutrient needed for growth and repair and for bile.

GLYCOGEN A polymer of glucose used as a reserve in muscle and liver cells. Glucose released from liver glycogen stores maintains the blood glucose level to ensure a supply of energy.

GLYCOLYSIS The conversion of glucose into lactic acid by a series of enzyme-catalyst reactions that occur in living organisms, as when making sauerkraut.

GOAT Goat rearing has increased in popularity in recent years. They are bred primarily for the quality of their milk, which is more digestible than cows' milk and contains higher amounts of niacin and thiamine.

Goats' milk, cheese and yogurt have all become very popular recently.

The meat, which from a young animal can be as tender as lamb and is known as kid or chevon, is also in demand. It is worth roasting or broiling (grilling). The meat from older animals can be used in curries or stews.

GODIVEAU A fine mixture of veal and kidney fat pounded to a paste with egg white to produce quenelles and forcemeats for pâtés and terrines.

GOLDEN SYRUP A British golden-colored syrup with the consistency of thick honey. Used for pancakes, waffles and puddings.

GOLUBTSI Polish or Russian stuffed cabbage leaves filled with ground (minced) pork flavored with caraway seeds and onion, braised in the oven with stock and tomatoes.

GOOSE (Fr. OIE) Geese are large, web-footed, wild or domesticated birds. They are larger than ducks weighing from 9lb (4kg) to 27lb (12kg). The female is called a goose and the male a gander while the young are referred to as goslings.

In France, geese are mainly reared for foie gras and making confit.

Geese are best roasted on account of their high fat content. This fat is good for frying potatoes and preserving confit.

Roast goose is served normally with chestnuts and sprouts with an accompaniment of Cumberland sauce made with Port wine, orange juice and redcurrant jelly melted together.

Goose giblets are used in many ways, but particularly in stews. The neck can be boned and stuffed like a sausage.

Typical dishes: Ballotine d'oie aux marrons, cassoulet d'oie aux petits oignons, roast goose with apricot stuffing, pâtés de foie gras en brioche.

GOOSEBERRY (Fr. GROSEILLE À MAQUEREAU) The fruit of a thorny shrub. It can be made into jams, pies, mousses or a puréed sauce to be served with broiled (grilled) mackerel.

A variety of red gooseberries is particularly sweet and ideal for desserts.

Gooseberry pickle

This pickle will keep in the refrigerator for 1-2 weeks.

½ tsp asafoetida powder
1 tsp fenugreek seeds
⅔ cup/5fl oz/150ml sesame oil
1/½ tsp mustard seeds
½ tsp turmeric powder
1 green or red chili pepper, seeded and chopped
8oz/225g unripe gooseberries
3 tbsp/2oz/50g salt

Serves 6

Dry-roast the asafoetida and fenugreek seeds in a frying pan for 2 minutes to develop flavor. Grind in the food processor to obtain a powder.

In a heavy frying pan heat the oil, add the chili pepper, gooseberries, the mustard seeds, ground turmeric, salt and the spice powder. Mix thoroughly and cook for 5 minutes. Do not overcook.

GORGONZOLA CHEESE A strong Italian blue cheese. It can be used in béchamel sauces and dips.

GOUDA CHEESE A semi-hard Dutch cheese similar to Port Salut.

GOUGÈRE A savory choux pastry containing with Gruyère or Emmental cheese. It is served warm as a light lunch or snack.

GOULASH This was originally a thick meat soup. As it developed through decades of variations, it became a famous Hungarian beef stew flavored with paprika and onion and tomatoes. Potatoes are added 30 minutes before the meat is cooked.

GOURD A vegetable belonging to the same family as squash; cook like zucchini (courgettes) when young, if left for too long they are too tough to eat.

GOYÈRE A Maroilles cheese tart from northern France.

GRAISSE Beef and pork fat cooked with vegetables and herbs and preserved in pots. A speciality of Normandy, northern France.

GRAMOLATE A granula sherbet (sorbet) made from fruit syrups.

GRANADILLA A fruit similar to and in the same family as passion fruit. It has smooth orange, inedible skin and aromatic yellow flesh with edible black seeds.
Granadilla can be used for mousses and sherbets (sorbets).

GRANITA A sorbet made without egg whites or meringue and more grainy and less sweet than a gramolate.

GRAPE The fruit of the vine. Grapes grow in bunches on a stalk. The skin may be green, yellow or purple and encloses a sweet flesh with usually between one and four seeds.
There are grape varieties grown exclusively for drying to produce raisins, golden raisins (sultanas) and currants — a significant proportion of the worlds' annual grape crop of roughly 50 million tons is grown for this purpose.
Other grape varieties are grown for eating raw or for using as desserts;

some of these varieties have a pronounced muscatel aroma while others are sweet and acid.

Seedless grapes are now grown successfully and are gaining favor with many children and old people.

Grapes should be washed in water which has been acidulated with vinegar or lemon.

Grapes can be eaten with cheeses and used in savory dishes with fish, small feathered game and duck livers, as well as cheesecakes, and can be used to make a tasty jam.

Wine is made from grape varieties grown specifically for that purpose.

Typical dishes: Foie de canard aux raisins, confiture de raisins, tartelette aux Muscat, sole à la Véronique.

GRAPEFRUIT (Fr. PAMPLEMOUSSE) After oranges, the most widely grown citrus fruit in the world. Most grapefruits are grown in tropical and subtropical regions such as Jamaica, Florida, Israel and Asia.

They can be served at breakfast, as an appetizer for any light meal or used in fruit salads.

GRATIN A dish cooked in the oven or under the grill (broiler) so that it develops a brown crust. A thin covering of breadcrumbs and grated cheese, or chopped nuts, or the coagulation of cream and egg are the usual agents for the formation of the crust.

Typical dishes: Cauliflower cheese, gratin de pomme à la Dauphinois, coquille Saint Jacques au gratin, sole et homard au gratin.

GRAVELAX A Swedish method of preserving oily fish. It is eaten raw and flavored with mustard seeds, salt, sugar and dill.

GRAVY Pure gravy should be made from the meat juices left in the pan (tin) after cooking a roast. The juices are reduced to a glaze then deglazed by adding stock. It can be supplemented by meat extracts or bouillon cubes.

GREASEPROOF PAPER A type of paper used in Britain to line cake pans (tins) before baking, to wrap stored foods and to cover foods cooked in the oven.

GREENGAGE (Fr. REINE-CLAUDE) The best eating variety of plum on the market. It has a green skin, sometimes tinged with yellow, red or purple and greenish yellow flesh. A very sweet fruit when mature. It used for jams and tart fillings.

GREENS The term greens includes all

G

the leaves of edible plants including cabbage, spinach, the tops of carrots, turnips and chard, lovage leaves and many more.

Greens provide essential fibers in the diet and most need very little water to cook in; while some such as spinach, do not require any water at all.

GREEN TEA Green teas are mainly produced in China and classed according to the size and condition of the leaf and the district where they were grown, such as Twankay. They are very astringent because they contain tannin.

Drunk with a slice of lemon, green teas are the perfect beverage, refreshing when served chilled and stimulating when served hot as a night cap.

Compotes made with a green tea syrup have a better flavor.

GRENADIN A thick slice of veal about ¾in/2cm thick and 2⅔in/7cm long, cut from the loin or the thick part of the leg of pork or veal.

Grenadins can be larded with fat or wrapped in bacon, and slowly shallow-fried, or braised in a casserole.

GRENADINE A syrup of pomegranate juice and used as a refreshing drink with iced water or lemonade.

GRISSINI Crisp Italian bread sticks.

GROUPER A large family of fish which inhabit the warm Mediterranean and Pacific seas. Groupers are related to bass and can grow to huge size. They are best baked in a casserole.

GROUND NUT *See Peanut.*

GROUND RICE Rice grains ground to a powder. Cooked in milk to make puddings they are served with compotes.

GROUSE (Fr. TÉTRAS) British species include the red grouse, black grouse and capercaillie. The common French species is the hazel grouse (gélinotte), and in the south the pin-tailed grouse (ganga) is found. In North America and Canada, there are many species including the ruffed grouse, blue grouse and sage grouse.

Grouse is rated higher than partridge as a feathered game. In Britain the grouse shooting season begins on 12 August and ends on 10 December.

Grouse are best roasted for 15-17 minutes so they are slightly underdone and served with gravy, game chips and bread sauce. *See also Game birds.*

GRUYÈRE CHEESE A popular hard

cheese originating in Switzerland and now made in made in France as well.

French Gruyère contains more, smaller holes than the Swiss variety. Gruyère is an ideal cheese for cookery and especially for making fondues.

GUACAMOLE A Mexican dip of puréed avocado, chopped tomatoes, chili pepper and onion, acidulated with lime juice. It can be served as a filling for tacos and tortillas.

GUAR A gum produced from a leguminous plant. It is used as stabilizer in ice creams, and a texturizer and thickener in chutneys and sauces.

GUAVA (Fr.GOYAVE) The guava grows wild in the West Indies and in India. There are many varieties, some pea-shaped, some apple-shaped and some are shaped like walnuts. The seeds are edible but the green or yellow skin should be discarded.

Guavas make delicious jellies and fruit butters.

GUINEA HEN (Eng. GUINEA FOWL, Fr. PINTADE) A bird which originated in Africa. Although still sometimes considered as a game bird, it is now farmed in Europe.

Guinea hen are prepared like chicken but are often hung for three days to develop their flavor.

Typical dishes: Pintade au Porto et pruneaux, terrine de pintade aux pistaches, blanc de pintade aux reinettes.

GUMBO *See Okra.*

GURNARD (Fr GURNET) All gurnards have a cylindrical body and a big head in relation to the tail. They are reddish in color and should not be confused with goatfish (red mullet). They are best used in fish soups, bouillabaisse or bourride. cabbage, spinach, the tops of carrots, turnips and chard, lovage leaves, and many more.

H

HABANERO An extremely fiery chili pepper which is shaped like a lantern. It is a native of the Caribbean and South America. Like all chili peppers and bell peppers the color changes from green to bright orange and red on ripening. It is used in stews and sauces.

HACHUA A Spanish Basque dish of bacon-wrapped beef braised in red wine.

HADDOCK (Fr. AIGLEFIN, ÉGLEFIN) A close relative of cod, with a thinner skin and a distinctive black line along the body. Haddock has light-textured white flesh. It is excellent when freshly cooked in butter.

Finnan haddie (smoked haddock) is usually poached in milk and served for breakfast, when mixed with rice this becomes kedgeree. It can also be made into soufflés, pies or mousses.

HAGGIS A kind of Scottish sausage which has a globular shape because the ingredients are packed in a cleaned sheep's stomach. It is made from sheep's heart, lungs and liver mixed with cooked barley, onions, herbs and lots of black pepper.

Traditionally haggis is eaten on Burns Night — 25 January — when it is boiled and served with a purée of mixed potatoes and rutabaga (swede) to the accompaniment of bagpipes.

HAKE (Fr. MERLU, COLIN) French cooks acclaim this fish as white salmon because it can be cooked in similar ways and served with rich sauces.

Hake has a blackish skin and can be as large as cod. It can be cooked by all cooking methods.

Typical dish: Hake with capers.

HALIBUT (Fr. FLÉTAN) The largest of the flounder family. It can be cooked in the same ways as turbot and brill. Halibut is also smoked.

Typical dishes: Suprême de flétan au caviar, blanc de flétan au sauce paloise.

Smoked halibut salad
There is a wide range of smoked fish that can be served in a similar way. Look for smoked tuna, swordfish, monkish and eel.

1 bunch of watercress leaves
3 tomatoes, sliced
8 oz/225g smoked halibut, very
  thinly sliced

Dressing
2 tbsp olive oil
1 tbsp balsamic vinegar
1 tbsp cream
salt and pepper

Arrange the watercress leaves around four plates, with alternative slices of tomatoes. Place the fish in the center.

To make the dressing, whisk all the ingredients together. Pour over the fish and tomatoes.

Halibut and pumpkin roll
This fish savory is made like a jelly (Swiss) roll using pumpkin and beaten eggs as a wrapping for the filling.

Roll
¼ cup/2oz/50g butter
scant 1 cup/3½ oz/95g all-purpose
  (plain) flour
1¼ cups/½ pint/300ml milk
8oz/225g cooked puréed pumpkin
¼ tsp grated nutmeg
¾ cup/3oz/75g Cheddar cheese,
  grated
4 eggs, separated

Fish filling
1lb/450g smoked halibut fillet
⅔ cup/5fl oz/150ml milk
1 tbsp mayonnaise
1 tbsp cream cheese or fromage frais
1 tbsp basil, parsley and tarragon
  chopped
1 tbsp lemon juice

Line the bottom and sides of 10 x 12-in/25cm x 30cm jelly (Swiss) roll pan (tin) with baking parchment (greaseproof paper).

Melt the butter, add the flour and stir constantly over heat to make a roux. Remove from the heat and gradually stir in the milk. Return to the heat and cook, stirring, until thickened.

Blend the pumpkin purée, grated nutmeg, cheese and egg yolks. Transfer to a large bowl.

In a clean bowl, beat the egg whites until stiff. Fold gently into the pumpkin purée.

Pour the pumpkin mixture into the jelly roll pan and spread it evenly with a palette knife. Bake at 400°F/200°C/gas mark 6 for 12 minutes.

Meanwhile, make the filling: poach the fish in the milk until it flakes easily, this should take 5 to 10 minutes. Drain the fish; flake it and then let it cool.

Mix the fish with the mayonnaise,

H

cream cheese or fromage frais, herbs and lemon juice.

Turn the roll onto a clean dish towel (tea-towel) and peel off the paper while the roll is hot.

Spread the fish filling over the hot roll. Roll it and wrap it in the towel to keep its shape. Set aside until cold.

HALUMI CHEESE A firm, white Greek cheese popular in Middle Eastern countries.

HALVA A very rich Mediterranean and Middle Eastern candy (sweet) made with ground or whole sesame seeds.

HAM The leg of a pig that is removed from the carcass and preserved by pickling, and sometimes drying or smoking.

Quality ham is pickled using salt, herbs, spices and sugar, honey, molasses or other sweeteners. Sodium nitrate is used as a preservative and gives ham its characteristic pink color. The curing process can take as long as 1 month, with repeated doses of salt being added until the ham becomes saturated.

In Britain, Yorkshire and Suffolk-cured hams have the sweetest flavor and are of the highest quality. American hams from Virginia are cured in hickory smoke. Ardennes ham from France and Belgium, and Prague hams are also famous for their distinctive taste.

Raw hams such as the Italian Parma ham can be served as appetizers with melon, and cooked hams, especially when baked in hard cider or Champagne, can be served with fruits such as apples, apricots, peaches and pineapples.

Ham and chips is a good stand-by which will remain popular irrespective of the source of the ham.

Typical dishes: Prosciutto di meloni, jambon à la crème, jambon en croûte, jambon de Paris aux épinards, honey-baked York ham with peaches.

HARD-BALL STAGE The stage when a sugar syrup reaches 250-265°F/121-130°C.

HARD-CRACK STAGE The stage when a sugar syrup reaches 295°F/146°C and hardens to brittle threads.

HARD SAUCE A buttercream flavored with brandy and served with Christmas pudding.

HARE A mammal larger than rabbit and more sanguine. Hares are found all over the world except Australia. It is an ideal game food for the winter. Excellent pies can be made as a change from jugged hare cooked in wine.

HARICOT BEAN (Am. NAVY BEAN) Navy (haricot) beans belong to the kidney bean family, and are one of the most widely eaten pulses in the world today. They can be purchased in cans as a saving in fuel and time.

The variety Soissons has been favored in France for centuries as part of the traditional cassoulet. In America navy beans are used for baked beans.

Navy beans are available dried, or canned in brine for convenience. The former need soaking for about 5 hours before use.

HARICOT VERT, FRENCH BEAN Slender, tender pod of a variety of low-growing bean that has an intense flavor. It does not have any strings down the sides so only the ends need to be trimmed. They are are best blanched for 5 minutes and tossed in butter, or served hot with French dressing.

HARISSA A fiery Moroccan condiment made of pounded cumin, garlic, chili powder, sesame seeds, olive oil and dry mint. It is used as a condiment all over Northern Africa particularly with dishes such as couscous.

HARUSAME Japanese transparent rice or potato flour noodles.

HASH A mixture of chopped cooked meat, usually the leftovers from the previous roast, mixed with onions, potatoes and perhaps other vegetables and herbs, reheated gently in left-over gravy or a sauce.

HAYACA A Venezuelan stuffed corn-meal pancake filled with a rich ground (minced) meat with corn, nuts and raisins served around Christmas.

HAZELNUT A small nut that grows wild; cultivated varieties are called cobnut or filbert. Hazelnuts are used in caramel confectionery, to make dacquoise and praline.

HEAD (Fr. TÊTE) The head of cattle, pigs and sheep have been choice food for people who like the gelatinous texture. Calves' heads are usually used for cooking whole, and in France they are often sold boned and rolled, and may be stuffed and baked.

The flesh and tongue can be pickled in brine then boiled until tender, then cut in small pieces and served with

H

French dressing or hot sharp sauces.

Pig's head is used to make head cheese (brawn) molded in a terrine.

HEALTH Good health is the attainment and maintenance of the highest state of mental and bodily vigor of which any given individual is capable.

Some people have learned to discipline their natural instincts to eat more than they need and have adapted themselves to be content with eating simple foods in just large enough amounts to maintain their body in good condition.

Generally, long before middle-age, most people have contracted some defects of the body or constitution that arise from their bad habits or from their surroundings.

The preservation of health should begin very early in life because infants are more easily affected by improper feeding than by any other physical influence; the care of the child in this respect is of the greatest importance. Children even at an early age will develop eating fads, such as refusing to eat certain vegetables, which, if unchecked, can become undesirable habits.

Food that is high in quality and in amount is paramount. Far too much junk food is allowed in the home today, leading to the usual craving for fried and sweet items, and making children obese before they reach adulthood.

Food may be an emotional stop-gap, an expression of love, it may bring memories of happiness, warmth, reward, mother, love and comfort, or it may be an instant and temporary cure for boredom, sadness, depression or excitement.

Most of us love to eat — we live to eat, but we hate being fat and the thought of dying early as a result of over-eating is distressing.

To the seasoned dieter the mere word 'diet' evokes memories of hunger and deprivation. None of us is going to suffer from lack of eating, and health demands that you stop indulging in food your body does not actually need.

Discipline in controlling the normal diet is tough. So a mental attitude must be developed by not listening to the eulogy of the food romantic. Tell yourself that you want to live a longer life and healthy one at that. Say to yourself that being fat is unnecessary and undesirable.

Train your unconscious mind to accept a plain and small amount of food. Plan your menus as you would plan a battle. To win in life is to be healthy and capable of resisting temptation in all its deceptive forms.

It is important for everyone to learn about nutrition before cooking food; until you can know how your body works, you cannot know how to keep it going like a well maintained motor.

Overeating may lead you to having ulcers and suffering the inconvenience of gastrotomy unless you can control your eating habits.

HEALTH FOOD SHOP A shop serving groceries for vegetarians and people who want natural organic foods.

HEART The most tender of hearts come from calves and sheep. Heart can be sliced and stewed or stuffed and braised. Ox hearts are tougher and require longer stewing at a lower heat.

HEAT ENERGY The energy required to raise temperature. Heat energy is transferred by conduction, convection and radiation.

HEAT TREATMENT As well as making food more tender and more palatable, cooking food prior to consumption is a form of food preservation because it kills a large proportion of the harmful bacteria and the natural enzymes. Most food that is cooked can therefore can be kept for longer, provided it is protected from recontamination.

Cooking generally will not sterilize food, and so even if protected from recontamination food will spoil within a comparatively short time. However, this time is prolonged if cooked foods are refrigerated correctly. The toxin produced by *Clostridium botulinum*, the most heat-resistant of the food poisoning organisms, is destroyed by exposure to moist heat at boiling point, 212°F/ 100°C, or above for at least 10 minutes. *See also Blanch, Pasteurization, Sterilization.*

HEN (Fr. POULE) Traditionally, a castrated female chicken.

HERB Aromatic herbs have for centuries been considered invaluable for their stimulating, medicinal and culinary properties.

A whole range of aromatic herbs are used to flavor food, including coriander, basil, parsley, thyme, tarragon, mint, lovage, sage, bay leaves and fennel. They are used in composite butter pastes, stews, casseroles, forcemeats, omelets, quiches, terrines and pâtés.

Thyme, sage, lavender and tarragon are the best herbs to keep for drying, since they retain their aroma particularly well.

H

Culinary herbal classification

GROUP ONE
Containing cineole.
Bay
Rosemary

GROUP TWO
Containing eugenol.
West Indian bay
A fresh spicy herb with a strong clove-like character, warm and pungent but with a bitter after-note. Widely used in Asian sauces, chutneys and also in fish mousses.

GROUP THREE
Containing thymol and carvacol.
Oregano
Savory
Clary sage
Thyme
Mexican sage
This latter has a very strong, distinctive flavor. It is used with tomato dishes, chutneys and pickles, in soups and stews, cereals, pasta and rice dishes and with fish and vegetable terrines.

GROUP FOUR
Sweet herbs containing a mixture of balsamic, thymol and cineole extracts.
Basil
Marjoram
Parsley
Sage

GROUP FIVE
Containing thujone.
Dalmatian sage
A wild species of common sage

GROUP SIX
Containing menthol.
Mints such as:
Spearmint
Apple mint
Peppermint.

Green herb sauce
Serve with eggs, pasta, fish and poultry dishes.

2 cups/2oz/50g mixture of chopped herbs such as mint, basil, parsley, watercress and spinach
1¼ cups/½ pint/300ml fish stock
⅓ cup/3fl oz/75ml sour (soured) cream
salt and black pepper

Gently boil the herbs in the stock for 5 minutes.
Remove from the heat and stir in the sour (soured) cream and seasoning.

HERBAL INFUSION A drink made by steeping therapeutic herbs and flowers of plants such as chamomile in boiling water.

HERRING (Fr. HARENG) One of the most nourishing, as well as the cheapest and most versatile fish there is. Herrings are delicious broiled (grilled) and pickled.

Bismark herrings are herring fillets marinated in spiced vinegar; rollmop herrings are marinated raw in salted vinegar; matjes herrings are pickled in a sweet and sour vinegar brine.

Hard and soft herring roes are also great delicacies, fried in batter and served as snacks. *See also Bloater, Kipper.*

Typical dishes: Harengs marinés au vin blanc, smoked herring fillets, Swedish-style herrings baked with sliced potatoes and cream.

HICKORY NUT Exported from the United States, hickory nuts are used like pecan nuts.

HISTIDINE An amino acid not essential to adults although it might be necessary for children.

HOLLANDAISE SAUCE An emulsion of hot clarified butter and eggs lightly heated until beginning to coagulate and thicken the sauce. A good hollandaise sauce should have the consistency of a smooth custard when served warm.

Hollandaise sauce is traditionally-served with poached fish.

Many variations can be produced from hollandaise sauce, such as Béarnaise, and paloise sauce with mint.

⅓ cup/3fl oz/75ml fish stock
1 tbsp lemon juice
4 shallots, very finely chopped
6 egg yolks
1 cup/8oz/225g sweet (unsalted)
warm clarified butter (See
Clarification)

Boil the stock with the lemon juice and shallots until reduced to one third of its volume.

Remove from the heat stir in the egg yolks. Gradually add in the butter, whisking until the sauce thickens.

The sauce cooks best if the pan is placed in a deep metal tray half-filled with hot water; this helps the egg yolk to coagulate to a thick sauce while the butter is being added.

Be careful not to over heat the mixture as the sauce will curdle and spoil. If this does happen, add 1 tablespoon of cold fish stock or water and whisk again. Strain the sauce through cheesecloth.

H

Variation

Paloise sauce. Strain the sauce then add 1 tablespoon of finely chopped mint.

HOMINY GRITS An American corn-meal porridge served for breakfast.

HONEY (Fr. MIEL) Honey has been used for sweetening food long before sugar was processed and refined. Indeed, gingerbread and honey cakes were made centuries ago.

Honey is the thick nectar processed from pollen by honey bees, *Apis mellifica*, and consists principally of a mixture of glucose and fructose. Beekeeping takes its name of apiculture from the Latin for bees.

Honey takes its flavor from the type of flowers from which the bees have collected the pollen:

ACACIA HONEY is exceptionally delicate in flavor and aroma.

BRITTANY is a brown honey called is made from bees that have fed on buckwheat.

COMB AND CHUNK HONEY these are the best type of honey and also the most expensive. They contain bits of the waxy comb itself.

ORANGE BLOSSOM HONEY is highly flavored and aromatic.

PINE AND HEATHER HONEYS are the strongest of all. The flowers also affect the color and usually the paler the honey the milder the flavor.

Honey may be clear and runny, or it may be set. Runny honeys have often been heat treated to keep them liquid and to prevent them from crystallizing, which they will do if kept in cold conditions. This can be easily reversed by warming the honey.

In savory cookery, honey is used to flavor carrots or glazed ham and duck. Honey is used in sweet cookery for ginger and honey cake, French pain de miel, and German lebkuchen.

HOP Hops are grown primarily for making beer but young hops can be boiled and served as a vegetable.

HORS D'OEUVRES These are the appetizers of French gastronomy. A tomato salad with one egg mayonnaise does not make an hors d'oeuvre. It takes a whole collection of charcuterie and delicatessen items to produce a fine assortment.

The range of hors d'oeuvres is vast. It includes vegetable and fish terrines, meat liver pâtés, sausages, smoked fish and smoked ham, melons, mousses, salads, quails eggs, foie gras, caviar, Provençal ratatouille, mushrooms à la Grecque, tarts, tartlets.

Dips such as tapenade, taramasalata and hummus and those made with ground peanuts, mushrooms, creamed sweet potatoes, cauliflowers, broccoli, asparagus and artichokes, and fish dips of creamed smoked fish purées or pounded shellfish. Small pieces of fried fish such as sole in breadcrumbs can be served with a dip of tartare sauce.

An hors d'oeuvre usually consists of cold items but hot savory morsels such as hot bouchées, croquettes, crêpettes, soufletons or fritters can also be included.

All kinds of smoked fish can be garnished or served with seasonal fruits, for instance smoked salmon with lime and fresh strawberries, smoked mackerel with gooseberry chutney, kipper pâté with grapefruit segments. a wedge of melon with three jumbo shrimp (king prawns) or half a pawpaw filled with lobster.

Be subtle when making a dressing; it can be a sweet and sour sauce for carrots with scallops; when using mint think of the many different types of mint leaves; smoked mackerel can be enlivened with horseradish cream with a little ginger; salmon and bass can be marinated with galingale and garnished with scallion (spring onion) blossoms (flowers).

In short, explore your herb garden to make your hors d'oeuvre come alive with fresh fragrance, flavor and imaginative decoration

Salmon roe roll

Salmon roes are salted in the same way as caviar and are bright orange-pink. They are the next best thing to strugeon caviar.

Pancake batter

1 whole egg and 1 egg yolk
½ tsp celery salt
½ cup/4fl oz/100ml light (single) cream
½ cup/2oz/50g self-raising flour
2 tbsp butter for cooking

Filling

4oz/100g salmon roe as caviar, drained
1 cup/8fl oz/225ml mixed sour (soured) cream and thick (double) cream
2 tsp scallion (spring onion), chopped
1 wedge of lemon
8oz/225g smoked salmon, sliced thinly

H

Garnish
3 tbsp French dressing made with
  lemon juice
a good mixture of salad leaves such
  as:
lettuce, cress, radicchio, endive
1 tbsp mixed parsley, tarragon and
  dill

Serves 6

Make a pancake batter (*See page 40*).

Using 1½ tablespoons batter per pancake, cook 6 pancakes in a little butter in a 6in/15cm pancake pan for about 35 seconds a side.

To make the filling, mix the salmon caviar with two-thirds of the cream mixture and a good pinch cayenne or black pepper.

Spread the filling over the pancakes and roll them up. Place on 6 plates.

To make the garnish, use the dressing to dress the salad leaves. Arrange the salad on the plates and scatter across the chopped herbs. Serve with the remaining cream mixture.

HORSERADISH A strong-tasting root which is used as a condiment and in pickles with beets (beetroot) and red cabbage.

It can be grated and mixed with vinegar to serve with smoked fish or with boiled corned (salt) beef.

Horseradish sauce
1¼ cups ½ pint/300ml hot velouté
  sauce
1 tbsp horseradish cream
½ tsp Dijon mustard

Flavor the velouté sauce with the horseradish cream and mustard. Do not reboil. Serve with broiled (grilled) smoked fish.

HUCKLEBERRY An American type of cranberry that is very similar to a blueberry. The berries are used for canning, and in pies and tarts.

HUMMUS A Middle Eastern dip made from puréed garbanzo beans (chick peas), olive oil, garlic and tahini.

HYDROLYSED PROTEIN This has been broken down by acid hydrolysis and is widely used as a flavoring by the food industry.

Hydrolysed vegetable proteins such as soya are used to improve the nutritional value of vegetarian products.

HYDROMETER *See Saccharometer.*

HYGIENE This is the persuit of absolute cleanliness, which is vital when handling food to prevent contamination from all kinds of bacteria.

I

IAGO A small sponge cake filled with coffee flavored confectioners' custard, brushed with apricot glaze and coated with coffee colored fondant.

ICE A solidified mass of frozen water. A clear block of transparent solid ice is used for ice carving decorations for the adornment of cold buffets.

The tools required for ice carving and sculpting are the same as those used for wood carving, plus iron bars which are heated and used to accentuate grooves and hollow lines in the ice.

ICE CREAM Frozen cream, custard and syrup are the base of most varieties of frozen desserts. The sugar content must not exceed 50 percent to produce the right texture.

Ice creams can be flavored with fruit essences or purées, chocolate, coffee or with liqueurs. Candied fruits and nuts can also be used in special iced gâteaux or bombs.

Sherbets are made from fruit syrups with a density of 14°C Beaumé.

Electric sorbetières for ice cream making are available as well as soft ice cream apparatus.

Typical dishes: Glace au praline, bombe aux marrons glacés, cassata, omelette Norvegiènne, baked Alaska, coupe Melba.

ICING The coating on a cake or gâteau. It can be glace, fondant or royal icing.

INDIANERKRAPFEN. A classic small Austrian pastry baked in a fluted pan (tin), filled with whipped cream and coated with chocolate.

INOSITOL An essential nutrient for micro-organisms and many animals so it is classed as a vitamin, although there is no evidence that it is essential. It is a part of the Vitamin B complex. Use as a remedy for baldness.

INSULIN The hormone produced in the pancreas that controls the metabolism of sugar in the body.

When injected into the blood stream by diabetics, it lowers the blood sugar level and so relieves the symptoms of *Diabetes mellitus.* Insulin is one of the

I

few proteins the detailed structure of which is known.

INULIN A soluble polysaccharide consisting of fructose units. It occurs in many plants as stored food. Used in making bread for diabetics.

Inulin has been found in Jerusalem artichokes and the roots of the sun flower.

INVERT SUGAR A mixture of glucose and fructose produced by hydrolysis of sugar by an acid or enzyme. It occurs naturally in honey.

IODINE An essential trace element, needed by the thyroid gland for the synthesis of thyroid hormones. Kelp and other seaweeds are rich sources of iodine. Dietary insufficiency can result in goitre.

One drop of iodine in a cup of hot milk is a remedy for a sour throat.

IPURUMA A sago-like flour used in South Africa.

IRRADIATION A method of preserving food by irradiating it with gamma rays.

The treatment destroys micro organisms and inactivates the enzymes and thus sterilizes the food. It is used to stop potatoes sprouting in store and to clean spices such as pepper. The method is also used to preserve soft fruits like strawberries.

IRISH COFFEE This coffee is served in a glass, with a good measure of Irish whiskey added and heavy (double) cream slowly poured on top so that it floats. A spoon can be placed across the top of the glass to conduct the heat away. If Irish coffee does not warm the cockles of your heart, nothing else as good will.

IRISH MOSS *See Carrageen.*

IRISH STEW A hotpot of alternate layers of lamb, potatoes and onions with just enough water to cover. Neck, middle cutlets and some pieces of breast and shoulder are the best lamb cuts for Irish stew.

It is the finest stew ever created in this green island of song and laughter, and a world famous dish more popular than some of the wine stews of Burgundy.

IRON A mineral needed for red blood cell formation. The richest sources of easily absorbed iron are black puddings, liver, sardines, egg yolks, wholegrain cereals, pulses, nuts and spinach when eaten raw in salad. Lack of iron in the diet may cause anaemia.

IRON AMMONIUM CITRATE Dietary iron supplement.

IRON OXIDE Added to food as red, yellow and orange coloring.

ISOLEUCINE An essential amino acid in the daily diet rarely limited in foods.

ITALIAN CHEESES The best known are Parmesan, blue Gorgonzola, Bel Paese, Stracchino, Ricotta, Fontina, Caciocavallo, Mozzarella, creamy Mascarpone, and Dolcelatte.

There are many other Italian cheeses similar to French cheeses made from goats' and ewes' milk.

JACKFRUIT A relative of the breadfruit and fig, this fruit is a native of India and is cultivated today in south-east Asia, Brazil and parts of Africa. It has a yellow-green skin covered with small knobs, and yellow edible flesh that can be eaten raw or baked.

A jackfruit can weigh as much as 90lb/40kg when ripe. Unripe jackfruit are cooked like green mangoes in curries. The seeds are cooked in the same way as chestnuts.

JAFFA CITRUS FRUITS The superiority of Jaffa citrus fruits is recognised by all consumers of fruit. The recent work of the Jaffa research department in Isreal into plant technology has demonstrated that many different hybrids can be produced that are seedless and sweeter and thinner-skinned than ever before.

JAGGERY An unrefined, very dark brown sugar from India. It is obtained

J

by boiling and evaporating the sap of sugar cane and certain palms. Jaggery is usually refined by further treatment, but in India it is sold in the bazaars and used as an important ingredient in vegetarian curries.

JAILLES A Swiss pork and apple stew flavored with aromatic herbs.

JALOUSIE This is not another temperamental scene over who is the best pastry cook, but a strip of pastry cut like the slatted blind of a French house, filled with apples, apricots or jam.

JAM For centuries jams of all kinds have been made to provide an easy spread for bread.

Jam must be boiled until the temperature reaches 220°F/105°C, which is known as the setting point. However, fruits low in pectin may need to be reinforced with additional pectin to ensure the jam sets.

Acid must be used to bring out the color of red fruits. A good jam should contain around 66 percent sugar when completed.

All fruits, including bananas, may be made into jams.

Cane sugar makes better and brighter jam than beet sugar. *See also Jelly, Marmalade.*

Apricot and ginger jam
7lb/3kg apricots, not too ripe
2 ½ cups/1 pint/600ml water
¾in/2cm piece of fresh ginger
*   root, grated*
7lb/3kg sugar

Makes 9½ cups/7lb/3kg

Wash, halve and pit the apricots. Crack a few of the pits and remove the kernels.

Simmer the apricots and reserved kernels in the water until tender and the mixture is reduced by half, about 15 minutes.

Stir in the sugar until dissolved and boil until setting point is reached (*See page 212 in Jellies for full details of the setting point*), about 10 minutes.

Pour into warm sterilized jars. Cover. Process in a water bath for 5 minutes.

Let the jars cool. Store in a cool, dark place.

JAMAICA PEPPER *See Allspice.*

JAMBALAYA A Creole dish made of rice, bell peppers, chili pepper, fish and chicken. It has a Spanish origin, from paella, but it is the spices and the chili pepper which contribute to its poplarity in New Orleans and Central America.

JAMBONNEAU The boned knuckle of ham or gammon, boiled and rolled in breadcrumbs.

JAMÓN SERRANO A Spanish ham which can be eaten raw like the Italian Parma ham.

JAPANESE ARTICHOKE *See Crosne.*

JAPANESE COOKERY Japanese food relies on its aesthetic appeal and in many respects Japanese cooks are more like artists than culinarians in the strict sense of the word. Their aim is to catch the eye rather that the palate. Japanese cooks are dedicated artists, sculpting beautiful shapes out of vegetables and transforming prosaic turnips into chrysanthemums and carrots into cherry blossoms.

Japanese dishes range from snacks, such as sushi to festival dinners, from frugally economical meals to lavish dinners, yet all have one thing in common — the meticulous care of their presentation.

The Japanese have made the custom of eating raw fish universally acceptable, but it does require total and absolute freshness to the point of using live fish.

Another outstanding characteristic of Japanese food is the minuteness of the portions, although the overall amount of food eaten is no smaller than at a Western meal. However the variety of dishes makes up for the small amounts.

No fat is used in the making of soups and stews.

Many Japanese ingredients, methods and ingredients, such as bean curd, are derived from China but most of their repertoire has been modified and influenced by the gastronomy of the Pacific Islands and their economic ties with European and American countries. In this potpourri the Japanese present their case for simplicity and relationship with natural products.

Imagine the appearance of a sumptuous Japanese restaurant: the sushi room where ingredients and their preparation are religiously pristine. Famed matsuzaka beef and peak-quality vegetables are cooked to order with balletic precision under the broilers or on the grills; the tempura is lined with garnishes such as small eggplants (aubergines), okra, the plumpest shrimp (prawns), ginko nuts, tiny mushrooms and other vegetables.

A carved ice bowl bears a chrysanthemum on which rest furled petals of raw tuna and snapper; squares of silver flying fish enclose slices of fragrant matcutake pine mushrooms with

J

shoots of pale-pink fresh ginger; and an iced Champagne coupe holds a purée of sweet-sharp Asian pear crowned with emerald cubes of kelp. All these dishes are produced by Japanese cooks, complete masters of all the arts of food technology.

JAPANESE CAKE *See Daquoise.*

JELLY 1) A soft-firm semi-transparent sweet or savory dish set with gelatin or agar. Fish, poultry and meat jellies are set with aspic from their own bone gelatin. Most fish produce their own jelly from the cooling stock in which they were poached. Savory jellies can be molded with vegetables and diced meat while fruit jellies can be studded with diced fruits. *See also Table jelly.*

2) A clear, smooth, set preserve. Some people prefer fruit jellies to jams and marmalades because they do not contain pieces, and often the flavor is more pronounced and the texture lighter yet spreadable.

To produce a well-set jelly you must use fruit which is rich in pectin and sugar and acid. Suitable fruits are tart apples, blackberries, crab apples, cranberries, currants, gooseberries, grapes, quinces, kiwi fruits and tart plums.

Sweet apples, apricots, cherries, strawberries, pears, peaches, figs, pineapples and huckleberries are lacking either in quantity or quality of pectin. In some of these fruits, such as apricots and peaches, particularly when ripe, the acid also is insufficient. Additional pectin and acid and an increased amount of sugar have to be added to compensate.

In order to produce a clear jelly, all traces of flesh and skin must be removed by straining the cooked fruit through a jelly bag or a double thickness of cheesecloth.

The equipment needed for jelly making is the same as for jam except that jelly needs a bag for straining the fruit pulp. A thick flannel bag which can be fitted to an inverted bench or tripod would be ideal. Several layers of cheesecloth are needed as well as a large non-reactive strainer.

Use attractive jars in which the jelly can be taken to the table instead of having to transfer the jelly into a different serving dish.

To make fruit jellies

• Preparing the fruits. All pectin-rich fruits such as apples, crab apples, quince and tart plums should be cut in small pieces unpeeled for the maximum extraction of pectin.

All berries should be washed. Gooseberries need not be topped and tailed. The skin can be left on kiwi fruits but the fruits must be cut up.

• Simmer the fruit, until soft. Add sufficient water to hard fruits.

• Strain the whole mixture through a muslin, cheesecloth or flannel bag, letting the juice drip for several hours. Do not squeeze the pulp through as it would cloud the jelly. The pulp can be reboiled with some water for the maximum yield.

• Test the jelly for pectin content: put one tablespoon of the juice in a bottle, add 5 tablespoons of grain alcohol (methylated spirits). Shake the bottle. If the pectin forms a ball there is enough pectin in the juice to make a jam or jelly. If the pectin forms small flakes the pectin needs to be concentrated by boiling.

Measure the juice as it is important to the amount of sugar that has to be used.

• For every 2½ cups/1 pint/600ml of juice add 2 cups/1lb/450g of sugar.

• Boil the juice and sugar until the temperature reaches 220°C/105°F; this usually takes about 10 minutes but quinces take longer (*See recipe overleaf*). Over-boiling would make the jelly too rubbery.

To test for set without a thermometer, remove the pan from the heat, pour a few drops of jelly onto a small cold plate, and wait for 1 or 2 minutes. Push gently with your finger – if setting point is reached the surface of the jelly will wrinkle.

• Discard any scum from the top of the jelly with a slotted spoon dipped in boiling water and then shaken.

• Pour the jelly into warm sterilized jars slightly tilted to avoid air bubbles. Cover at once with non-reactive lids. Process in a water bath for 5 minutes. Remove jars and let set.

Do not move the jars until the jelly is set and cold. Store in a cool, dark, dry place.

Blackcurrant jelly
2 ¼ lb/1kg blackcurrants
2½ cups/1 pint/600ml water
about 4½ cups/2¼ lb/1kg sugar
1 tsp citric acid
            Makes 5½ cups/4lb/1.75kg

Simmer the blackcurrants in two thirds of the water for 20 minutes. Strain through a double thickness of cheesecloth without pushing the pulp through. Boil the pulp again with the remaining water and strain once more.

Measure 2 cups/1lb/450g of sugar per 2½ cups/1 pint/600 ml of clear juice. Add the citric acid and boil until the jelly sets.

Pour the jelly into warm sterilized

J

jars slightly tilted to avoid air bubbles. Cover. Process in a water bath for 5 minutes.

Remove the jars and let cool. Do not move the jars until the jelly is set and cold. Store in a cool dark place.

Variations

1) Replace the blackcurrants with blackberries and follow the recipe.

2) Replace the blackcurrants with loganberries and follow the recipe.

Quince jelly

Quinces have a distinctive flavor which need not be tempered with another fruit.

> 2lb/1kg (quince
> 8⅔ cups/3½ pints/2 liters water
> about 4½ cups/2¼ lb/1kg sugar
> Makes 2¾ cups/2lb/1.2kg

Cut the quinces into small pieces without peeling or coring.

Gently simmer the quince in the water until soft, takes about 1 hour.

Strain through a double thickness of cheesecloth.

Measure 2 cups/1lb/45g of sugar per 2½ cups/1 pint/600ml of clear juice. Bring to a boil and simmer for 45 minutes. Strain again through cheesecloth.

Pour the jelly into warm sterilized

jars slightly tilted to avoid air bubbles. Cover. Process in a water bath for 5 minutes.

Remove the jars and let cool. Do not move the jars until the jelly is set and cold. Store in a cool dark place.

Variations

1) Use crab apples instead of quinces. Follow the recipe.

2) Use crab apples and 12 finely chopped mint leaves. Follow the recipe.

After boiling with the sugar, strain the jelly and color with green coloring or mint liqueur.

Redcurrant jelly

This jelly is usually served with roast lamb. It can be flavored with Port wine or mixed with crab jelly for a better texture.

> 3lb/1.5kg red currants or mixture
> of white and red currants
> ⅔ cup/5fl oz/150ml Port wine or
> orange juice
> about 6 cups/3lb/1.5kg sugar
> Makes 5½ cups/4lb/1.75kg

Boil the red currants without their stems in the port wine or orange juice for 15 minutes. Strain through a double thickness of cheesecloth.

Measure 2 cups/1lb/450g of sugar per 2½ cups/1 pint/600ml of clear juice. Add the citric acid and boil until the jelly sets.

Pour the jelly into warm sterilized jars slightly tilted to avoid air bubbles. Cover. Process in a water bath for 5 minutes.

Remove the jars and let cool. Do not move the jars until the jelly is set and cold. Store in a cool dark place.

Variations

1) Use gooseberries or peeled kiwi fruits instead of redcurrants and follow the recipe.

2) Combine equal amounts of redcurrants, raspberries and cranberries and follow the recipe.

JERAAD Boiled locusts are sold for food in Morocco. These are like shrimp (prawns) and considered a great delicacy by the local inhabitants.

JERKED BEEF *See Tassejo.*

JERUSALEM ARTICHOKE (Fr. TOPINAMBOUR) The tuber of a member of the sunflower family. It has a nutty, sweet flavor and can be used raw or lightly cooked as a vegetable or in salads.

Jerusalem artichokes can also be mixed with eggs and made into a gratin, or served with asparagus or watercress sauce. *See also Globe artichoke.*

Jerusalem artichoke and jumbo shrimp (king prawn) salad

Langoustines can be used instead of jumbo shrimp (king prawns).

1lb/450g Jerusalem artichokes, peeled, sliced, washed and dried
1lb /450g jumbo shrimp boiled and shelled
⅓ cup/3fl oz/75ml mayonnaise
1 tbsp yogurt
2 tbsp chervil, chopped
boiled sliced small potatoes to serve

Scald the artichokes for 1 minute in boiling salted water. Drain and mix with the shrimp in a bowl.

Stir in the mayonnaise and yogurt and add the chervil. Serve with a border of boiled sliced small potatoes.

JICAMA, MEXICAN POTATO A bulbous root vegetable similar to the sweet potato. It can be baked in the skin or peeled and mashed together with cheese or herbs.

JOHN DORY (Fr. SAINT PIERRE) This is an ugly fish with long, sharp needles and fins.

J

However, it has an exquisite flesh which lends itself to baking whole like turbot, but with herbs, garlic and tomatoes. It also has a wonderful texture when steamed.

JOHNNYCAKE A small cornmeal cake made from a cornmeal batter and cooked on a griddle.

JORDAN ALMONDS These are the most highly esteemed almonds available.

JOULE A unit of energy. 4.184 joules equals 1 calorie.

JUGGED HARE Hare cooked in the wine in which it has been marinated for at least 4 hours. The sauce is thickened at the last minute with a mixture of the hare's blood and liver but the stew must not be allowed to boil after the mixture has been added.

JUICES There are different presses or juice extractors on the market which are ideal to extract the maximum juice out of fruits. A blender is also useful for making vegetable juices.

Mix the juice with 10 percent freshly boiled water and then strain.

If liked, salt can be added to vegetable juices and sugar to fruit juices.

Apricots, blueberries, cherries, figs, gooseberries, kumquats, lychees, melons, nectarines, oranges, pears, rhubarb, strawberries, raspberries, currants and blackberries are good for fruit juices.

Carrots, beets (beetroot), spinach, firm lettuce and tomatoes are all good for vegetable juices.

JULIENNE Thin strips of vegetables 1¾ in/4.5cm long and ¼in/5mm are used as garnish, for example on consommé.

JUNIPER BERRY (Fr. GENIÈVRE) The fruit of a low, fine-leaved resinous shrub. The berries contain small seeds and require two years to grow. They are ripe when they are dark purple and the size of blackcurrants.

Juniper berries are mainly used in the manufacture of gin, but the flavor is appreciated in pickles such as sauerkraut and in German dishes.

Juniper berries are available dried.

JUNKET The simplest dessert to prepare by curdling warm sweetened and flavored milk with rennet.

KADIN GOBEGI Turkish sponge fritters fried until golden brown then soaked in syrup, or dusted with confectioners' (icing) sugar.

KAFFIR CORN *See Millet.*

KAHWA This is the real Turkish coffee, finely powdered and infused in boiling water. It is drunk without the coffee being strained, and can be flavored with a crushed cardamom pod but is usually heavily sugared.

KAIFA An Asian blancmange made of potato flour, sago, salep, rice flour, cocoa, sugar and agar.

KAKI A type of persimmon with reddish-orange fruit the size of a tomato that, like other persimmons, can be tart or very sweet. It is very common both fresh and dried in China, where it is called shizi.

KALE Sea kale can be recognized by its frilly leaves arranged like a bouquet. It has white stems that can be boiled like asparagus and served with butter or Hollandaise sauce. It tastes rather like a white cabbage.

KALTSCHALE A German cold fruit soup made with many different types of fruits. It can be served as an appetizer or a dessert.

KARI The French word for curry.

KARMANDINE A Middle Eastern fruit paste made from apricot pressed into thin sheets.

KASHA Russian dish made from boiled cereal, often buckwheat or barley.

KATABOLISM Part of the metabolism dealing with the chemical decomposition of complex substances into simple components, such as the breakdown of fats into fatty acids and the breakdown of starched into mono saccharides.

KEBAB Meat, poultry, fish or vegetables threaded onto kebabs and broiled (grilled) or fried. Turkish doner kebab is made with slices of marinated lamb threaded onto skewers so they are tightly packed, then cooked on a rotat-

K

ing vertical spit. Thin slices are carved off as the outside cooks.

KEDGEREE A traditional English breakfast dish of Indian origin. Today it is made of finnan haddie (smoked haddock), boiled rice and hard-cooked (hard-boiled) eggs. Sometimes it is flavored with curry, or it may be only lightly seasoned.

KELP, KOMBU A seaweed that is available dried and useful as a source of iodine. It is an essential ingredient of the Japanese stock, dashi, and is used as a wrapping for sushi.

KEMIRI A term used in the Pacific Islands and Australia for a wide range of nuts, which includes candlenuts and macadamia nuts.

KEFTEDAKIA, KEFTEDES Greek meat balls that are shallow-fried or broiled (grilled) and served with tomato sauce.

KETCHUP (Am. CATSUP) A thick fruit sauce made with one or two main ingredients and less spicy than most other fruit sauces.

It is usually bottled and kept under refrigeration, but if processed in a water bath they can be kept for longer. *See recipes on page 87.*

KHOSHAF The classic Arab dried fruit compote of apricots, prunes, seedless raisins and pistachios flavored with rose water syrup.

KHOURABIA Turkish crescent made with sweet pastry and stuffed with walnuts and baked until golden.

KIBBEH A Lebanese and Syrian lamb dish in which the meat is ground (minced) and pounded with cracked wheat, spices, onions, walnuts, pine nuts and seedless raisins.

It can be eaten raw, fried or broiled (grilled), stuffed or baked. Kibbeh is served with salad and hummus.

KIDNEYS Kidneys are popular in many dishes in which they appear. They are distinguished by their conformation: beef and calves' kidneys are multi-lobed while those of lamb and pigs are single lobed. The kidneys from young animals are more tender than those from older ones.

Wash kidneys with water acidulated with vinegar before cooking.

Beef kidney is used with beef in steak-and-kidney pie or pudding. Calves' kidneys are more tender and can be shallow-fried in a few minutes and served with a wine, cream and mustard sauce.

K

Both lamb and pigs' kidneys are usually broiled (grilled) on kebabs or with bacon and cutlets.

KING PRAWN (Am. JUMBO SHRIMP)
The largest of the shrimp (prawn) family which include tiger prawns. Not to be confused with langoustines.

KISSEL A Russian and Scandinavian dessert made of a purée of fruit such raspberries thickened with potato starch.

It is served with sour (soured) cream and almond tuiles or duck, boiled rice and hard-cooked (hard-boiled) eggs.

Sometimes kissel is flavored with curry, otherwise it may be only lightly seasoned.

Raspberry kissel
8oz/225g raspberries
1¼ cups/½ pint/300ml red wine
½ cup/4oz/100g sugar
2 tbsp potato starch mixed with ½
*   cup/4fl oz/100ml water*
fresh red berries to decorate
⅔ cup/5fl oz/150ml heavy (double)
*   cream*

Boil the raspberries with the wine and sugar for 4 minutes.
Blend to a thin purée. Reboil and stir in the starch mixed with the water. Boil for 4 minutes.

Pour into six 1 cup/8fl oz/225ml ramekin dishes and chill until set.
Decorate with the berries and serve with the cream.

KIWANO Inside the spiky, orange skin the flesh is emerald green with a jelly-like texture and delicate flavor.
Serve the fruit cut into halves with the flesh scooped out.

KIWI FRUIT A fruit which looks like a large, long, fat gooseberry with a furry yellowish-brown skin.

It has juicy green flesh which can be used for mousses, fruit salads or chutneys or made into a sauce to serve with smoked fish or pork and duck.

KNACKWÜRST A German sausage made of beef and pork flavored with cumin and parsley. It is shorter than a frankfurter.

Knackwürst can be eaten poached or broiled (grilled).

KOEKSISTER A German pastry made like a biscuit (scone) but triangular and shaped like snail.

It is fried, drained and soaked in lemon syrup.

KOFTA Middle Eastern ground (minced) lamb ball that can be broiled

K

(grilled) or braised and served with rice and a tomato sauce.

KOHLRABI A root vegetable that is cooked like turnip or rutabaga (swede).

KOLA NUT The brown, bitter seed of a native African tree, which resembles a chestnut tree. The pods grow in clusters of 10 to 12.

Kola nut contains caffeine. Powdered kola can be mixed with cocoa and ground coffee to increase the caffeine content and therefore stimulating effect.

KOMBU *See Kelp.*

KOSHER A Jewish system of controlling the production and preparation of food on religious grounds. Food for Jews must be prepared (or in the case of meat and poultry, killed) by Jews and approved by a rabbi.

Meat and poultry are slaughtered by having their throats cut without prior stunning, so they bleed to death. Meat and poultry may be soaked in salted water to remove any last traces of blood.

Kosher regulations forbid the eating of pork, shellfish and fish without scales, and the mixing of dairy products with meat.

KOUMISS A fermented drink made from the milk of mares or asses, and now sometimes cows. It was used by the Tartars, Kalmucks and other tribes of Northern Asia.

A simpler version can be made from yogurt mixed with carbonated (soda) water.

KOUNAFA A baked Indian pastry filled with hazelnuts and pistachio nuts and then soaked with syrup.

KOURAMBIEDE A Greek butter cookie (biscuit) that can contain walnuts and be flavored with rose water.

1 cup/8oz/225g sweet (unsalted) butter
4 cups/1lb/450g confectioners' (icing) sugar
1 egg yolk
2 tbsp brandy or ouzo
5 drops of vanilla extract
3¼ cups/13oz/375g flour
1 tsp baking powder
1 tsp rose water
¾ cup/3oz/75g chopped walnuts

Beat the butter until fluffy. Gradually beat in ¾ cup/3oz/75g of the sugar, the egg yolk, brandy or ouzo, vanilla extract, flour, baking powder and rose water.

Add the walnuts and knead a little.

Roll the dough into a log shape. Chill for 30 minutes.

Cut into rounds and place on baking sheets lined with baking parchment (greaseproof paper).

Bake at 350°F/180°C/gas mark 4 for 5 minutes. Turn the baking sheets round and bake for another 5 minutes.

Set the cookies (biscuits) aside until cold. Dust them on both sides with the remaining confectioners' (icing) sugar.

KRAPFEN A German jam doughnut.

KUGELHOPF A fruited German yeast cake baked in a fluted tube pan (tin). After baking a kugelhopf is dusted with confectioners' (icing) sugar.

KULICH A delicious Russian Easter yeast cake studded with candied fruits and flavored with saffron, cardamom, mace and vanilla.

Kulich is dusted with confectioners' (icing) sugar after baking.

KUMQUAT, CUMQUAT A small orange originating in China. Kumquats are usually pickled in syrup or made into a special marmalade.

KWASHIORKOR A protein deficiency disease that mainly affects children.

L

LA BOUILLE   A comparatively new cheese from Normandy. It has 60 percent fat, is firm to the touch and has a strong aroma.

LABELLING OF FOOD The laws on the complete and exact labelling of food products are now very strict throughout all the European countries and in the United States of America.

The rules that all food must be described properly are enforced with heavy penalties for false or lack of prescribed information.

For example, in Britain food packages must list all the ingredients in descending order, including all chemical names, chemical additives and the amounts of calories, protein, carbohydrates and fat.

LABNA A soft, fresh Middle Eastern yogurt made from ewes' or goats' milk.

LABSKAUS   A German meat hotpot made from fried pickled pork or beef and onions and mixed with mashed potatoes and vinegar.

It may be served with poached eggs, picked beets (beetroot), rollmop herrings and dill pickles.

LACTASE The enzyme that catalyzes the conversion of lactose into glucose. It is present in the digestive juices of mammals.

LACTIC ACID This is formed by the action of bacteria on the lactose of milk during souring, and on the glycogen in meat after it has been slaughtered, so tenderizing it.

It is also produced during the fermentation of sauerkraut and helps to preservative it.

LACTOSE The sugar in milk.

LADDOO A small fritter made with a garbanzo bean (chickpea) flour batter. It may be soaked in saffron syrup, and sprinkled with cashew nuts and raisins.

LADIES FINGERS *See Okra.*

LADY FINGERS Sponge fingers made with separated eggs, sugar and flour.

The batter is piped onto oiled baking trays and baked until golden. They are used for charlottes, trifles, or served with ice cream desserts.

> 4 eggs, separated
> ½ cup/4oz/100g superfine (caster) sugar
> 3 drops of vanilla extract
> 1 drop of almond extract
> ½ teaspoon cream of tartar
> 1¼ cups/5oz/150g flour
> pinch of salt
> confectioners' (icing) sugar for dusting
>
> Makes 24

In a bowl beat, the egg yolks with one quarter of the sugar, until the mixture thickens, about 5 minutes. Add the vanilla and almond extracts.

Whisk the egg whites and salt until semi-stiff. Sprinkle over the remaining sugar a teaspoon at a time, beating the whites all the time until stiff.

Carefully fold one quarter of the meringue into the egg yolk mixture. Then fold in the flour and remaining meringue.

Oil 2 baking sheets and line them with baking parchment (greaseproof paper). Oil the paper and dust with flour. Shake off the surplus flour. Half-fill a pastry (piping) bag fitted with a large tube (nozzle) and pipe fingers of the batter 2¾in/7cm long and ¾in/2cm apart as they will spread on cooking. Bake for 12-15 minutes.

Cool and dust with confectioners' sugar. Store in airtight container.

LAMB Lamb comes from a sheep that is less than one year old. Baby lamb is customarily slaughtered at between six to eight weeks. Spring lamb is killed between three and five months.

Lamb is completely 'free -range' and therefore has a seasonal cycle.

From earliest times the sheep industry has served mankind well, providing both meat and clothing. Over the years sheep have been interbred and now there are well over 200 breeds. Modern breeds provide better meat and wool than their predecessors.

Regional variations of taste and cooking methods mean than different cuts of meat exist in different countries. Lamb is a popular meat to serve on all occasions, from the humblest to the most grand.

Where once it was only possible to buy large roasts (joints) of lamb, the meat is now also packaged in a variety of convenient forms — ready ground (minced) for moussaka, burgers and stuffing, small or large cutlets (chops), and fillets.

L

Because of the popularity and versatility of lamb it is used in many delicious dishes from around the world.

When buying lamb, look for meat with firm flesh, white fat and no unpleasant, rancid smell.

The best cuts for broiling (grilling) are rib cutlets and British loin chops.

For roasting use the leg, saddle and best end of neck.

Diced shoulder, breast, and neck and middle cutlets are best stewed.

For kebabs, use the thick part of the leg or the loin.

Typical dishes: Gigot d'agneau aux haricots panaches, côtelettes aux herbes, selle d'agneau au gratin Savoyard, rosette d'agneau pommes de terre sautées, Irish stew, fricassée d'agneau, moussaka, Lancashire hotpot, noisette d'agneau aux asperges.

Surf and turf kebab pacific
Enhance the Asian flavor of this striking dish by serving it with stir-fried julienne vegetables. These kebabs could also be barbecued and served with a mixed green salad.

8 x 6oz (175g) lamb loin steaks
20 jumbo shrimp (king prawns),
* peeled*
2 large green bell peppers, seeded
* and cut into 1in/2.5cm squares*

3 tbsp sunflower oil
1 tbsp sesame oil

Sauce
1 tbsp sunflower oil
2 large red bell peppers, seeded and
* chopped*
1 - 2 green chili peppers, seeded,
* and chopped*
½tsp Szchwan peppercorns or
* crushed black peppercorns*
1 x 14oz/400g can chopped
* tomatoes*
2 tbsp dry Sherry

Serves 8

To make the sauce, heat the oil in a frying pan and fry the bell peppers, chili peppers, onion and peppercorns until the vegetables are tender. Purée the vegetable mixture with the tomatoes and sherry.

Reheat when required.

To make the kebabs, cut each piece of lamb into 6 equal portions. Thread 3 pieces of lamb and 2 shrimp (prawns) on each skewer and interspace with green bell peppers. Serve 2 kebabs per portion.

Place the kebabs under a hot preheated broiler (grill) and cook for about 8 to 10 minutes, turning occasionally and brushing with oil.

Serve the kebabs with the sauce.

Lamb cutlets in aspic

Lamb in aspic is always a popular buffet dish. Select best quality lean lamb from the loin, or best end cutlets. The meat can be boned and stuffed with a rich mushroom and cheese duxelle. Roast the lamb the day before it is required to be pink or medium, as preferred. Serve in a delicate aspic flavored with white Port wine.

*1lb/450g lamb cutlets, trimmed
  and prepared (chined)
salt and pepper
2 tbsp oil
1¼ cups/½ pint/300ml aspic jelly
⅓ cup/3fl oz/75ml white Port wine
1 small bunch of tarragon
slices of carrot and truffle for
  decoration
¾ large cucumber
3 tbsp French dressing, optional
8oz/225g blackcurrants*

Season the lamb.

Heat the oil in a frying pan and brown the meat for 8 minutes. Remove the meat and cool completely. When cold, neatly trim off the fat.

Bring the aspic jelly to a boil and pour in the Port wine. Pour 1 tablespoon into each of 8 oval 1 cup/8fl oz/225ml dishes. Place in the freezer for 15 minutes to set.

Lay a few tarragon leaves and slices of carrots and truffles on the set jelly. Put a cutlet on top and fill the dishes with the remaining hot aspic. Chill overnight.

Peel the cucumber and cut a few rounds that, by removing the seeds, can be shaped like boats. Cut the remaining piece of cucumber in half, slice it thinly and toss the pieces into the salad dressing.

Unmold each cutlet onto a plate and garnish with the cucumber. Pour a little more aspic jelly, or French dressing, over the cucumber as a glaze. Garnish with blackcurrants.

LAMB'S LETTUCE, CORN SALAD, MÂCHE. This salad leaf goes very well with a mixture of celery and beets (beetroot).

LAMPREY A cartilaginous eel-like fish. The flesh is very oily and can be smoked and served as an hors d'oeuvre. Lamprey is also stewed in wine.

LANCASHIRE CHEESE A more crumbly British cheese than Cheddar. When fully matured Lancashire cheese has a loose texture and a characteristic mellow flavor. It is a particularly good cheese to use for making quiches and sauces.

L

LANGOUSTE *See Crawfish.*

LANGOUSTINE, DUBLIN BAY PRAWN, SCAMPI This large shrimp (prawn) looks like a lobster and lives in burrows in a muddy sea bed for protection. They are caught in trawl nets or pots when they come out to feed. Large quantities are caught annually in off Dublin Bay in Ireland, hence the name sometimes used in Britain, of Dublin Bay prawns.

Langoustines can be served boiled in the shell as an appetizer with mayonnaise. Peeled langoustines can be coated in breadcrumbs or batter, deep-fried and served for cocktail parties, with tartare sauce as a dip.

They can also be cooked in tomato sauce, sautéed in butter or broiled (grilled) on skewers.

LANGUE DE CHAT A light cookie (biscuit) made with egg whites, flour and sugar, piped onto an oiled baking sheet and dusted with flour before baking. They are usually shaped like cat's tongues, hence the name.

½ cup/4oz/100g soft butter
½ cup//4oz/100g superfine (caster) sugar
3 small egg whites
generous 1 cup/4½ oz/125g cake flour
3 drops of vanilla extract
2 drops of lemon extract
1 drop of almond extract
confectioners' (icing) sugar for dusting

Makes 24

Beat the butter and sugar until fluffy then mix in the egg whites, flour and extracts to make a soft batter which can be piped onto a baking sheet.

Oil a baking sheet and line it with baking parchment (greaseproof paper). Dust with flour and shake off the surplus. Pipe small fingers of the batter at ¾-in/2cm intervals.

Bake at 350°C/180°C/gas mark 4 for 8-10 minutes.

Cool and dust with confectioners' (icing) sugar.

LAQUERED FOOD A Chinese term to describe food such as duck which have been glazed with a syrupy gravy.

LARD 1) The melted fat of pork that is use for frying.

2) The hard back fat of pork used for larding lean meat. It is used either in strips with a needle or as a wrapping for meat or birds with the intention of moisturizing and protecting the meat during cooking.

LASAGNE A wide pasta with plain or ripple edges, and yellow or green color. It is poached before being layered with meat, vegetables or fish and a sauce.

LATENT HEAT The quantity of heat absorbed or released in an isothermal transformation phase. This is the reason why cooked foods continue to cook after they have been removed from the source of heat.

LATIN AMERICAN GASTRONOMY It is surprisingly easy to trace the origins of the cooking styles in all the Central and South American countries where Africans, Aztecs, French, Italians, Portuguese and Spanish have left a rich mix of their languages and culture. Out of this potpourri emerged a very distinctive highly spiced, colorful and tasty cuisine.

All Latin American countries use corn, beans, cassava, squashes, chili peppers and sweet potatoes, with the addition of all the products of the sea along the coasts.

Argentineans eat more beef than the other countries. There is roast beef on the spit and barbecued kebabs, churrasco, served with salads. The main cheese is called tafi, which is like Cheddar.

Bolivia and Peru are the countries of origin of the potato and more than 350 varieties are grown there. Their notable specialities include rabbit stews, conejo estirado, roast sucking pig or goat, and pachamanca, a mixture of meats and fish cooked in a pit dug in the ground and lined with bricks and a layer of aromatic grasses.

Peru is the country for ceviche (marinated fish). Pawpaw and banana chutneys are traditionally served with meat and poultry.

There is more to Brazil than brilliant football played by the descendants of African slaves. These same people have improved the local food, especially the festival food which is cooked to celebrate mardi gras when many good things are eaten particularly with pancakes. Fried seafood such as a mixture of oysters, shrimp (prawns) and crab are very popular.

Other specialities include chicken stew with peanut sauce. Basic dishes are bean purée with bacon fried like croquettes and for dessert, cream cheese or ice cream served with guava jelly.

The same type of food is enjoyed in Paraguay and Uruguay alongside bori bori, the national dish of meat balls stewed in a spicy sauce and served with corn.

L

LATKE A Jewish dish — a small potato pancake made with grated potatoes, matzo crumbs and eggs. It can be flavored with caraway seeds.

LAVENDER OIL An aromatic oil with a pleasant aroma. It is used to flavor ice creams and light desserts.

LAVER, NORI A seaweed available dried in sheets. It has a fresh, tart-sweet flavor and a dark color.

Dried laver should be crisped under a hot broiler (grill) or by holding it over a flame. It is used in soups and in fritters made for snacks.

When chopped it can be mixed with eggs and made into omelets, or it can be made into a dough for laver bread.

LEAVENING (RAISING) The operation of aerating flour confections and bread using a leavening (raising) agent such as baking powder, baking soda (bicarbonate of soda) or yeast.

When heated, the leavening agent produces carbon dioxide that expands and lifts the batter or dough, making it lighter.

LEBKUCHEN Small German spiced honey cakes. The dough is set aside to rest for 3 hours before baking. The cake can be decorated with almonds.

⅔ cup/10oz/300g honey
2½ cups/10oz/300g all-purpose (plain) flour
6 tbsp rye flour
2 tsp baking soda (bicarbonate of soda)
4 tbsp milk

Heat the honey over medium heat until it begins to bubble. Let cool.

Beat the flour, rye flour, baking soda (bicarbonate of soda) and milk into the honey. Rest overnight.

Put the dough into a greased 5 cup/2 pint/1.2 liter square cake pan (tin). Bake at 350°F/180°C/gas mark 4 for 30 minutes.

Cut into squares to serve.

LECITHIN A phospholipid composed of glycerol and two fatty acids — phosphorus and choline. It is found in egg yolks, mustard seeds and soya flour and helps to from emulsions as when making mayonnaise and hollandaise sauce.

LEEK A biennial plant of the onion family. Leeks can be used in soups, in fillings for quiches and in casseroles.

Young leeks can be boiled and eaten with hollandaise sauce or French dressing (*see page 315*) and are as good if not better than asparagus.

Leek sauce

Serve with poached cod or haddock or with boiled chicken and creamed potatoes.

½ cup/2oz/50g butter
¾ cup/5oz/150g white of leeks, chopped
1 ¼ cups/½ pint/300ml velouté sauce
1 tbsp heavy (double) cream
salt and white pepper

Heat the butter and cook the leeks for 5 minutes. Mix in the velouté sauce and boil for a further 10 minutes. Stir in the cream and season to taste.

LEGUME (Fr. LÉGUME) A plant that has long seed pods that split on both sides when ripe. These include peas, beans and lentils. They contain useful amounts of vegetable protein and starch, plus Vitamin B and minerals.

LEICESTER CHEESE A smaller British cheese than Cheddar with a more flaky texture, but not as flaky as Cheshire.

LEMON (Fr. CITRON) There are over thirty varieties of lemon. Lemons keep better when wrapped in soft tissue paper.

In cookery lemon juice is used in French dressings, fish sauces, sherbets (sorbets), curds and marmalades. Lemon syrup is made in many countries and can be diluted with water for a refreshing drink.

Typical dishes: Lemon curd, lemon marmalade, avgolémono, confit de citron, lemon meringue pie, lemon sherbet (sorbet), lemonade.

LEMON GRASS A lemon-flavored grass that is used as a herb or spice in Asian and modern cuisines.

LEMONADE A carbonated drink made from lemon juice (or flavoring), carbonated water and sugar.

LENTIL There are many varieties of lentil, some of which are quite large. The colors also vary, but they are most often brown or green when whole. Inside they are yellow, cream, orange or red. Lentils are classed as a pulse. They are grown in France, Italy, Egypt, North Africa and India.

Lentils are available whole, split or ground to flour. They are good sources of vegetable protein and contain Vitamin A, thiamin and riboflavin.

Old lentils may need soaking but this should not normally be necessary. They cook in about 20 minutes, depending on age. Hot lentils are delicious served with a French dressing.

LETTUCE There numerous varieties of lettuce, for example Boston, bibb, buttercrunch, crisphead or iceberg, and Cos, to name but few.

Lettuce must be rinsed quickly in water and drained well. Never leave them soaking in water for longer than two minutes.

Lettuce is an ideal salad ingredient, yet the desire to eat more can only be stimulated if the seasoning and flavor of the dressing are good.

Whole heads of lettuce can be cooked, but the best way to use them in cooked dishes is to shred them for pancakes, omelets and stir-fried dishes. *See also Corn salad, Arugula, Chicory.*

LEUCINE An essential amino acid.

LEUCOCYTES White blood cells that contain no haemoglobin. Their function is to combat infection.

LEVULOSE *See Fructose.*

LEYDEN CHEESE A large Dutch cheese flavored with cumin. It is used for open sandwiches and canapés and can be made into a Dutch fondue with Dutch gin and lager beer.

LIMA BEAN A popular flat green bean similar to the fava (broad) bean. It freezes well.

LIMBURGER CHEESE A German cheese easily recognizable by its reddish-brown rind. It is also manufactured in Belgium.

LIME A citrus fruit that is smaller than a lemon and retains its green color longer. The rind and juice are used for flavoring cream cheese desserts and creams.

Lime juice is available as a cordial or syrup.

LING Of the cod family, with softer flesh; made into quenelles and fish pâtés by grinding (mincing) the uncooked ling with egg whites and cream.

LINGUINI Very thin Italian pasta ribbons, either yellow or green.

LINOLEIC ACID An essential amino acid contained in fats.

LINZER TART A raspberry tart with a rich pie dough (pastry) containing ground hazelnuts and cinnamon.

LIPASE An enzyme that can split fat.

LIPID The chemical name embracing natural fats and oils, sterols, glycerol and phospholipides. They contain essential fatty acids that cannot be synthesized naturally in the body.

All fats yield 9.3 calories per gram and are the highest source of energy in the diet. Lipids are used for energy, for the structure of all cells and are essential for the absorption of Vitamins A, D, E and K.

The word lipid is sometimes used to distinguish fatty substances in the body from fat in the diet.

LIPOCAIC A hormone in the pancreas which plays a part in the metabolism of fat. Without it, fat would accumulate in the liver and interfere with its functioning.

LIPTAUER CHEESE An Hungarian cheese flavored with paprika, onion, garlic and herbs.

LIQUORICE The liquorice root is used for candies (sweets) and in cola drinks.

LITCHI *See Lychee.*

LITER A metric liquid measurement equal to 2¼lb/1kg of water.

One liter is the equivalent of 4⅓ cups/1¾ pints. *See also Appendices.*

LIVAROT CHEESE A popular strong cheese made in Normandy.

LIVER For quality and texture goose and duck livers are considered the best, then come turkey, chicken, guinea hen (fowl) and game birds.

Of the meat livers, calf's liver is the most tender and has the best color and taste. The most common liver for pâté is pig's liver, followed by lamb's liver. Beef liver is rarely used for pâtés but can be made into delicious stews.

Calf's liver pâté
For a better flavor, lightly fry the onion in butter first, and add ½ teaspoon of mixed spice.

½ cup/4oz/100g calf's liver, ground (minced)
½ cup/4oz/100g ground (minced) pork and veal leg (shin)
1 tbsp chopped onion
1 garlic clove
1 egg, beaten
½ tsp salt
¼ tsp white pepper
2 tbsp whiskey or brandy
8 slices of bacon without rinds
4 bay leaves

Mix all the ingredients together, except the whiskey or brandy, bacon and bay

231

L

leaves, and grind (mince) them again. Add the whiskey or brandy.

Line an oblong 2 cup/1lb/450g terrine with 5 of the bacon slices and the bay leaves. Fill it with the meat mixture and cover it with the remaining bacon slices.

Cover the terrine and bake in a water bath in an oven at 350°F/180°C/gas mark 4 for 1 hour.

Cool and chill the terrine.

Typical dishes: Pâté de foie de porc, pâté de campagne, foie de veau aux raisins, foie d'agneau au poivre vert.

LIVERWURST A German liver sausage.

LOAF Any kind of ground (minced) mixture made of fish, meat or poultry baked in a terrine and served hot, as opposed to a terrine and pâté which are served cold and are richer and meatier.

Fish and meat loaves can be stretched with cooked rice or breadcrumbs and eggs, so making them economical and nutritious.

Typical dishes: Pain de volaille et carotte, pain de boeuf à l'ail et aux herbes.

LOBSTER Lobster are long-living crustaceans and can reach 22lb/5kg in weight. They inhabit rocky areas, seldom moving far, and have to be enticed into baited pots for capture.

The flavor, size and appearance of lobster give it the title 'king of crustaceans'. Despite this, it is simple to prepare.

The familiar red lobster you buy from the shops has already been boiled. Uncooked, they are an intense blue-black color. Choose a female lobster that has a broader tail with plenty of eggs (coral). This can give flavor to lobster sauces or soups. The liver is also a good flavoring for soups and sauces.

Lobsters can be boiled, broiled (grilled), stewed in wine and served cold with mayonnaise. Lobster is better for lunch rather than dinner because there is a saying 'never eat lobster or crab for dinner or you may turn into a spider, during the night'.

Delicious soups flavored with Sherry can be made from the shell and the coral, the lobster eggs. The coral and liver — called tomalley — can be blended with butter and added to the lobster sauce to give it more color and flavor.

Typical dishes: Homard thermidor, homard à la Newburg, homard à l'Américaine, vol-au-vent de homard à la Parisienne, lobster timbale, lobster and asparagus salad.

Lobster Newburgh quiche

This is absolutely one of the nicest quiches there is.

1lb/450g savory pie dough (short
crust pastry) (See recipe page 273)

Filling

1 cup/8oz/225g lobster meat, cut in
slices
⅔ cup/5fl oz/150ml shrimp or
lobster sauce
1 tsp tarragon, chopped
salt and pepper
3 eggs, beaten
¼ cup/3oz/75g white mushrooms,
sliced
3 tbsp medium Sherry
3 tbsp heavy (double) cream

Roll out the pie dough (pastry) and use it to line a 6in/15cm quiche pan (flan tin). Line with baking parchment and fill with dried beans. Bake blind at 400°F/200°C/gas mark 6 for about 10 minutes.

Cool the tart shell and remove the beans. Arrange a layer of lobster meat and mushrooms in the tart shell.

Boil the sauce and tarragon for 5 minutes. Let cool. Check the seasoning and add the eggs, cream and Sherry. Pour two thirds of the sauce over the lobster meat.

Bake at 400°F/200°C/gas mark 6 for 12 minutes. Add the remaining sauce and continue baking until the filling is set like a custard. Serve hot or cold.

LOCUST Fried locusts are one of the tastiest foods one could possibly eat. There are two edible species: the smaller one has green wings and a silver belly; the larger species has a red head and legs.

Locusts are eaten broiled (grilled), roasted, boiled like shrimp (prawns); and dried and ground to a powder or a paste. They are also used as a condiment with garlic and chili pepper.

LOCUST BEAN *See Carob.*

LOGANBERRY A cross between a blackberry and a raspberry. It can be served with cream as a dessert, used as a filling for tarts or made into cream puddings or ice creams.

LOIN The part of an animal along the back from neck to rump. All loins can be made into roasts (roasting joints) as the meat is tender.

LOQUAT A fruit that comes from the same species as medlar and originates in Japan. It has a peculiar astringent taste between pineapple and tamarind.

L

It is best made into jam or jelly. It must be very ripe to be edible.

LOTUS   An Asian plant popularly known as the water lily. Its large seeds are boiled, or broiled (grilled) while the root is prepared in the same way as celery. The leaves can be cooked like spinach.

LTCHKI   Yugoslavian bread made of equal amounts of cornmeal and wheat.

LUAU   A Pacific island feast of sucking pig, barbecued fish and fruits.

LUMACHE   Italian pasta shaped like snails which can be stuffed with mixtures of fish, chicken or cheese.

LUMPFISH   An ugly fish full of bones but the roes are preserved in the same way as caviar and used as a cheap alternative to it for garnishing canapés and hors d'oeuvre.

LYCHEE, LITCHI   One of the Chinese precious fruits. The thin, brittle shell has many small nobbles or spines. The taste of the flesh resembles that of a plum. It has a large stone. Lychees are available fresh or canned in syrup. They can be served with smoked fish, pork or duck, or as a dessert.

LYONNAISE   1) à la: A garnish of onions fried in butter.

2) An onion sauce or soup.

3) Pommes de terre Lyonnaise. A potato dish.

LYSINE   An essential amino acid needed in the daily diet for growth and repair and the formation of new body proteins.

M

MACADAMIA NUT The fruit of an Australian tree. It is used in curries, stews, nougat and caramels.

MACAIRE The mashed flesh of a baked potato mixed with butter and made into a cake, then baked for 10 minutes.

MACARONI A tubular Italian pasta which is available in various sizes. The generic Italian name for all tubular pasta is maccheroni.

MACAROON A small, crisp almond cookie (biscuit) made with ground almonds and egg whites with sugar.

Macaroons are baked on baking sheets lined with wafer paper (rice paper) or baking parchment. They can be flavored with cocoa powder or a few drops of vanilla and almond extract.

Ground nuts can be used as a substitute for the almonds.

4 egg whites
pinch of salt
1½ cups/12oz/350g superfine
* (caster) sugar*
2 cups/8oz/250g ground almonds
                                    Makes 48

Lightly whisk the egg whites and salt. Fold in the sugar and ground almonds. Pipe or spoon the mixture onto a baking tray lined with wafer (rice) paper or baking parchment.

Bake at 350°F/180°C/gas mark 4 for 15 minutes. Cool completely.

If baking parchment has been used dampen the underside of the paper using a damp cloth. After a few minutes, carefully remove the macaroons from the paper. Store until use in airtight containers so they don't go soft.

MACE (Fr. MACIS) A spice with a flavor similar to nutmeg.

MACÉDOINE A mixture of vegetables or fruit cut into ½in/1.2cm dice and combined for their color and taste. A vegetable macédoine can be stirred into a rich mayonnaise and served as a salad.

Fruit macédoine is made of a similar variety of fruits. It is available commercially canned in syrup, where it is found under the name of fruit cocktail.

M

MACKEREL (Fr. MAQUEREAU) An oily fish that can be pickled, or broiled (grilled) and served with a fruit sauce such as gooseberry.

Mackerel and leek salad
4 mackerel fillets
2 large leeks, white parts only sliced into rings
⅔ cup/5fl oz/150ml court bouillon

Mustard dressing
6 tbsp French dressing
1 tbsp cream
I tsp mustard

Poach the mackerel and leeks in the court bouillon for 8 minutes. Let cool in the liquid.

To make the mustard dressing, mix all the ingredients together.

Serve the fish and leeks with a little of the stock spooned over, and the dressing separately in a jug for each to help themselves.

MACROBIOTIC A special diet inspired by Japanese Buddhists based on balancing male and female elements. Meat, fruits and alcoholic drinks are forbidden but tea is allowed.

Dieticians have not approved this strange diet on the grounds that is is unbalanced and even unhealthy.

MADEIRA CAKE The perfect Madeira cake is made using equal weights of butter, sugar, eggs and flour, with lemon juice and rind as as flavorings.

MADELEINE A light sponge cake baked either in a shallow, shell-shaped pan (tin) for French madeleines, or in dariole molds for English madeleines; these are coated with jam and rolled in shredded (desiccated) coconut.

MADRAS CURRY POWDER A typical blend may consist of coriander, chili pepper, asafoetida, black or white peppercorns, cumin, fenugreek, yellow mustard seeds and curry leaves pounded together.

MAFALDA An Italian broad, flat, ripple-edged noodle.

MAGLIETTE A short, curved Italian pasta tube.

MAGRET The boned breast of duck. Magrets are broiled (grilled) until the flesh is slightly underdone but the fat must be almost melted.

MAGNESIUM A mineral which is required for all metabolic processes and is essential for the health of the nervous system.

Magnesium is found mainly in whole grain cereals, soy beans and nuts.

MAGNESIUM HYDROXIDE A white crystalline substance that is used as an emulsifier or stabilizer.

MAID OF HONOUR A small English tartlet with an almond filling.

MAIZE *See Corn.*

MALABSORPTION A digestive disorder resulting in the failure of the body to absorb nutrients into the blood stream.

MALAGA RAISIN Sun-dried muscat grape; reputed to be the best raisin.

MALIC ACID The acid in apples.

MALNUTRITION Ill-health brought about by a failure to eat a balanced and nourishing diet.

MALT EXTRACT A thick syrup prepared from barley or wheat. It is a mixture of starch breakdown products containing mainly maltose (malt sugar).

Malt extract has a delicate flavor and is high in vitamins and iron and is widely used as a supplement.

MALTESE SAUCE Hollandaise sauce flavored with blood orange juice.

MALTOSE A sugar converted by the enzyme maltase.

MAMALIGA A staple food of the country people of Romania. It is made from a cornmeal dough and is almost a bread.

Mamaliga is served with stews and sauces, made into dumplings, or fried. Mamaliga is very similar to Italian polenta.

MANCHEGO CHEESE The most popular Spanish cheese. It is made from the ewes' milk of La Mancha. Curado is four months old and viego is older and harder.

MANDARIN An orange, fragrant, sweet small citrus fruit.

MANICOTTI Italian pasta tubes which can be stuffed.

MANGO (Fr. MANGUE) A delicious sweet fruit that is served as a dessert and made into sherbets (sorbets) or cream desserts. It is also added to curries and used for pickles, jams and other preserves. In India it is made into a wide variety of chutneys.

M

MANGOSTEEN A fruit with a thick, dark skin and sweet, dark rose-colored flesh that is delicately scented and similar to lychee. The thick skin should be discarded.

Mangosteens are used for desserts and salads.

MANIOC *See Cassava.*

MANNA The manna of modern commerce is the sweet juice which exudes like gum from the trunks and branches of the manna-ash Tamarisk tree that is abundant in Sicily. It is used as a sweetener.

This, or something very similar, is believed to have been the manna of the Israelites.

MANNITOL A white sweetener used for thickening, stabilizing and flavoring commercial food products.

MAPLE SYRUP This is made from the sap of an American variety of maple tree. The sap is boiled, clarified and packed in cans or bottles.

Maple syrup has many uses, such as to sweeten pancakes and waffles as well as puddings.

MARASMUS An illness resulting from starvation.

MARENGO (À LA) A casserole of veal or chicken cooked with white wine, tomatoes, onions and olives. It is traditionally garnished with crayfish. The casserole was created by Durand, Napoleon's Swiss chef.

MARGARINE Modern margarine is made by the hydrogenization of oils. By law, margarine must contain not more than 16 percent water and a minimum of 80 percent fat. The best brands have butter added for flavor, but the butter content must not exceed 10 percent.

Hard margarines contain high levels of saturated fatty acids, and are best for making Danish and puff pastries.

On health grounds, some margarines have fewer saturated fatty acids. *See also Fats and oils.*

MARGUERITE Italian pasta with a narrow ripple side.

MARINADE A liquid for flavoring and tenderizing fish, meat and game. A marinade should contain an acid, either lemon juice, vinegar or wine, oil for lubrication, and appropriate herbs and spices.

The fresh juice of fruits that contain enzymes capable of breaking down protein, such as pineapple and kiwi fruit, are useful for marinating tough meats.

Pineapple marinade
½ cup/4fl oz/100ml pineapple juice
1 green chili pepper, chopped
6 tbsp olive oil
I tsp yeast extract (optional)
1 tsp salt

Mix all the ingredients together and use it to marinate fish or brush it during cooking.

Variations
1. Add peanut butter to the basic marinade.
2. Add 2 anchovy fillets, pounded into a paste, to the basic marinade.

MARINIÈRE (À LA) 'Sailor's style' cooking for seafood, usually mussels, using white wine, shallots, garlic and herbs.

MARJORAM (MARJOLAINE) Sweet or knotted marjoram is a fragrant herb used in southern European cooking.

MARMALADE A preserve made from citrus fruits. The word marmalade is derived from marmelo the Portuguese word for quince.

There is a vast selection of mar-malades to choose from including the clear lemon, lime and orange marmalades containing fine shreds of peel, to dark ones containing thickly-cut chunks of orange.

MARRONS GLACÉS Candied chestnuts made in Italy and France.

They are ideal for serving in a selection of petits fours, or adding to desserts and cakes. *See Candy.*

MARROW 1) A large winter squash. On account of their high water content marrows are best blanched for 2 minutes, then tossed in butter. They can be flavored with onion and tomato, fried in finely chopped almonds or served plain.

Marrow can also be stuffed or made into jam flavored with ginger.
2) A delicate fatty substance found inside marrow bones.

MARROW BONE The shin (shank) bone, which is hollow and contains the delicate marrow. The bone should be wrapped in cheesecloth and boiled for 20 minutes then the marrow removed, sliced and served on toast or as a garnish for steaks.

MARROW FAT PEAS Dried, whole peas. They are available dry and canned.

M

MARSCAPONE CHEESE A creamy, rich Italian cheese that is served with soft fruits, or used in cheesecakes and rich chocolate desserts.

MARSHMALLOW A candy (sweet) made with meringue and gelatin and colored pink or white.

Marshmallows toasted on skewers are a barbecue favorite, especially with children.

Strawberry marshmallow
3 tbsp powdered gelatin
1¼ cups/½ pint/300ml water
1¼ cups/10oz/300g sugar
1 tbsp powdered glucose
4 egg whites
1 tsp vanilla extract
3 drops of edible red food coloring
½ tsp strawberry flavor, if available
confectioners' (icing) sugar

Dissolve the gelatin in the water. Add the sugar and boil to 225°F/107°C.

Add the glucose and boil to 245°F/118°C.

Beat the egg whites until stiff. Slowly pour the syrup into the egg whites, stirring constantly. Add the vanilla extract.

Divide the mixture in half. Add red coloring, and strawberry flavor if available, to one batch.

Pour both mixtures into baking pans (tins) to make a 1in/2.5cm thick layer. Cool. Cut in cubes. Dust with confectioners' (icing) sugar. Store in an airtight container.

MARUZZE Italian pasta shaped like seashells.

MARZIPAN *See Almond paste.*

MASA HARINA Mexican cornmeal that has been treated with lime. It is used for making tortillas.

MASALA An Indian blend of herbs, spices and seasoning. A masala can be a paste or a powder, and it can be made from any number of combinations of spices out of any number of different ingredients.

MASHLUM BISCUIT A Scottish biscuit (scone) made with a mixture of flours such as rye and wheat.

MAYONNAISE An emulsion of egg yolks, oil and mustard. It can be made with any kind of oil, such as peanut, soybean, sunflower or walnut, or mixed with the best olive oil. Some modern cooks use any good salad oil (to reduce the calories) or mix a cheap oil with olive oil for flavor.

Mayonnaise can be flavored with aromatic herbs or spices or colored with tomato paste (purée) or curry sauce.

1 tsp Dijon mustard
salt and white pepper
2 egg yolks
1¼ cups/½ pint/300ml lukewarm
  vegetable oil
juice of ½ lemon

Mix together the mustard, salt and pepper and egg yolks. Stir in the oil in a slow stream at first while beating until the mixture begins to thicken as the emulsion takes place.

Increase the flow of the oil slightly and beat in the same direction until all the oil is used and the mayonnaise is very thick. Add the lemon juice.

MEAL   Coarse or finely ground grain or pulse used for breads, cakes, soups and porridges, or as fillers for force-meats and fritters.

MEASUREMENTS   *See Appendix.*

MEAT Good meat can only come from healthy, well-reared livestock.

Tough meat is due to the thickness and density of muscle fibers and connective tissues. Thickening occurs with use and activity so the meat from old animals tends to be tougher than the meat from younger ones.

Less tender cuts of meat come from the neck and legs of an animal because they do most exercise. The more tender cuts come from the back.

Tenderness can be improved by hanging the meat for 10 days at temperatures a little above freezing point. Injections of enzymes and hormones can also be used to tenderize meat.

Grading is done on the basis of conformation, age and finish. Tenderness, juiciness and palatability are considered when designating quality.

The conformation deals with the form or shape of an animal; those having broad, large full muscles with a relatively smaller proportion of bone are graded the highest. The 'finish' is the amount, quality and color of the fat within and around the tissues.

Fat becomes yellower with age, so whiter fat is graded higher than creamy or more yellow fat. In beef of the same age, yellow fat may also indicate that carotene, in the form of sugar beet, rutabaga (swedes) or carrots, was used in the feed.

MEAT COOKERY   Meat is cooked to make it tender, palatable and safer to eat. Tender cuts of beef and lamb are

M

usually cooked rare or medium in order to retain their juices. Pork must be cooked through. Meat can be braised, boiled, roasted, broiled (grilled) and shallow-fried.

Tips for cooking meats in liquids
• Add the garnish vegetables for boiled or poached meat 30 minutes before the meat is ready. Vegetables that are being used as flavoring (onions, leeks, celery, carrots) can be cooked for the same length of time as the meat.

• Meat boiled on the bone will produce a better-flavored stock.

• Cool tougher cured meats such as ham in the liquid in which they were cooked.

• Use the stock of all boiled meats for soups and sauces. This stock can be frozen in small containers and used as and when needed.

• Always use fresh bones, meat and vegetables.

• Remove the scum, which is coagulated albumen, as it rises.

• Remove any fat as it surfaces.

• Keep the liquid under boiling point. Add cold water if the liquid begins to bubble, and replace liquid lost through evaporation.

• Desalt all cured meat by soaking in cold water overnight.

• Any meat that is to be boiled should not be seasoned with salt until after it is cooked. Before or during cooking, season the meat only with peppercorns.

• For maximum flavor ensure that the quantity of solids is equal to the quantity of liquid.

MEAT EXTRACT Meat, poultry, fish or fish juices boiled and reduced until thick. It is used to strengthen broths, to rectify a weak sauce, spread on toasted bread, or taken as a hot drink.

MEAT PIES Hot meat pies are covered with pie dough (short crust pastry) or puff paste. The most popular are steak-and-kidney, chicken-and-ham and lamb-and-leek. From these three pies a large number of variations can be made by substituting one ingredient for another.

The meat for the filling is always cooked first then cooled before being covered.

The pie dough for cold meat pies can be either hot-water crust paste (*See recipe page 274*), or savory pie dough (shortcrust pastry) enriched with eggs. The pies should be jellied by pouring in melted aspic after baking, to retain the moisture in the meat.

They can be made in rectangular,

oblong or fluted oval-shaped pans (tins) or molds with removable, hinged sides.

Typical dishes: Steak-and-kidney pie, cottage pie, shepherd's pie, pork pie, ham-and-veal pie, liver pie, game pie.

MECHOUI A Middle Eastern method of roasting animals on the spit. It is a form of barbecue.

MEDALLION A thick oval French cut of meat.

MELON Melons are grouped as dessert melons and watermelons.

DESSERT MELONS have a number of different flesh colors; they may be scarlet, green, white or orange. The skin may be netted, ridged or smooth.

Examples are musk melons, which encompass citron, cantaloup, nutmeg and pineapple melons, charentais melon with a very sweet flesh and greenish skin, and yellow-skinned honeydew.

WATERMELONS usually have red or pink flesh but newer varieties may be white, pink or even orange flesh. Black seeds are embedded in the flesh.

Melons can easily be made into sherbets (sorbets) when very ripe. They can also be served with smoked ham or smoked salmon.

MENTHOL One of the series of organic compounds of the camphor group. A white crystalline substance that occurs in the volatile oils of members of the mint family. It has a minty taste and is used as mint flavoring for confectionery.

MENU A list of the foods or dishes to be served, arranged in courses.

Menus today reflect the current attitude and desire to pursue a healthier, more balanced diet without neglecting the pleasures of gastronomy. Meals are not as fatty or starchy as they used to be, consequently butter and cream have been reduced in recipes in accordance with the current eating trends.

In addition more and more restaurants and hotels are following the fashion towards ethnic and foreign cuisines and fewer are printing their menus in French.

The names of the dishes these days are self-explanatory whereas before when classical French names were used a knowledge of cuisine was essential; for example, chicken Nantua would simply be written as chicken

M

with crayfish, bisque d'écrevisse is now a freshwater crayfish soup.

MERINGUE There are three kinds of meringues:

HARD MERINGUE made with ¼ cup/2oz/50g sugar per egg white, for baking until dry in a cool oven.

ITALIAN OR COOKED MERINGUE made by beating syrup at 250°F/121°C into egg whites, then baking in a cool oven until as dry as a cookie (biscuit). Use 6 tablespoons of syrup per egg white.

SOFT MERINGUE made with 2 tablespoons/1oz/25g sugar per egg white and used for soufflés, cream fillings or covering pies.

Meringue-making

Egg whites can make the stable foam necessary for making successful meringues because they have low surface tension, low vapor pressure, and a tendency for the surface to solidify, giving rigidity and permanence.

Fresh egg whites should be used as they are more viscous than stale ones.

With light whipping the incorporated air bubbles are large and the egg white appears foamy yet transparent, is very runny and still flows readily.

After longer beating the air bubbles become smaller and the mixture becomes less transparent and whiter. It still flows if the bowl is partly inverted however.

The egg white becomes stiffer with continued beating until it becomes very white and begins to lose a little of its moist, shiny appearance and is instead stiff and rigid. If the bowl is inverted the egg white does not run out but remains attached to the bowl. This is called the dry stage.

If the meringue is left standing for a while, some liquid will appear in the bottom of the bowl. After this stage is reached continued whipping causes increased breakdown of the foam with greater drainage.

To test whether a meringue is ready for cooking — assess the appearance, the height of the peaks, the rate of flow when the bowl is partly inverted and the extent to which they bend over when the egg beater is lifted out of the beaten white.

A skillful cook working frequently with egg whites soon learns to judge the degree of stiffness by these simple methods, and the degree of proficiency that can be attained is surprising.

The addition of a small amount of salt will help to produce stiff egg whites for savory dishes. For sweet dishes 1 teaspoon of an acid such as cream of tartar, vinegar and lemon juice per four egg whites help to make a stiffer foam.

Adding sugar to the foam increases its stability. The sugar should be added when the egg white begins to hold in the whisk, then the addition should be done a spoonful at a time and each spoonful thoroughly beaten in.

Frozen egg whites which have been thawed will produce a good foam as some of their moisture has evaporated during the freezing process.

MESCLUN A mixture of wild salad leaves and herbs such as curly endive, dandelion, radicchio and Belgian endive (chicory), oak leaves, corn salad, lollo rosso, arugula, chervil and purslane. They are tossed in French dressing containing walnut or olive oil and wine vinegar.

Fried croûtons, broiled (grilled) bacon, quails' eggs, chicken livers and broiled (grilled) goats' cheese go well with this salad.

METABOLISM The chemical change that goes on in living cells, with the growth of new tissues and the breakdown of old tissues producing energy.

Basal metabolism is the term used for the amount of energy used to maintain the body, this varies enormously from person to person.

METHIONINE An essential amino acid. It is needed for the synthesis of other important substances, for example choline, which is usually classed as a vitamin.

METTWURST A soft, spreadable German meat sausage made of pork and flavored with coriander and white pepper.

MEZZANI Italian pasta with very short curves.

MEZZE Middle Eastern hors d'oeuvre.

MICROWAVE COOKING Microwaves are electromagnetic waves of radiant energy, like the waves that carry radio and television programmes. Like light they travel in straight lines.

Microwaves are reflected by metals, pass through air and many, but not all, types of glass, paper and plastic materials but they are absorbed by several food constituents including water. When this happens the microwaves transmit their energy to the absorbing medium in the form of heat.

When microwaves are reflected they do not heat the reflecting medium,

M

which is why dishes can stay cold even when food is cooked in a microwave oven. The heat in a microwave is generated quickly and quite uniformly throughout the food.

Since their introduction in the early 1960s, microwave ovens have developed many features including turntables for more even cooking and provisions for browning foods.

The best results are obtained when microwaveing foods that contain a reasonable amount of liquid. Baked apples and potatoes should be pierced before cooking to prevent them splitting whilst cooking.

Raw foods cook in a fraction of the time taken in a conventional oven but the main uses of microwave ovens are for rapidly reheating food and defrosting frozen food.

Never try to cook eggs in their shells as they will explode.

When purchasing a microwave oven you need to know its power output, whether 400 watt, 550 watt or 700 watt.

MILANAISE (ALLA) 'In the style of Milan'. Popularly, fish or veal scallops (escalopes) coated in breadcrumbs, then fried and served with spaghetti.

MILK Milk consists of about 87.4 per-

cent water, 3.3 percent protein, 3.9 percent fat, 4.5 percent lactose and 0.9 percent mineral salts.

Fresh milk is pasteurized and available semi-skimmed, skimmed or whole. It is packaged in paper cartons and plastic or glass bottles.

Milk can be homogenized, sterilized, evaporated or condensed and sold in cans, or dried to make dry milk solids (milk powder).

Milk is used in batters for pancakes and fritters, in soups and for making béchamel sauce, porridge and similar cereals, and is most important for all types of custards and set creams.

Milk is also used in conjunction with water in yeast cakes, scones and other baked goods.

MILLAS A kind of porridge prepared with cornmeal and semolina. When set it is molded into cakes and fried.

MILLE-FEUILLE Two or three layers of puff pastry sandwiched with cream and sometimes fruit. The top is covered with frosting (icing).

MILLET A cereal which is grown in Africa. It is rich in magnesium, iron and Vitamins A and B. It is sold as grains, flakes and flour.

Millet is cooked with twice its volume of liquid, such as water, stock or milk, for 20 minutes to make a nourishing porridge.

MIMOSA 1) The bright yellow blossoms (flowers) of the mimosa tree can be fried as fritters.

2) Hard-cooked (boiled) egg yolk passed through a strainer (sieve) and used as a garnish.

MINCEMEAT Originally this was a mixture of ground (minced) meat and dried fruits. Modern mincemeats consist of a mixture of sugar, dried fruits, candied peels, apple, suet and spices. It is used in various British pastries and puddings.

MINERAL WATER Mineral water springs from the earth in various parts of the world and are naturally charged with an aerating gas.

The medicinal value of these waters is due to the mineral salts they contain. Of all natural mineral waters the alkaline are the most numerous and used for therapeutic purposes.

MINESTRONE An Italian vegetable soup with garlic and tomatoes and a quick-cooking pasta such as vermicelli. It is served with grated Parmesan cheese.

MINT One of the most useful, easily grown and popular of all the garden herbs. Numerous mints are available and used for different flavoring purposes in the kitchen.

Lemon mint, spearmint, peppermint and pennyroyal are chiefly used in confectionery.

Mint sauce
2 cups/5oz/150g mint leaves,
  chopped
2 tbsp brown sugar
1¼ cups/½ pint/300ml malt vinegar

Mix together the mint, sugar and vinegar and bring to a boil. Let cool. Serve with roast lamb.

MIRABELLE A small yellow plum grown in France and Germany and used for tarts and jams.

MIREPOIX A mixture of cut vegetables, usually onion, carrot and celery and sometimes bacon or ham, used as a bed on which to braise meat.

MIRIN A sweet Japanese rice wine used for cooking.

MISO A Japanese paste made from soya beans and fermented like soy sauce. It is used in soups and sauces.

M

MIXED SPICE A finely ground mixture of cinnamon, cloves, nutmeg, mace, ginger, coriander and allspice. It is used for rich fruit cakes and puddings.

MOCHA COFFEE *See Coffee.*

MOLASSES (BLACK TREACLE) The syrup left from the refining of sugar. It varies in color from dark yellow to very dark brownish-black. It gives a strong, characteristic taste to dishes.

MOLD A container for food that is to have a distinctive shape after being cooked or chilled. Molds can be plain or fluted, round or oblong or square. In modern cookery individual molds are preferred. Whatever the shape, metal molds must be cleaned and never allowed to become rusty.

MOLE POBLANO The national dish of Mexico. The sauce is made with three kinds of chili peppers, onions, tomatoes, raisins, nuts, seeds, spices and chocolate, which are pounded together until smooth. Diced cooked turkey is simmered in the prepared sauce.

MONASTIC COOKERY A great deal is owed to monks of the past for their creation and production of foods which are now taken for granted.

They were also the culinary teachers who recorded all the best recipes for producing all kinds of food.

Monks perfected the production of honey, which was used as a sweetener and in making cakes and cookies (biscuits). In addition monks improved the shelf-life of cheeses by creating methods of making harder types such as Saint-Paulin, Saint-Nectaire, Port Salut and Munster.

The third area of their researches covered pastries, cakes, breads and wafers. *See also Saints in food.*

MONGOLIAN HOTPOT A Chinese fondue where guests cook raw meat in a simmering stock in a pot placed over an alcohol (spirit) lamp on the dining table.

MONKFISH, ANGLER FISH (Fr. LOTTE) This fish may look monstrous with its ugly head, but the flesh of the tail is tender and as good as turbot but firmer. It is therefore expensive.

It can be roasted on a bed of sliced potatoes and basted with butter for serving for lunch or dinner.

Alternatively it can be threaded on skewers with mushrooms and then grilled over a barbecue.

Better still, monkfish can be poached in Champagne flavored with star anise and served with a delicious sauce made from the cooking liquid.

Typical dishes: Escallope de lotte au muscadet, filet de lotte à l'estragon, coulibiac de lotte aux épinards.

MONOSACCARIDE The simple sugars fructose, galactose and glucose, synthesized by plants, animals and microbes. They are absorbed into the blood stream.

MONOSODIUM GLUTAMATE, MSG AJI-NO-MOTO A flavor enhancer much used in food manufacture in the East. Monosodium glutamate is made from wheat gluten and is frequently heavily used in Chinese, Japanese and southeast Asiasn cuisines.

MONSTERA, MEXICAN BREADFRUIT A fruit with a conical shape and a flavor of mango and pineapple. It should be eaten when ripe.

MONT-BLANC A dessert of sweet chestnut purée topped with whipped cream. Chestnut purée may be piped over the dessert, or it can be served with chocolate sauce.

MONT-DORE Potato purée blended with egg yolks, cream and grated Cantal cheese. It is baked until golden.

MONTER 1) To emulsify a sauce in order to increase its volume.

2) Whipping egg whites or cream to increase their volume.

MORCILLA A Spanish black pudding.

MOREL (Fr. MORILLE) A sponge-like wild mushroom that should be washed several times in cold water to remove the sand that can collect in the pits of the cap.

Morels with dark caps are the most highly prized.

Typical dishes: Morilles à la crème; saumon aux morilles.

MORNAY Béchamel sauce to which egg yolks, cream and cheese are added. It is served with cauliflower, leeks and poached fish, and used for potatoes au gratin.

MORTADELLA An large Italian cooked sausage made of pork and veal containing a proportion of chopped fat.

MOSCOVITE (À LA) A style of cooking whereby fruits are embedded in gelatin and molded in fluted bowls.

Many French chefs who made their names in Moscow before 1914, created jellied dishes for special buffets and their ideas were incorporated into a

M

huge repertoire of mousses, bavaroise, chartreuse and fruit macédoines coated with aspic or sweet fruit jelly.

MOSTACCIOLI   Italian pasta tubes about 1¼in/4cm long.

MOTHER OF VINEGAR The vinegar 'plant' which promotes the production of vinegar from wine, cider or beer by oxidzing the alcohol into acetic acid.

A vinegar mother is a cellulose substance produced by an organism closely resembling the mycoderma (acetobacter) but can produce a jelly-like substance from either glucose, fructose or mannite. *See also Vinegar.*

MOUCLADE Mussels in a creamy white wine sauce flavored with saffron or curry powder. It comes from the Charente region of France.

MOUSSAKA A Greek dish of sliced eggplants (aubergines), tomatoes and ground (minced) lamb highly flavored with spices. The top can be covered with grated cheese and browned in the oven or under the broiler (grill).

MOUSSE A mousse is made from any kind of purée, such as fruit, vegetables, fish, poultry or meat, mixed with an equal quantity of whipped cream or, for sweet mousses, meringue.

Mousses must have a light consistency somewhat similar to that of a marshmallow. This is a particularly attractive and spectacular way to present food for a dinner party or for a special occasion.

Mousses can be cooked in a water bath or set with either gelatin or agar. The amount of gelatin used should be no more than two or three percent of the total weight of the mousse mixture; this means that you should use about 1 tablespoon gelatin for every 1¼ lb/500g of the mixture. In hot weather the amount of gelatin used may need to be increased slightly.

Mousses can be made in a large mold and then unmolded onto a plate with a suitable garnish or decoration.

To unmold a mousse, let it stand for at least 1 hour in a cool place. When the mousse is ready, dip the mold into hot water for 30 seconds, then carefully wipe the sides and turn it quickly on to a plate. Garnish the unmolded mousse with thinly sliced cooked vegetables or hard-cooked (boiled) eggs.

Before beginning to put on the garnish place the cut vegetables on a small plate with melted aspic jelly. The plate should stand over a pan or bowl of hot water to keep the jelly liquid. With the point of a small knife pick up the cuttings and garnish as required.

Mousses can also be served in individual containers, like dips. In this instance the amount of gelatin used can be reduced.

Mousses can also be used as a filling or stuffing for tart shells, avocados, papayas, tomatoes, cucumbers, or bell peppers, which can be cut once the mousse filling is set.

Basic savory mousse

*1 cup/8oz/225g lean cooked meat
  or fish
1¼ cups/½ pint/300ml heavy
  (double) cream
½ tsp salt
¼ tsp white pepper
1 tbsp gelatin
6 tbsp meat or fish stock*

Grind (mince) the meat or fish twice then chill for 30 minutes.

Beat in the cream and seasoning.

Dissolve the gelatin in the stock and stir into the cream mixture. Chill.

MOUSSELINE 1) A sponge cake or brioche lightened by the addition of egg whites.

2) Mayonnaise or hollandaise sauce lightened by the addition of whipped cream.

3) A hot mousse made from raw ground meat, poultry or fish in a similar way to a mousse. It is cooked in a water bath until set with the texture of a marshmallow, yet still elastic enough to bounce back to shape when touched.

Basic mousseline

*1 cup/8oz/225g raw meat, poultry
  or fish
1 egg white.
⅔-1¼ cups/¼-½ pint/150-300ml
  heavy (double) cream
1 tsp salt
¼ tsp white pepper*

Grind (mince) the meat, poultry or fish twice and beat in the egg white. Chill for 30 minutes.

Beat in the cream. Add the seasoning to taste.

The mousseline can be cooked in small china ramekin dishes at 350°F/180°C/gas 4 for 30 minutes.

Alternatively they can be used as dumplings or quenelles, poached for 10 minutes in stock in a deep tray for easy removal with a slotted spoon.

MOUSSERON A white field mushroom with a delicate flavor.

MOZZARELLA CHEESE An Italian semi-

M

soft cheese made from buffalo or cows' milk. It can be shaped into balls or loaves of varying sizes, and is kept in salted water or whey.

MUESLI A Swiss breakfast mixture of rolled oats, plus other grains, dried fruits and nuts, served with milk or yogurt.

MUFFIN American muffins are made with baking powder and baked in individual muffin pans (tins), while English muffins are made with a yeast batter that is formed into rounds and cooked on a griddle.

MULBERRY A dark purple berry that is usually made into jams or jellies, or a coulis to serve with desserts.

MULLET (Fr. MULET, ROUGET) There are two groups of mullet: in the first group there are the grey and the golden mullet. These are prepared like bass and best baked in the oven with butter and fennel.

The second group includes the red mullet (rouget), which is closely related to the American goatfish. They are usually baked in foil with herbs and butter or filleted and broiled (grilled) and served with a salad alongside as an appetizer.

MUNG BEAN A small dried pea that can be green, brown or black with yellow flesh. It is commercially sprouted for bean sprouts, or grown at home as a sprouting vegetable in the same way as mustard and cress.

Ground mung beans are used to make noodles and a variety of Indian pancakes and fritters.

MUNSTER CHEESE A cumin-flavored, soft square cheese made in Germany and Alsace.

MUSCOVADO SUGAR A soft, dark brown unrefined sugar with a rich flavor. It can be used for dark puddings and cakes.

MUSHROOM (Fr. CHAMPIGNON) Edible fungi which reproduce by the production of spores. Mushrooms have very little food value.

Wild varieties have a better flavor than cultivated types. The majority of mushrooms that are eaten in Britain and the USA are cultivated, but in recent years some of the edible wild mushrooms have become popular, such as ceps, morels, chanterelles, oyster and shiitake mushooms; the last two are now cultivated and widely available in supermarkets.

Dried mushrooms have a stronger

M

flavor than fresh ones and need soaking before they can be used.

Mushrooms should not be soaked in water but washed under the tap; to bring out their flavor, cook them with a little thyme and garlic.

Mushrooms can be made into a catsup (ketchup), or duxell with herbs for stuffing, terrines, pâtés, mousses and omelet fillings.

Typical dishes: Champignons à la Grecque, soufflé aux champignons, caviar de champignons, champignons sous cloche, crème cappucine de champignons.

MUSSEL (Fr. MOULE) A quick-cooking bivalve. The best known mussel dish is moules à la marinière, mussels cooked in white wine with shallots and herbs.

Mussels are particularly popular in France and wherever they are available. They are tasty, economical and easy to prepare as an appetizer or light lunch. They can be stuffed with garlic butter and broiled (grilled), coated in breadcrumbs or batter and fried, or poached for 5 minutes with herbs, onion and dry white wine.

The shell is oval, smooth, blue-black in color and has two separate halves held together by a powerful muscle. Mussels grow by attaching themselves by their beard to any surface.

Discard any mussels that do not close when tapped. Wash well in several changes of water and remove the beard with a sharp tug. Then brush the mussels hard to remove grit and any small attached shells. Discard all empty, broken and dead shells.

Stuffed mussels Italian style
16 large mussels, cleaned
⅓ cup/3oz/75g butter
3 garlic cloves, chopped
8 pine nuts, chopped
8 tbsp chopped cooked spinach, well-drained
2 anchovy fillets, chopped
salt and pepper
2 tbsp oil
2 tbsp grated Parmesan cheese

Open the mussels and discard the top shells.

Heat the butter and lightly stir-fry the garlic for 15 minutes. Mix in the pine nuts, spinach, anchovy fillets and seasoning to taste. Cook for 4 minutes. Let cool.

Remove the mussels from their shells. Fill the empty shells with the spinach mixture. Put the mussels on top.

Brush the mussels with olive oil and sprinkle over the Parmesan cheese. Broil (grill) for 3 minutes, or cook in

M-N

an oven at 400°F/200 °C/gas mark 6
for 10 minutes.

MUSTARD There are three varieties of
mustard seeds: Black mustard seeds,
which are spicy and piquant, brown
seeds which are less piquant and white
mustard seed, which are more bland
but bitter.

Whole mustard seeds are used in
Indian cookery where they are tossed
in the pan with other spice seeds to
develop a more piquant flavor.
Mustard seeds are also used in making
pickles.

Typical dishes: Lapin à la Dijonnaise,
céleriac rémoulade, poulet à la
moutarde, saucisse à la moutarde;
rognons à la moutarde et crème.

MUTTON The meat of sheep older than
one year. *See also Lamb.*

NAAN *See Nann.*

NACHO Although more of an
American dish than a Mexican one,
nachos have a Mexican identity.

Nachos are deep-fried quartered
corn tortillas topped with cheese and
chili peppers or pickles and baked in a
hot oven until the cheese melts.

NAGE (À LA) Literally 'swimming', the
term applics to large shellfish such as
lobster poached in a wine-enriched
court bouillon with herbs and other
flavorings, and served with the poaching liquid.

NANN, NAAN, NAN Indian tear-drop
shaped flat bread that is lightly leavened by a natural yeast starter developed from airborne yeasts. Nann are
baked in a tandoori oven. They can be
plain or stuffed with various fillings
such as garlic or nuts and sultanas.

NANTAIS A small, round almond cookie (biscuit) from the area of Nantes, western France. It can be decorated with candied fruits.

NANTUA A sauce made with crayfish, similar to the Américaine sauce for lobsters.

Typical dishes: Sole à la Nantua, charlotte d'ecrevisses à la Nantua.

NASEBERRY, *See Sapodilla.*

NASHI PEAR *See Asian pear.*

NASI GORENG A rice dish. Many versions are found in Indonesia, Malaysia and all nearby islands.

The most common style is rice, shrimp (prawns) mixed with chicken, chili peppers and peanuts. If noodles are used instead of rice the dish becomes babmi goreng.

NASTURTIUM A plant belonging to the watercress family. The blossoms (flowers) and leaves are edible, but not the root. Nasturtium seeds and buds are pickled like capers.

NAVY BEAN (HARICOT BEAN) Navy (haricot) beans belong to the kidney bean family, and are one of the most widely eaten pulses in the world today purchased in cans as a saving in fuel and time.

The variety Soissons has been favored in France for centuries as part of the traditional cassoulet. In America, navy beans are processed and used for baked beans.

Navy beans are available dried, or canned in brine for convenience.

NEAPOLITAN SLICE A layered pistachio, strawberry and chocolate ice cream cake. It is shaped in an oblong pan (tin) lined with baking parchment for easy removal. It is served cut in thick slices.

NECTARINE (Fr. BRUGNON) A delicious fruit sometimes incorrectly believed to be a cross between a plum and a peach because it has the skin of a plum and the stone of a peach.

NÈGRE EN CHEMISE A small chocolate cake or mousse covered with whipped cream and dark chocolate.

NEUFCHÂTEL CHEESE A French cream cheese produced in Neufchâtel in the Bray region of France.

NEW ZEALAND SPINACH, SUMMER SPINACH A native leaf vegetable of New Zealand and Australia it is best

N

cooked without water, drained, rinsed and reheated with butter.

NEWBURG (À LA) An American lobster dish featured at the Delmonico restaurant in New York in the early part of this century. It was made popular in almost every restaurant in the world by the great chef Escoffier.

The dish consists of a sauce with Sherry, cream, egg yolks, fish stock and the coral and liver of the lobster. It has become a classic worth keeping.

NIACIN *See Nicotinic acid.*

NIÇOISE (À LA) A style of cooking with local Nice products, primarily olives, anchovies, capers, tomatoes and garlic. It is greatly influenced by Italian gastronomy and heritage.

NICOTINIC ACID, NIACIN Once called Vitamin B3, its food sources are liver, kidneys, oily fish, milk, pulses, eggs, bran and peanuts. A deficiency of nicotinic acid causes pellagra.

NIGELLA The aromatic seeds can be used as a seasoning for soups or cakes.

NITRATE *See Saltpeter.*

NITROGEN One of the elements and part of the amino acids, nitrogen is found in leguminous plants (members of the pea family) which are rich in protein. Nitrogen is also an element in the flesh of land and sea animals.

In the so called vegetarian sources of protein nitrogen is found in all cereals, nuts, pulses as well as in eggs and milk products.

Liquid nitrogen is used in commercial food freezing.

NOISETTE 1) Potatoes scooped into balls with a Parisian knife.
2) A cut of lamb taken from the loin or best end minus the bone.

Typical dishes: Noisette d'agneau grillé aux fonds d'artichaut, noisette d'agneau aux épinards en branche.

NOIX 1) French for walnut.
2) A butcher's term for a cut from the round roast (topside) of veal or beef.

Typical dishes: Noix de veau aux endives, noix de veau braisé à la bourgeoise.

NONSTICK COOKWARE This is made possible by special coatings that are applied to pans to prevent foods sticking. Non-stick frying pans are especially useful as they eliminate the need to use fat for frying

NOODLE The Chinese invented noodles but they were popularized by the Italians as pasta. As well as being made in China, noodles are made in Japan and south-east Asia from many types of starches, such as wheat, buckwheat, yam, soybean, rice flour, potato flour, rice and mung bean, which is used for cellophane noodles.

Basic wheat flour noodle dough
The same dough can be used for making ravioli.

4 cups/1lb/450g bread (strong)
flour
1 tsp salt
4 eggs, beaten
1 tbsp olive oil
1 tbsp lukewarm water

Mix the flour and salt together in a bowl. Add the eggs, olive oil and water and knead the dough until smooth, about 10 minutes.

Roll the dough into a ball. Cover and let rest for 1 hour.

Divide the dough into 4 pieces and roll each piece to a paper-thin rectangle. Cut the rectangles into ribbons. Separate the ribbons.

Let the ribbons dry on a clean towel on a tray until brittle, this will take several hours.

Fresh pasta cooks within a few minutes in gently boiling water.

Variations
1) To make green pasta, add green spinach juice instead of the water.

2) To make red pasta add tomato juice instead of the water.

NORI A Japanese variety of laver.

NORMANDY One of the most celebrated regions in France, particularly well-known for its dairy products and seafood dishes.

Typical dishes: Sole à la Normande, tripe à la mode de Caen, marmite à la Dieppoise, poulet à la Normande, faisan aux pommes et Calvados.

NORWAY HADDOCK *See Redfish.*

NOUGAT A candy (sweet) made with boiled sugar and egg whites and usually containing nuts or candied fruits. Brown nougat is a type of caramel with nuts.

NOUVELLE CUISINE Nouvelle cuisine sprung to life in the 'sixties and remained a very popular style of eating for about a decade and a half.

Nouvelle cuisine totally rejected the complicated and indigestible dishes

N

loaded with fat and starchy thickeners that are no longer suitable for the health-conscious generation of people more educated and aware of the risk of heart diseases.

The new gourmets espoused authenticity, simplicity and freshness, and preferred naming their dishes using descriptive titles rather that the pomposity of calling a dish by the name of a personality otherwise unconnected with that particular dish or food.

The old-fashioned chefs and many of the 'old school' uphold the principle that chemistry, medicine and dietetics are essential parts of haute cuisine, and believe that a greater understanding of science can help in improving the general standard of cookery.

Nouvelle cuisine advocated cooking vegetables quickly, a practice supported by dietitians because it retains maximum nutritional value and taste. Asian cooks have practiced this for centuries.

Elegant food artistically presented, as done by nouvelle cuisine chefs, is fine to a point as long as the food is nutritious and healthy. Some cooks, however, seemed to miss the point of nouvelle cuisine and were instead motivated by self-promotion.

Sadly, it is only too easy for the pretentious chefs to become ridiculous in their efforts to surprise, provoke, and stimulate jaded palates.

Good cooking will always draw its inspiration from well-devised recipes that have been tasted and developed by generations of gourmets. True gastronomes will remain faithful to the classic dishes and to what is simple and harmonious.

Life must go on and while accepting the craftsmanship of the new generation we must not forsake the great chefs, who have spent more time in the kitchen than the new cooks who have hardly had time enough to learn their craft in depth.

NUT Any large fruit with a hard shell and edible kernel is called a nut. A great number of nuts are used commercially for various purposes, principally as food or a source of oil.

Many of the edible species such as pecan, Brazil, walnut, coconut, pistachio and almond are rich in fat, while others such as chestnuts and water chestnuts are rich in carbohydrates.

In cooking nuts are used in confectionery, desserts, cakes, cookies (biscuits) and snacks.

The flavor of most nuts is intensified and improved by toasting, or frying and salting for snacks. *See also individual varieties of nuts.*

NUTMEG (Fr. MUSCADE) A nut which is a pleasant spice. It is grated and used in rice or milk puddings, and over greens and potato purées.

NUTRIENT A substance in foods that provides nourishment, which supplies building materials and energy for the synthesis and maintenance of living matter. The nutrients needed by humans are protein, carbohydrates, fat, minerals and vitamins, all taken in the proper proportions.

OATCAKE A cake made with fine oats, butter and water, shaped into a circle then cut in triangular shapes and baked, or cooked on a griddle. It is also known also as havercake in the north of England.

OATMEAL Ground dried oats that are produced in three grades, coarse, medium and small. Oatmeal is usually made into porridge for breakfast and served with milk or cream and salt, or sugar or honey according to taste.

OATS (Fr. AVOINE) Oats are the seeds of a cereal of which there are many varieties. Oats are used for porridge, oatcakes, flapjacks and cakes such as parkin. Oat flour is used for griddle cakes.

OBESITY A condition caused by over-eating and lack of exercise or by faulty hormones. Overweight may precipi-

O

tate gout, diabetes and heart disease.

This is the reason why the nouvelle cuisine was created, to cook with less fat and sugar to produce better diets.

O'BRIEN POTATOES An Irish dish of potatoes fried with onions and bell peppers in the best Irish butter.

The name O'Brien comes from one of the ancient kings who ruled the regions of Ireland before it was invaded by Vikings, Normands and English.

The descendants of this king still live at Dromoland Castle, now converted into a luxurious hotel producing some of the finest food in Ireland.

OCTOPUS (Fr. POULPE) A mollusk that is related to squid and cuttlefish.

The younger the better for tenderness; young octopus are eaten raw by the Japanese but are more often pickled and lightly poached.

The eight tentacles and the body are edible but the eyes, mouth and entrails are discarded. The ink sac contains a black liquid that can be used to color and flavor dishes such as fish soups, pasta and stews.

Prepared fresh and frozen octopus has become quite easily available.

OFFAL (Am. VARIETY MEATS) Variety meats (offal) are the edible parts and some extremities of an animal which are removed before the carcass is dissected. They are divided into white and red meats:

RED VARIETY MEATS include the kidneys. heart, liver, tongue, lungs, and spleen.

WHITE VARIETY MEATS (offal) includes bone marrow, animelles (testicles), brain, mesentery (the membrane which holds the intestines together), feet, sweetbreads, stomach and head.

Tripe and the intestines are also used in many countries.

The pig provides the most variety meats (offal), and cows provide a good return with cow's heels, tripe and kidney. Veal variety meats are more delicate .

All the variety meats are used as gastronomic meals, especially kidneys, sweetbreads and liver. Sheep and calves brains are much prized.

OILS Oils used in cooking include coconut, groundnut (peanut), olive, palm nut, corn, sesame, sunflower and walnut to name but a few.

Oils should not be exposed to heat, light or air for long as they deteriorate due to oxydation. Keep them covered in a cool, dark place. *See also Fats and oils, Volatile oils.*

OILY FISH A category which includes herrings anchovies, shad, sardines, whitebait, mackerel, bonito, tuna, swordfish, salmon and trout.

Oily fish can be smoked for flavor and preservation, and they can be canned in brine or savory sauces.

Oily fish are best suited to broiling (grilling) on account of their richness. Use only the best quality fish, especially whole fish such as herrings, trout and sardines. Make sure also to oil the bars of the broiler (grill) rack to prevent the fish from sticking and being damaged.

Small fish should be broiled quickly. Larger fish are cooked at the highest heat to seal the outside, then the fish should be cooked more slowly, and basted regularly with a little oil and lemon juice.

Finally dust the fish with seasoned flour, shake off the excess, then coat the fish on both sides with oil.

The best sauce to serve with broiled oily fish is tartare sauce.

OKRA, GUMBO, LADIES FINGERS (Fr. BAMIA) The unripe fruit of a tropical plant that is used as a vegetable.

Okra is the chief ingredient in the dish called 'gumbo' a soup-stew that can be made of fish or chicken, and oysters. The tender pods can be cooked gently in butter, or boiled in salted water for 8 minutes.

Okra and corn casserole
8oz/225g okra, trimmed and sliced
2 tbsp oil
1 onion, chopped
2 garlic cloves, chopped
1 large tomato, skinned, seeded and
  chopped
½ green chili pepper, seeded and
  chopped
2¼ cups/18fl oz/500 ml water or
  chicken stock
8oz/225g okra, trimmed and sliced
⅔ cup/8oz/225g corn kernels
salt and pepper

Blanch the okra in boiling water for 2 minutes. Drain well.

Heat the oil in a frying pan and fry the onion for 2 minutes.

Add the garlic, tomato, chili pepper and water or stock. Bring to a boil and mix in the okra and corn. Boil for 12 minutes.

Season and serve in a deep plate.

OLIVE A fruit that is cultivated mainly around the Mediterranean for its precious oil and is also pickled in brine.

O

Green olives, which are less ripe than black olives, can be pitted and stuffed with red bell peppers or anchovies.

Olives are served with cocktails or used as garnish for many dishes.

OLLA-PRODIDA One of the richest stews in Spanish cookery made with several types of meat and poultry, and garbanzo beans (chickpeas).

OMELET (Fr. OMELETTE) The name comes from the Latin ovamelita, giving by elimination the word omelitta, and then finally omelet.

Eggs for omelets should be well beaten, cooked quickly, stirred two or three times and served fluffy and neatly folded with pointed ends. The center should be creamy and soft. Nothing is worse than an overdone, rubbery omelet.

The filling may either be placed on the top of the omelet, with a little gash in the center of the omelet, around the omelet, or inside it before the omelet is folded. A cordon of sauce can be poured round the omelet.

COUNTRY OMELET also known as paysanne or Spanish omelet is made with potatoes and onions, left flat and cooked on both sides like a thick pancake.

SOUFFLÉ OMELET is made by beating the egg whites separately then folding them into the egg yolks. The omelet will puff up on being cooked, first over a burner before being folded and transferred to a baking dish to finish cooking in the oven.

This is a more spectacular type of omelet; it is often stuffed with strawberries and flamed with brandy or rum.

Literally hundreds of different fillings can be used for omelets.

Typical dishes: Omelette soufflée au foie gras, omelette baveuse aux asperges, omelette au homard sauce Américaine, omelette aux mousserons, omelette surprise aux fraises.

Chili frittata
A Mexican-style flat omelet popular as a snack, and often served with a tomato and avocado salad.

4 tbsp oil
8oz/225g goatfish, red mullet or
*   bream fillets cut in small pieces*
1 large potato, peeled, washed and
*   grated*
1 small onion, chopped
1 tbsp coriander, chopped
1 green chili pepper, chopped
2 tbsp olive oil
6 eggs, beaten

O

½ *cup/2oz/50g smoked cheese,
 grated*

Heat the oil and fry the fish, potato, onion, coriander and chili pepper until cooked through, about 5 minutes. Remove from the pan.

In a clean 6in/15cm omelet pan, heat the olive oil then add the beaten eggs. Stir a few times and when it begins to set add the fish and vegetable mixture. Sprinkle over the grated cheese.

Place the pan under a preheated broiler (grill) to brown the top. Turn out on a platter and divide into triangular pieces.

ONGLET A French cut of beef that is equivalent to the flank. It is a cheap cut taken from the small muscles joined by an elastic membrane. It makes an acceptable steak when the skin is removed and the steak has been beaten with a meat bat.

ONION (Fr. OIGNON) Onions have been the staple food of the country farm worker for centuries; eat bread, cheese and onion and you will be healthy.

There are many types of onions, such as scallions (spring onions) and Spanish onions. Red onions can be fried, sweetened with sugar and made extra tart with vinegar to bring back the red color and produce a very tasty sweet and sour accompaniment.

Onions are used as flavorings in stews, soups and casseroles, Cornish pasties, onion tarts and pizzas.

Boiled stuffed onions are a nutritious dish for vegetarians when the onions are filled with rice, mushrooms or nuts and cheese. The famous soubise sauce served with veal contains onion purée. Onion soup glazed with grated cheese is a very stimulating appetizer. *See also Shallot.*

Typical dishes: Onion farci en duxelle, tarte aux oignons Alsacienne.

ONO *See Wahoo.*

ORANGE Oranges grow in semi-tropical and tropical countries and today there are huge orange groves in North Africa, Israel, Florida and California. The technology of plant development has produced high quality fruits without seeds (pips) and even sweeter than ever.

Citrus fruits that are orange hybrids include clementines, tangerines and satsumas.

Orange juice is a source of Vitamin C and so is an ideal morning drink.

Orange segments are used in salads and as a garnish for many dishes such

O

as duck with orange sauce. and baked ham.

Typical dishes: Caramelized oranges, duck with orange sauce

ORANGE BLOSSOM (FLOWER) The orange flower is very fragrant and the volatile oil made from it is used in the perfume industry.

However, the oil is also diluted and sold as orange flower water for use in confectionery, desserts and in particular in a wide variety of Middle Eastern pastries to which it adds a delicate aroma.

ORANGEADE A diluted orange juice mixture with carbonated (soda) water.

ORGANIC COMPOUND A natural substance containing living cells, such as fertilizer which is made up of organic matter — manure, compost and natural phosphates, pulverized rock, wood ash and bird droppings.

Organic farmers carefully mix and rotate their crops by alternating demanding crops and plants which need weeding, with those that enrich the soil, such as leguminous plants which are nitrogen fixers.

ORGEAT This is a syrup made from almonds.

ORLEANS VINEGAR A superior French vinegar made by the traditional slow method which involves maturing the vinegar in wooden barrels.

ORMER *See Abalone.*

OSMAZOME The meat and poultry flavor extracted from the flesh, skin and bones during the cooking process.

OSMOSIS The diffusion of two miscible solutions through a semi-permeable membrane to equalize their concentration without rupturing the membrane. An example is found in the process of candying fruits and peels. (*See page 79*).

OSTRICH The biggest African bird laying the biggest egg. The flesh is treated like beef and can be very succulent when braised.

The eggs can be eaten in omelets or made into cakes. Ostrich are now farmed commercially.

OUKHA A Russian broth made with strained fish bones and vegetables, then garnished with chopped eggs and caviar.

OVENS A variety of ovens are available, including microwave ovens, and conduction and steam injecting ovens for bread.

All modern ovens should be fitted with improved temperature control.

OX-GALL A sac in the liver that contains bitter bile which is used for absorption and digestion.

Great care must be taken to remove this black or dark greenish sac from chicken liver as bursting it would make the liver inedible.

OX TAIL The tail of beef is trimmed of the fat and cut into small pieces. This is stewed with carrots and onions in wine and stock for three hours.

Ox tail can be served as a main course, or made into a delicious meat soup; the meat and vegetable are puréed in the cooking liquid as a rapid short-cut. But, to have the meat soft and easy to remove from the bone, the cooking process has to take a long time in a low oven.

OX TONGUE The tongue is usually best pickled in brine and soaked overnight. It is boiled for 2 hours and the outer skin is removed.

Tongue is served with piquant brown sauces.

OXALIC ACID A simple acid in foods that is insoluble with calcium and magnesium in the digestive system, rendering these minerals unavailable to the body. Rhubarb leaves contain toxic quantities.

OXYGEN One of the elements contained in the air. Oxygen can cause changes leading to discoloration in potatoes, avocados and fruits such as apples particularly after cutting, and rancidity in fats through the activity of the enzyme oxidase.

OYSTER (Fr. HUÎTRE) A bivalve mollusk. There are over 50 varieties of oysters around the word. Those grown in cool climates are much finer-flavored than the coarser Pacific and Portuguese oysters, which are canned in brine or smoked and best used for sauces and stews.

In the United States, wild oysters are still dredged by the bushel in the Gulf of Mexico and the Chesapeake Bay. Native northwest oysters include the Pacific and the tiny Olympia.

Regional eastern oyster names include Virginia, Blue Point, Cape Cod and Chinoteague.

The main type of oyster now grown in Europe is the flat, or 'native', oyster. These are seasonal, spawning during the summer months from May until

O

August, when they are not for sale, besides at this time the flesh is milky and not at its best.

The best French 'natives' are Belons and Marennes oysters and the best English ones are Colchesters and Whitstables. They are in season when there is an 'r' in the month.

The ancient Greeks in Athens counted their votes with oyster shells. From the Latin word for oyster — ostrea — comes the word ostracism; God forbid that we ban such delicious bivalves from our table!

Some large oysters found in Pacific waters contain pearls, but the only pearl you may find on your plate is caviar; an oyster served on its shell coated with Russian caviar is a super hors d'oeuvre.

Buying and storing oysters

When buying oysters, make sure that the shells are firmly shut. If any shells are open slightly, tap them sharply and discard any oysters that do not close immediately.

Although best eaten when very fresh on the day of purchase, oysters will keep for 5 or even 7 days if kept cool, loosely covered with fresh seaweed or a damp cloth, and placed in the bottom of the refrigerator with the flat shell uppermost to retain their juices.

How to open oysters

Hold a folded cloth in your left hand. Place the oyster in it and insert an oyster knife between the two shells where they join, passing them lightly with the fingers of the left hand. The blade not the point goes between the shells.

Then insert the point of your knife by rotating the blade and lifting it up against the top shell to loosen the oyster flesh. Scrape the inside of the top shell, then raise it and pull it away. Take care not to cut into the head of the oyster. The knife should not touch the flesh but rotate in a scraping motion across the top shell.

Oysters are best eaten raw, served cold on crushed ice with lemon juice of a spiced vinegar dressing made with shallots. They can also be served hot. Some chefs broil (grill) oysters on skewers with bacon as 'another way of spoiling some good oysters' according to Brillat Savarin many years ago.

Typical dishes: Angels on horseback, fritot d'huîtres aux amandes, oyster chowder.

Oysters in champagne

24 oysters

Sauce

*¼ cup/2oz/50g sweet (unsalted)
  butter*

⅓ small carrot, cut in thin strips
1 small piece of fennel, cut in thin
   strips
1 small piece of white of leek, cut in
   thin strips 1in/2.5 cm long
juice of 1 lemon
⅔ cup/5floz/150ml dry Champagne
I tsp mint, chopped
2 egg yolks
6 tbsp heavy (double) cream
2 tsp cornstarch (cornflour)

To make the sauce, heat the butter.
Add the carrot, fennel and leek and fry
for 1 minute.

Stir in the lemon juice, Champagne
and mint. Boil gently for 4 minutes.

Strain the vegetables; reserve the liquid and vegetables.

Stir together the egg yolks, cream
and cornstarch (cornflour).

Slowly pour in the reserved liquid.
Boil until cleared and thickened, this
should take about 3 minutes.

Open the oysters and strain their liquid into the sauce.

Put 2 oysters in each deep oyster
shell. Add some of the reserved vegetables. Cover with the sauce. Put the
oysters under a preheated broiler
(grill) for 2 minutes.

Oyster sauce
Serve with stir-fried fish strips.

1¼ cups/½ pint/300ml white wine
   sauce
4 fresh or smoked oysters

Process the sauce with the oysters in
a blender. Heat through.

OYSTER PLANT *See Salsify.*

P

PACKAGING Packaging can be a method of preservation in itself, and indeed faulty packaging will undo all that a food processor has attempted to accomplish by the most meticulous of manufacturing processes.

Packaging materials for foods include aluminum, glass bottles, jars, rigid, semi-rigid and flexible plastics, paper and laminates, or multi-layers which may combine paper, plastic and foil to achieve properties unattainable with any single component.

The essential requirement of food packaging material is that it is non-toxic, yet compatible with the specific food that it contains. Also that it provides protection against moisture, fat, gas and in some cases light.

Furthermore packaging must be tamper-proof, but still easily opened and poured from if by the consumernecessary. Finally it must be light and easy to dispose of.

PAELLA A Spanish saffron-flavored rice dish containing shrimp (prawns), chicken, peas, bell peppers and garlic. It can also include lobsters, scallops, mussels, chorizo sausage or squid.

In modern cookery paella is sometimes modified by adding too many foods that are too expensive.

PAKORA An Indian savory fritter.

PALATE The human palate is the instrument which assess es the taste of food in the same way as the nose responds to aromas. The effects of contact with food can remain for some time after the food has left the mouth.

There is a wide range of words to describe a variety reactions to food qualities: solid, soft, crisp, blunt, thin, heavy, dry, moist, rough, rubbery, smooth, syrupy, sticky, sharp,and above all, hot and cold, sweet and sour.

A good example is of tasting fresh cream. The words to describe the sensation are unctuous, mellow and rich, whereas if the same cream is whipped the predominent sensation changes to smoothness.

The sensation of heat is experienced when eating fresh ginger, radishes, watercress and chili peppers, coolness is felt when eating very juicy, acid fruits and the sensation of heaviness is apparent with fat, oily or greasy food. The viscosity of syrupy liquids gives a different, weighty sensation. There is also the biting touch, the feel of teeth crunching and chewing.

With bread, the feelings can be crisp, soft, dry, moist or spongy, whereas meat can be chewy, tough and even rubbery.

PALM OIL Oil extracted from the palm tree. It is used for making hard margarines and soap.

PALM SUGAR Sugar obtained from the sap of the date palm genus *Phoenix dactylifera*. It is called date sugar and jaggery.

PALMIER A folded sweet pastry made with puff paste (pastry) and sugar.

PALMITIC A wax fatty acid found in palm oil and many other natural saturated fats.

PAMPEROLADA This Italian sauce is made of bread, garlic and water.

PAN BAGNA The name of this Provençal filled bread rolled means 'bathed bread'.

The roll, or a small loaf, is soaked with olive oil from the filling, which can include anchovies, black olives, tomatoes and haricots verts (French beans).

PANCAKE A thin, flat fried cake made from a batter of flour, eggs and milk or beer. Wheat flour is usually used, but buckwheat flour is used for Russian blinis and Breton crêpes.

Pancakes must be as thin as possible. 2¼ cups/18fl oz/500ml batter will make 12-16 pancakes in a 5in/12.5cm omelet pan.

Chinese pancakes are made with a dough that contains 10 percent fat. The dough is shaped into small balls and rolled 2 balls at a time to a diameter of 4in/10cm.

The pancake is then baked or cooked on a griddle. They are kept hot in a wooden basket covered with a towel. Chinese pancakes are the garnish for Peking duck.

PANCETTA A type of bacon made in Italy. It can be eaten raw, unlike the British and American versions of bacon.

PANCREAS The most important functions of the pancreas are to produce pancreatic juice to help in the digestive process and insulin which is vital for the digestion of starches and sugars.

P

When the pancreas is not working properly the serious condition of *Diabetes mellitus* occurs. *See also Sweetbread.*

PANDOWDY An sweet apple batter pudding flavored with spices. It is baked until well puffed up then dusted with confectioners' (icing) sugar and cinnamon before serving.

PANETTONE A rich Italian yeast cake studded with candied peel and seedless raisins and flavored with lemon. It is baked in a cylindrical mold. A perfect cake to be enjoyed at any time of the day.

PANTIN PIE A pie made without a mold. The pastry is wrapped around the filling and baked on a baking sheet. Fillings include salmon and egg, pheasant and pork, and venison and pork.

PANTOTHENIC ACID An important member of the Vitamin B complex. It occurs in rice, bran and plant and animal tissues.

Pantothenic acid is essential for the growth of healthy cells.

PAPAIN Enzyme extracted from paw-paws and used as a meat tenderizer.

PAPILOTTE (EN) Cooking of individual portions of fish, meat, or poultry in a package. Herbs, vegetables or wine can be included for extra flavor.

The Chinese and Japanese use the method of wrapping fish in banana leaves or alginate skins, and steam them. Aromatic mushrooms and potatoes can also be wrapped in pastry then in foil and baked in the ashes of a bonfire.

But the real papillote of the French chi-chi showmanship cuisine is exemplified by the effect and raison d'être of this method.

Fold a large sheet of foil or parchment paper (greaseproof paper) in two and cut into a heart-shape with scissors. Fry a goatfish (red mullet) stuffed with mushrooms quickly on both sides then wrap in a slice of ham and place in the center of the foil or paper heart with some dill and fennel.

Fold the foil or paper over the fish and twist the edges together to seal. Cook the package in the oven and within 10 minutes the hot air inside the wrapping will blow the package up like a balloon.

When presented to the guests, there is a round of applause as the balloon is burst or opened with the fish — exuding a wonderful perfume of aromatic herbs.

PAPETON A Provençal eggplant (aubergine) custard baked in a mold and served with tomato sauce.

PAPPADUMS *See Poppadums.*

PAPRIKA A variety of red bell pepper grown in Hungary for making the red spice of the same name. It varies from mild to very hot.

Typical dishes: Veal goulash, chicken paprika.

PARATHA An Indian bread that is shallow-fried or cook on a griddle.

PARCHMENT PAPER A heavy grease- and moisture-resistant paper used for lining can pans (tins) and baking trays or cooking food en papillote.

PARFAIT 1) An ice cream of egg yolks and saturated syrup flavored with coffee, chocolate or nougatine.

2) Pure liver pâté, especially of foie gras.

In French, parfait literally means perfect, but in any form of art nothing should ever be described as such because it can never be achieved, even in gastronomy.

PARMA HAM The true prosciutto and one of the best hams in the world. The best brand comes from Lanhirano. Parma ham is cured in brine and air-dried without being smoked.

PARMESAN CHEESE A hard Italian cheese used with pasta and as a garnish for many Italian vegetable soups such as minestrone.

PARSLEY (Fr. PERSIL) A culinary herb of which there are many varieties, such as Hamburg, common or curly-leaved parsley, and flat-leaved or Continental parsley, which is considered to have the best flavor.

Parsley should be washed and well drained before it is chopped. It is used in composite butter pastes, with garlic or shallots in duxelles and in bouquet garnis and can be cooked like spinach. It is widely used as a simple garnish for many dishes.

Parsely has a stimulating and diuretic effect.

PARSNIP (Fr. PANAIS) A white biennial root vegetable. It has an unusual and quite sweet taste.

The best way to cook parsnips is to blanch and then deep-fry them, or roast them like potatoes. Parsnips after cooking can also be mixed with an equal weight of mashed potatoes and made into croquettes.

P

PARTRIDGE (Fr. PERDREAU) A member of the grouse family that is considered one of the finest game birds. There are two main species, the grey partridge, which is traditional in Britain, and the red-legged partridge, which is considered inferior.

PASHKA A Russian cream cheese dessert decorated with candied fruits and nuts that is served at Easter.

PASSION FRUIT (Fr. FRUIT DE LA PASSION) A fruit much over-rated by snobbish food enthusiasts. It is grown in the West Indies, Kenya, Zimbabwe and South Africa.

The fruit is ripe when the skin becomes wrinkled. It is usually eaten raw but can be puréed and used for sherbets (sorbets) and sauces. It is a traditional ingredient in rum punch and fruit drinks.

PASTA An important part of Italian cuisine, pasta is made from durum wheat flour, water and sometimes eggs.

Pasta should be boiled in salted water until 'al dente', just tender; the timing depends on the thickness of the pasta. Small pasta shapes take only 3 to 5 minutes to cook, thin spaghetti should be cooked for 10 minutes but the thicker macaroni and ravioli take 14 minutes.

Pasta can be served simply with butter and grated cheese, or with pesto sauce, tomato-flavored sauces, or a meaty sauce like Bolognese. *See also Noodle, and individual types of pasta.*

Bell pepper sauce for pasta
1 tbsp olive oil
2 tbsp mixed red and yellow bell peppers, cut into thin strips
1 clove garlic, chopped
1¼ cups/½ pint/300ml stock or velouté
1 tbsp tomato paste (purée)
3 white mushrooms, sliced
salt and pepper
juice of ½ lemon
1 tbsp basil, chopped

Heat the oil and stir-fry the bell peppers for 4 minutes Add the garlic for 30 seconds, then stir in the stock or sauce, tomato paste (purée) and mushrooms. Boil for 10 minutes.

Season to taste and add the lemon juice and basil.

PASTEURIZATION Partial sterilization. It involves heating to a temperature sufficiently high to kill bacteria but not their spores, at 145°F/65°C for 30 minutes or 161°F/72°C for 15 seconds,

P

then rapid cooling at 40°F/50°C. The later method, called high temperature short time (HTST) has less adverse effects on the flavor of the product.

PASTICCIO DI MACCHERONI ALLA POPE
This pontifical pasta dish must have been blessed by every pope of the holy city of Rome.

It is made of cooked ground (minced) beef mixed with a tomato sauce and pitted black olives, covered with a layer of cooked short macaroni and an egg sauce. The dish is sprinkled with grated Parmesan cheese and baked until golden brown.

PASTRAMI Cold pickled, smoked brisket of beef highly seasoned with spices and garlic.

Pastrami can be served as part of a cold buffet, or used for sandwiches or snacks.

PASTRIES There are several kind of pastries divided in two main categories, savory and sweet, and short and flaky.

Typical dishes: Apple boats, pretorias, Yorkshire curd tartlets, Danish pastries, almond tartlets, apple frangipane tartlets (filled with apples and coated with frangipane cream), custard tart, fruit tartlets.

Savory pie dough (short crust pastry)
¾ cup/6oz/175g butter or
  margarine
2 ½ cups/10oz/300g all-puprose
  (plain) flour
1 pinch of dry mustard powder
½ tsp salt
1 large egg, beaten

Cut the butter or margarine into the flour, mustard and salt until the mixture resembles crumbs. Stir in the egg. Mix but do not knead like bread. Roll the dough on a floured board or counter (work top). Chill for 30 minutes before using.

Sweet pie dough (short crust pastry)
Used for cookies (biscuits), shortbread, fruit tarts and Bakewell tart.

⅔ cup/5oz/150g unsalted butter
⅓ cup/2oz/50g confectioners' (icing)
  sugar
1 large egg, beaten
1 pinch salt
2 cups/8oz/225g all-purpose
  (plain) flour

Beat the butter and sugar together. Stir in the egg and mix well. Add the salt and flour. Shape the dough delicately into a ball, sprinkle with flour and refrigerate for 30 minutes.

P

Puff paste (puff pastry)
Use for millefeuilles, apple turnovers, Eccles cakes and cheese straws.

⅓ cup/3oz/75g margarine
4 cups/1 lb/450g bread (strong)
* flour*
½ tsp salt
1¼ cups/ ½ pint/300ml water
1 tsp lemon juice
1¼ cups/14oz/400g unsalted butter

Cut the margarine into the flour and salt to resemble crumbs.

Stir in the water and lemon juice and knead the dough. Let stand for 15 minutes.

Roll the dough to a rectangule. Cut the butter into slices and cover three quarters of the pastry. Fold over the quarter to cover the butter. Complete by folding again. There should be 3 layers of pastry enclosing the butter.

Repeat this process at 15 minute intervals, each time giving 2 turns. Refrigerate the paste before using.

Hot-water crust pie dough (pastry)
This pie dough is used for traditional British pies (*See recipe page 289*), usually pork or game, that have a tightly-packed meat filling and are served cold. If lard is available, substitute it for 2 tbsp/1oz/25g of the margarine.

This recipe will produce enough pie pastry for two x 18oz/500g pies with a little over for pastry trimmings to cut decorative items like leaves.

scant 1¼ cups/9fl oz/225ml water
½ cup/4oz/100g margarine
4 cups/1lb/450g all purpose
* (plain) flour*

Boil the water, margarine and salt until the margarine has melted. Sift the flour into a bowl and stir the hot liquid. Beat together to make a dough. Knead well on a floured board or counter (work top).

Let cool then chill for 1 hour. Use as ordinary pie (pastry) dough.

PÂTÉ A cooked mixture of liver and raw forcemeat served cold as a spread if smooth or sliced if coarse.

Basic liver pâté
Any type of liver can be used.

½ cup/4oz/100g liver, chopped
2 tbsp brandy
¼ cup/2fl oz/50ml oil
1 onion, chopped
1 garlic clove, chopped (optional)
1 cup/8oz/225g pork sausagemeat
3 tbsp heavy (double) cream
1 tsp salt

½ tsp black pepper
½ tsp mixed spice
1 egg, beaten
6 slices bacon without rinds

Serves 8

Marinate the liver in the brandy for 1 hour.

Heat the oil and fry the onion without browning for 30 seconds.

Grind (mince) the liver, onion and garlic with the sausagemeat. Add the seasoning, spice, egg and cream. Line the bottom of an earthenware terrine with 3 bacon slices and fill it with the liver mixture. Cover with the remaining bacon and a lid.

Cook in a water bath in an oven at 350° F/180°C/gas mark 4 for 1¼ hours.

Let cool and chill overnight.

Variation

For a smooth mousse-like pâté, grind (mince) the cooked pâté and then add ¼ cup/4fl oz/100ml heavy (double) cream, whipped. Chill again and use immediately.

PATHOGEN An organism that causes disease.

PATNA RICE A long-grained variety of rice which is four or five times as long as it is wide. It comes from Bengal.

Patna rice cooks in boiling water in 15-17 minutes.

PATTY-PAN A small, round cup-shaped summer squash with a scalloped edge. It is yellow-green in color.

The best way to cook patty-pan squash is whole with a little butter and lemon juice.

PAUPIETTE A thin slice of meat, poultry or fish spread with a savory stuffing and rolled up. It can be secured with string or wooden toothpicks (cocktail sticks). In the United States it may also be called a 'bird' and in Britain an 'olive'.

A delicious version can be made with a slice of salmon and a raw mousseline of white fish.

Typical dishes: Paupiette de volaille aux champignons, paupiette de dindon aux châtaignes, paupiette de saumon aux fines herbes.

PAVLOVA An Australian dessert of a crisp meringue with a soft center, filled with whipped cream and fruit such as strawberries.

PAWPAW (Fr. PAPAYA) A pear-shaped fruit that is native to Malaysia and is now cultivated in other tropical countries, America and the Caribbean

P

islands. It contains grey-black seeds that are not eaten.

Pawpaw are cooked when green, and served cold as a fruit when ripe. They can also be served like avocados with shrimp (prawns) or other fillings, grated and served in salads, or made into a purée or even cold soups.

PAYASAM A southern Indian dessert of milk simmered with cashew nuts, cereals, sugar and seedless raisins.

PAYSANNE (À LA) A traditional French cooking style, with root vegetables such as onions, carrot and turnips.

PEA (Fr. POIS) At the time of Louis XIV the peas were served as a dish fit for the royal table. They were treated with respect, but now are used like potatoes and served as a regular vegetable. However, peas are a good source of vegetable protein and the popularity of vegetarianism may well revive the use of peas in dishes.

In modern cuisine snow peas (mangetout) have taken over from the French petits pois, both of which can be eaten whole. But frozen peas are now universally used as the quickest way of producing a good vegetable — especially when they are flavored with fresh mint leaves and a little sugar.

A delicate purée can also be made with peas, potatoes and scallions (spring onions).

In the north of England, mushy marrow fat peas are traditionally served with fish and chips.

Typical dishes: Potage Clamart, potage Saint Germain.

PEA FLOUR A flour made from the peas. It is used for soups.

PEACH (Fr. PÊCHE) A fruit that grows in many temperate countries including France, Spain, Italy, Greece, parts of India and in California. The French Montreuil peach has white flesh and is more acid than yellow fleshed varieties. Fresh clingstone peaches keep longer than freestone varieties.

Peaches are usually in season from June to August or September.

Peaches are very versatile and the famous Peach Melba created by Escoffier at the Carlton Hotel has done a lot to promote it as a first class dessert. White fleshed peaches are preferred for Peach Melba. New trends in presentation of this dessert have modified it by caging the peach in a web of caramel or spun sugar.

Peaches can be used as a garnish for boiled or baked ham or gammon, duck and pork chops.

PEANUT (Fr. ARACHIDE) The fruit of the arachide, a leguminous plant no way connected with the nut family. Peanuts are good sources of vegetable proteins so should be used in stews, pilaffs and sauces. When toasted they also add a rich flavor.

An excellent dip can be made by grinding toasted peanuts and blending with creamy mashed potatoes.

Toasted peanuts are a snack which children should be encouraged to eat instead of candies (sweets).

Peanuts are ground for their oil, which is used in salad dressings, mayonnaise and for frying.

PEANUT BUTTER A paste made from cooked peanuts, sometimes mixed with salt, oil and sugar. It can be diluted with water or vegetable stock to produce a vegetarian brown sauce.

PEAR (Fr. POIRE) Pears should be fully ripe in order to develop their full flavor and sweetness.

Hard pears are best poached in syrup flavored with strong tea or wine, and served with ice cream and chocolate sauce, or baked in flans.

PEARL BARLEY Barley which has been milled to remove the husk. Pearl barley is used in soups.

Flaked barley are also available for porridge and rich country stews.

PECAN NUT This looks like a walnut and can be made into delicious desserts, cookies (biscuits) and cakes.

Pecan nuts can also be ground and made into paste like almonds.

PECORINO CHEESE A hard Italian cheese made with ewes' milk. It has a more pungent taste than Parmesan.

Pecorino cheese can be grated and used with pasta.

PECTASE The enzyme that converts pectin to pectic acid.

PECTIN A class of natural jellying substances found in many fruits, some vegetables such as split peas and lentils, and the pith of citrus fruit rind. Some fruits are rich in pectin, such as apples, and other have a low pectin content, such as strawberries.

To extract pectin from fruits, the fruit, including any skin and seeds (pips) because they are rich in pectin, must be boiled so the protopectin is broken up and changes into pectin.

The absolute minimum amount of water must be used for boiling the fruit to concentrate the pectin. Hard fruits like crabapples, quinces and

P

apples should be cut in small pieces. The extraction is more complete if acid is present in the fruit, or is added to fruits that do not contain much acid.

In Britain liquid pectin extract and sugar containing pectin can be bought.

PEKING DUCK A Chinese dish preparing by blowing air between the skin and flesh of a duck, like a balloon. The duck is then dipped in salted and sweetened water then hung for 24 hours until the skin is dry.

After this the duck is roasted at a high temperature to make the skin crisp. When cooked, the skin is cut into squares or strips and served with the duck meat wrapped in Chinese pancakes. A sweet and sour sauce and raw scallions (spring onions) are served as accompaniments.

PELLAGRA Nutrional disorder caused by a deficiency of nicotinic acid.

PELMIENI A Russian pasta turnover filled with meat, fish, vegetables or cream cheese. The dough must be kept cool all the time.

Pelmieni come in all shapes from squares to triangles. They are poached in salted water and can be served with sour (soured) cream or lemon flavored meat gravy.

PEMMICAN Powdered dried meat that was originally made by American Indians, who also developed the art of smoking meat and fish.

PENICILLIN A beneficial mold obtained from cereals and used as an antibiotic. It is the mold used to make blue cheeses.

PENNYROYAL A variety of mint that is used as a culinary herb for mint sauce.

PEPERONATA An Italian dish of red and green bell peppers, tomatoes and onions cooked in olive oil. It can be served hot or cold.

PEPERONI A peppery Italian salami made with pork and beef.

PEPINO MELON This sweet fragrant melon grows in California, New Zealand and other tropical regions. It is used in salads or appetizers with smoked fish or ham.

PEPITA Edible pumpkin seeds with the husks removed. They can be served at cocktail parties to be nibbled as a snack in the same way as peanuts.

PEPPER (Fr. POIVRE) A spice and seasoning that is native to tropical Asia.

The principal commercial varieties are Mangalore, Tellichery, Malabar and Alleppy.

BLACK PEPPERCORNS are the unripe berries left to dry and darken.

GREEN PEPPERCORNS are unripe berries. They are available dried, and in cans and jars.

GROUND PEPPER is judged by aroma, color and free-running qualities.

WHITE PEPPERCORNS are the ripened berries with the outer casing removed. The berries are dried, resulting in a less aromatic heat.
See also Pink peppercorns.

PEPPERMINT A variety of garden mint with a strong flavor.

PEPPERPOT SOUP A national Jamaican soup made with salt pork or beef, and shrimp (prawns) with vegetables including yams and spinach or callaloo leaves, and spices and chili peppers cooked in coconut milk.

PEPSIN An enzyme present in the gastric juice that digests proteins. It is usually prepared as a light yellowish powder that has a faint but not disagreeable odor and saline taste. This is used to help people digest protein foods who are unable to do it themselves. It is also used in cheesemaking.

PERCH (Fr. PERCHE) One of the best river fish, and belonging to the same family as bass.
Perch must be scaled and cleaned as soon as they are caught. They can be shallow-fried in butter.

PERIGOURDINE (À LA) A French garnish of truffles to which foie gras is sometimes added. It is named after the region of Perigord famous for truffles and foie gras.

PERIWINKLE (Fr. BERNIQUE) Sea snail of which there are many species of various sizes. They are boiled in the shells and served for the guests to extract the meat with a needle.

PERSIMMON (FR. KAKI) A fruit from a tree that grows best in the southern states of America and Japan. It looks like a large orange-red tomato and has soft flesh. *See also Kaki fruit.*

PESTO, PISTO An Italian paste made with pine nuts, Parmesan cheese, basil, olive oil and garlic. It is used with pasta and in fish soups.

P

8 basil leaves
½ cup/2oz/50g pine nuts
¼ cup/1oz/25g Parmesan cheese
⅔ cup/5fl oz/150ml olive oil
black pepper

Pound the ingredients to a paste.

PETIT FOURS No confectionery is so little understood and appreciated as petits fours. Their production is a testing ground for the artistry and imagination of a pâtissier with knowledge of sugar and chocolate work.

A petit four must be small enough to be eaten in one mouthful.

Petits fours are divided into dry, like cookies (biscuits) and macaroons and glacé, glazed with caramel or fondant.

Petits fours dry can be made in five classes: cookies, meringues, marzipan, puff pastry and short pastry.

Petits fours glacés are grouped as:

DRY petits four with a glaze or
  cream.
CHOUX PASTRY filled and glazed.
GENOESE.
SMALL TARTLETS and nut meringues.

There are three types of petits fours that are not baked:
CARAMELIZED FRUITS
FONDANTS

CANDIES (jellies) like Turkish delight and fruit pastes. The best are made of chocolate and flavored with mint or filled with liqueurs, fondant or nougat.

Petits fours can be served with a decoration of pulled sugar, with blown sugar designs or nougatine sculptures.

A collection of petits fours can be served with a fancy title after coffee as mignardises de dame, friandises or plaisirs d'amour as long as the occasion justifies the title.

Savory petits fours are really canapés and cocktail tit-bits based on the sweet petits fours.

PEZENAS PIE A sweet mutton and kidney pie from the Languedoc region of France. It can be served hot or cold.

PHEASANT (Fr. FAISAN) A feathered game bird which can be prepared like chicken. It has to be matured a little to develop a gamey flavor. The hens are smaller and more delicate than the cock birds. Pheasants can be bred like chicken.

Typical dishes: Faisan à la Normande, chartreuse de faisan.

PHOTOSYNTHESIS The highly complex process by which plants manufacture carbohydrates from atmospheric carbon dioxid, and water in the presence of sunlight.

When light falls upon green plants the greater part of the energy is absorbed by small particles called chloroplasts, which contain a variety of pigments amongst them compounds called chlorophylls.

The cholorophylls transform the energy of the light into chemical energy by a process that is not fully understood but it is known to involve the photolysis of water and the activation of adenosine triphosphate (ATP). The energy-rich ATP subsequently energizes the fixation of the carbon dioxide after a series of reactions, so that sugar molecules are formed.

Animals are unable to fix atmospheric carbon dioxide in this way, so they depend for their carbon on the plants that they eat. Photosynthesis is thus essential to all the higher forms of life, either directly or indirectly.

PHYLO *See Filo.*

PHYSALIS *See Cape gooseberry.*

PICADILLO A popular Mexican way of cooking ground (minced) meat. It is often used as a filling for chili peppers rellenos and empanadas.

PICCALILLI A pickle of mixed vegetables, mainly cucumber, cauliflower and onions, in a characteristic thick yellow mustard sauce.

PICCATA A small Italian veal scallop (escalope) shallow-fried in butter and glazed with Marsala and lemon juice.

PICKLED HERRING Fresh gutted herring packed in salt and used for rollmop herrings, which are marinated in white vinegar, onions and a little sugar and dill.

PICKLED PORK, SALT PORK Pork preserved in brine or kosher (coarse) salt to which 10 percent saltpeter may be added.

PICKLES These include the familiar condiments found in most grocery stores, such as mixed pickles, pickled onions, piccalilli, dill pickles, chow-chow, pickled red cabbage, beets (beetroot) and sweet pickles of fruits such as mango. The preservative ingredient of pickles is vinegar.

It is the crispiness of the vegetables which scores marks in competitions.

Some fruits are pickled in sweet spicy vinegar and used as condiments for oily fish, meat, game or poultry. For example crab apple, pears, peach-

P

es, apricots, plums, melon, and water melon rind, olives and tomatoes.

To make pickles

• Buy or prepare the spiced vinegar according to the recipe 3 weeks ahead. Wrap all the spices in cheesecloth for easier removal.

• Prepare the vegetables: peel onions and garlic; grate or chop cucumber; divide cauliflower into florets; cut root vegetables into slices or chunks; leave small beets (beetroots) whole and dice or slice large ones. Chop or shred vegetables such as cabbage and celery. Prick them with a stainless steel fork or skewer for easier penetration of the vinegar.

• Most vegetables should be soaked in kosher (coarse) salt or a brine made with 8 tbsp/4oz/100g of kosher (coarse) salt per 4⅓ cups/1¾ pints/1 liter of water. Dry-salting is recommended for watery vegetables like cucumber and zucchini (courgettes).

• Leave the vegetables for 24 hours then rinse in running water. Drain.

• Pack the vegetables in sterilized jars leaving a space of 1in/2.5 cm at the top. Fill with spiced vinegar to within ½in/1.2cm of the top.

• Cover and seal the jars with non-reactive lids as soon as they are filled. Store in a cool dark place.

To make sweet fruit pickle

• Use under-ripe fruit and prick with a stainless steel fork or skewer for easier penetration of the vinegar.

• Simmer the fruit in sweet pickling vinegar so it remains crisp.

• Strain the vinegar into another saucepan. Boil for 8 minutes to a syrupy consistency.

• Pack the fruit into hot sterilized jars. Pour in the vinegar to cover. Close with a non-reactive lid and seal.

Pickled red cabbage
*1/½lb/750g red cabbage, cored
  and shredded, washed and
  drained well in a colander
1 red onion, finely chopped
1 small boiled beet (beetroot),
  peeled and finely chopped
1 apple, peeled, cored and grated
1 clove garlic, chopped
2 tbsp brown sugar
1 small red chili pepper (optional)
6 white or pink peppercorns
4⅓ cups/1¾ pints/1 liter red wine
  vinegar*

Makes 4 lb/1.75 kg

Mix all the ingredients in a large non-reacative bowl. Let stand for 1 hour then pack into jars. Cover tightly with non-reactive lids.

Set aside for 2 weeks.

Variation

For pickled white cabbage, replace the red onion with a white onion and a peeled mouli for the beet (beetroot). Use distilled white vinegar and 1 teaspoon of caraway seeds. Omit the chili pepper and use white sugar instead of brown.

PICKLING SPICE A mixture of a number of spices such as mustard seeds, black peppercorns, coriander, cloves, chili peppers and mace added in various proportions when making pickles, chutneys and bottled sauces. Pickling spice can be bought or home made.

PICNIC HAMS Boned shoulder gammons or hams pickled and boiled.

PIE (Fr. PÂTÉ) A pie can be sweet or savory, hot or cold. Generally pies have a pastry covering, but in America pies can have a pie dough (pastry) base.

Savory pies may be covered with mashed potatoes or they can include pasta. *See also Meat pies, recipe on page 289, Pastries.*

PIEROGI A miniature Russian pastry filled with ground (minced) pork, cream cheese, vegetables, fish or rice. They are baked or fried.

PIG The Chinese and the Romans were probably the first people to use pork extensively in cooking. They developed a complete range of pork products from sausages to cured ham and bacon.

The cottage pig sustained much of rural Britain and Europe for centuries until the Industrial Revolution. It was common for a pig to be kept in the cottage garden, fed on kitchen scraps and fattened on windfall apples from the nearby orchards. The pig was cheap to keep and ready for slaughter at Christmas. A boar's head often had pride of place on the festive table.

Not so long ago the main meal of poor people in Europe often consisted of pork drippings spread on top of thick slices of bread because it was the cheapest and most filling food available for poverty-stricken families who could afford little variety in their diet.

Pigs thrive best in temperate climates and are bred in huge numbers in America, Canada and Russia as well as most European countries.

Most pigs are sold between 6 and 12 months of age, and the majority of pigs are marketed in the winter. Although pork is now available all year round pork dishes tend to be eaten more in the winter than in the summer months.

P

PIGEON (Fr. PIGEONNEAU) Young pigeons, or squab, can be cooked like broilers (small chicken) and either broiled (grilled) or served en cocotte with peas.

They can also be boned, stuffed and wrapped in pastry shaped to their original form and served cold.

PIGEON PEA A pulse that is used dried, either whole or split and polished. Pigeon peas can replace garbanzo beans (chickpeas) and split peas in recipes.

PIKE (Fr. BROCHET) The flesh of the freshwater pike is used for mousselines, fish terrines and quenelles because of its plastic texture.

Typical dishes: Terrine de brochet, brochet au beurre blanc, quenelles de brochet aux écrevisse à la Nantua.

PIKELET A type of biscuit (scone) made in various parts of Britain, particularly the north. In Yorkshire, it is the name for a crumpet, but in other parts it is made with a batter containing baking soda (bicarbonate of soda) as a leavening (raising) agent, and is cooked on a griddle.

In Scotland, pikelets are similar to griddle-cooked pikelets but are made with a yeast batter.

PILCHARD A large sardine. It is usually canned in tomato sauce.

PIMENTO See *Allspice*.

PIMIENTO Another name for the capsicum family of bell peppers.

PINE NUT (Fr. PIGNON) The nut of the pine tree much used around the Mediterranean and in the southern Latin countries. Pine nuts are one of the ingredients of the pesto paste used with pasta and fish soup.

PINEAPPLE (Fr. ANANAS) This fruit contains an enzyme used to tenderize meat and curdle milk. Pineapples are used in many desserts.

Typical dishes: Riz condé à l'ananas, ananas glace et confit à la bavaroise.

PINK PEPPERCORN This is not a true pepper, but a berry coming from the Baies rose plant cultivated in Madagascar — *Schinus terebinthifolius*. Pink peppercorns are available dried or in cans and jars — they are often mixed in with real peppercorns.

PINTO BEAN A bean with streaks of reddish-brown on a pinkish-colored background. It is often cooked with rice and bell peppers.

PIPÉRADE A Basque dish of scrambled eggs flavored with diced bell peppers, garlic, onion and tomatoes.

PIPPIN The name of a large family of dessert apples. The most well-known is Cox's Orange Pippin.

PIRI-PIRI A Portuguese chili sauce made with red chili peppers, tomatoes and garlic pounded together with vinegar; a little sugar may also be added.

Piri-piri can be made at home but is also available commercially in bottles.

PIROSHKI Filled Polish and Russian pastries that are served with soups.

The ingredients for the filling can be cheese, fish, meat, poultry or game, but mainly they are taken from the main ingredients of the soup. For instance piroski served with bortsch made with duck would contain duck liver and leg meat.

Moscow piroshki

8oz/225g puff paste (pastry)
½ cup/4oz/100g cooked duck meat
¼ cup/2oz/50g duck liver
⅔ cup/5oz/150g sausagemeat
1 small piece of onion, chopped
1 egg, beaten
1 tbsp dried mixed herbs

Roll the puff paste into a rectangle 12 x 5in/30 x 12.5cm. Brush the edges with cold water.

Combine the remaining ingredients and shape on a floured board to a sausage 12in/30cm long and 1¼in/3cm in diameter. Place it on the edge of the pastry.

Roll up the pastry leaving a small border. Press the pastry edges together to seal. Cut the roll into 2in/5cm long pieces.

Place the pieces on an oiled baking sheet and bake at 400°F/200°C/gas mark 6 for 20 minutes. Serve hot.

PISSALADIÈRE A Provençal tart traditionally made with a yeast dough base covered with fried onions and garnished with anchovies, black olives and capers. It is often referred to as a French version of the Italian pizza.

PISTACHIO Pistachio nuts have a characteristic flavor that is exploited by Italian ice cream makers.

Pistachios are also a part of rich terrines of foie gras and truffles. They are made into pastes and used in baklava.

PISTO A Spanish vegetable stew of bell peppers, tomatoes, onions and garlic cooked together in olive oil like a French ratatouille.

P

PISTOU *See Pesto.*

PITA BREAD An oval, flat, unleavened Middle Eastern bread. It forms a hollow when cooked and puffs up, forming a pocket that can filled, usually with savory ingredients.

PITAHAYA *See Prickly pear.*

PIZZA A Italian disc of yeast dough traditionally covered with savory ingredients such as tomatoes, eggplants (aubergines), bell peppers, salamis, Mozarella cheese, herbs, olives and anchovies, then baked.

PLAICE (Fr. PLIE) A white fish with reddish-brown spots on the dark skin on its back that is the most common flatfish eaten in Europe.
   Plaice has a soft flesh and is best fried or broiled (grilled).

PLANTAIN A coarse species of banana which is cooked and eaten as a vegetable or in stews.

PLOVER'S EGG A small, green, spotted egg that is a delicacy served hard-cooked (boiled) with celery salt.

PLUM (Fr. PRUNE) There are over 300 varieties of plum. They are used for tarts, other desserts and making jams.

PLUM PUDDING *See Christmas pudding.*

POACHING A gentle moist method of cooking, usually with the minimum of liquid. The liquid is kept at just below simmering point so that it shivers in one or two places rather than bubbles.
   Delicate foods that break up easily, such as fish, eggs and fruits should be poached.

POBLANO CHILI One of the best quality chili peppers grown in Mexico. It is available in cans.

POCHOUSE A Burgundian stew of river fish, usually pike, carp and perch, poached in white wine.

POGNON A rich brioche cake studded with mixed candied fruits such as angelica, peel, pineapple and cherries.
   It can be served with a raspberry coulis and ice cream as a dessert.

POIRAT A French double-crust pear pie with cream poured in through a hole in the top just before the pie is taken out of the oven.

POIVRADE A black peppercorn sauce

made from the wine used to marinade the meat, an equal amount of reduced brown sauce, and well-flavored with crushed black peppercorns, vinegar and cayenne pepper.

POJARSKI A false cutlet made of chopped meat, chicken or fish mixed with onions, herbs and breadcrumbs soaked in milk. It is shaped like a cutlet and fried.

POLENTA An Italian cornmeal porridge that varies considerably in thickness depending on how it is to be used.

It can be made like a thick porridge and served as an accompaniment, or made thicker, spread in a baking pan (tin) and left to cool. It is then cut in fancy shapes and fried in butter.

When polenta is cooked like this it is often served with tomato sauce and sprinkled with Parmesan cheese. For such a meal some cooks add eggs to bind the polenta.

POLKA A small cake made of sweet pie dough (pastry) lined with a ring of choux pastry and filled with caramel-flavored confectioners' custard.

POLLACK (Fr. LIEU) An excellent member of the cod family which is prepared like cod and haddock.

The yellow pollack is found in the Atlantic and the Bay of Biscay. Black and grey pollack are coarser and more like hake.

Scandinavian fish processors produce dried pollack under the name of kilppfisch.

POLONAISE (À LA) A garnish of fried breadcrumbs mixed with parsley and chopped hard-cooked (hard-boiled) eggs that is sprinkled over many hot vegetables, such as cauliflower, broccoli, French beans and asparagus.

POLONY An inexpensive cooked sausage encased in a red skin. It is boiled and served hot.

POLYSACCHARIDE The most complex sugar consisting of many simple sugars jointed together.

Some polysaccharides, such as starch, dextrin and glycogen can be split down to their constituent sugar — glucose, during digestion.

Other polysaccharides like cellulose, pectin and inulin cannot be digested and so contribute instead to dietary fiber.

POMEGRANATE (Fr. GRENADE) A fruit with a hard skin reddish seeds and tart juice.

P

The juice is made into a syrup sold commercially as grenadine.

Grenadine is also delicious when used in rhubarb pie.

POMELO The largest member of the citrus family. It is the ancestor of the grapefruit.

POMMEL A small, soft, double cream cheese made in France weighing about 2oz/50g.

POMPE A round yeast cake soaked in rum or kirsch and served in the south of France at Christmas.

POMPONNETTE A small savory pastry.

PONT L'ÉVÊQUE CHEESE A square, fermented soft French cheese that has a much stronger and more pronouced flavor than Camembert. It is made in Neufchâtel in Normandy.

PONT-NEUF POTATOES Fried potatoes ½in/1.2cm thick and 6cm/2½in long (slightly bigger than regular pommes frites).

Pont-neuf potatoes should be blanched in hot oil for 4 minutes, left until wanted for serving, then quickly refried until brown and crisp. *See also Deep-frying.*

POP-CORN Corn kernels cooked in hot oil until they burst due to the expansion of the moisture in the starch cells on being heated.

Pop-corn is usually sweetened and covered with caramelized sugar, though it is also sometimes salted.

POPOVER Batter baked in individual pans (tins) in America, and similar to English Yorkshire pudding.

POPPADOM, PAPPADUM, PAPAR A savory crisp and brittle Indian pancake made from dal.

Poppadoms are sometimes spiced. They are deep-fried and drained of fat just before serving.

POPPY SEEDS These have a grey-blue color and are sprinkled on breads.

PORK (Fr. PORC) In the days before refrigeration, pork was only eaten when there was an 'r' in the month — that is in the winter.

All parts of the pig can be used for food — head, feet, flesh, variety meats (offal) and fat for lard — a truly economic investment!

The most popular cuts are the fillet, loin, cutlets and leg. The belly is best used for bacon or spare ribs. Pig's trotters are considered gourmet food.

Blood sausages, also known as black puddings and German sausages are much-prized by lovers of big fried breakfasts!

When buying pork look for pieces with fat that is less than ½in/1.2cm thick. The flesh should be bright pink and fine textured.

Pork can be stored for 3 days under refrigeration and can be frozen for up to a year. Bacon and ham will keep for longer; the length of time depends on the cure and whether it has been smoked, which increases the shelf-life.

In Britain roast pork with crackling is a popular Sunday meal but in France the rind is often removed and used to make stock. Also in France roasts (joints) are usually completely defatted and pot-roasted with vegetables before serving with a sauce made from a wine or vinegar base.

Various parts of the pig are served as appetizers in France. Chitterling sauages known as andouille and andouilette, black pudding flavored with rum, and herb sausages made from a mixture of pork, chicken and venison, are all considered to be gourmet foods.

Chinese pork dishes have become very popular in the West; particularly spare ribs in sweet and sour sauce and pork dumplings.

Pork pies

This recipe makes large traditional British pork pies. They have solid meat fillings and are always served cold. Use equal amounts of pastry and filling. The raw diced meat can be marinated for 2 hours in fresh pineapple juice to tenderize it.

1 recipe hot-water crust pie dough
(pastry) for 1lb/450g filling
(See recipe page 274)

Filling

generous 1 cup/9oz/250g diced lean
* pork*
generous 1 cup/9oz/250g sausage
* meat*
1 tbsp chopped onion
1 tsp salt
¼ tsp mixed spice
¼ tsp black pepper
1 pinch of dry sage
1 tsp aspic powder
2 tbsp Sherry or water
  Makes two x 1¼ lb/500g pies.

Grease two hinged 2½ cup/1¼ lb/500g pie molds. Reserve some of the pie dough (pastry) to make decorations for the crust.

Line the molds with the pie dough, keeping a third of the pie dough to cover the pies.

P

Mix the sausagemeat with onions, salt and spices. Add the pork.

Divide meat filling in half. Fill each pie mold with the filling.

Wet the edges of the pie dough and cover with a pie dough top. Make a hole in each covering.

Roll our the reserved pie dough and make decorations to go on top of the pies.

Brush the tops with milk. Chill for 2 hours.

Bake the pies at 350°F/180°C/gas 4 for 1½ hours.

Cool the pies. When cold remove the pie molds.

Dissolve the aspic powder in the Sherry or water and then carefully pour into the pies.

Chill the pies overnight to develop flavor and tenderness. Serve sliced.

PORRIDGE A semi-soft to thick mixture of any kind of cereal cooked with water or milk. The thickness of the porridge depends on the amount of cereal used.

For example, as a general guide, to make polenta corn meal ⅔ cup/4½oz/125g corn meal is used per 4⅓ cups/1¾ pints/ 1 liter water, and to make semolina ⅔ cup/4oz/100g per 4⅓ cups/1¾ pints/1 liter water is needed.

Porridge may be enriched with cream and egg yolks; but savory or sweet, porridge should be well salted.

PORT-SALUT CHEESE A French semi-hard cheese.

PORTUGAISE (À LA) A generic name given to a variety of dishes from Portugal, or in the style dominating Portuguese gastronomy. For example, cabillaud à la Portugaise (with a rich onion and tomato sauce) and broiled (grilled) sardines with tomatoes and a wine dressing.

POT ROASTING (Fr. POÊLÉ) Meat or poultry that is first roasted in a little butter or oil until a golden color, then basted with stock or wine and covered with a lid for the remaining cooking time.

POTASSIUM A trace element present in the human body in considerable amounts. It is found in a wide variety of foods so there is very little risk of a deficiency.

Rich sources of potassium are wheat germ, molasses (black treacle) and dried fruits.

POTASSIUM HYDROGEN TARTRATE Used in baking powder and as an emulsifyng agent.

POTASSIUM SODIUM TARTRATE Used as an emulsifier.

POTATO (Fr. POMME DE TERRE) A root vegetable that belongs to the same family as eggplants (aubergines) and tomatoes. There are over 1,500 varieties of potatoes.

Potatoes with a firm waxy texture are best for roasting and frying, while those which have a floury texture are more suitable for making mashed potatoes.

Potatoes cooked in their skins are more flavorful and are more nutritious than potatoes that are peeled before cooking. Furthermore, the flavor of soups is improved if potatoes are used as the thickening agent.

Potatoes are often regarded as a fattening food, but a ¼ potato/2oz/50g of potato has only 40 calories whereas ½ cup/2oz/50g of cheese contains 210 calories.

More than 1,000 recipes for potatoes would not do justice to this tuber the shortage of which caused famine in Ireland in 1848.

Typical dishes: Pommes soufflées , pommes Dauphine, pommes Anna, pommes à la Sarlat, pommes à la Lyonnaise, pommes fondantes; pommes à la boulangère, pommes à la Savoyarde, pommes à la crème, pommes mousseline, French fries, potée à la Flamande, potée à l'Alsacienne, potée à l'Auvergnate, potée à la Bourguignonne, potée à la Bretonne (with lamb).

Soufflé potatoes

These potatoes are so-called because they puff up after deep-frying twice.

4 large potatoes
oil for deep frying

Cut the potatoes into ¼in/5mm thick slices. Wash and pat dry.

Heat a deep-fat fryer half-filled with oil to 325°F/160°C and add the potatos slices in batches while gently shaking the fryer. When the potato slices are soft but not brown — about 3 minutes — remove the potato slices and then drain well.

Reheat the oil to 375°F/190°C and re-fry the potatoes, still shaking the pan gently; the slices will puff up like balloons. Drain well.

Potée à l'Amiènoise

8⅔ cups/3½ pints/2 liters water
1lb 4oz/500g rib of beef
2 onions, studded with cloves
1 bouquet garni
2 carrots
2 leeks

P

2 turnips
1 small cabbage, quartered
1lb/450g potatoes
1 small head of celery
salt and pepper

To serve
4 slices of whole wheat (wholemeal)
  country bread
pickles
mustard
kosher (coarse) salt
grated sharp (mature) cheese

Pour the water into a large saucepan and bring to a boil. Remove the scum as it rises. Add the studded onions and bouquet garni.

Boil for 2 hours until the meat is almost tender. Add the remaining vegetables and boil for 30 minutes. Season to taste.

Serve in the following order :

• Soak the bread in a soup tureen with 2½ cups/1 pint/600ml of the beef broth. Pour in the remaining broth and serve as the appetizer.

• Carve the meat and place on a platter. Serve with pickles, mustard, kosher salt and grated cheese.

• Serve the vegetables separately.

POTTED FOOD Potting has for a long time been a way of preserving fish, poultry or meat without using salt or smoke. A layer of fat was poured over the top of the cooked food making an hermetic seal that prevented the entry of bacteria.

Potted foods could therefore provide people with pleasing and tasty dishes in the winter.

Typical dishes: Morecambe Bay potted shrimps, confit de canard, rillettes.

POULTRY The collective name for birds that are reared commercially — that is chicken, turkeys, ducks and geese.

Quail and guinea hen (fowl) are also reared commercially but they are usually still classed as game, because that is what they were until fairly recently and how they are still thought of.

POUND CAKE A cake made with completely equal weights of butter, sugar, eggs and flour.

POZOLE A thick, chunky Mexican soup containing hominy, pork, chili peppers and vegetables.

PRALINE Sugar-coated almonds.

PRAWN In America large shrimp (prawns) may be called jumbo prawns, whereas in Britain the name prawn is given to a range of sizes of shellfish from those that are just larger than shrimps, to langoustines and large warm-water tiger prawns.

PRESERVATIVE Permitted additive used to preserve foods from bacterial infection and growth. *See Sodium nitrate, Benzoic acid, Sulphur dioxide.*

PRESERVE A general term for jams, jellies, marmalades, candied fruits, and canned (bottled) fruits and vegetables which can be stored.

PRESSURE COOKER A thick, lidded saucepan used to cook food in steam or a liquid under specific pressures and therefore at higher temperatures; the higher the pressure the higher the temperature at which water boils. They need to be treated with respect.

Using a pressure cooker reduces the time needed to cook foods, but meat may not be as tender as when braised or pot-roasted. A pressure cooker is also useful for sterilizing foods.

Most pressure cookers have a regulator that can adjust the pressure: 2.5kg for low, 5kg for medium and 7.5kg for high pressure.

All pressure cookers have a saftey valve which releases surplus steam in case of malfunction.

PRICKLY PEAR, BARBERRY The fruit of a cactus plant. It is acid and ideal for sherbets (sorbets). It can be eaten raw when mature and ripe.

PRIMEUR First early spring vegetables such as baby carrots and turnips and green beans.

PRIMROSE A small plant with pale yellow blossoms that can be eaten in salads. A natural food coloring is made by infusing the blossoms in water.

PRINCESSE (À LA) A garnish of asparagus and truffles used for salmon, poultry and veal scallops (escalopes).

PRINTANIÈRE (À LA) A mixture of early spring vegetables, such as carrots, turnips, green beans and peas.

PROFITEROLES Small choux pastry buns filled with whipped cream and coated with chocolate sauce.

PROSCIUTTO Italian ham. Prosciutto cotto is cooked and prosciutto crudo is raw but dried and ready to eat. Special prosciuttos are Parma and San Daniele hams.

PROTEASES A group of enzymes capable of breaking proteins into amino

P

acids, of building amino acids into proteins and of substituting one amino acid for another in protein molecules.

PROTEIN A class of complex nitrogenous organic compounds of high molecular weight, which are of great importance to all living matter. Protein molecules consist of hundreds or thousands of amino acids joined together by peptide linkage into one or more inter-linked polypeptide chains, which maybe folded in a variety of different ways.

About 20 different amino acids occur in protein and each protein molecule is likely to contain all of them arranged in a variety of sequences. It is the sequence of the different amino acids that gives individual proteins their specific properties.

The particular sequence of the amino acids in protein is determined by the sequence of the nucleotide in the nucleic acids of the chromosomes, three nucleotides coding for each amino acid.

Most proteins form colloidal solutions in water or dilute solutions, but some, notably fibrous proteins, are insoluble.

Enzymes are a particularly important group of proteins as they determine the chemical reactions that will take place in a cell, therefore the characteristic that it will have,

PROTEOLYSIS The hydrolysis of proteins to amino acids by acid, alkali or enzymes.

PROVENÇAL (À LA) A style of cooking using southern French foods such olive oil, tomatoes, olives, anchovies and garlic.

Typical dishes: Sauté de veau à la Provençal, tapenade, oursinade, bouillabaisse, pissaladière.

PRUNE (Fr. PRUNEAU) Special varieties of plums are grown for drying as prunes; those from Agen or California are the best.

Prunes should be soaked in freshly-made tea soaked until well swollen.

PTARMIGAN A feathered game bird, belonging to the grouse family, with very tasty flesh. It is best roasted when young and casseroled when old.

PTYALIN The enzyme contained in saliva which changes starches into sugar, preparing them for absorption in the stomach.

PUCHERO A Latin American stew made with beef, mutton, sausages and ham, with chili peppers and vegetables in a highly seasoned sauce.

PUDDING There are two kinds of puddings in British cookery, savory and sweet.

They are both made in heatproof bowls, which are lined and covered with a pie dough that contains suet rather then butter or margarine, with baking powder as a leavening (raising) agent.

The pudding is cooked by boiling or steaming. They remain popular old-fashioned dishes, especially in winter.

Typical dishes:
SAVORY — steak-and-kidney pudding, bacon-and-onion pudding.

SWEET — cabinet pudding, apple pudding, Christmas pudding, bread-and-butter pudding, treacle pudding, summer pudding.

PUFF PASTE A layered pie dough (pastry) made with equal quanities of butter or hard margarine and flour. The dough is rolled and folded six times. *See recipe page 274.*

PULLED SUGAR Sugar boiled with glucose to the hard crack stage then poured onto a cold oiled slab. The syrup is cooled slightly then pulled and stretched by hand until it has a glossy satin shine. It can then be used for making decorations.

PULQUE A drink made from the fermented juice of the prickly pear.

PULSE The generic name for dried beans, peas and lentils.

PUMPERNICKEL A dark German bread made of rye flour.

PUMPKIN (Fr. POTIRON) Pumpkin can be cooked in butter without water, or boiled quickly to retain its flavor and texture.

Pumpkin purée can be sweetened with honey and made into a filling for pumpkin pie. One of best puréed soups can be made with various varieties of pumpkin.

Pumpkin seeds can be toasted and used as an ingredient for vegetarian pilaffs or pasta dishes.

PUNNET A container like a box without a lid in which soft fruits are sold in Britain.

PURÉE Fruit, vegetable, meat or fish which has been pounded, processed in a blender or strained until smooth.

P-Q

PURGATIVE A drug or food laxative. Examples are fibrous foods, fruits with the skins, nuts, whole wheat (wholemeal) bread, oats, figs, passion fruit, tamarind, prunes, rhubarb and castor oil.

PURI A deep-fried Indian flat bread which puffs up like a balloon when cooked.

PYRIDOXINE Part of the Vitamin B complex, pyridoxine is essential for growth, blood formation, protection against infection, and healthy skin and nerves.

Good sources of pyridoxine are yeast, liver, mackerel and tuna, peanuts and bananas. *See also Vitamins.*

QUAHOG *See Clam.*

QUAIL (Fr. CAILLE) A small bird that is usually referred to as game but is now more likely farmed than wild. Quails average 11in/28cm in length. They are nearly round in shape, with short tails and heavy bills. In the wild they feed on grass, seeds and clovers but, like other commercially-reared birds, they are fed on cereals enriched with mineral and vitamin supplements to balance their diet and to produce good quality meat and eggs.

Quails are trussed and covered with small slices of bacon and roasted for 10-14 minutes. They can also be boned and stuffed and served hot or cold.

Quails' eggs are served poached if very fresh, or hard-cooked (boiled) in salads or as an hors d'oeuvre.

Typical dishes: Cailles aux raisins, cailles en cassolette, caille farcie au foie gras en aspic.

QUARK A fresh cream cheese made by coagulating heated milk with lemon juice. It can be used for cheesecakes.

QUASI A French butchery cut from the rump of veal.

The veal should be well larded and cooked in a casserole or sautéed.

QUATRE-ÉPICES A French mixture of four specific ground spices, pepper, nutmeg, cinnamon and cloves. It is used for flavoring terrines and also in pâtés.

QUENELLE A light rounded dumpling made of finely ground (minced) and pounded fish, veal or chicken mixed with heavy (double) cream and eggs before cooking in water or stock.

The texture of the mixture is important as it determines whether the quenelles are coarse or superfine. Furthermore the fat content governs the lightness of a quenelle.

The meat must be well ground (minced) and pounded to a paste in a mortar, with eggs added to coagulate the mixture. Then heavy cream or butter equal the weight of the ground ingredients, is added. Cream gives a better result than butter.

The mixture can also be used as a filling for sausages.

Superfine quenelles

2 cups/1lb/450g skinless raw finely ground (minced) chicken
2 whole eggs, beaten
1¼ cups/½ pint/300ml heavy (double) cream
½ tsp celery salt
½ tsp white pepper
½ tsp ground mace
chicken stock for poaching

Pound the chicken then chill it for 10 minutes in the freezer, 1 hour in a refrigerator or over ice cubes.

Beat in the eggs and cream and season to taste. Chill again for a further 45 minutes.

Shape quenelles with two spoons or pipe onto a roasting pan (tin) lined with oiled baking parchment. Half fill the pan with chicken stock. Bring to a boil over low heat then poach for 15 minutes.

Remove the quenelles with a slotted soon and serve with an appropriate sauce.

QUESO The Spanish word for cheese. The name is used in all Spanish speaking Latin countries.

Queso anejo is a crumbly goats' cheese served with Mexican tortillas; queso de bola — in the shape of a ball, it is a semi-hard cheese similar to

Q

Edam; cabrales is a Spanish blue cheese similar to and probably as good as Roquefort, and further south in Venezuela, queso de mano is wrapped in banana leaves.

All of them show that excellent cheeses can be made when fresh milk is readily available from healthy, well-tended animals.

QUICHE A very popular savory tart with a custard filling. It can contain fish, meat or poultry, or can be made as a vegetarian dish.

The original quiche was first featured in Lorraine, the eastern region of France known for its culinary specialities. The word quiche is derived from the German word kuchen.

Quiche Lorraine

8oz/225g pie dough (short crust pastry)
melted butter for brushing
2 slices bacon, diced and blanched
2 eggs, beaten
⅔ cup/5fl oz/150ml heavy (double) cream
salt, white pepper and ground nutmeg

Grease a 9in/22cm quiche pan (flan tin). Line with the pie dough (shortcrust pastry). Crimp the edges and raise the dough on the sides by ½in/1.2cm.

Brush the tart shell with melted butter to prevent it from becoming soggy.

Put the bacon in the tart shell.

Beat the eggs, cream and seasoning and pour into the tart shell.

Bake at 400°F/200°C/gas mark 6 until golden and set, this takes about 35 minutes.

Variations

1) Replace the bacon by ½ cup/2 oz/50g grated sharp (mature) cheese.

2) Use 1 cup/2oz/50g sliced white mushrooms instead of the bacon.

3) Use ⅓ cup/3oz/75g smoked salmon, finnan haddie (smoked haddock), or cooked meat such as cold roast chicken.

4) Parsley, garlic, dill, basil and oregano as well as other herbs can be used to flavor quiches according to the type of filling used.

QUICK BREAD A bread that is leavened (raised) with a mixture of an acid and an alkali, such as baking powder, instead of yeast. The battter can, therefore, be baked as soon as it is prepared without having to be left to rise and prove for an hour or more.

Quick breads are more like cakes than a yeasted bread.

5 cups/1¼ lb/500g all-purpose
(plain) flour
1 tbsp baking powder
⅓ cup/3oz/75g sugar
salt
⅓ cup/3oz/75g butter
⅔ cup/5fl oz/150 ml buttermilk

Stir the flour, baking powder, sugar and salt together in a bowl. Cut in the butter until the mixture resembles crumbs.

Add the buttermilk and stir to make a dough.

Knead a little and divide into two loaves. Glaze with milk Place on a well-greased baking sheet.

Bake at 450°F/230°C/gas mark 8 for 15-20 minutes.

QUINCE (Fr. COING) A relative of the pear with the same shape, but the flesh is astringent and not edible when raw.

Quinces are used for their aromatic fragrance and setting properties, which the Spanish and French exploit by making a preserve that is so thick that is cut into squares; this is called cotignac in French and membrillo in Spanish.

Quince jelly can also be made. *See recipe on page 214, and Alva.*

QUININE An extract from the bark of a Peruvian tree. It is a tonic and stimulant which, when taken in moderation, can be an excellent aperitif.

QUINOA A grain grown in South America. It has a high protein content and contains more essential amino acids than wheat grains. It is boiled like rice. Quinoa can be used in soups or as an accompaniment to meat or vegetables.

QUINTESSENCE A word used by cookery writers and restaurant critics to describe the excellence of a particular food or dish. There is a saying 'beware of flatterers, they may try to gain your favor for a free dinner'.

Nothing in the world can ever be as good as the quintessence. The best compliment one can pay to a chef is to find fault.

R

RABBIT (Fr. LAPIN) Rabbit flesh is white and lean. Wild rabbits are smaller than farmed rabbits and can be tough, especially when old. Farmed rabbits are tender and can be used for the same recipes as veal and poultry.

Wild rabbits often have flesh flavored with the wild thyme on which they feed. Young rabbits, between three and four months old, have short necks, large joints and well-developed paws with a small knob underneath. Their ears are soft, thin and easily torn and their jaws are narrow.

Rabbits can be hung for a few days to develop their flavor. The rabbit should be hung by the fore-legs to retain the blood in the body.

Rabbit cuts

FILLET The whole fillet is removed from both sides of the saddle. It can then be cut lengthwise into two or three slices.

FRONT LEGS When large, these are cut from the body and used for casseroles and pies. When small, they are not cut off individually, but used as part of the ribs on the underside.

FRONT RIBS. Generally used for stock or in a stew.

HIND LEGS Cut close to the body, trimmed and larded in the usual way. Legs of young animals are used for sautées and casseroles; those of old animals for jugged rabbit and for game stuffings.

PAUPIETTE A thin fillet beaten to flatten it, then stuffed and rolled up.

SADDLE The body portion after the legs have been removed.

Before using as a saddle, cut off the portion containing the lungs, heart and liver, and then trim the sides, cutting all the ribs very short. With the point of a filleting knife, remove all the skin and sinews from the back and underside. A saddle should be larded with thin strips of fat.

Typical dishes: Gibelotte de lapin aux pruneaux, lapin rôti aux pommes reinettes, terrine de lapin aux trois herbes.

RABOTTE *See Talibur.*

RACAHOUT An Arabic thickening that can be of salep, potato starch and sweet acorn flour. It is used to thicken soups or milk puddings.

RACK, BEST END OF NECK (FR. CARRÉ) A cut of lamb that contains the ribs from the 7th–13th; the last rib bone is removed. It is a joint which should be trimmed with spinal bone and skin removed before cooking and the ends of the rib bones scrapped clean of flesh and fat.

Typical dishes: Carré d'agneau pommes Sarladais, rack of lamb with ratatouille.

RACLETTE The name of a group of Swiss cheeses that are used to make a dish of the same name.

The cut surface of a piece of cheese is exposed to the heat of a fire to soften it so that it can be scrapped onto a dish and served immediately to waiting guests. Boiled potatoes, pickled onions and pickled gherkins are served as accompaniments.

RADIANT COOKING A dry method of cooking by exposure to direct heat as when cooking under a broiler (grill).

Tender foods like fish, poultry and the best meat cuts can be broiled. They are placed close to the source of heat at the beginning of cooking to seal the surface and retain their natural juices. Except for thin cuts, the pieces are moved further away from the heat source to finish cooking. *See also Conduction, Convection.*

RADIATORE A short, thick Italian pasta with rippled edges, resembling tiny radiators.

RADICCHIO A reddish member of the endive (chicory) family which has become fashionable for its decorative leaves. It is often mixed with other salad leaves to form a bed for cold appetizers of fish, shellfish or meat.

There are two main types of raddicchio, Castelfranco with Burgundy-red leaves, and Treviso with narrow, pointed leaves.

RADISH A native of China, radishes are salad ingredients used with French dressing. The black skin radish is a French variety with a stronger flavor than red radishes. *See also Mouli.*

RAGI FLOUR A flour made from millet in India. Ragi flour gives pancakes a crispiness and brittleness that they do not have when made with wheat flour.

R

RAHAT LOKHOUM *See Turkish delight.*

RAISIN Dried grape. Good quality raisins are sold seedless. The best sources of raisins are California, Greece, Malaga, Valencia and Australia.

Raisins are used in cakes, desserts, pastries and chutneys.

RAISING (Am. LEAVENING) Aerating flour confections and bread using a leavening (raising) agent such as baking powder, baking soda (bicarbonate of soda) or yeast. All of these produce carbon dioxide during cooking that expands and lifts the batter or dough as they get heated, making the mixture lighter and greater in depth.

RAMBUTAN A very pleasant and refreshing fruit that originated in Malayasia. It is used the same way as lychees in salads or as a garnish for pork and duck dishes.

RAMEKIN An earthenware dish that is used for soufflés, custards or mousses. Various sizes of ramekins are available.

RAMPION A root that can be used raw in salads or boiled as a vegetable. The leaves can be cooked in butter like spinach.

RAPESEED, COLZA A biennial member of the cabbage family with long edible roots and leaves. It is grown for the oil which can be made from the seeds.

RAS MALAI A delicate Indian dessert of cream cheese dumplings poached in syrup then served wth a sauce of milk boiled until thickened.

RASAM A southern Indian highly seasoned lentil broth that is either drunk as a soup or mixed with rice before being eaten.

RASPBERRY A fruit that is closely related to the blackberry and loganberry. It is used for syrups, coulis, sherbets (sorbets), tartlets, mousses, soufflés and charlottes.

A flavored dressing is made by macerating raspberries for 1 week in wine vinegar, sugar and water.

RASPINGS (Fr. CHAPELURE) Bread crumbs used as a coating for fish, croquettes or fried dumplings.

RASSOL'NICK A light Russian ox kidney soup flavored with pickled cucumbers and the juice in which the cucumbers were pickled. Sour (soured) cream is stirred in to the soup just before serving.

RASTEGAI Small Russian fish pies made with yeast dough, similar to pirozhki but larger.

RATAFIA An almond-flavored cookie (biscuit) similar to a macaroon but made with bitter almonds as well as sweet almonds.

RATATOUILLE The most characteristic Mediterranean mixture, consisting of tomatoes, eggplants (aubergines), onion, zucchini (courgettes) and bell peppers cooked gently in olive oil and served either hot or cold.

RAVIGOTTE SAUCE 1) A piquant hot French sauce made of a velouté sauce, shallots, herbs, white stock and vinegar boiled until reduced by two-thirds.

2) A piquant cold sauce similar to mayonnaise and flavored with shallots, dill pickles (gherkins), capers and herbs.

RAVIOLI A small Italian pasta 'pillow' filled with meat, spinach or cheese mixtures.

Ravioli are boiled in water, then simmered in tomato sauce. Ravioli tastes better and is more tender if cooked a day in advance and reheated in the sauce when required.

RED CABBAGE There are several varieties of red cabbage with different hues. They can be pickled in sweet vinegar flavored with grated horseradish, or braised with apples and wine.

If boiled in water red cabbage changes to an unattractive brownish color. To prevent this use a few beets (beetroot) and a little vinegar to enhance the red color.

RED HERRING A heavily salted and smoked herring that is served for breakfast, or early supper in the winter accompanied by boiled potatoes.

RED MULLET (Fr. ROUGET) A fish which does not need to be gutted and can be cooked whole like a sardine.

However, there are many recipes where only the fillets are used. The skin is left on because of its attractive appearance.

Goatfish is similar to red mullet and can be substituted for it in recipes.

Typical dishes: Rouget en mille-feuille, rouget grillé sauce aïoli, rouget en chartreuse, terrine de rouget aux asperges.

Red mullet with asparagus and bean sprouts
Goatfish or red snapper fillets may be used instead of red mullet.

R

2 tbsp olive oil
4 red mullet, filleted and cut in
strips
12 small asparagus tips, blanched for
4 minutes
1 garlic clove, chopped
4 large mushrooms, sliced
2 tbsp soy sauce
salt and black pepper
pinch of grated fresh ginger root
1 cup/8oz/225g bean sprouts
juice of 1 lime

Heat the oil and stir-fry the fish for 4 minutes. Add the asparagus tips, garlic and mushrooms and cook for 3 minutes. Stir in the soy sauce and seasoning to taste and add grated ginger root to taste.

Arrange the bean sprouts on 4 plates. Add the fish mixture. Squeeze over the lime juice at the last minute.

REDCURRANT A small red version of the blackcurrant. Redcurrants are used for jellies, jams and sauces.

REDEYE GRAVY A south American gravy made from the cooking liquid of braised ham, or brown stock and fresh coffee boiled until thickened. It is served with ham, hot buttered grits and biscuits (scones), or sometimes corn bread.

REDFISH, Norway haddock A plump fish with a large spiny head and sharp fins. It is bright pink with a silvery sheen and has lean, firm flesh that resembles crabmeat in taste.

REFRIGERANT A liquid used in the refrigerating cycle of a refrigerator. It is usually a liquid that will vaporize at a low temperature, such as Freon.

REFRIGERATING CYCLE The cycle that takes place in a refrigerator. The refrigerant absorbs heat from the cold chamber and its contents, which causes it to vaporize. It is then pumped to a compressor where it gives up heat and condenses back to a liquid. This passes to the cold chamber, so making a continuous cycle.

REFRIGERATION Refrigeration influences the practices of agriculture and marketing and without it many countries would not be able to export or import perishable foods.

A few hours delay between harvest or slaughter and refrigeration is sufficient for food to deteriorate in transit. To remedy this, fruits and vegetables pass through a hydro-cooler where they are sprayed with a jet of cold water. The water may also contain a germicide to inactivate surface micro-organisms. The cooled products are then transported in refrigerated trucks to refrigerated warehouses. Naturally, this adds to the cost of the foods.

Refrigeration equalizes food prices throughout the year. Without it prices would be low at the time of harvest but extremely high later on, if indeed the foods were available at all.

Refrigerated storage will preserve perishable foods for days or weeks depending upon the food.

At 32°F/0°C most perishable foods such as meat, poultry and fish, and many fruits and vegetables may last two weeks.

At 42°F/3°C storage life is often less than one week. On the other hand, at 72°F/20°C or above these foods may perish within a day or two.

It is recommended that domestic refrigerators should be kept at below 41°F/5°C. Most food spoilage micro-organisms grow rapidly at above 50°F/10 °C, but some grow slowly at temperatures down to 38°°F/3°C.

Psychrophilic organisms will grow slowly down to 15°F/-8°C, provided the food is not solidly frozen. These organisms will not produce food poisoning or disease but even below 25°F/-5°C will cause the food to deteriorate.

Below 15°F/-8°C there is a gradual decrease in the numbers of living organisms in food. Micro-organisms still alive in frozen food will multiply rapidly when the food is thawed, which can lead to food spoilage.

Refrigerating foods also helps in controlling chemical and enzymatic reactions. This is the case in the cool ripening of cheeses and cool ageing of beef.

Refrigerating citrus fruits reduces changes in flavor during extraction and straining of fruit juices. It also improves the ease and efficiency of meat cutting and bread slicing. If water for drinks is cooled before carbonating the solubility of carbon dioxide is increased.

Refrigeration is the gentlest method of food preservation. By and large it has relatively little adverse effect upon taste, texture, color or nutritive value. Some foods are even improved when served cool or chilled, provided simple rules are followed and storage periods are not too excessive.

It is not always economical or practical to separate foods in a refrigerator and provide each with their optimum temperature and humidity requirements. Pack or wrap all foods properly, especially those with strong odors such as fish and bacon, to minimize the spread of one smell to another.

R

REINDEER Reindeer meat is similar to venison. The meat should be marinated in wine with juniper berries for a special flavor.

Steaks can be quickly cooked but big joints need 2 hours braising in moderate heat. Smoked reindeer tongues are esteemed by gourmets. All the gazelle and antelope species are used in a similar way.

REINE A garnish of chicken, white mushrooms and truffles in a creamy sauce.

RELIGIEUSE A pyramid of small éclairs filled with coffee flavored confectioners' custard.

RELISH An acid condiment or pickle of vegetables or fruits with pieces.

RÉMOULADE SAUCE Made from mayonnaise with chopped hard-cooked (boiled) eggs, gherkins, capers, parsley, tarragon and shallots and sometimes also anchovy fillets. It is served with fried fish, vegetables and cold cuts (meats).

RENNET Extract of calves' stomachs. Rennet contains the enzyme rennin, which coagulates milk and is used to make junket and cheese.

RETES A type of strudel filled with a various fruits such as cherries, plums, apples and raisins, and poppy seeds.

RHUBARB (Fr. RHUBARBE) The stalks of the fruit are used in jams, pies and tarts; rhubarb tarts topped with strawberries or raspberries are attractive and tasty.

Combined with apples or gooseberries, rhubarb can be made into chutney or fruit catsup (ketchup).

Rhubarb leaves are toxic as they contain oxalic acid.

RIBBON The ribbon stage is reached when a whisked egg and sugar mixture will support the weight of a trail left by the lifted whisk.

RIBOFLAVIN Once called Vitamin B2, it is needed for growth, body maintenance and for healthy skin and eyes. It is found in yeast, liver, milk, eggs, cheese, pulses and cereal germs.

RICE (Fr. RIZ) Nutritionally rice is one of the poorest cereals, yet it is the staple diet in far Eastern countries. It is absorbed easily and so is a useful food in certain diseases of the alimentary tract. Rice must be served with fish, eggs, dairy products or meat to become a nourishing diet.

Brown rice, which is rice that has been de-husked but not polished, has more fiber and nutrients than white rice; it also takes longer to cook, about 40 minutes.

Most white rice is cooked in 12-20 or 25 minutes, but rice milk puddings are best if cooked gently rather than boiled, for 1 hour. The cooking water from boiled rice should be retained and used in soups or sauces as it contains thiamin.

Rice flour is used for milk puddings, as a binder for forcemeats and for cakes.

There more than 1,500 varieties of rice produced and sold all over the world. *See also individual varieties.*

Typical dishes:

SAVORY: paella, timbale de poulet au riz safran, risotto, nasi goreng, pilaff, dolmas.

SWEET: riz à l'Impératrice, riz Conde, rice pudding.

Indian rice pancakes
Use as a wrapping for fish fillets.

2 ¼ cups/1lb/450g long grain rice
2½ cups/1 pint/600ml water
1 cup/5oz/150g black gram dal,
  washed and drained
2 tsp fenugreek seeds
salt
oil for cooking
        Makes about 20 thin pancakes

Soak the rice in twice its volume of water for 6 hours. Drain completely and purée with 425ml/¾ pint/scant 2 cups of the water.

Meanwhile, soak the dal and fenugreek for 6 hours. Drain and purée with the remaining water. Combine the two batters. Add salt to tast .

Heat 2 teaspoons of oil in a pancake pan. Pour in 2 tablespoonsful of the batter and cook on both sides for 2 to 3 minutes. Repeat with the remaining batter.

RICE PAPER An edible, smooth white brittle paper made from the pith of a tree peculiar to Taiwan. Macaroons and similar cookies are baked on it and the paper is eaten with the cookie .

RICOTTA A soft, fresh Italian cheese made from whey. The word ricotta means recooked.

Ricotta has a slightly sweet taste. It is used in pasta dishes as well as cheesecakes and cassata.

RIGATONI An Italian pasta resembling macaroni but bigger.

R

RIJSTTAFEL A Dutch-Indonesian meal of various meats, fish, egg and vegetable dishes with accompanying sauces and condiments, served with a large bowl of boiled rice.

RILLETTE French potted pork, duck or goose made by roasting pork belly until golden brown. It is then ground (minced) and mixed with salt and spices. Rillons are made in the same way, but they are coarser.

RIMOT(T)E A type of polenta made in south west France. It can be left until cold then cut into squares and served with stews, or it can be sweetened and served cooked fruits.

RISO Italian for rice.

RISOTTO An Italian rice dish made of arborio rice simmered slowly for 20-25 minutes, with the water or stock being stirred in gradually.

A risotto can be flavored with many savory ingredients, such as cheese, mushrooms and shellfish.

RISSOLE Savory pastry with a force-meat or cooked filling, which can be either fried or baked. It can be made more luxurious by using shellfish, fish roes and other delicate morsels.

ROASTING Cooking by dry heat in an oven or on a spit over a fire.

When roasting in the oven, meat, poultry and game should be seared at 425° F/220°C/gas mark 7 for the first 20 minutes to develop flavor and color on the outside, then cooked at 350°F/180°C/gas mark 4 for 10 minutes per 1lb/450g for beef, lamb and venison, and 15-20 minutes per 450g/1lb for pork, veal and poultry.

Lean meat, poultry and game should be basted frequently during roasting to prevent them becoming dry. Use butter or olive oil for poultry. Oil and the drippings from the meat can be used for meats and game.

How to roast meat

Position the shelves in the oven so that the meat is in the middle. Preheat the oven to 425°F/ 220°C/gas mark 7.

Weigh the joint and calculate the cooking time. When cooking a stuffed roast (joint), weigh the roast after it is stuffed and calculate the cooking time accordingly.

Place the roast , uncovered, on a rack in a roasting pan (tin) so that the largest cut surfaces are exposed and any fat is on top. In this way the roast will be basted by its own fat during cooking. Cook in the oven for the calculated time.

A meat thermometer is very useful for checking whether the meat is sufficiently well cooked. Take the temperature toward the end of the cooking time — using a pair of gloves, carefully insert the thermometer into the middle of the roast at the thickest part of the joint and leave for a few seconds for the temperature to stabilize.

The internal temperature readings should be:

BEEF	rare	*125°F/51°C*
	medium	*140°F/60°C*
LAMB	well-done	*160°F/70°C*
VEAL		*160°F/70°C*
PORK		*170°C/75°C*

ROCAMBOLE A plant of the same family as onions that is used in salads.

ROCHER Confectionery made to look like a rock. It can be made of coconut and fondant, as for congolais, or chocolate truffles with finely chopped almonds.

ROCK SALT Salt extracted from mines on land, as opposed to sea salt which is evaporated from the sea. It is used for pickling.

Rock salt was traditionally mixed with pounded ice and used to keep ice cream cold while freezing.

ROCKET *See Arugula.*

ROCKFISH A large family of fish found mainly along the coasts of America. The flesh can vary from fairly firm to soft and difficult to handle. For this reason, rockfish is often used in soups.

In the United States, the name rockfish is sometimes given to the striped bass and the scorpion fish family.

ROE The eggs of fish and shellfish. Fish roe is usually salted, smoked or made into caviar. The roe, or coral, of lobsters is used to flavor shellfish sauces, such as Newburg and Américaine.

Herring roe is usually broiled (grilled) on toast as a savory. Another tasty dish that is made from smoked cod's roe is taramasalata. *See also Caviar, Lumpfish.*

ROGNONNAD A French butchery term to describe a roast (joint) of loin meat that encloses the trimmed kidney.

ROQUEFORT CHEESE One of the best known blue cheeses made in France from ewes' and goats' milk.

ROSE WATER A natural flavoring made from the distillation of scented Damask rose petals.

R

Rose water is used to flavor Turkish delight, and used frequently in Middle Eastern cooking.

ROSEMARY (Fr. ROMARIN) An aromatic herb used to flavor roast lamb. It can also be used in stuffings, pâtés and fillings for pies.

ROSETTE A cut of meat taken from the loin of lamb or venison and tied with string into a round.

ROSHGULLA An Indian sour milk and flour dumpling poached in rose water syrup.

RÖSTI A Swiss potato cake made from the grated flesh of a part-baked potato that has been fried in butter so that butter is the dominating flavor. Using part-baked potatoes are the key to making correct rösti; raw grated potatoes do not taste the same.

ROTELLE Italian pasta made in the shape of small wheels.

ROTINI Italian pasta in the shape of small spirals.

ROUILLE A southern French chili pepper and garlic mayonnaise served with shellfish soups and stews, such as bouillabaisse. A little of the fish stock can added to the sauce to improve the flavor and texture.

2 tbsp strong fish and saffron stock
2 garlic cloves, chopped
1 red chili pepper, chopped
1¼ cups/½ pint/300ml mayonnaise

Boil the stock, garlic and chili pepper for 5 minutes.

Process in a blender or food processor and let cool.

Mix with the mayonnaise.

ROULADE A French term also used in Britain that refers to a cake batter, or a vegetable or soufflé mixture rolled around a filling in the same way as a jelly (Swiss) roll. Small roulades can also be made with thin slices of whole wheat (wholemeal) bread and smoked salmon or herb-flavored cream cheese.

ROUND (RUMP, Fr. CULOTTE) A cut from the hind quarters of beef. It can be roasted or served as steaks.

ROUX A thickening paste made of shortening (fat) and flour cooked together briefly over low heat when making sauces.

When making béchamel sauce the roux is cooked until sandy-textured but not colored; when making a velouté sauce, the roux is cooked until straw-colored and for a brown sauce, it is cooked for 5 minutes until it reaches a golden stage.

The liquid is gradually whisked or stirred into the roux to prevent lumps forming. It is then boiled and stirred until the sauce thickens.

ROWAN BERRY The berry from the mountain ash tree that can be used for jellies and jams.

The juice of freshly-squeezed rowan berries can be added to gin in place of Angostura bitters to make pink gin.

ROYAL ICING A type of icing made of confectioners' (icing) sugar and egg whites. It is often used to cover wedding cakes.

ROYALE A molded savory custard which is cut in thin slices and used as a garnish for consommés.

  2 whole eggs
  4 egg yolks
  1¼ cups/½ pint/300ml consommé
    or milk
  salt and pepper

Mix all the cold ingredients together.
  Strain and pour into dariole molds.

Cook in a water bath in an oven at 350° F/180°C/gas mark 4 for 25 minutes until set.

Let cool then cut into the desired shapes.

RUGULA *See Arugula.*

RUMP (**ROUND, Fr. CULOTTE**) A cut from the hind quarters of beef. It can be roasted or served as steaks.

RUNNER BEAN A climbing plant producing attractive scarlet flowers followed by long green edible pods which can be eaten hot or cold.

To prepare runner beans, trim them and remove the strings on both sides. They are usually cut into thin slices slantwise before boiling.

The young beans are stringless and more tender, but to get them like this they have to be home-grown.

RUOTE Italian pasta shaped like small wheels.

RUSK This is made by baking bread slices until crisp and dry.

RUSSET A name given to dessert apples that have reddish-brown skins.

RUTABAGA (**SWEDE**) A plant whose

S

large, round roots, with their yellow or white flesh, resemble turnips.

RYE Rye flour has a lower protein content than wheat flour, so it produces dense loaves and cakes unless it is combined with wheat flour. Caraway seeds are often used to flavor rye breads.

In Russia and some parts of Scandinavia roasted rye was mixed with chicory to make a type of coffee.

SABAYON A thick, foamy sauce made from egg yolks, sugar and white wine beaten together while being heated in a water bath.

SABLÉ A rich and very crumbly shortbread cookie (biscuit). The handling of a sablé dough is very delicate and but if it is well chilled, lightly kneaded, with hands that are very cold, the results can be very rewarding in the variations that can be obtained from a such a simple recipe.

> 1 cup/8oz/225g sweet (unsalted)
>   butter, softened
> 1 cup/4oz/100g confectioners'
>   (icing) sugar
> 2 large egg yolks
> ½ tsp vanilla extract
> 2 drops of almond extract
> 2 cups/1lb/450g all-purpose
>   (plain) flour

Makes 16

Beat the butter and confectioners' (icing) sugar together.

Beat in 1 egg yolk at a time. Add the extracts then mix in the flour to make a dough. Knead the dough very lightly. Roll to a ball, wrap and chill.

Roll the dough into 2 long sausage shapes about 2in/5cm in diameter. Cut into ¼in/5mm thick slices.

Place the slices on baking trays lined with baking parchment or greased greaseproof paper.

Bake at 325°F/170°C/gas mark 3 for 10 minutes. Lower the oven temperature to 300 F/160°C/gas mark 2 and bake for 10 minutes more.

Let cool then store in an airtight container.

Variations

The dough can be flavored with vanilla, cinnamon or ground almonds.

SACCHARIN A white crystalline powder made from coal-tar. It is used as a substitute for sugar. It has been reliably estimated that the sweetening power of saccharin is 200-500 times stronger than sucrose.

SACCHAROMETER, HYDROMETER An instrument for measuring the density of a syrup. It floats higher in a dense liquid than in a lighter one. A saccharometer is graduated in various units, such as Baumé, Brix or SG (specific gravity).

SACHERTORTE An Austrian chocolate layer cake sandwiched with apricot jam and whipped cream, and coated with dark chocolate.

SADDLE Two loins of lamb, rabbit or hare left attached at the backbone.

SAFFLOWER This is primarily grown for the oil which can be extracted from the seeds. Safflower oil is low in saturated fatty acids but it has a strong flavor unless it is deodorized, which it is for sale in the west.

Safflower leaves can be used to manufacture a red dye, or used as an inferior substitute for saffron.

SAFFRON (Fr. SAFRAN) The dried thread-like stigmas of a type of crocus. The best-quality saffron comes from Spain. It is the worlds' most expensive spice because of the high costs involved in growing and harvesting it, and the low yield.

Saffron should be infused in a hot liquid in a cup then added to the main ingredients. Saffron is used in breads, cakes, soups, sauces and many rice dishes and curries.

S

New potatoes cooked in butter with shallots and saffron taste better than when cooked with mint.

SAGE (Fr. SAUGE) A small, shrubby garden perennial. The leaves have a very strong, sweet, camphoric aroma and taste. It is used in pork and cheese dishes, sausages and stuffings. It is also infused as a medicinal drink.

SAGO A starch that is extracted from the hollow trunk of a palm that grows in southern Asia. The pith is scraped from the trunk, ground up then washed, drained and dried.

Sago is available as a flour or as granules of pearl sago, which are used for making sago pudding.

Sago is less nutritious than rice but it can be digested easily. Cooked in milk it is a good food for invalids.

SAINTS IN FOOD Many foods have saints names, such as gâteau Saint - Honoré, pieds de porc à la Saint-Menehould (pigs' feet fried in breadcrumbs), and the cheeses Saint-Nectaire, Saint-Florentin, Saint-Paulin, Saint-Maure and Saint-Marcellin.

Butchers have their own saint, Saint Anthony, and Saint Hubert is the patron saint of game.

SAKE Both the name for Japan's most popular beverage and the word that refers to to all Japanese alcholic drinks. Sake wine is made from fermented rice and is sligtly sweetened. It is used extensively in Japanese cooking.

SALAD APPETIZERS A healthy salad should not be one of abstinence, denying the pleasures of appetizing and luxurious ingredients, but rather should combine enjoyment with sensible eating.

The therapeutic values of herbs, vegetables and seafood have been recognized since Hippocrates said that food was our best medication.

My grandmother Mathilde never ceased to remind me of the value of dandelion salad with hot flaked kippers or bacon slices. The lettuces of her garden were milky, and the cores, eaten with salt were like eating crisp radishes. We had salads at every meal, but those that were most memorable contained eggs mixed with vegetables and served with langoustines, scallops or mussels.

Surf and turf mingle happily when both are freshly gathered. My personal choice could be a cold skate vinaigrette or trout in a vermouth dressing with melon, smoked salmon with asparagus or, better still, cold lobster with artichoke bottoms or Jerusalem artichokes in a lemon dressing.

Canned tuna or pilchards with crisp lettuce leaves have been a favorite light meal when expensive seafood is out of the question.

An appetizing way to serve canned sardines in olive oil is with a garlic tomato salad.

SALAD BURNET An aromatic herb with serrated leaves. It is used like parsley to flavor salads, sauces and stews.

SALAD CREAM A commercial British salad dressing that must by law contain one percent acetic acid. This makes it more acidic than mayonnaise.

Commercial salad creams are homogonized so they hold the maximum of oil, and have special stabilizers added to prevent separation. A similar fresh product can bc made at home mixing sour (soured) cream, or fresh cream and lemon juice, into béchamel sauce.

Salad cream can be flavored with blue cheese, celery, shallots, garlic, herbs, nuts, seeds and spices.

SALAD DRESSING A basic French salad dressing is made with three parts mild-flavored oil and one part wine vinegar.

To make it milder less vinegar can be used and a proportion of lemon juice and sugar added.

For a superior flavor walnut and olive oil are used with lemon juice and mustard. Herbs, garlic, shallots and onions add aromatic flavors.

Dijon dressing
1 tsp Dijon mustard
½ tsp salt
coarsely ground black pepper
6 tbsp olive oil
2 tbsp wine vinegar
I tsp sugar
I tbsp parsley, chopped
juice and grated rind of ½ lemon

Place all the ingredients in a bowl and whisk to obtain a good emulsion.

Variations
1. Add 1 chopped hard-cooked (boiled) egg.
2. Add 2 chopped garlic cloves.
3. Use balsamic or sherry vinegar instead of wine vinegar.
4. Add 1 tablespoon of finely chopped basil and 2 tablespoons of minced almonds or pine nuts.

SALAD LEAVES A large variety of salad leaves can be bought all the year round besides iceberg, romaine (Cos) and

S

butterhead. For example, spinach and fresh coriander can be eaten in salads with a lemon dressing.

Wash all salad leaves and drain them well both in a colander and with a cloth. Wrap the leaves in a plastic bag and refrigerate.

Salads should be crunchy and nutritious, which is why the addition of eggs, fish, meat, cheese and nuts can make a world of difference to salad leaves.

Do not toss a salad with the dressing until 5 minutes before serving.

SALEP A gelatinous starch used as a thickener for soups, sauces and milk puddings.

SALINE PRESERVATION Preserving with dry salt or in brine was for many centuries the standard means of storing foods such as meat, fish and vegetables for the winter. It is is still one of the cheapest methods of food preservation. The canning industry uses brines for canned beans, garbanzo beans (chickpeas), root vegetables, artichokes and asparagus.

SALLY LUNN Yeast bun reputed to have been invented by a girl named Sally Lunn in Bath, in the west of England.

SALMAGUNDI An old English dish of diced meat, chicken and fish mixed with cooked and raw vegetables, flavored with a dressing.

SALMON (Fr. SAUMON) An oily fish which can be farmed or caught in the rivers when it returns from its sea journey to lay its eggs. The main varieties of salmon are Pacific and Atlantic, and the varieties chinook, coho, chum and sockeye.

Salmon can be filleted or cut across on the bone into steaks. It is also available canned, frozen or smoked.

Broiling (grilling) and stir-frying are good methods of cooking salmon.

Typical dishes: Escalope de saumon sauvage au poivre vert, gravelax, rilletes de saumon, coulibiac, darne de saumon au sauce hollandaise, salmon and asparagus mousse.

Salmon tartare

8oz/225g smoked salmon
¼ cup/2fl oz/50ml thick yogurt
½ tsp made sweet mustard
½ cucumber, peeled, halved
  lengthwise, seeded and sliced
juice of 1 lemon
1 tbsp sunflower oil
salt and black pepper
dill and lime for garnish

Chop the smoked salmon coarsely. Mix with the yogurt and mustard. Season to taste.

Put a plain 2in/5cm diameter cookie (pastry) cutter on a plate and press the mixture in it. Remove the cutter and repeat with the remaining mixture. Chill them all.

Toss the sliced cucumber in lemon juice and oil with a little seasoning. Arrange slices of cucumber around each salmon tartare. Garnish with dill and lime.

Smoked salmon and strawberries
*1lb/450g smoked salmon, thinly
  sliced
4 Chinese leaves, shredded
8oz/225g strawberries, washed and
  well drained
2 limes, thinly sliced
3 tbsp olive oil
juice of 1 lime*

Arrange the salmon on 4 plates. Surround with a border of Chinese leaves. Garnish with sliced strawberries and slices of lime.

SALMONELLA A bacteria which can cause food poisoning. It is found in eggs from infected hens, and raw meats, and can be spread by cross-contamination. Salmonella can survive in brine and in the refrigerator but is destroyed by heat.

SALTPETER, SODIUM NITRATE, POTASSIUM NITRATE A meat preservative used in cured meats, to which it gives the characteristic pink color.

SALPICON A French term for a mixture of meat or poultry cut into small pieces and used for vol au vent fillings, or for garnishes.

SALSA VERDE A piquant Italian green sauce made of olive oil, vinegar and herbs such as parsley, mint and chives, anchovy fillets and capers.

SALSIFY, OYSTER PLANT (Fr. SALSIFIS) An edible root that must be peeled and immersed in acidulated water to prevent discoloration by oxidation. Salsify can be par-boiled and fried in butter with herbs or made into fritters.

SALT, SODIUM CHLORIDE Although chemically the term 'salt' means any combination of an acid with a salifiable base, the word 'salt' in ordinary use is confined to the well-known seasoner and preserver of food.

Salt is produced in much the same way today as it was 1,000 years ago from bay or sea salt, rock or mine salt,

S

and natural brine or pit salt. Salt is available as fine, free-running table salt and coarser sea salt, which is obtained by evaporation and has a distinct flavor. Kosher salt is additive free and has coarse crystals.

The preserving quality of salt is due to its power of attracting moisture from foods, which hardens them. The salt itself softens as it absorbs water, and loses its flavor. Salt is soluble in 8.82 times its weight of cold water, and in 2.76 times its weight of boiling water.

The level of salt to preserve olives in brine can be as high as 15-18 percent, and 7-10 percent in cucumber and gherkins, but in sauerkraut 2.0-2.5 percent dry salt is used. In these products salt aids the action of lactic acid-producing organisms, which can prevent destructive bacteria spoiling the brine.

The same principle applies in cheese making. Salt is usually added to the curd to control the action of organisms that breakdown proteins during the ripening period, which in some cases may be more than a year.

Soybean pastes and sauces are also preserved with salt as are matured sausages (sometimes they are also smoked). Usually 4-5 percent salt is used in salamis and similar long-keep-ing sausages. The same amount is used for bacon.

Salted butter has 2 percent salt added to improve its shelf life.

Salted beans

3 lb/1.5kg French green beans, snap
  beans or English runner beans,
  ends snipped off, washed and
  pat-dried
1lb 4oz/500g cooking salt

Either leave the green beans whole or cut them into halves. Snap beans and English runner beans should be sliced thinly.

Place a layer of salt about ½in/1.2cm thick in the bottom of a non-reactive container. Cover with a layer of beans 1in/2.5cm thick, or about double the thickness of the salt used. Repeat these alternate layers of salt and beans until the container is packed full up to the brim.

Press the mixture down and put a saucer or lid on top with a heavy weight, such as a large food can to keep the beans immersed in salt. When the level of mixture has sunk, add more beans and salt to keep the container as full as possible.

Remove the weight after 4 days and seal the top with plastic wrap (cling-film) and waxed paper.

Variations

Other vegetables can be salted in this way such as asparagus, bell peppers, flageolet beans and mushrooms.

Sauerkraut

3lb/1.5kg white Savoy cabbage or
* firm cabbage*
3 tbsp/1½oz/40g coarse salt

Cut the cabbage into very thin shreds including the core. Place in a clean non-reactive bowl.

Mix the salt with the cabbage. Put a non-reactive lid or plate on top and let ferment in a room at 75°F/24°C for 5 days. Remove the scum as it rises as a result of the fermentation.

Add 2 tablespoons of salt mixed with 2¼ cups/500ml/18fl oz water. Cover again with a non-reactive lid or plate and leave at the same temperature for 10 days. The plate must always be covered by the brine. If this does not happen add salt and water in the same ratio as before: 2tbsp salt to 2¼ cups/500ml/18oz water.

After 10 days the sauerkraut can be eaten. Rinse it in cold water and cook with frankfurters and bacon.

SALTIMBOCCA An Italian dish of fried veal scallops (escalopes) topped with prosciutto and sage leaves, either left flat or rolled up. Some versions include sliced cheese.

SAMBAL Small Indonesian and Malayasian side dishes and condiments such as chutneys and salads.

SAMBAL UDANG An Indonesian dish of skewered shrimp (prawns) coated in a chili pepper and shrimp paste, then barbecued.

SAMOSA A fried Indian pastry filled with potatoes and vegetables, fish or meat and served as a snack.

SAMPHIRE, GLASSWORT (Fr. FENOUIL MARIN) A sea plant that can be boiled and used like asparagus, or pickled in sweet vinegar and used as a pickle.

SANDWICH The sandwich was named after John Montagu, fourth Earl of Sandwich, who demanded some cold meat between two slices of bread while refusing to move from the gaming table of a casino. His simple idea caught on and the sandwich has become a major part of our diet, particularly for grabbing a quick meal.

Innumerable types of sandwiches can be made. Popular sandwiches include club sandwiches and toasted triple-deck sandwiches with three

S

slices of bread and two layers of different fillings.

If bread is chilled overnight it will be easier to slice.

SANCOCHO A Venezuelan and Chilean stew made up of beef, green bananas and thickened with cassava.

SAPODILLA A plum-like fruit native to Mexico and Central America. It makes a delicate sherbet (sorbet).

SARDINE A small oily fish belonging to the herring family. It can be broiled (grilled) without first removing the bones, which are an excellent source of calcium.

Unfortunately more sardines are available canned in olive oil than are available fresh in the shops.

Sardines à la Provençal

16 fresh sardines, slightly scaled but
*   not gutted*
2 tbsp olive oil
salt and black pepper
4 large sweet tomatoes, sliced
*   horizontally*
2 garlic cloves
½ cup/4floz/100ml French dressing
1 red onion, sliced in rings
2 tbsp parsley, chopped
French bread to serve

Wash the sardines in salted water. Drain and pat dry. Brush with oil and broil (grill) for 8 minutes.

Place the tomatoes in a salad bowl. Sprinkle with chopped garlic and stir in the French dressing.

Arrange the onion rings over the tomatoes and sprinkle with parsley. Serve the sardines with this salad and French bread.

SASHIMI A Japanese hors d'ouvre of raw fish served with a dipping sauce and wasabi, a hot horseradish-like paste.

SATAY SAUCE An Asian sauce made with ground peanuts, coconut milk, garlic, ginger, shrimp paste, chili powder and seasoning.

SATSUMA PLUM A prolific Japanese red plum. It can be made into a condiment with vinegar and sugar.

SAUCE The varieties of sauces are innumerable and diverse. For example, mayonnaise and all its many derivatives such as tartare and rémoulade sauces, aïoli, chasseur, horseradish, pesto, tomato, mornay, Américaine, Newburg, Béarnaise, hollandaise, Bordelaise, Bercy, and Bourguignonne to name but a few.

Sauces can be frozen, bottled, canned, powdered or reduced by boiling to make extracts and glazes. The consistency of a sauce is obtained by deglazing, reduction and concentration, by adding coagulating ingredients such as eggs, butter, cream, gelatin, agar, flour, a roux or beurre manié. *See also Bottled sauces.*

SAUERKRAUT Fermented cabbage which is served with frankfurter sausages, boiled bacon and potatoes. It is available in cans or jars. *See details on page 282.*

SAUSAGES Sausages are made from meat, poultry, game or fish packed into skins. They can be fresh (sometimes they can contain preservatives), or they can be cooked or smoked to be reheated or eaten without cooking as hors d'oeuvres.

Modern sausages are packed in casings made from edible alginate (seaweed) rather than animal intestines. The varieties of sausages are legion:

ANDOUILLE AND ANDOUILLETTE are highly seasoned French pork sausages. They are served cold.

BAVARIAN SAUSAGES made with pork and veal.

BOILED LIVER SAUSAGE made from pig's or calves liver or goose liver.

BOILED LUNCHEON SAUSAGE which can be eaten cold.

BOLOGNA SAUSAGE is a large ready-cooked Italian sausage, served thinly sliced as an hors d'oeuvre.

BRITISH SAUSAGES made from pork, beef or a mixture of beef and pork.

CHIPOLATAS are small, thin, beef or pork sausages.

FISH SAUSAGES, made fresh to be broiled (grilled) or poached.

FRANKFURTER HOT DOG SAUSAGES ready-cooked and made with mixed meat. They are reheated in hot water for eating.

GARLIC PORK SAUSAGE that is boiled and ready to be eaten.

SALAMI made from beef and pork are smoked and dried so they are ready to eat cold without any preparation other than slicing.

SMOKED LYONS SAUSAGE is made from beef.

S

Fresh British sausage

This mixture must be well ground (minced), mixed and refrigerated for 6 hours before use to give it time to develop its full flavor.

2¼ lb/1kg neck or shoulder pork meat, finely ground (minced)
9oz/250g hard pork fat
3½ cups/7oz/200g fresh bread crumbs
1 cup/3oz/75g minced parsley
1 egg, beaten
30g /salt
1tsp black peppercorns, coarsely ground
½ tsp ground mixed spices

Mix all the ingredients together. Fill into sausage skins. Cook under the broiler (grill) or gently fry in a skillet.

Variations

1) Instead of being filled into sausage skins the mixture can be wrapped in pig's caul or made into burgers.

2) Add 2 chopped garlic cloves, 2 tbsp chopped parsley, ½ cup/2oz/50g chopped nuts, 1 small onion, 1¼ cups/4oz/100g chopped mushrooms or ¼ cup/2oz/50g cooked spinach.

3) Instead of all pork the mixture can be made with beef, venison, lamb, veal, pig, lambs' or calves' liver, chicken, duck or game.

SAUTÉ To cook small pieces of food in a special straight-sided pan over high heat in butter or oil, shaking and tossing the pan so the food literally jumps.

SAVELOY Boiled sausage originally made with sheeps' brain but now made from pork. Saveloys are similar to frankfurter sausages but are coarser.

SAVORY (Fr. SARRIETTE) 1)An aromatic plant that is grown the same way as marjoram.

Winter savory is a perennial while summer savory is an annual. Both plants are full of aromatic oil and fresh or dried make a pleasant and different seasoning for soups, beans, salads and stuffings.

2) In classic menus, especially in Britain, savories were served at the end of a meal.

Typical savories are small portions of Welsh rarebit, scrambled eggs with anchovy fillets, mushrooms and cheese au gratin, a light cheese soufflé mixture baked in a small tartlet case, small cheese and mushroom kebabs or even cheese or cauliflower fritters.

Savories can also be served as hot

appetizers for a buffet or as snacks.

Typical dishes: Angels on horseback, Scotch woodcock, soft roes on toast, York ham and mushrooms on toast.

Croque My Lord

4 slices of smoked salmon
8 slices of toast with crusts removed
4 slices of mozzarella cheese
lemon wedges for garnish

Place a smoked salmon slice on each of 4 pieces of toast. Put a slice of mozzarella cheese on top of each one.

Cook under a broiler (grill) until brown and top with another slice of toast. Cut into triangles.

Serve immediately garnished with lemon wedges.

French bread pizza

1 small French loaf
4 canned sardines, split in half lengthwise
1 tsp Dijon mustard
2 tbsp mayonnaise
2 tbsp grated Gruyère cheese
1 red onion, thinly sliced into rings for garnish

Cut the loaf into 4 pieces. Split each piece in half lengthwise. Toast the bread on one side only. Top the bread with the sardines.

Mix the mustard into the mayonnaise and spread over the sardines. Sprinkle over the cheese and broil (grill) until the cheese is melted.

Garnish with red onion rings.

SCALLION (SPRING ONION) Seed onion harvested when young. The white bulb and stem and some or all of the green leaves can be used. The size and shape of a scallion varies according to the variety. The flavor is more delicate than regular onions. It is used a lot in Chinese cookery.

SCALLOP (Eng. ESCALOPE) 1) A thin slice of lean, tender meat, traditionally veal but now is also applied to similar slices of pork, chicken and turkey.
2) A bivalve mollusk (Fr. Coquille St. Jacques) found in many parts of the world. The firm, white flesh takes less than 5 minutes to cook.

Small scallops such as bay scallops and queen scallops are often barbecued on kebabs, or fried, but they are also delicious in white wine sauce.

To open scallops, place them on top of the stove or in a hot oven until they open, or place a knife between the two shells, rotate the blade on the flat shell to prize the scallop apart.

Remove the top shell by cutting the adhering flesh right against the shell.

S

Wash the scallops.

Typical dishes: Coquille St. Jacques sauce au vinaigre de Xérès, coquille St. Jacques Bretonne, coquille St. Jacques marinière.

Scallops with pasta and pesto sauce

8 large scallops, cleaned
seasoned flour
¼ cup/2oz/50g butter or olive oil
2 shallots, chopped
1 garlic clove, crushed
⅔ cup/5fl oz/150ml Italian medium
   vermouth
2 large tomatoes, skinned, seeded
   and chopped
½ cup/4fl oz/100ml heavy (double)
   cream
salt and pepper, grinded to taste
8oz/225g pasta noodles preferably
   in 3 colors

Pesto sauce

8 basil leaves
1 bunch of parsley
12 pine nuts
1 garlic clove,
2 anchovy fillets
black pepper
4 tbsp olive oil

Wash the scallops and pat dry. Toss in seasoned flour; shake off the surplus so as not to overwhelm the mollusks.

Heat the butter or oil in a frying pan and shallow-fry the shallots for 1 minute. Add the garlic, vermouth and tomatoes and cook for 4 minutes.

Add the scallops and poach gently for 4 minutes. Add the cream, stir well and season.

Meanwhile, boil the pasta for 8 minutes. Drain and keep hot while preparing the pesto. To make the pesto sauce, purée all the ingredients to make a thin sauce. Toss the pasta in the pesto.

Serve the scallops and their sauce on the pasta.

Scallop mousseline Monte Carlo

This is one of the most sophisticated and delicate of dishes. The scallop flesh is pounded into a paste and blended with heavy (double) cream and egg white.

8oz/225g scallops, cleaned
5oz/150g haddock fillet, skinned
2 egg whites
⅔ cup/5fl oz/150ml heavy cream
salt and white pepper

Sauce

⅔ cup/5fl oz/150ml velouté sauce
   made with fish stock
1 small sachet of saffron
2 tbsp taramasalata
2 tbsp double cream

Garnish

8oz/225g spinach purée seasoned with grated nutmeg, salt and pepper

4 x 2in/5cm baked puff pastry tartlet shells

Grind (mince) the scallops with the haddock. Mix with the egg whites then add the cream. Place over a bowl half filled with ice cubes and chill for 1 hour.

Fill 4 x 2in/5cm oiled ramekin dishes with the scallop mixture.

Gently poach in a water bath in an oven at 350°F/180°C/gas mark 4 for 20 minutes.

Blend the fish velouté sauce with the saffron and taramasalata. Boil for 3 minutes. Check the seasoning and strain.

Heat the spinach purée. Season with nutmeg, salt and black pepper.

Turn out the mousses into the pastry tartlet shells. Coat with a little sauce. Pour a pool of the remaining sauce beside the tartlets. Add the spinach purée.

Scallops in whisky

Scottish malt whisky gives a special tang to the scallops.

1lb/450g bay (queen) scallop meat, fresh or defrosted

⅔ cup/5fl oz/150ml fish stock

2 tbsp malt whisky

1 tbsp fine oats

2 tbsp basil, chopped

juice of ½ lemon

1 tsp honey, preferably heather-flavored

2 tbsp slivered almonds

Clean, trim and wash the scallops. Pat dry and cut each in 2 slices horizontally. Poach in stock for 3 minutes.

Drain the scallops; reserve the stock. Put the scallops in shallow individual dishes.

Pour the reserved stock into a small saucepan. Stir in the whisky and oats, and cook for 4 minutes until thickened. Add the basil, lemon juice and honey.

Pour some of the sauce over each scallop and sprinkle with flaked almonds. Broil until lightly browned.

Seafood in aspic

Fish in aspic is very popular in Russian and Dutch cookery.

Bearing in mind that some fish are more gelatinous than others, eel, turbot, brill and trout are especially suitable for making attractive seafood in aspic, providing the jelly is clarified before it sets.

S

½ cup/4oz/100g peeled, cooked
  jumbo shrimp (king prawns)
½ cup/4oz/100g flaked cooked
  salmon
2oz/50g short grain rice, boiled
⅓ cup/2oz/50g green beans, cooked
  and diced
¼ red bell pepper, cooked and diced
⅓ cup/3fl oz/75ml thick mayonnaise
1¼ cups/½ pint/300ml fish stock
6 tbsp fish stock
1 package powdered gelatin
6 tbsp water/
salt and pepper

Aspic
1¼ cups/½ pint/300ml fish stock
2 tsp powdered gelatin
3 tbsp medium sherry

Mix the shrimp rice, beans, bell peppers and mayonnaise in a large bowl.

Heat the fish stock and dissolve the
gelatin. While it is still warm, add two
thirds to the fish mixture. Chill until
set.

Pour 1 tablespoon of the remaining
aspic into 4 x 2 cup/8fl oz/225ml
ramekin dishes. Chill to set.

Fill the dishes with fish mixture.

Chill until needed then turn out the
ramekins onto plates or attractive
glasses with a garnish of assorted salad
leaves.

SCALDING 1) Pouring boiling water
over food to clean it, loosen hairs or
remove the skin.

2) Heating milk to just below boiling
point, to retard souring or to infuse it
with another flavor.

SCAMPI *See Langoustine.*

SCORPION FISH (Fr. RASCASSE) A
Mediterranean red fish particularly
used in bouillabaisse. Gurnard can be
used instead.

SCRAG Pieces of neck meat, usually
lamb, with the bones still attached that
are used for stews.

SEA BASS (Fr. BAR) An oily fish which
can be baked with fennel or broiled.

SEA-BREAM *See Bream.*

**SEA CUCUMBER, BALALO, TREPANG (Fr.
BÊCHE DE MER)** A great delicacy much
favored by the Chinese. Sea cucumbers are available canned in Chinese
stores.

SEA URCHIN (Fr. OURSIN) A spiny
marine invertebrate commonly known
in France as châtaigne de mer or sea
hedgehog. Only the coral and the juice
are edible, raw with lemon juice. The

coral can also be used to flavor sauces or fish mousses.

SEAL To fry meat, poultry and fish to form a crust on the outside and so improve the flavor.

SEARING Browning meat, poultry or fish quickly in a little hot oil for a good flavor and color.

SEASONING One of the most important operations of cooking. Other flavorings as well as salt and pepper should be used.

SEAWEED (Fr. ALGUES) Seaweeds are among the last major natural resources still generally unexploited by man, but as the population of the world expands and food famine becomes everybody's concern, seaweeds will soon become part of our everyday life. Japan, Ireland and Wales have used seaweeds for generations. *See Agar, Carrageen, Kelp, Laver.*

SEED An embryo enclosed by an integumentary covering or seed coat. An endosperm containing reserve foods may also be present within the seed coat.

Seeds develop from the ovule, the embryo resulting from the fertiliza-tion of the megagamete (egg) by the microgamete (sperm). The resultant zygote (fertilized egg) undergoes nuclear and cellular divisions and develops as the embryo sporophyte.

The nutrient material which supplies the embryo with food during the initial stages of germination may be located in the cotyledons. In some cases, such as mustard seeds, the cotyledons are thick and fleshy and the seed is said to be exalbuminous.

When the food reserves are in storage tissues that are not a part of the embryo, that is, in the endosperm or perisperm, the seed is said to be albuminous. The type of food stored in seeds depends upon the species of plant; carbohydrates, fat and proteins may occur in various proportions.

Starch is the most common food reserve; the endosperm of cereals and the cotyledons of legumes are especially rich in this form of carbohydrate.

Sugar, usually sucrose, may occur in smaller amounts in some seeds such as chestnuts and peas. Proteins form a part of the food reserves of all seeds but are especially abundant in legumes.

Sometimes an additional seed covering — the aril — to the seed is formed after fertilization. In the nutmeg this is called mace.

S

There is a wide variation in the viability and longevity of seeds. Although some seeds will germinate as soon as they mature, notably in certain cultivated plants such as beans and peas, most seeds require a period of dormancy that may range from a few days to a few months.

Some seeds retain their viability for several years and there are cases of 100 year-old seeds still germinating; cassia seeds are a prime example.

Germination of seeds depends on a supply of water, oxygen and a suitable temperature, exactly the same conditions required for yeast growth. Some seeds grow better in light and others in darkness.

Many seeds are used in cookery for their aromatic flavor, especially in stir-fried dishes, such as mustard, celery and lovage seeds.

Other familiar edible seeds are sesame, pumpkin and sunflower seeds, wheat, garbanzo beans (chickpeas), kidney beans, lentils, and buckwheat, fenugreek, mung beans, alfalfa and adzuki beans.

Many seeds can be sprouted for salads or garnishes for a number of Asian dishes. Sprouting seeds were the first true crops harvested by man; bean sprouts were known in China more than 5,000 years ago.

As an easy-to-grow, cheap and nutritious food crop, sprouting seeds can hardly be bettered. They sprout easily in trays or jars; first moisten the seeds, then cover and keep them warm without too much light. They are ready within a few days.

SEEDS DE MELONE Italian pasta shaped like melon seeds.

SEETHING (Fr. SAISIR) Gently cooking food in foaming butter.

SEMOLINA (Fr. SEMOULE) This is made from wheat flour milled to varying degrees of fineness.

Usually hard durum wheat flour is used, but some soft wheat flour semolina is available. *See also Couscous..*

SESAME SEED A small seed that has been eaten throughout India and the Middle East for thousands of years. It is used in vegetable dishes, breads, chutneys and with rice. It is also ground for its oil.

Toasted sesame seeds, called gomashio in Japan, are mixed with spinach. *See also Tahini.*

SCONES (Am. BISCUITS) Small buns leavened (raised) with baking powder and served with cream and jam. Biscuits (scones) may be baked in the oven or cooked on a griddle.

SCOTCH BROTH A soup either of chicken broth with barley and vegetables or mutton and oatmeal.

SHAD (Fr. ALOSE) A migratory fish caught in rivers. It is baked or broiled and served with spinach or sorrel.

SHANK (SHIN, Fr. JARRET) The end of the leg used for stock or to make beef consommé .

SHARK (Fr. REQUIN) A scavenger fish which Asian and Indian cooks use in stews and soups. Sharks' fins are an expensive Chinese delicacy.

SHELLFISH There are a very large number of shellfish throughout the world, some edible, some not. The main categories of shellfish that are eaten are crustaceans and mollusks.

SHEEP (Fr. BRÉBIS, MOUTON) From earliest times sheep have served mankind well, providing both meat and warm clothing.

Over the years sheep have been interbred from the many ancient species to produce the over 200 breeds which now exist. Modern breeds of sheep provide better meat and wool than their predecessors.

Sheep are completely 'free range' and therefore have a seasonal cycle. *See also Lamb.*

SHALLOT (Fr. ÉCHALOTE) A bulbous sweet member of the onion family.

It has small cloves and a more delicate flavor than onions. Shallots are used for shallot sauce for serving with oysters, and various fish or meat sauces such as Bércy sauce.

SHALLOW-FRYING Frying with the minimum fat. *See also Sauté, and Stir-frying.*

SHARON FRUIT A variety of the persimmon which may be eaten soft. It has an edible bright orange or red skin and very sweet-tasting flesh.

Sharon fruit can be made into pies, jams and jellies as well as sweet and sour sauces.

SHELF (OVEN) The position of the shelves in the oven determines the place where the food will be cooked to best advantage, the top being the hottest place and the bottom relatively the coldest.

The exception are convection or fan

S

ovens where the heat is more evenly distributed and less variable.

Use an oven thermometer to check the temperature of shelves at the top, center and bottom of the oven.

SHERBET (SORBET) A water ice flavored with lemon or other fruit juices. The addition of egg whites, gelatin or Italian meringue will lighten a sherbet (sorbet) and make it less grainy.

SHIÏTAKE Originally from Asia shiitake mushrooms are now cultivated in America and Europe.

Shiitake mushrooms have a resilient texture and meaty flavor. They can be stir-fried, sautéed in butter, broiled (grilled) or used in stews. In China and Japan they are dried to become black mushrooms.

SHORTBREAD A rich butter cookie (biscuit) made by either cutting the butter into the flour, or by beating the sugar and butter together before adding the flour. Confectioners' (icing), superfine (caster) or granulated sugar can be used depending on the texture required.

SHOULDER (Fr. ÉPAULE) The part of an animal to which the front legs are attached. A shoulder can be boned, rolled and filled with a stuffing, or diced and used in stews.

Beef and veal shoulders can be roasted and braised or even cut into steaks or scallops (escalopes).

SHREWBURRY CAKES Small round cookies (biscuits).

SHRIMP (PRAWNS) Over 100 different species of shrimp (prawns) of different sizes are caught around the world, and many of these are farmed. They feed on small organisms or food particles in the water, so the vast majority are caught with trawl nets.

Small shrimp can be boiled and eaten simply with whole wheat (wholemeal) bread and butter as an ideal lunch appetizer. Stir-fried prawns are served with rice, and striped jumbo shrimp, also called tiger prawns, can be broiled (grilled) on skewers and served with barbecue sauces, or used for dipping (they are ideal for this because of their size). The tail meat of these shrimp changes to a delightful coral and white color on cooking.

Stir-fried shrimp (prawns), bamboo and broccoli
1lb/450g shelled frozen striped
    jumbo shrimp (tiger prawns)
2 tbsp oil

1 onion, chopped
1⅓ cups/8oz/225g canned bamboo,
  sliced
2 cups/8oz/225g broccoli florets,
  blanched for 4 minutes
8oz/225g white button mushrooms
2 garlic cloves, chopped
6 tbsp fish stock
I small piece of fresh ginger root,
  grated
Sauce
3 oysters
1 tbsp soy sauce
6 tbsp fish stock
2 tsp cornstarch (cornflour) blended
  with 2 tbsp cold water
salt and pepper

Using a sharp knife, cut down the backs of the shrimp (prawns) and remove the dark intestinal thread.

Heat the oil and stir-fry the shrimp and onion for 3 minutes.

Add the bamboo, broccoli, mushrooms, garlic, fish stock and ginger. Cook for 4 minutes.

To make the oyster sauce, boil the oysters in the soy sauce and fish stock for 2 minutes.

Stir in the cornstarch (cornflour) and water and boil for 4 minutes to thicken the sauce.

Purée the sauce and add to the shrimp mixture. Season to taste.

SHRIMPS (Am. SMALL SHRIMP, Fr. CREVETTES) In Britain shrimps applies to the smallest member of the crustacean family.

Shrimps are either boiled in the shell for 4 minutes, or peeled and tossed in butter with cayenne or chili pepper and eaten on toast.

SHROPSHIRE CHEESE A hard cheese made in the county of Shropshire, England. Blue Shropshire cheese is made as well as white.

SILICON DIOXIDE An anti-caking agent used in dry cake batter mixtures.

SIMNEL CAKE A British Easter cake. A layer of almond paste is baked between two layers of rich fruit cake. The top of the baked cake is covered with almond paste and decorated with eleven almond paste balls that are said to represent Jesus' disciples, minus the traitor, Judas.

SINIGANG A soup-like meat or fish and vegetable dish from the Philippines. The cooking liquid is made tart with tamarind and fruits such as green guavas.

SKATE (Fr. RAIE) Only the wings are used for cooking. The fish should be

S

soaked in cold water with white vinegar and rinsed well to remove the smell. Skate can be poached in a court bouillon, drained and coated with vinegar, capers and fresh herbs, or fried in butter.

SKIRRET A perennial plant with a long, white root that is used as a vegetable. It can be par-boiled and tossed in butter or deep-fried.

SKIRT STEAK (Am. FLANK) A lean cut of beef that is taken from the abdomen and chest cavity. After trimming the steak is beaten with a meat bat to tenderize it and providing it is broiled (grilled) or fried underdone it will be tender enough.

SLIMMING DIET A severely restricted diet designed to reduce the weight of those eating it.

SLOE (Fr. PRUNELLE) A small, very acid type of plum. It is usually made into a liqueur called sloe gin.

SMELT (Fr. ÉPERLAN) A small fish that is usually about 4-6in/10-15cm long when sold. It is usually deep-fried.

SMOKED FISH Smoked fish should look fresh and glossy and should have a pleasant smoky smell from natural wood smoke and not artificial smoke powders. Fish can be hot or cold smoked.

COLD SMOKED FISH are smoked in a kiln at a temperature below 85°F/30°C to avoid cooking the flesh. Cold smoked fish does not need to be cooked before it is eaten.

With this method the fish is often only lightly colored during the smoking process and so permitted edible colorings are usually added to make the fish more attractive. Color-free fish are also available.

Cold smoked fish include smoked cod, finnan haddie (smoked haddock), kippers, bloaters, red herrings, ling, smoked mackerel and whiting.

HOT-SMOKED FISH is smoked in a kiln to a temperature of about 180°F/82°C, which partially cooks the flesh. Hot-smoked fish needs no further cooking and are ready to eat cold.

Hot smoked fish include smoked cod's roe, smoked eel, Arbroath smokies, buckling, smoked mackerel, smoked oysters, smoked salmon and trout, smoked halibut and tuna.

SMOKING Curing food by exposure to wood smoke. The smoke can be from oak, hickory or any type of fruit tree. For extra flavor aromatic herbs such as sage, rosemary or dried mint can be added. Fish takes less time to smoke than meat and poultry.

There are two types of smoking:

COLD SMOKING at temperatures from 50-85°F/10-30°C. To keep the temperature low, the fuel that provides the smoke is kept on the outside of the smoker. Commercially cold-smoked foods include kippers, poultry, ham and bacon.

HOT SMOKING at temperatures from 200-250°F/93-121°C, which is enough to lightly cook the food. It is used for duck, goose, chicken and meat as well as firm fish. The food is only partially preserved so should be eaten within a few days.

SMÖRGÅSBORD Swedish cold table laden with a sumptuous spread of appetizer-style dishes.

SMØRREBRØD Danish open sandwiches: smorrebrod literally means 'buttered bread'. These are often made with pumpernickel bread.

There are many different kind of fillings including fish, shellfish, meat, poultry, cheese and eggs. They may be garnished with attractively arranged fruits, herbs or vegetables.

SMYRNE RAISIN A type of sun-dried raisin that is a speciality of Smyrna in Greece. These raisins are used to make a strong sweet wine.

SNAIL (Fr. ESCARGOT) There are two kinds used as food: the small grey snail and the large escargot de Bourgogne which is found in vineyards.

Snails are usually starved for 36 hours then boiled in the shell before being stuffed with garlic and herb butter. They are served on special snail plates which have indentations to hold the snails, a set of tongs and a special two pronged fork to extract the meat from the shells.

Snails can also be served in a sauce without the shells.

SNAKE Snakes have the same oily and gelatinous flesh as eels. They are edible and eaten, irrespective of whether they are poisonous or not. A snake should be skinned and gutted like fish.

China and other Asiatic countries have many recipes for snakes, all based on fish cookery.

SNAPPER There are about 250 members of the snapper family and the best known, particularly in America and Australia, are the grey snapper and the red snapper. These salt water fish can grow up to 38lb/17kg.

Snapper are best filleted and either braised or broiled.

SOCCA The flour made from garbanzo beans (chickpeas) and used for purées, porridge or tart fillings.

SODA WATER Water carbonated by the injection of carbon dioxide. A special piece of equipment can be purchased to carbonate the water.

SODIUM A dietary essential which is almost always satisfied by a normal diet.

Sodium is used in the preparation of sodium compounds. *See individual entries.*

SODIUM BENZOATE A food preservative effective only in a slightly acid environment.

SODIUM BICARBONATE An alkali that is used in baking powder.

SODIUM CHLORIDE *See Salt.*

SODIUM CITRATE An antioxidant, buffer and emulsifying agent.

SODIUM NITRATE *See Saltpeter.*

SOLE Dover sole is a flat fish of great gourmet appeal. Both the skin and fins are removed before cooking. The fish can be cooked whole in wine and stock or fried in oil and butter.

Alternatively, it can be filleted and deep-fried in batter.

Lemon sole is considered an inferior fish, it has softer flesh and is best fried.

Typical dishes: Sole à la bonne femme, sole Bercy, sole Colbert, sole à la Dieppoise, sole Florentine, sole à la Joinville, sole à la Nantua, sole mornay, sole Walewska.

Sole soufflé Conil
The combination of Dover sole fillets with a salmon soufflé mixture is one of the highlights of fish gastronomy and a credit to the cook. This is one of the best dishes that can be served for a party dinner. The soufflés are unmolded onto plates so the ramekins must be well-buttered.

4 Dover sole fillets
¼ cup/2oz/50g butter, softened

Sauce
⅔ cup/5fl oz/150ml fish stock
⅔ cup/5fl oz/150ml fish velouté
salt and pepper

Soufflé mixture

*⅓ cup/3oz/75g salmon fillet, ground
(minced) and chilled*
*⅓ cup/3fl oz/75ml heavy (double)
cream*
1 egg white
3 mint leaves, chopped
salt, pepper and paprika

Sauce

⅔ cup/5fl oz/150ml fish stock
⅔ cup/5fl oz/150ml fish velouté
salt and pepper

Garnish

8 asparagus tips
4 slices fresh truffle

Serves 4

Place the sole fillets top side downwards, between sheets of plastic wrap (clingfilm) and beat with a meat bat to flatten them and break the fibers slightly.

Coat the insides of 4 x 1 cup/8fl oz/225ml ramekin dishes or individual soufflé dishes with the softened butter. Line each dish with a sole fillet, pressing it firmly against the wall of the dish, to leave a large cavity for the soufflé mixture.

Refrigerate the fillets for 20 minutes while preparing the soufflé mixture, sauce and garnish.

To make the sauce, boil the fish stock and fish velouté together until reduced by one third. Strain, season and keep warm in a water bath.

To make the soufflé mixture, place some ice cubes and water in a bowl. Put the salmon in the bowl and gradually beat in the cream and egg white. Add the mint leaves and season with a pinch of salt, white pepper and paprika. Adjust the pink color with a little tomato paste (purée) or catsup (ketchup). Fill the sole-lined dishes.

Place the dishes in a deep roasting pan (tin) half-filled with hot water and bake at 400 °F/200°C/gas mark 6 for 15-20 minutes.

Boil the asparagus for 6-7 minutes until tender. Drain well.

Unmold the sole fillets carefully onto four plates, using the blade of a small knife to ease the fish out of the dishes. Coat each one with reduced sauce. Garnish with a thin slice of truffle and place 2 asparagus tips, crisscrossing each other by the side.

SOP KACANG MERAH A thin, puréed Indonesian red bean and coconut milk soup flavored with ginger, galingal and garlic.

SOPAIPILLA Deep-fried Mexican pastry fritters that are served immediately

S

they are cooked, with a hot syrup poured over.

SORBET (Am. SHERBET) A water ice flavored with lemon or other fruit juices. The addition of egg whites, gelatin or Italian meringue will lighten a sherbet and make it less grainy.

SORBITAN MONOSTEARATE An emulsifier, stabilizer and glazing agent.

SORGHUM A grass related to millet that is a staple for the poor of Africa and India. Sweet sorghum has a stem rich in sugars, so it is crushed to extract the sugar, which is boiled down to make sorghum syrup.

SORREL (Fr. OSEILLE) A leafy plant that is acidic because it contains oxalic acid. It can be used as a filling for omelets and soups. Sorrel turns yellowish on cooking.

SOSATI A South African lamb kebab that is marinated before broiling.

SOUBISE Onion and rice purée served as an accompaniment to various cuts of meat.

SOUFFLÉ The basis of most soufflés is an egg custard mixed with three times the volume of beaten (whisked) egg white. Use 1 cup of confectioners' custard and 2 cups of whipped egg whites as a guide line, and twice as many egg whites as egg yolks.

The ability of a soufflé to remain risen for at least 20 minutes depends on the gluten content of the flour used, so bread (strong) flour should be used for best results.

Very light fruit soufflés can be made with fruit purées.

Popular savory soufflés include spinach, mushroom, cheese, salmon and broccoli. Popular sweet soufflés include vanilla soufflé served with a chocolate sauce or Grand Marnier soufflé served with oranges in syrup, ginger served with lychees, and strawberry soufflé served with strawberries.

Smoked trout soufflés
A tomato sauce makes a good accompaniment to these soufflés.

¼ cup/2oz/50g soft butter for the
  soufflé dishes
½ cup/2oz/50g chopped almonds

Soufflé mixture
2 tbsp/1oz/25g butter
3 tbsp/1oz/25g bread (strong) flour
⅔ cup/5fl oz/150ml light (single)
  cream

1 whole egg, beaten

2 egg yolks

⅔ cup/5oz/150g chopped smoked trout flesh

⅔ cup/3 oz/75 g cooked chopped spinach, well drained and pressed

2 tbsp grated Parmesan cheese

1 garlic clove, finely chopped

salt, black pepper and grated nutmeg or celery salt

6 egg whites

Serves 4

Coat the inside of the 4 individual soufflé dishes with the butter. Sprinkle the almonds over the inside of the dishes and put them in a deep baking pan (tin).

To make the soufflé mixture, melt the butter in a saucepan. Stir in the flour and cook for 30 seconds.

Gradually stir in the cream and simmer to obtain a smooth paste.

Remove from heat and beat in the whole egg, the egg yolks, fish, spinach, Parmesan cheese, garlic and seasoning. Reheat the mixture until it begins to bubble, stirring continually. Pour into a large bowl and beat well. Cool.

In a clean bowl, beat the egg whites with a pinch of salt until they cling to the whisk. Fold half into the fish mixture and mix thoroughly.

Fold the remaining egg whites carefully and lightly into the fish mixture. Fill the soufflé dishes. Smooth the tops.

Bake at 400°F/200°C/gas mark 6 for 20 minutes, until well risen above the top of the dishes.

SOUP A soup is a broth made with vegetables, or a purée of vegetables, fish, shellfish or seafood, or a thickened meat or chicken stock plus the ingredients that characterize the soup, such as potatoes or tomatoes.

Most soups are served hot as appetizers or stimulants, but heavier soups are best served as a meal by and in themselves.

Centuries ago, soups were stews of meat and vegetables cooked in their stock. The liquid was drunk first, soaked in bread, and the solid food eaten afterwards as the main meal. Hence the saying: 'Eat your soup' instead of saying drink it .

Although there are many commercial dried and canned soups on the market, with a blender there is no excuse why people should be deprived of the flavor and taste of a freshly-made soup.

Soups may be broadly classified into two main groups, clear and thick.

CLEAR SOUPS include broths with

S

appropriate diced or strips of meat and vegetables, consommés made of clarified stocks with more decorative garnishes such as attractively-cut vegetables, rice or savory custards cut in geometric patterns.

COLD SUMMER SOUPS can also be in a class of their own as refreshing appetizers for buffet or picnic lunches.

Examples are Spanish gazpacho, the French vichyssoise and Jewish beet (beetroot) soup served with sour (soured) cream, and jellied consommé served without a garnish.

SOUP-CUM-STEW is another broad category which includes such delights as Russian borstch, French bouillabaisse, and chowders of clams and mussels.

THICK SOUPS include bisques made with shellfish and thickened with ground rice; brown soups thickened with brown roux; cream soups thickened with purées; soups thickened white roux and cream; velouté soups thickened by the coagulation of egg yolks, plus starch and cream.

Soups can be made with any kind of vegetable, fish, meat, poultry, game, pulse or cereal.

Most vegetable and fish soups can be produced very rapidly, and with the help of an electrical blender they can be puréed. *See also Bisque, Bourride and Minestrone.*

Potato and leek soup
¼ cup/2oz/50g butter
1 large leek, shredded
1 potato, finely chopped
2¼ cups/18fl oz/500ml chicken stock
2 ¼ cups/18fl oz/500ml milk or light (single) cream
salt and white pepper
chives for garnish

Melt the butter and fry the leek for 4 minutes. Add the potato and cook for 4 more minutes. Stir in the stock and boil for 12 minutes until the vegetables are soft.

Add the milk or cream and reheat the soup. Season to taste.

Serve the soup hot or cold as it is or purée it. Garnish with chives.

Variations
1) Use watercress instead of leek.
2) Use onions instead of leek.
3) Replace the leek with garlic.

Lentil soup
4 tbsp oil
1½ red onions, chopped

1 carrot, chopped
3 slices of bacon, chopped
1 garlic clove, chopped
1 cup/4oz/100g split yellow or red
   lentils
4 ⅓ cups/1¾ pints/1 liter brown beef
   stock
salt and black pepper

Heat the oil and fry the onions and carrot for 5 minutes. Add the garlic, bacon and lentils. Cook for another 5 minutes.

Stir in the stock and boil for 30 minutes. Purée the soup and reheat. Season to taste.

Variations

1) Replace lentils with split green peas and add a few spinach leaves to improve the color.

2) Replace the lentils with beans.

Cream velouté soup

¼ cup/2oz/50g butter
generous ¼ cup/1½ oz/40g flour
4⅓ cups/1¾ pints/1 liter white veal
   stock
⅔ cup/5fl oz/150ml heavy (double)
   cream
salt, white pepper and grated mace

Melt the butter and stir in the flour. Cook for 2 minutes until it becomes the color of sand. Stir in the stock gradually and simmer for 20 minutes.

Add the cream and seasoning. Strain.

Variations

1) To make chicken soup, use chicken stock instead of veal stock and add ½ cup/4oz/100g of cooked ground (minced) chicken to the soup for a better flavor.

2) Add 4oz/100g fresh asparagus tips to chicken soup in Variation (1). Purée the soup.

3) To make German velouté soup, mix 2 egg yolks with ½ cup/4fl z/100ml heavy (double) cream. Gradually stir into chicken soup in Variation (1) while whisking. Reheat until the soup begins to boil.

4) To make crème capucine, toss 1¾ cups/4oz/100g white mushrooms in 2 tbsp/1oz/25g butter and add to German velouté soup in Variation (3).

SOURDOUGH STARTER A small amount of dough, alive with beneficial yeasts and bacteria that cause fermentation. The starter is increased for use by the addition of flour and water.

SOUS-VIDE A food-packaging system in which food is vacuum-sealed and then cooked with a very rapid heating

S

and cooling so that much of the flavor and aroma of the fresh ingredients are retained under vacuum then immediately chilled.

This form of cooking has been tried in industrial restaurants to reduce the numbers of kitchen staff.

SOUVAROV (À LA) A French method of cooking game or poultry in a casserole with foie gras. The lid of the casserole is sealed with flour and water paste to retain the aroma.

SOY SAUCE A Chinese sauce made from a paste of ground soybeans and wheat flour fermented in water for several months until the liquid turns black.

SOYBEAN A native of China, Java and Japan, where it has been cultivated for centuries. It was later introduced into India, southern Europe and America. A new hybrid is now being grown in colder countries such as Scandinavia.

Soybeans are used to make bean curd, and soy protein has been extracted commercially for using as a meat replacement. *See Textured vegetable protein.*

SPAGHETTI An Italian pasta extruded like strips, in various thicknesses.

Spaghetti should be boiled 'al dente' for 10-12 minutes depending on the thickness, then drained and reheated with butter and grated cheese. The sauce is always made separately and poured onto the prepared pasta.

SPANAKOPITA A layered Greek pie made of feta cheese, spinach and filo pastry.

SPANISH ONION A large, sweet onion. It can be parboiled, stuffed with meat and baked, but it is mostly used for flavoring soups, stews and sauces.

SPARE RIBS These come from the breast of pork. They can be cooked Chinese-style soaked in a sweet and sour marinade flavored with garlic, ginger and five spice powder, then roasted.

SPÄTZLE Small German and Alsatian noodles. The noodle batter is poured through a special spätzle colander into boiling water to cook until they rise to the surface.

SPICE (Fr. ÉPICE) Aromatic dried roots, buds, seeds, bark, berries and other fruits that contain a volatile oil, for example cloves, nutmeg and cinnamon. *See individual entries.*

SPICED VINEGAR A vinegar flavored with spices and herbs such as coriander, tarragon, mustard seeds, celery seeds, cumin, caraway, thyme, mint and fennel. *See also Pickling spice, Vinegar.*

SPINACH (Fr. ÉPINARDS) Spinach should be washed well to rid it of any grit. It is best cooked without water but with a little butter, garlic and lemon juice. Spinach is better frozen rather than canned.

Typical dishes: Épinards en timbale à la Viroflay, crème d'épinards, soufflé d'épinards aux noix et fromage, quiche aux épinards, garbanzo beans (chickpeas) with spinach, spinach salad with hard-cooked (hard-boiled) eggs.

SPINY LOBSTER *See Crawfish.*

SPLIT PEA Certain varieties of pea are grown specially for splitting, which consist of stripping off the cellulose by friction to get the pea to split.

Split peas are served as a purée or used in soup flavored with bacon stock. *See Dal.*

SPONGE CAKE Sponge cakes and gâteaux are always popular, particularly in the afternoon. There are many types such as Savoy sponge, jelly (Swiss) roll, Victoria sandwich and Genoese.

If possible, use a cake flour with a low protein content. Do not use bread (strong) flour as it makes sponges tough in texture.

In some sponge recipes, whole eggs are beaten (whisked) together until very thick. In other recipes, the eggs are separated, beaten separately then folded together for a lighter cake. The flour should be sifted and lightly stirred into the eggs.

Plain sponge

5 eggs
1¼ cups/9½ oz/275g superfine (caster) sugar
4 drops of vanilla extract
2¼ cups/9½ oz/275g all-purpose (plain) flour
jam and whipped cream for the filling
confectioners' (icing) sugar for sifting

Line an 8in/20cm cake pan (tin) with baking parchment (greaseproof paper). Butter the parchment and sprinkle it with flour. Turn the pan upside down and bang the bottom to remove surplus flour.

In a grease-free bowl, beat the eggs, sugar and vanilla extract until very thick. Sift the flour onto a piece of

S

paper. Sprinkle it onto the egg mixture while mixing lightly with a large metal spoon. Do not beat in the flour.

Pour the batter into the cake pan and bake at 400°F/200°C/gas mark 6 for 20 minutes until golden brown.

Cool on a rack. When cold split the cake vertically. Spread with jam and whipped cream. Dust the top with confectioners' (icing) sugar.

SPRAT Small fish of the sardine family. A sprat has no axillary scales to the ventral fins, which are common to both the herring and sardines.

Sprats are cured and smoked and eaten as an hors d'oeuvre.

SPRING ONION (SCALLION) Seed onion harvested when young. The white bulb and stem and some or all of the green leaves can be used.

The size and shape of a scallion (spring onion) varies according to the variety. The flavor is more delicate than regular onions.

SQUASH These often quite large, water-filled fruits are generally used in the kitchen as vegetables. Ginger, garlic and tomatoes are the best flavoring ingredients for all kinds of squash.

Squash blossoms (flowers) can be stuffed or used as a garnish.

They are classified as:

SUMMER SQUASH such as zucchini (courgettes), patty pan and crookneck. These have a thin edible skin and tasty seeds.

WINTER SQUASH such as pumpkin, butternut, acorn, hubbard and turban. Both the thick skin and seeds are discarded.

SQUID (Fr. CAL(A)MAR) A relative of cuttle fish.

SQUILL-FISH A crustacean related to crawfish found in the Mediterranean, they can reach 18in/45cm. They have no claws, the tail only is used boiled, stewed or grilled.

STABILIZING AGENT An ingredient used in the food industry to improve the texture and consistency of commercially made emulsified sauces, creams, and ice creams.

Examples of natural stabilizing agents are lecithin extracted from soybean flour and egg yolk, tartaric acid, alginate, pectin, carob, tamarind and guar gum.

STAR ANISE A spice much used in China as one of the ingredients of five spice powder. Star anise is particularly used to flavor seafood.

STAR APPLE A fruit native to the West Indies and Central America, it has always been prized for its ornamental value as well as its fruit.

STAR FRUIT, CARAMBOLA, BARBADINE A bright yellow, waxy-looking, star-shaped and very acid fruit. It is used for garnishing dishes such as smoked fish appetizers, or in fruit salads.

STARCH (Fr. FÉCULE) A carbohydrate stored in the seeds, stalks, roots and tubers of numerous plants such as wheat, cassava, potato, banana, yam and pulses. Starch, either in the food or in the form of flour is used for thickening sauces, soups and gravies, and in custards and molded desserts.

Starches vary in size, shape and properties such as the thickening capacity, adhesiveness, ease and rate of dehydration, and the rate of hydrolysis by diastase.

During gelatinization the starch changes from an opaque suspension to a translucent gel. Rice is likely to be more translucent and tender but cornstarch (cornflour) is the firmest. Both corn and sago gelatinize at about the same temperature as potato starch.

Only cornstarch can be used for sauces which are going to be frozen or kept warm in a water bath as sauces thickened by a roux or other starches will thin down.

Normally acid breaks down starch-thickened sauces or soups. When this happens the starch changes into simple sugars.

STARVATION This is deprivation of food for a long period causing loss of weight, dryness of the mouth and headaches. Normal adults can survive without food for about six weeks; thin people for less and emaciated hungry people for only few days. *See Famine, Malnutrition.*

STEAK According to one legend, steaks became popular after the Battle of Waterloo when the occupying British forces claimed that broiled (grilled) fillet and loin steaks were needed for a good meal.

Steack au poivre was created at the Hotel Monte Carlo in 1905 by the chef Prosper Montagné, then Parisian chefs made tournedos Rossini (tournedos with foie gras) and Châteaubriand steak fashionable.

Carpetbag steak, which is stuffed with oysters, is a particular favorite in Australia.

S

A meat bat is used to flatten tougher steaks such as skirt to tenderize them.

STEAMING   The cooking of foods in moist heat. It is an economical and nutritious method of cooking.

Foods which are suitable for steaming are fish, vegetables such as sea kale, asparagus and snow peas (mangetout), tender meats and poultry. Some savory and sweet puddings are also steamed *See Puddings.*

The food to be steamed must not be in direct contact with the boiling water.

There are a number of different designs of steaming basket but a Chinese lidded wooden steamer is the simplest and cheapest.

Steamed pork dumplings

Lean pork can be used for pies and puddings. This dish is popular with children and the elderly because it is easy to eat and is as tasty cold as hot.

2 tbsp oil
8oz/225g lean pork, cut into 1in/2.5 cm cubes
½ cup/4oz/100g diced lean bacon
1 onion, chopped
1 tbsp flour
salt and pepper
⅔ cup/5fl oz/150 ml water

1 piece of fresh ginger root, grated
2 tbsp parsley, chopped
1 garlic clove, chopped
⅔ cup/4oz/100g baked beans in tomato sauce
stir-fried or steamed vegetables to serve

Pastry

4 cups/1lb/450g self-rising (self-raising) flour
1 tsp salt
⅔ cup/5oz/150g margarine
1 egg, beaten
3 tbsp cold water

Heat the oil in a pan and stir-fry the pork, bacon and onion together for 5 minutes.

Sprinkle the flour, ginger, parsley, garlic and seasoning over the meat. Stir in the water and simmer for 15 minutes. Mix the beans into the tomato sauce. Drain away any surplus sauce and let the mixture cool completely.

To make the pastry, place the flour and salt in a bowl and cut in the margarine until the mixture resembles crumbs. Stir in the egg and water to make a dough.

Roll out the dough to ¼in/5mm thick. Cut out 2in/5cm rounds

Place a spoonful of the meat mixture in the center of each round. Brush the edges with water and fold over. Crimp the edges. Put each half-moon-shaped dumpling on a piece of baking parchment (greaseproof paper) and steam for 45 minutes.

Serve immediately with stir-fried or steamed vegetables.

STEARIN A fatty acid present in most animal and vegetable fats as triglyceride.

STERILIZATION The complete destruction of micro organisms. This may require a heat treatment of up to 250°F/121°C by pressure cooking for 15 minutes.

STERLET A small species of sturgeon. It is baked, fried or poached like hake or salmon.

STICKY RICE *See Glutinous rice.*

STILTON CHEESE This British cheese is one of the finest blue cheeses made anywhere in the world.

Stilton is cylindrical in form, about 7½ in/18cm in diameter and 11in/28cm high. It is usually cut into portions for marketing.

When ripe, Stilton should be kept in a refrigerator. It should be cut with a wire and not a knife.

STEWING A long, slow, gentle, moist method of cooking. It tenderizes tough meat so it is ideal for cooking cheap cuts such as the shoulder, neck and breast of beef, veal, pork and lamb. Stewing may be done over direct heat or in the oven. There are three types of meat stews:

BROWN STEWS with meat or game.

SPICY STEWS such as curries, goulash and chili con carne.

WHITE STEWS with pork , veal, poultry and lamb.

Coarse fish like conger eels can be stewed in wine.

Stews are good value both nutritionally as the sauces and vegetables complement the meat, and economically as they are prepared with the cheapest cuts of meats.

The most suitable temperature for stewing is 200°F/95°C on the stove top or 300°F/150° C/gas mark 3 in the oven. The liquid should never boil but simmer gently, and the dish must always be covered with a lid. Herbs must be added only 15 minutes before the meat is ready.

Typical dishes: Boeuf à la bourguignonne, blanquette de veau, fricas-

S

sée d'agneau, ox tail casserole, veal goulash.

STIR-FRY A quick operation of frying ingredients while stirring them. Stir-fried vegetables are usually cooked until they are crisp and slightly undone.

STOCK Basic stock is the foundation of all good soups and sauces. A protein content gives stock a good flavor, while vegetables, herbs and spices also provide extra refinement. Different kinds of stock are prepared for different dishes depending on the principal ingredient.

BROWN STOCK The vegetables must be shallow-fried to caramelize their sugar content. Beef bones are generally used for brown stock.

When making meat stock add ½ cup/2oz/50g diced bacon and 8oz/225g of roasted shank (shin) or knuckle bones cut in small pieces. Brown stock requires at least 2 hours simmering.

CHICKEN STOCK Made with chicken wings, giblets, bones and skin, which can be lightly roasted prior to boiling for a better flavor. Chicken stock requires at least 2 hours simmering.

FISH STOCK Use 8oz/225g mixed white fish bones and a small anise star; the vegetables should include fennel. Fish stock can be prepared in 30 minutes.

GAME STOCK The trimmings, neck and bones of game can be used. If a marinade has been prepared, this can also be added providing vinegar has not been included as this would make the stock too acid. Game requires at least 2 hours simmering.

VEGETABLE STOCK can be prepared in 45 minutes.

WHITE STOCK The ingredients are boiled for just long enough to extract their flavor. Veal bones are generally used for white stock; then add ½ cup/2oz/50g of diced bacon and 8oz/225g shank (shin) or raw knuckle bones cut into small pieces. Simmer together for about 2 hours.

All stocks should have a bouquet garni consisting of a bay leaf, celery leaves, thyme and parsley, 1 onion studded with 4 cloves, and about 1 cup/7 oz/200g in total of mixed celery, carrot and onion per 4⅓ cups/1¾ pints/1 liter water.

The ratio of ingredients for a good stock is 30 percent bones and meat, 60 percent water and/or wine, and 10 percent vegetables, including the bouquet garni.

After shallow-frying or roasting the bones pour away all the fat.

Remove any scum from the stock as it rises, and let the stock simmer at just under boiling point to extract the maximum flavor.

The bouquet garni can be added 15 minutes before the stock is ready.

Care must be taken to remove all the fat; to do this either blot it off the surface with absorbent kitchen paper, or let the stock cool then lift off the fat.

Never season a stock with salt or pepper; the seasoning is done later when preparing the sauces.

Meat extracts or bouillon (stock) cubes can be added to a stock if the flavor is too weak. Mushroom skins and stalks, and tomato skins and seeds can be added, depending on the finished dish.

Stock can be strained and will freeze well for further use; it is a good idea to freeze stock in convenient amounts such as 2½ cups/1 pint/600ml.

STOCK CUBE (Am. BOUILLON CUBE) Numerous types of powdered bouillon (stock) cubes are available. They are usually made of seasoning and soluble hydrolyzed protein made from soya, meat or fish concentrate.

Aromatic herbs, leek, onion, thyme and celery could be used to add flavor to their rather bland taste.

STOCK SYRUP A syrup that is used in making sherbets (sorbets) and some candied fruits.

Use a saucepan with good heat conductivity this will discourage the accumulation of undissolved sugar crystals. Suitable materials are tin-lined copper, stainless steel or thick aluminum

The syrup can be colored or flavored according to your requirements.

Alternatively, clear fruit juices can be used instead of water for fruit pastes.

To allow the sugar to be boiled at a high temperature without browning, a maximum of 10 drops of tartaric acid can be added. Measure ¼ teaspoon of tartaric acid with ¼ teaspoon water and use 10 drops only of this solution.

6¾ cups/1.3kg/3lb sugar
5 cups/1.2 liters/2 pints water
1 cup/8fl oz/225ml liquid glucose

Gently heat the sugar in the water, stirring, until dissolved. Add the glucose and boil for 4 minutes.

Strain the syrup through cheesecloth. Pour into sterilized bottles. Close tightly and store in a cold place.

S

STOCKFISH Fish dried in the cold open air until hard is one of the oldest methods of preserving fish without refrigeration. Cod, hake and haddock can be made into stockfish. They must be soaked in cold water to regain their original moisture content.

STRAWBERRY (Fr. FRAISE) There are many ways to use strawberries apart from mousses, ice creams and tartlets. They can enrich fruit salads and be used as an attractive garnish for smoked salmon and other smoked fish.

Strawberries can also be mixed with rhubarb for a pie, but the best ways to eat them are fresh picked with whipped cream, or steeped in red wine or Champagne.

STRICHETTI An Italian pasta used for soups.

STRUDEL A classic Hungarian filo pastry roll filled with either apples, cherries, or cream cheese. The pastry is stretched very thinly across a large sheet before being rolled up and the dough brushed with melted butter to prevent it drying. *See Apple strudel.*

STUFFATU A Corsican mixed meat stew with onions, tomatoes and herbs.

STUFFING A mixture of ingredients such as breadcrumbs or cooked rice, herbs and eggs used to fill poultry, meat or vegetables.

STURGEON (Fr. ESTURGEON) A fish that lives in the sea and migrates to rivers to spawn. It is famed for its roes, which are salted as caviar — a popular Russian condiment.

The sturgeon itself has a good flesh which can be used for quenelles or baked or braised with wine.

SUBRIC Small fried croquette made from a thick béchamel sauce mixed with eggs, diced cooked chicken meat or other white meat.

Sweet subrics can be made of semolina and eggs and served with a jam sauce.

SUCCESS One of the finest French cakes made with baked nut meringue sandwiched with coffee praline buttercream.

SUCCORY Wild endive (chicory).

SUCCOTASH A mixture of corn kernels and lima beans, cooked together.

SUCKING PIG A piglet, which is usually oven roasted or spit-roasted whole.

SUÉDOISE Similar to Muscovite this is a molded fruit jelly dessert decorated with whipped cream.

SUGAR The most common sugars in foods are fructose, glucose, maltose and lactose. Mannose is found in mana. The juice from sugar cane and sugar beet is refined into pure sucrose.

BROWN SUGAR includes demerara and Barbados.

JAM SUGAR Now being produced by sugar manufacturers, it contains pectin and preserving sugar which takes a long time to dissolve.

WHITE SUGAR Available on the market are superfine (caster), granulated and confectioners' (icing) sugar.

Sugar is also extracted from dates and from an African fruit called taumathosin reputed to be 200 times sweeter than sucrose.

It is possible to dissolve just under 4½ lb/2kg sugar in 4⅓ cups/1¾ pints/1 liter water at 65° F/19°C, and nearly 5kg at 212°F/100°C.

Sugar caramelizes at above 340°F/170°C and even before if a particle of sugar becomes colored on the side of the saucepan.

SUGAR PASTE A sweet gum paste used for decoration. It is made from confectioners' (icing) sugar, gelatin and gum tragacanth.

SUGAR SNAP PEA A pea that is slightly bigger and fatter than snowpeas (mangetout) and can be eaten whole.

SUKIYAKI A Japanese fondue. Ingredients such as mushrooms, onions, carrots, bamboo shoots, beans and edible chrysanthemum leaves, as well as meat or fish, are cut into small thin pieces (not cubes) and cooked in dashi. The mixture of sweet and sharp stock makes it more interesting.

It is served with rice and a dipping sauce.

SULTANA (Am. GOLDEN RAISIN) Dried pale raisin.

SUMMER SPINACH *See New Zealand spinach.*

SUNDAE A celebrated American ice cream dessert that consists of scoops of ice cream, plus fruit or chocolate sauce and nuts with whipped cream spooned over the top.

Classic ice cream sundaes include peach Melba with one scoop of ice cream, half a peach and a spoonful of

S

raspberry sauce and perhaps a few toasted nuts and a little whipped cream; and pear Hélène which is half a banana with ice cream and chocolate sauce.

SUNFLOWER SEED Shelled, roasted and salted it is eaten as a snack like peanuts. Sunflower seeds contain 24 percent protein.

SUPRÈME 1) A béchamel sauce with added cream boiled until reduced.

2) A neatly dissected breast of poultry minus skin and winglet.

3) A suprème of fish is the large broad fillet of turbot, brill and similar thick flat white fish.

SUSHI A Japanese speciality of circles or rectangles of boiled rice flavored with sweet vinegar and wrapped with a wide range of different ingredients, such as seaweed, sliced vegetables or omelets.

SUZETTE Who could ever forget Suzette, the soprano of the Lyric Theatre in Paris after whom this thin flambéed pancake was named?

In the modern version of crêpe suzette, the pancake is tossed in a butterscotch sauce flavored with reduced orange juice and orange liqueur and then flamed with brandy. This is a spectacular dish when done with style.

SWEDE (Am. RUTABAGA) A yellow turnip which can be mashed or diced or mixed with mashed potato as a tasty purée.

SWEET (Am. CANDY) Sugar confection of which there are many varieties, such as caramels, taffies (toffees), butterscotch, fondant, almond paste and coconut fondant. *See Candy.*

SWEET AND SOUR SAUCE This type of sauce originated in China and still has an important place in far eastern and Asian cooking.

Honey or sugar, and vinegar are added to a sauce to bring about a contrasting flavor and accentuate the aromatic spices and herbs. Ginger and garlic play a part in these flavors together with pineapple, orange and tomato juices.

SWEET CORN The British term for corn kernels or whole corn cobs. The cob is boiled and served with butter. The loose kernels can be boiled and mixed with cream or used in a macédoine.

SWEET POTATO There are a number of

varieties of sweet potato. They vary in size and shape and the color may be white, yellow or purple. The flesh is sweeter than that of a regular potato They are either eaten boiled, roasted or fried.

SWEET SOP A fruit of the custard apple family that is very common in the West Indies, where it is made into sherbets (sorbets) and popularly used in fruit salads.

SWEETBREAD (Fr. RIS) The thymus (throat) gland and the pancreatic (near the stomach) gland of calves, lamb and pigs. The thymus sweetbread is elongated while the pancreatic sweetbread is larger.

Both the thymus and pancreas are cooked in the same way; they are blanched, refreshed, trimmed and either shallow-fried or braised. They can be used as a filling for vol au vents or served as an appetizer or light lunch.

Typical dishes: Ris de veau en casserole aux olives et champignons, salpicon de ris de veau à la crème.

SWISS CHEESES The Swiss produce about 150 different types of cheese such as Gruyère, Emmenthal, Sbrinz, Appenzeller and Raclette.

Semi-hard cheeses include Tilsit, Vacherin de Friboug and Vacherin Mont d'Or.

SWORDFISH (Fr. ESPADON) A fish with a long needle-like nose. The flesh can be prepared like tuna.

SYLLABUB A rich creamy dessert made by flavoring heavy (double) cream with medium Sherry and lemon juice while beating the mixture. It is served with shortbread.

SYRUP A concentrated solution of sugar in water. Syrups differ in density depending on the amount of sugar in relation to the volume of water.

Syrups are used for sherbets (sorbets), Middle Eastern pastries, desserts and cakes, pancakes, fritters, fruit compotes and candies (sweets). *See also Baumé, Brix, Saccharometer.*

SYRNIKI Russian cheese dumplings.

SZECHUAN PEPPERCORNS Chinese peppercorns with a rather different flavor and a more pungent aroma than conventional peppercorns. They come from a prickly ash tree and are not related to the peppercorn family.

They are marketed in Chinese stores.

T

TABASCO A branded sauce made with fermented red chili peppers, seasoning and preservatives. It is extremely hot and must be used with caution. It comes in a small glass bottle.

Tabasco has a distinctive fiery flavor due to the taste of the chili peppers, which cannot be duplicated in the kitchen.

TABIL A mixed spice powder of coriander, garlic, caraway and chili pepper. It is used in Middle Eastern cookery for stews, fava (broad) bean purées, salad dressings, and shellfish soups.

TABLE JELLY A commercial product sold as flavored crystals or concentrated gum-like paste which only need to be dissolved in boiling water.

TAB(B)OULEH A Middle Eastern salad made by soaking burgul in hot water

for about 12 minutes then draining and squeezing it dry. It is then mixed with scallions (spring onions), olives, tomatoes and herbs.

TACO A crisp, fried folded Mexican tortilla that can be filled with various mixtures of meats, beans and guacamole. It is a popular snack.

TAGETES The Aztec marigold used as a coloring agent.

TAGINE The name of both a North African earthenware cooking pot with a conical lid, and the spiced meat and vegetable stew cooked in it.

A tagine may also contain fruits such as dates and apricots.

TAGLIATELLE Long, thin flat Italian egg pasta about ¼in/5mm wide. It is available plain or colored with a number of foods, such as spinach purée (green) and tomato paste (purée) (pink).

Taglarini is narrower.

TAHINI, TAHINA An oily paste made of ground sesame seeds.

Tahini is used in Middle Eastern puréed dips such as hummus, and in soups and stews. It also has a binding effect on purées.

TALIBUR, RABOTTE A French apple dumpling.

TALLOW Clarified beef or lamb fat. It can be carved for buffet decorations, and used for making candles.

TALMOUSE One of the oldest curd cheese tartlets.

TAMALE A small Mexican package of cornmeal dough and filling wrapped in a corn husk and steamed. The sweet version contains dried fruits and nuts and sometimes cream cheese and egg.

TAMARILLO A fruit with a bitter reddish-yellow skin and golden-pink flesh that, although sweet, is allayed by acidity. Tamarillos are used for both savory and sweet dishes.

TAMARIND The flesh around the seeds of this fruit has a fruity-tart taste, and is used for chutneys.

TANDOORI An Indian method of cooking chicken that has been marinated in a coating of red spices and yogurt, then baked in a clay oven called a tandoor. The chicken or fish are served with salads and chutney.

TANGERINE A British name for the Mediterranean mandarin. It is light in color, with a good flavor but tend to contain a lot of seeds (pips). Tangerines can be made into sherbets (sorbets) or used in fruit salads.

TANNIN The astringent constituent of tea. It is also found in the roots and seeds of plants and immature fruits like grapes. Tannin darkens when oxidized and will precipitate gelatin from solution and form insoluble compounds.

On the good side, tannin gives a slight bitter taste to food so can counterbalance too much acidity.

TAPAS A Spanish selection of hors d'oeuvres and appetizers.

TAPENADE A Provençal paste of black olives, capers and anchovy fillets. It is spread on canapés or toasted French bread.

TAPIOCA A starch extracted from cassava roots, partially cooked and sold as pearls. It is used in milk puddings and broths. It can be ground and used as starch to thicken sauces.

TARAMASALATA A Greek or Turkish paste of cod's roe, olive oil, garlic and lemon juice.

T

TARATOR A Turkish sauce made by pounding walnuts, bread, olive oil and sometimes yogurt into a thick consistency.

It can be used as dressing for cucumber, served with vegetables or made into a soup by adding crushed ice and flavoring with dill or mint.

TARO A root grown in tropical countries and used in the same way as potato. It can be stuffed and steamed, fried, or stewed with other vegetables and meat.

The grated pulp is used to bind acras, which are fritters made with raw fish, not unlike potato and fish cakes.

TARRAGON (Fr. ESTRAGON) A very fragrant thin-leaved herb used in vinegars, dressings, eggs in aspic, fish and poultry dishes such as poached chicken in cream sauce, lobster Amèricaine, chicken chasseur and mussels cooked in wine and tarragon.

TART (Fr. TARTE) An open pie shell, filled with various fruits according to season. Tarts can also be baked blind before adding the filling.

Typical dishes : Tarte à la Normande, tarte aux cerises, tarte aux mirabelles, German gooseberry tart, tarte au citron, rhubarb and strawberry tart.

TARTAR OF SALMON TROUT The Japanese and Scandinavians have popularized the eating of raw fish.

The fish for making tartar must be absolutely fresh. It has replaced beef tartar as appetizer in recent years. The fish must be alive and killed just before use to be as fresh as possible.

TARTARE SAUCE A piquant svariation of mayonnaise that is flavored with chopped hard-cooked (boiled) egg, gherkins, herbs, anchovy fillets, capers and shallots.

It is served with broiled (grilled) fish, meat and poultry, or can be used as a dip.

1 hard-cooked egg, chopped
1 small shallot, chopped
6 capers, chopped
1 small gherkin, chopped
I tbsp parsley, chopped
2 anchovy fillets, chopped
1¼ cups/½ pint/300ml thick mayonnaise
1 tbsp sour (soured) cream, optional

Combine all the chopped ingredients together in a bowl and gradually stir in the mayonnaise as well as the sour (soured) cream if you decide to use it.

Check and adjust the seasoning if necessary.

TARTARIC ACID The acid of cream of tartar. It is used in sugar confectionery to prevent crystallization, and as an acid for drinks.

To use tartaric acid for syrups in sugar confectionery mix it with an equal quantity of water.

For 4½ cups/2 ¼ lb/Ikg of sugar, 10 drops of the tartic acid solution and ½ cup/4floz/100ml of liquid glucose are needed; use for pulled and blown sugar.

TASSAJO, JERKED BEEF Salted sun-dried beef produced in Argentina and other Latin American countries. It has to be soaked overnight when required.

TASSO A Cajun speciality. Beef or pork is flavored with Cajun spices and smoked for 2 days. The meat is used like bacon, and broiled (grilled) or fried with eggs, or used in stews.

TATIN A caramelized upside-down apple tart named after two sisters who lived in Lamotte-Beuvron, south of the river Loire in France although it had been made throughout France for many years.

The pan (tin) is sprinkled inside with sugar and the same amount of butter. Apples cut into wedges are placed in concentric circles in the pan. The tart is covered with a pie dough (shortcrust pastry) and baked like a pie. When cooked it is turned upside-down so the caramelized apple is on top.

TCHORBA *See Chorba.*

TEA A drink made from the dried leaves of an evergreen shrub.

Tea originated in China and has been drunk for several thousand years. It contains tannin and caffeine, which give it a stimulating effect.

To produce dried tea leaves the shoots of the shrub are withered, rolled, fermented and dried.

Tea can be made into a syrup and used for soaking yeast cakes such as rum babas or for any kind of fruit compote.

Iced tea with lemon is a refreshing drink and more healthy than hot tea with milk. *See also Green tea.*

TEA MELON A tiny, sweet fruit which looks like a small cucumber. It can be eaten raw or preserved in honey.

TEAL (Fr. SARCELLE) A wild duck cooked like mallard with spicy fruit sauces.

TEMPERATURE The temperature of a body is a measure of its hotness. It is

T

recorded using either the Fahrenheit or Centigrade scale.

To convert from Fahrenheit to Centigrade subtract 32 from the Fahrenheit reading, multiply by 5 and divide by 9.

Example: 65°F - 32 = 33, 33 x 5 = 165: 165 ÷ 9 = 18.3°C.

To convert Centigrade to Fahrenheit multiply the Centigrade by 9, divide by 5 and add 32.

Example: 30°C x 9 = 270 ÷ 5 = 54; 54 + 32 = 86°F.

A sugar thermometer can register the temperature up to 350°F/180°C.

TEMPERING 1) A term used in Indian cooking, meaning to stir-fry whole grains or seeds with a little fat to develop their flavor.

2) In chocolate confectionery. *See Chocolate.*

TEMPURA A Japanese dish of small pieces of fish, shrimp (prawns) and vegetables, dipped in batter and quickly deep-fried until crisp.

TENCH (Fr. TENCH) A very tender freshwater river fish with small, delicate bones.

Tench is best cooked in butter or poached and served with hollandaise sauce.

TENDERLOIN *See Fillet.*

TENDRON A French cut of veal taken from the rib. Veal tendrons are usually braised and served with pasta.

TERIYAKI A Japanese dish of strips of meat, poultry or fish marinated in lime juice, ginger, garlic and soy sauce. The meat, poultry or fish is drained and broiled (grilled), or stir-fried.

The marinade liquid is thickened with a little cornstarch (cornflour) to make a sauce to serve with the dish.

TERRAPIN (Fr. TORTUE) A species of fresh water turtle esteemed as food in North America. Both the eggs and flesh are eaten. A delicious soup is made by boiling the flesh in a broth flavored with sherry and herbs such as savory, mint, sage, thyme and basil.

TERRINE A modern terrine is cooked in an oblong or oval earthenware baking dish. It is made of equal quantities of uncooked mousseline and either diced or strips of meat or fish. The dish is usually lined with blanched spinach or cabbage leaves, or thin slices of bacon.

Meat terrines can also be made with a forcemeat containing liver or foie gras as well as poultry, game or meat.

Seafood terrines may be made with white or pink fish. Roes or caviar can be incorporated into a fine fish mousseline, which can be wrapped and shaped like a long sausage. It is then frozen to firm it.

The unwrapped roll is placed in the center of the terrine for an attractive mosaic pattern.

Alternatively, strips of pink salmon and white fish can be embedded in the mousseline.

Terrine of salmon and sole

1lb/450g spinach leaves, blanched
and dried
1 cup/8oz/225g mousseline made
of raw flounder (whiting) or
haddock
4oz/100g raw salmon, cut into
strips
4oz/100g sole fillets, cut into strips
⅔ cup/5fl oz/150ml fish aspic

Line 2½ cup/1 pt/600 ml oblong terrine with the spinach leaves. Place a layer of mousseline on top.

Cover with alternate strips of salmon and sole. Repeat the layers until the terrine is full.

Pour the fish aspic into the terrine.

Cover with a lid and bake in a water bath in an oven at 350°F/80°C/gas mark 4 for 45 minutes.

Cool and chill.

Chicken and ham terrine

8 very thin slices of cooked ham
1 cup/8oz/225g mousseline made
with raw chicken
1 cup/8oz/225g ham cut into strips
⅔ cup/5fl oz/150 ml chicken aspic

Line a 2½ cup/1 pt/600ml terrine with the ham.

Place a layer of the mousseline on top. Cover with a layer of ham strips.

Repeat the layering until the terrine is full.

Pour in the chicken aspic. Cover with a lid and bake in a water bath in an oven at 350°F/180 °C/gas mark 4 for 1 hour.

Cool and chill.

Variations

Both of the above salmon and chicken terrines can be made more exotic with the addition of pistachios or some diced truffles stirred into the mousseline mixture.

Typical dishes: Terrine de canard aux kumquat confit, terrine de foie de canard Rouennaise, terrine de légumes.

T

TEXTURED VEGETABLE PROTEIN, TVP
This is a meat substitute which is made from vegetables — most usually soy beans. Textured vegetable protein usually takes on the flavor of the other foods with which it is cooked.

THEOBROMINE A white substance found in cocoa that has the same stimulating properties as caffeine.

THERAPEUTIC DIET A diet prescribed to cure complaints like obesity, diabetes, malfunctions of metabolism, gout, heart disease, dyspepsia, ulcers and food allergies.

THERMOSTAT An instrument for maintaining a constant temperature by cutting off the supply of heat when the required temperature is exceeded and automatically restoring the supply when the temperature falls.

THICKENING AGENT There are four thickening agents that are most commonly used for sauces and stocks:

CORNSTARCH (cornflour) or arrowroot .

EGG YOLKS AND FLOUR. Use 2 teaspoons flour with 2 egg yolks and 6 tablespoons heavy (double) cream for 2¼ cups/18fl oz/500ml sauce.

ROUX. This should be used for acid sauces.

VEGETABLE PURÉES.

TEXTURIZING AGENT An ingredient added to products to improve the structure, consistency, density, fluidity and viscosity and hence the smoothness, oiliness and creaminess. It may be lecithin in chocolate, polyphosphates in pork and duck, agar in soups, sauces and ice creams, pectin in jams, or gum arabic in chutneys.

THERMIDOR A classic dish of lobster coated with a rich mustard and cheese flavored béchamel sauce.

THYME A herb belonging to the same family as mint. It has a pungent smell, even when dried. It is used in stocks, soups, stews and casseroles and to flavor cream cheese. The wild variety has the best fragrance.

TIGER LILY BUDS The dried golden buds of the tiger lily are used by Chinese cooks in many exotic stir-fried dishes.

TIMPANA A popular Maltese pie made

of cooked ground (minced) meat and pasta coated with a thick egg sauce and topped with puff pastry.

TINNED FOOD *See Canned food.*

TISANE A drink made by infusing herbs such as chamomile, marjoram, peppermint, or lime blossom, that are reputed to have therapeutic properties, in water.

TITANIUM DIOXIDE A food coloring agent.

TOAD-IN-THE-HOLE A simple dish of sausages baked in pancake batter. To make sure the sausages stay in the base of the roasting pan (tin), half-roast them without the batter, pour over half of the batter and bake for a further 10 minutes.

Add the remaining batter and bake for another 15 minutes.

TOCINO Spanish salted pork fat used in cooking.

TOCOPHEROL *See Vitamin E.*

TOFU *See Bean curd.*

TOMATILLO A Mexican fruit related to the cape gooseberry and tomato. The tomatillo has a thin skin and a tart lemon-apple flavor. It is used in salads, sauces and pickles.

TOMATO (Fr. TOMATE) There are many varieties of tomatoes with different sweetnesses and sizes. Cherry tomatoes are popular because of their size and Italian plum tomatoes are considered the sweetest of all.

Tomatoes are rich in Vitamin C. They can be sun-dried, canned, made into catsup (ketchup), purées, pastes, sauces, jams and sherbets (sorbets).

Green tomatoes can be made into jam or chutney with 25 percent each of sugar and vinegar.

TOMATO COULIS A smooth sauce made of skinned, seeded and finely chopped tomatoes.

It can be used raw or cooked by boiling until reduced to the required consistency. A little sugar or honey will improve the flavor.

Arrowroot diluted with stock can be added to give the right consistency. *See also Coulis.*

TOME(ME) A generic name for goats', ewes' and cows' milk cheeses, mainly from the French Alps. They are usually pressed, uncooked, and have a natural rind.

T

TONGUE (Fr. LANGUE) Tongue is cured by the same method as beef and pork, using saltpeter as a preservative so the tongue becomes scarlet-pink.

Tongue is available canned or smoked. Salted ox tongue served with rye bread and pickled cucumber is a particular Jewish speciality.

TONKA BEAN A fragrant seed used as an imitation vanilla.

TOOLS The main tools for the cook are knives of all sizes including a small one for trimming vegetables, a medium-sized knife for regular use, a filleting knife and two carving knives, one plain and one serrated, and a knife sharpener.

For pastry, a rolling pin and two sets of cutters, one plain and one fluted.

Also useful are a grater, lemon zester and a blender and/food processor, a sugar thermometer, a meat thermometer and spatulas. Keep a first aid box for cuts and burns handy.

TOPPING An commercial product used as an artificial cream for desserts.

TORTE German for filled or decorated cake.

Typical dishes: Sachertorte, zuger kirschtorte.

TORTILLA A Mexican pancake made from corn or wheat flour.

Tortillas are used as wrappers for many fillings of fish, meat or vegetables. They may include salad leaves, avocados, tomatoes and onion, all dressed with chilli sauce.

TOURNEDOS A trimmed cut of beef or veal fillet weighing a maximum of 5 oz/150g.

TOUS LES MOIS This is the starch of a tuberous root native of Peru and cultivated in the West Indies.

It is known by the name of achira and is used in Louisiana where it is characteristic of Creole cookery.

Tous les mois has the same dietary value as arrowroot, but it does not remain in jelly form for very long.

TOXIN Poison produced by bacteria. Toxins are destroyed by heat. When injected into animals in carefully controlled doses, they bring about the formation of substances called antitoxins, which neutralize toxins.

These substances in turn can be made into serum to combat some diseases.

TRAGACANTH These partially soluble gums are obtained from various species of *Astragalus* bushes known as goat-thorn grown in Crete, Turkey, Iran and Greece.

The gum is used in sugar confectionery to stiffen sugar pastes, and can be used to add texture to pickles, acid sauces and chutneys.

TREACLE, BLACK (Am. MOLASSES) This consists of the initially clear, reddish-brown diluted molasses filtered through cloth and charcoal. The mixture by then is very black and has been concentrated to the consistency of thick, viscous syrup.

TRENETTE A narrower version of the tagliatelle pasta.

TREPANG *See Sea cucumber.*

TRIGLYCERIDES Simple, neutral fats composed of esters of glycerol and three fatty acids.

Triglycerides can be modified to make emulsifiers and stabilizers.

TRIPE (Fr. GRAS-DOUBLE) The stomach of oxen, cows or sheep. In Normandy, France, tripe are cleaned, par-boiled and braised in cider with carrots and onions.

In the north of England, tripe are simmered in milk after they have been cooked in stock until tender.

TRIPOLINI Italian pasta bows with rounded edges.

TROTTER (Am. FEET, Fr. PIED) The feet of pigs, calves, cows and sheep are boiled and served with sharp sauces and enjoyed by many gourmets. Feet are used in stocks for making meat jellies and sauces.

TROUT (Fr. TRUITE) Oily fresh or sea water fish. Rainbow trout have delicate pink flesh and are farmed extensively; brown trout are caught wild from rivers; salmon trout is a family of several species, the brown trout, sea trout and lake trout.

Trout are best broiled (grilled) or fried. When poached they are served with hollandaise sauce and its many derivatives.

Trout lend themselves to many other light dishes such as mousses, pâtés, and hors d'oeuvres when smoked.

TRUFFLE A subterranean fungus that lives in symbiosis with certain trees, mainly oak, chestnut, hazel and beech. It is highly esteemed for its pleasant aromatic flavor when used fresh; canned truffles have less flavor and so are mainly decorative.

Truffles are used in foie gras pâtés, with chicken, veal and sweetbreads

T

and as a garnish for fish and salads. Truffles are extremely expensive in relation to their role as a garnish.

TRUSSING Preparing birds for roasting or poaching by tying up with string.

- Trim the sides of the wings. Remove the wishbone by pulling the flap of skin over the wishbone, then with the point of a knife, scrape the flesh over each of the forks of the bone.
- Insert the knife under one side of the bone, and cut downward to the junction of the wing. Repeat this on the other side of the bone. Once the two sides have been detached, continue to free the top of the bone. Pull the bone off the breast bone without damaging the flesh.
- Thread a large trussing needle with a piece of string three times the length of the bird. Hold the bird on its back with the legs firmly against the thigh. Insert the needle through the middle of the right leg, pass it through the carcass, to come out through the center of the other leg. Pull the needle out of the other side.
- Turn the bird onto its breast. Push the flap of the neck skin over the opening of the neck to extend down the back. Cover it with the outstretched wings.

- Secure both wings and flap together by threading the needle through the small end of one wing extremity, passing it through the flap then through the other wing.
- Pull out the needle, taking great care not to pull the string too tightly. Tie the two ends of string together securely with a double knot, so that the legs will be firmly attached to the carcass. If possible, the knot should be made without cutting the string, though this is not essential.
- Insert the needle through the flesh of the thigh, just underneath where the leg was pierced, and where a small cavity is found.
- Pull the needle through the other side of the other thigh under the leg. Pull the string over this leg and re-insert the needle just above the leg into the flesh under the breastbone, to come out the opposite side, immediately above the other leg.
- The tip of the breastbone should be lifted before this insertion is made to avoid piercing it with the needle. Join the end of the string with a double knot at the point where the string was first inserted. Finally, cut the string.

TRYPSIN An enzyme produced by the pancreas. During digestion it breaks proteins into amino acids.

TRYPTOPHAN An essential amino acid needed in the daily diet for the repair of proteins lost through wear and tear. It is found in animal foods, corn and sesame seeds, mung beans and lentils.

When added to bean curd or soya products it complements the essential amino acids normally lacking in vegetarian diets.

TUBETTI Fine tubular Italian pasta.

TUILE An elegant crisp, plain or almond-flavored cookie (biscuit) that is curved over a rolling pin while cooling. They should be no bigger than 2in/5cm in diameter

generous ½ cup/4½ oz/125g superfine (caster) sugar
¾ cup/3oz/75g flour
2 eggs, beaten
2 tbsp/1oz/25g melted butter
¾ cup/3oz/75g sliced almonds
confectioners' (icing) sugar for dusting

Makes about 36

Combine all the ingredients, except the confectioners' (icing) sugar for dusting, to make a pliable paste.

Butter 3 baking sheets. Drop about a small spoonful of the batter ¾in/2cm apart on the baking sheet. Dip a fork in cold water and flatten the tops.

Bake for 4 minutes at 350°F/180°C/gas mark 4.

Oil a rolling pin and place the tuiles on it to curl them. Set aside until cold.

Dust with confectioners' sugar and store in air tight container.

TUNA (Fr. THON) Tuna has a firm texture and is classified as an oily fish suitable for broiling (grilling) and roasting as a joint. It can also be poached and served in an olive oil dressing.

The three main varieties of tuna are albacore, bluefin and the striped bonito. The flesh of the albacore is white but the other two have pale pink flesh.

Tuna is available fresh and canned in brine or oil.

Tuna salad
⅔ cup/5oz/150g long grain rice
⅔ cup/5oz/150g canned tuna, drained, or boiled fresh tuna
1 fennel bulb, thinly sliced
⅓ cup/2oz/50g black olives, pitted
⅔ cup/5fl oz/150ml tartare sauce
salt and pepper
1 bunch of watercress
2 hard-cooked (boiled) eggs, chopped

Boil the rice for 18-20 minutes. Drain well and pat dry. Flake the tuna with a

T

fork into the rice. Toss gently.

Add the fennel, black olives and tartare sauce. Check the seasoning. Serve on plates garnished with watercress leaves. Sprinkle chopped eggs all over.

Variations

The tuna can be replaced by cold broiled (grilled) red snapper, bass or goatfish (red mullet), or lobster or shrimp (prawns).

Barbados fish salad
1lb/450g fresh tuna fillets, skinned and diced

Marinade
1 tsp salt
¼ cup/2fl oz/50ml dry sherry
¼ cup/2fl oz/50ml sherry vinegar or rice

Garnish
⅔ cup/5fl oz/150ml fresh or canned coconut cream
4 tomatoes, sliced
1 green bell pepper, seeded and sliced
1 red chili pepper, chopped
2 tbsp chives snipped
1 tsp sugar
Chinese leaves to serve

In a large bowl combine the marinade ingredients.

Wash the fish in running water. Add to the marinade and chill overnight.

Rinse the fish under running water and drain well. Fry the tuna for 5 minutes each side. Flake the tuna and let cool.

In a salad bowl combine the coconut cream, tomatoes, bell pepper, chili pepper, chives and sugar. Toss in the tuna.

Refrigerate until ready to serve on Chinese lettuce leaves.

TURBOT (Fr. **TURBOT**) A flat fish with white flesh and brown top skin.

Turbot is one of the very best flat fish and the most expensive. It is best poached and served with hollandaise sauce or broiled (grilled) and served with tartare sauce.

Typical dishes: Suprême de turbot à la cardinal, turbot poché hollandaise, turbotin farci aux mousserons.

Turbot filo rolls
½ cup/4½ oz/125g cooked spinach purée
1 cup/4 oz/100g feta cheese, crumbled
½ cup/4oz/100g cream cheese
1lb/450g cold poached turbot
½ cup/2oz/50g walnuts

salt, pepper and grated nutmeg
10 sheets of filo pastry
¼ cup/2fl oz/50ml olive oil

Purée the first 5 ingredients in a blender. Season to taste.

Brush each sheet of filo pastry with a little oil, layering 2 sheets together. Fold the 2 layered sheets in half, cut into 4 pieces. Repeat with the remaining pastry.

Place about 2 teaspoons of fish mixture across one corner of each piece of pastry and roll up the pastry, tucking in the ends. Lightly brush the rolls with oil, place on a greased baking sheet and bake at 375°F/190°C/gas mark 5 for 15-20 minutes.

TURKEY (Fr. DINDE, DINDON) The turkey is a native of North America, and was once classified as game. For preference, it should be hung for 48 hours to develop a better flavor.

Turkeys can be reared up to as much as 20lb/9kg, but size is not always a mark of high quality; as long as the breast is plump, a turkey can be bought from 13lb/6kg and still be in its prime.

Turkey is now sold in joints, small cuts such as scallops (escalopes) and individual portions.

Typical dishes: Turkey legs stuffed with chestnuts, turkey scallops (escalopes) with almonds, poached turkey with ravigotte sauce, ballottines de dindonneau aux pistaches.

TURKISH DELIGHT, RAHAT LAKHOUM A jellied candy (sweet) that is cut into cubes and coated in confectioners' (icing) sugar. It is one of the most appreciated petit fours served with Turkish coffee.

TURMERIC (Fr. CURCUMA) The rhizome from a member of the same family as ginger but turmeric does not have such a pungent flavor. It is mostly used to color curry mixtures yellow.

TURNIP (Fr. NAVET) A white root vegetable. The best are the early French varieties, or baby turnips. Turnips should be soaked in cold water with lemon juice or vinegar to remove any bitter flavor. The tops can be cooked like spinach.

TURTLE (Fr. TORTUE) A reptile that is appreciated for its flesh and eggs.

The flesh is available canned, frozen or dried for the use of soups and stews.

Turtle herbs are basil, marjoram, chervil and fennel, which can be used to make mock turtle soup. *See also Terrapin.*

T-U

TUSCAN OIL Italian olive oils from the Lucca, Florence and Leghorn districts are of great merit. Italian olive oils are more highly regarded than French and Spanish oils.

TUTTI-FRUTTI A mixture of candied fruits such as angelica, citrus peels, cherries and pineapple. They are added to cassata and other ice cream or ice cream desserts.

By extension the term is used by cooks for a mixture of fruits for salads including pears, bananas, cherries, pineapples, peaches and grapes.

TVP *See Textured vegetable protein.*

TWAROG A type of Russian cheesecake filling.

TYNDALLIZATION The sterilization in two or three short stages to kill not only harmful bacteria but also spores. It does not affect the food as much as sterilizing by one longer heating.

TYROPITTA One of the most popular Greek pies made of feta cheese, spinach and eggs layered with filo pastry.

TYROSINE A non-essential, white crystalline amino acid.

UGLI A citrus fruit with a thick skin. Ugli fruit are excellent for marmalade.

ULLUCO A South American tuber that can be cooked in the same ways as potatoes or yams.

UNSATURATED COMPOUND A compound that can form additional compounds. *See Fats and Oils.*

UPSIDE-DOWN CAKE Numerous versions of this cake make interesting desserts.

To make an upside down cake, coat a baking dish or cake pan (tin) with butter, add a layer of fruit such as apples, pineapple, apricots, peaches or bananas, arranged attractively and cover with a cake batter.

When baked, the cake is turned out on a dish to show the fruit. Serve with custard or cream.

VACHERIN 1) A round meringue gâteau filled with whipped cream and decorated with raspberries or strawberries.

2) Soft, very creamy cheese made in Switzerland and France.

VACUUM PACKING The exclusion of air from a container filled with food to make it keep longer. *See also Sousvide*

VADAI Small Indian fried snacks made of lentils or garbanzo bean (chickpea) flour. Grated vegetables and spices may be added.

VALESNIKI A Russian or Polish pancake filled with a cream cheese mixture and deep-fried.

VALINE An essential amino acid needed for the repair of proteins lost during the day.

VANILLA (Fr. VANILLE) Vanilla pods are cured and fermented until they have developed a strong aroma. It is one of the best aromatic extracts for confectionery and desserts.

Mexican Aztecs used vanilla long ago to flavor chocolate.

Six varieties of vanilla are known in Mexico: mansa, cimarrona, meztiza, pompona, puerca, and mono. Vanilla is also cultivated in Tahiti and in Madagascar.

A cheaper artificial flavoring is available but the flavor is vastly inferior.

VARENIKI A type of sweet or savory Russian ravioli made with a pelmeni dough. They are poached in salt water and served with a dressing or sauce.

VARIETY MEATS (OFFAL) Variety meats are the edible parts and some extremities of an animal which are removed before the carcass is dissected. The pig provides the largest range of variety meats, and cows provide a good return with cow heels, tripe and kidney.

Variety meats are divided into white and red:

RED VARIETY MEATS include the heart, liver, tongue, lungs, spleen and kidneys. Tripe and the intestines are also used in some countries.

V

VEAL VARIETY MEATS are more delicate and all the variety meats are used as gastronomic meals, especially the kidneys, sweetbreads and liver. The brain of both sheep and calves are also much prized.

WHITE VARIETY MEATS includes bone marrow, animelles (testicles), brain, mesentery (the membrane which holds the intestines) together, feet, sweetbreads, stomach and head.

VATROUSKA   Russian open-topped cream or curd cheese bun made with leavened (raised) dough and traditionally eaten with bortsch.

VEAL (Fr. VEAU) A meat that is particularly popular in Holland, France, Belgian, Italy and Austria. When buying veal look for cuts that are pale pink (in general, the darker the flesh, the older the animal), firm and with no unpleasant smell, and fat that is white and slightly pinkish.

Bones should also be pinkish and the cut surfaces of the meat should be moist. The connective tissue should be gelatinous, not hard, sinewy or bubbly (this indicates they contain air).

The younger the animal the more water its flesh contains and the lower its nutritional value; the Germans used to say that calf meat is half meat, but veal was in demand by classic chefs for grand dishes such as veal Orloff (sliced roasted or braised veal spread with onion purée, covered with a Béchamel sauce and cheese) and veal scallops (escalopes) with a rich Marsala wine sauce; rich wine sauces are more for veal than beef. However, flavor lies in the fat, which is why veal is often larded with pork or bacon fat.

Because veal comes from young animals, all cuts are tender but the prime cuts are the fillet, then the loin, followed by the top end of the leg.

Ground (minced) veal is tasteless unless it is mixed with pork fat and herbs. Veal and ham are good partners for hot and cold meat pies.

Typical dishes: Côte de veau à la Vallé d'Auge, côte de veau aux champignons, Viennese schnitzel, veal Orloff, sauté de veau Marengo, osso buco, médaillon de veau aux mousserons.

VEGAN   A person who does not eat any meat or animal products, such as eggs and all dairy foods. Vitamin B12 must be taken by vegans as there is no plant source.

VEGETABLE CUTS There is an accepted standard for shapes and sizes of cut vegetables. Each cut has a name which is recognized by professional cooks. *See also Brunoise, Julienne, Jardinière, Macédoine.*

VEGETABLE MARROW *See Marrow.*

VEGETABLE OILS These are obtained from the leaves, fruit or seeds of plants. They contain esters of fatty acids and glycerol.

VEGETARIAN DIET Much can be said in favor of eating meatless meals. This is a diet to be recommended for a number of periods throughout the year, providing sufficient protein is eaten in the form of milk, cheese and eggs combined with nuts, cereals and pulses.

Most vegetables provide energy and vitamins and add bulk to the diet.

VEGETARIANISM The rearing and slaughtering of animals are repugnant to vegetarians. Some people identify with every living creature in a spiritual fellowship where everything has the right to live a natural life.

Some religions, such as Hinduism and Buddhism, have as central tenets to their faith the belief that eating flesh, fish or fowl is sinful to the point of being criminal.

In Great Britain and America there is medical evidence that a vegetarian diet may be beneficial and can improve health. The best food in the world is found in countries blessed by the sun where olive, coconut and date trees have lasted for millennia. People in these countries are stronger and healthier and many live into their late nineties.

Many theories and arguments exist about why so many people in Western countries die in middle age. Many diseases might be avoided if less cholesterol and saturated fats, no meat and plenty of fiber were eaten.

Some people think they cannot live without a daily portion of meat, but the vast repertoire of vegetarian dishes from around the world shows that it is very easy to eat a varied, interesting and satisfying vegetarian diet.

In France alone it is easy to make menus for every meal of the year that will satisfy the most fastidious epicures. Providing adequate amounts of animal proteins from dairy foods and eggs are eaten everyone can survive from birth to death on a vegetarian diet.

The British Vegetarian Society was founded in 1847 on economic grounds. The Society urged that a vegetarian diet would support a larger

V

population and thus render Britain independent of foreign supplies.

An other point in favor of vegetarianism are that it is favorable to temperance and a peaceful disposition, it is economical and enables people to live better, it stops the horrors of killing animals and returns to when man originally lived on vegetables.

A piece of land produces more food if it is used to grow plants than if it is used for rearing animals for food. Animals supply only 10 percent as meat, 15 percent as eggs and 30 percent as milk, of the food value of the plants and vegetables they eat.

So a vegetarian diet is a good way to ease the present world food shortage. It is up to the cooks and food technologists to make vegetarian dishes and diets tasty, attractive and nutritionally balanced.

Nature provides delicious foods that not only taste better than meat, poultry or fish but look far more appetizing. Eve tempted Adam with a fruit and not with a piece of dead meat.

Some interesting research has shown that cruciferous vegetables such as broccoli, Brussels sprouts, cabbage and rutabaga (swede) may provide protection against certain cancers.

Typical vegetarian dishes: Potato and leek soup, gazpacho, minestrone, onion soup with cheese, asparagus with chopped egg dressing, globe artichokes with mushroom stuffing, hummus with sesame cookies (biscuits), eggplant (aubergine) gratin with Mozzarella cheese, ratatouille.

Stuffed pawpaw with nutty rice pilaff, spinach and cream cheese omelet, blue cheese soufflé, ravioli, pancakes stuffed with a poached egg, leek quiche, onion tart, lima (butter) bean soup, navy (haricot) bean timbale with rutabaga (swede) sauce.

Kidney bean terrine, garbanzo bean (chickpea) dumplings with bean sprouts and sesame seeds, stir-fried bean sprouts, pineapple and fried bean curd, flageolet beans and haricot verts in a rich olive oil dressing.

VELOUTÉ SAUCE A simple sauce that is the basis of a number of other sauces. It can be flavored with many ingredients, such as cheese, herbs, mushrooms and spices.

Cream and egg yolks can also be mixed into a velouté sauce. Sour (soured) cream and yogurt are sometimes used but must be added to the sauce away from the heat and not reheated as the acid would curdle the sauce.

Velouté sauce can be mixed with hollandaise sauce or mayonnaise to lighten it, or to make a particularly special dressing.

2 tbsp/1oz/25g butter
3tsp/1oz/25g all-purpose (plain) flour
2½ cups/1 pint/600ml fish or veal stock
salt and black pepper
juice of ½ lemon

Melt the butter then stir in the flour and cook to a sandy paste. Gradually stir in the stock and whisk to make it smooth. Simmer the sauce for 10 minutes. Season and add the lemon juice.

VENISON (Fr. VENAISON) Some farm-bred venison has all the attributes of wild venison, being high in flavor and low in fat, but at the same time, it is also very tender and its production has to meet rigorous standards of hygiene.

Fallow, red and sika deer are the principal breeds that are farmed. Apart from their size there is very little difference between them, so unless you buy your meat direct from the farm you are unlikely to know from which exact breed it comes.

The best meat is considered to be that from a buck or stag between 18 months and 2 years old. The meat is close-grained, dark in color and very lean. The meat does not have the marbling of fat present in beef.

Venison from an 18-month-old buck will have a fat content of 6 percent, meat from an older animal may have slightly more fat, but this fat is largely unsaturated. Venison is therefore a very useful meat for those requiring a low-cholesterol diet.

The flavor of the meat can be developed by hanging. Traditionally, venison from wild deer was hung for at least2-3 weeks to tenderize it and this was responsible for its gamey flavor. Nowadays, farmed venison is hung for 5 to 8 days.

The main cuts of venison are the haunch, leg, saddle, cutlets, médaillions, and stewing venison.

As venison is a lean meat cuts to be roasted or broiled (grilled) should be well larded before cooking. Marinating with herbs or spices, vinegar, wine, oil and seasoning is also recommended.

VERJUICE The juice of unripe green grapes which is used in place of vinegar for acidulating salad dressings and mustards.

VERMICELLI A thin Italian pasta mainly used as a garnish for consommés and soups such as minestrone.

V

VIENNESE COOKIES Cookies (biscuits) made from almond-flavored sponge, or Vienna batter, piped in various shapes.

VINEGAR An acid liquid usually made by the acetous fermentation of wine, beer and hard cider. The alcohol is oxidized by an enzyme or mother of vinegar, and the chief product is acetic acid.

Distilled white vinegar is based on dilute distilled alcohol and malt-based vinegar is the result of the fermentation of an infusion of barley malt or cereals whose starch has been converted to malt.

Vinegar can also be made very quickly by adding acetic acid crystals to wine, beer or hard cider.

The best wine vinegar is Orléans vinegar and the most expensive vinegar is balsamic vinegar. Sherry vinegar and fruit and herb vinegars are favored by many cooks.

Herb vinegars are made by macerating fresh strong herbs such as tarragon, dill, mint, celery, lovage, horseradish, garlic, basil or marjoram in vinegar.

The herbs should be bruised or chopped coarsely. Set aside for 6 weeks then strain. Fresh herbs can be used to replace those strained out.

Flavorings rather than fresh herbs are often used for commercial herb vinegars.

See Orléans vinegar, Pickling spice.

Fruit Vinegar

2¼ lb/1kg berries or currants
4⅓ cups/1¾ pints/1 liter wine
vinegar

Put the fruit and vinegar in a non-reactive container. Set aside to macerate for 3 days.

Strain the fruit through a non-reactive strainer without too much pressure. Boil the vinegar for 10 minutes.

Pour the vinegar into warm, sterilized bottles and cover with sterilized non-reactive lids.

Sweet pickling vinegar

Use for pickling melons, pears or stone fruits.

4½ cups/2¼ lb/1kg sugar
4⅓ cups/1¾ pints/1 liter vinegar
1 small stick of cinnamon or 4 cloves
½ cup/4fl oz/100ml vodka, gin or
brandy

Dissolve the sugar in the vinegar and heat to just below boiling point.

Add the cinnamon or cloves and vodka, gin or brandy.

Let cool. Pour into sterilized bottles, cover and keep in a cool, dark, dry place.

VITAMIN Organic material which must be supplied to the body in small amounts. Vitamins are divided into those that are fat soluble and those that are water soluble.

FAT SOLUBLE VITAMINS are A,D, E and K. Their absorption in the body depends upon the normal absorption of fat in the diet.

WATER SOLUBLE VITAMINS include Vitamin C and the members of the Vitamin B complex, including thiamin, riboflavin and niacin.

A good healthy diet should mean that vitamin supplements are unnecessary. However, people who for one reason or another omit food rich in some vitamins may need to take supplements to ensure that their health doesn't suffer.

In instances of ill health or special needs a doctor may prescribe supplements, otherwise you should think twice before taking any.

Be warned also that fat-soluble vitamins accumulate in the body and can be dangerous when taken in excess.

VITAMIN B6 Essential when carbohydrate is present in the diet, for helping the nervous system and metabolism and the formation of red blood cells. It is found in nuts, seeds, whole grains, fortified cereals, milk and eggs.

VITAMIN C, ASCORBIC ACID Contained in fresh citrus fruit in particular and most other fruits and green vegetables when eaten raw.

VITAMIN D Important for the absorption of calcium and phosphorus for bones and teeth. it is found in dairy products, margarine, eggs and oily fish such as herrings, mackerel and salmon, and also in cod liver oil.

VITAMIN E, TOCOPHEROL An important antioxidant.

Vitamin E is found in whole wheat (wholemeal) grain and flour and soya products such as miso, tamari and beancurd, beans, seaweeds, green beans, buckwheat and asparagus.

VITAMIN H *See Biotin.*

VOLATILE OIL, ESSENTIAL OIL This resembles a fixed oil in that it is soluble in ether or chloroform and is lighter than water. Volatile oils are extracted from plants and seeds by distillation and used as flavorings by the food industry.

Sources of volatile oils include anise seeds, caraway seeds, cloves, cinnamon, dill, eucalyptus, juniper berries, lavender, citrus rind, peppermint, rosemary, mustard seeds and vanilla.

In small doses most volatile oils are antispasmodic and analgesic and can be used as mild antiseptics.

WAFER A small crisp cookie (biscuit). It can be shaped like a cornet or molded with a special metal wafer iron.

WAFFLE Waffles can be made with an ordinary pancake pudding batter or a yeast batter. Waffle irons can be electric or designed for stove-top cooking.

Belgian waffles are often made with or beer or lager, enriched with eggs and milk and flavored with vanilla.

They are cooked in specially designed deep waffle irons.

All waffles should be served immediately they are cooked or their crispiness will be lost.

Brussels waffles
2 tsp dry (dried) yeast
⅓ cup/3fl oz/75ml warm water
2 cups/8oz/225g all-purpose (plain) flour

½ tsp salt
2 eggs, beaten
½ cup/4oz/100g butter, softened

Dissolve the yeast in the water and add half of the flour. Cover and let rise for 30 minutes. Add the rest of the flour, the salt, eggs and butter. Knead the dough and shape into a ball. Let rise again for 30 minutes.

Divide the dough into small balls the size of an egg. Let rise for 20 minutes.

Heat a greased waffle iron. Add balls of dough, which will take the imprint of the waffle iron. Close the lid and cook for 4 minutes.

Serve dusted with vanilla flavored confectioners' (icing) sugar.

WAHOO, ONO An oily fish native to the Gulf of Mexico. It weights an average of 30 lb/14 kg or more. It has white flesh with a tinge of pink and a rather sweet taste.

Wahoo can be filleted, cut in steaks, ground (minced) and made into burgers and served with broiled (grilled) pineapple, or wrapped in banana leaves and steamed or baked.

WAKAME Japanese seaweed used with cucumber in a salad. Dried wakame is soaked in cold water for 40 minutes until soft and then cut into squares.

WALNUT The kernel accounts for 35-50 percent of the total weight. Walnuts are available both in their shells and as kernels.

Walnuts are very fatty and yield an excellent oil which is rated as one of the best and most flavorsome, even better than olive oil and much more expensive.

Green, immature walnuts can be pickled in vinegar and spices.

WATER The best water comes from springs or deep wells, or is upland surface water. Tap water from reservoirs in urban regions is purified and may be fluoridated.

Some water contains insoluble minerals and is not considered to be very good for making tea but it is good for bread-making.

Soaking beans or pulses in hard water causes the beans to blister; if this is a problem, use distilled water. Hard waters are associated with a lower risk of mortality from heart disease.

Water is needed to balance losses in urine, perspiration and faeces. Most people need to drink at least 4¼ cups/1½ pints/750ml a day.

WATER BATH, BAIN-MARIE A bowl placed over a saucepan of hot water or in a deep baking pan (tin) half-full of boiling water. A water bath is used for cooking egg sauces or custards because they will cook gently, there is little danger of curdling or of over-cooking and no risk of the bottom of the mixture burning.

A water bath is also useful for keeping sauces hot.

WATER CHESTNUT An aquatic plant producing a nut looking like a chestnut. It is used in Chinese cooking and can be bought in cans.

WATER MELON A water melon has bright red flesh studded with black seeds. Arabs eat the black seeds as a source of protein.

The flesh can be puréed and made into sorbets, syrups and fruit juices.

WATERCRESS (Fr. CRESSON) Although classified as a salad plant it can also be used for soups with potatoes, such as the French soupe de cressonière.

WATERZOI A Dutch river fish and eel stew cooked gently in a court bouillon with carrots, onions and caraway.

WELSH RAREBIT A liquid paste of melted English Cheddar cheese, thickened with starch and mixed with beer or ale. It is then spread on toast and browned under the broiler (grill). A poached or fried egg can be served on top of the cooked cheese to make buck rarebit.

WESTPHALIAN HAM Delicious German ham flavored with juniper wood smoke and other fragrant woods.

WHEAT (Fr. BLÉ, FROMENT) There are over 200 varieties of wheat from which flour is extracted. They are divided into spring and winter wheats named after the season in which they are planted.

SPRING WHEAT is planted as soon as the winter ground softens and becomes dry.

WINTER WHEAT is planted in the fall (autumn), to permit development of a root system before winter dormancy, which gives the wheat an early start with the coming of spring.

A wheat grain consists of the kernel, the lower portion or germ which is high in fat, and the starchy portion, the endosperm, with a protein content varying from 7-18 percent.

Soft wheat is low in gluten and yields a weak flour; it is used for cakes and cookies (biscuits).

Hard wheat is higher in gluten and yields flour that makes strong, elastic dough; it is therefore used for bread-making, puff paste (pastry) and batters. *See also Flour.*

WHEY The liquid left after the removal of the curd when milk is curdled. Whey can be used in cheese making, in batters or as a beverage. *See also Buttermilk.*

WHISK The incorporation of air into a mixture to increase its volume and improve its texture.

WHITE PEPPER *See Pepper.*

WHITEBAIT (Fr. BLANCHAILLES) These tiny fish are young herrings and sprats. To cook them they are dipped first in milk then flour, then milk again, and finally deep-fried.

WHITEFISH Written as one word, this name is given to a large and varied family of mainly freshwater fish found in many parts of the world.

One of the most well-known is the lake whitefish from the Great Lakes. There is also a lake herring which has close, dark flesh. European whitefish are particularly abundant in Russia.

Whitefish are richer than most white-fleshed fish, with slightly flaky, pleasant-flavored flesh.

WHITING (Fr. MERLAN) A fish of the cod family, with excellent textured flesh which is ideal for cooking. Whiting is best deep-fried in oil or made into quenelles or terrines.

WHOLE WHEAT (WHOLEMEAL) FLOUR Flour that retains the bran and germ. *See also Flour, Wheat.*

WHORTLEBERRY A name that is occasionally given to both blueberries and cranberries. It makes excellent fruit pies and tarts.

WILD BOAR *See Boar.*

WILD RICE This is not a true rice but an aquatic grass. It is often sold mixed with regular rice and takes about 40 minutes in boiling water to cook.

WILTSHIRE BACON A complete side of pork cured as bacon. The term applies to bacon cured elsewhere other than Wiltshire, in southern England.

WINDSOR SOUP A classic brown soup with a calf's head as a base for the stock. Carrots, onions, celery, lovage and tomato are used for flavor.

W

WINE For centuries, cooks have used wine to marinate meat before cooking because wine makes meat more tender and tasty. It also adds considerable flavor and depth to sauces.

Fortified wines like Port, Sherry and vermouth also add their aromatic fragrance to other foods such as fish, shellfish, melons, custards and ice cream gâteaux.

White wine sauce

1¼ cups/½ pint/300ml fish or
   chicken stock
½ cup/2oz/50g white mushrooms,
   chopped
⅓ cup/3fl oz/75ml heavy (double)
   cream
1 egg yolk
1 tsp cornstarch (cornflour)
salt and pepper
juice of ¼ lemon
pinch of cayenne pepper

Boil the stock with the mushrooms for 5 minutes. Strain into another saucepan. In a bowl, mix together the cream, egg yolk and cornstarch (cornflour) and 6 tablespoons of the reduced stock.

Pour into the remaining stock in the saucepan. Bring to a boil, stirring continuously, to thicken it like a thin custard. Season with salt and pepper.

Add lemon juice and cayenne pepper to taste.

WINE VINEGAR A natural vinegar made when wine is exposed to the air. The bacteria *Mycoderma aceta* changes the alcohol into acetic acid at a temperature of 80°F/26°C.

The specific gravity of the vinegar should be 1.014 to 1.022.

WINGED BEAN, ASPARAGUS PEA A quick-growing member of the pea family that has an asparagus-like flavor when boiled for 5 minutes. It is a disease resistant member of the pea family and high in protein.

It has a four-sided pod which can be green, purple or red. The shoots, blossoms (flowers), root and leaves of the plant are all edible.

WOK A large bowl-shaped Chinese frying pan for tossing and stir-frying food over high heat.

WONTON A Chinese wrapper for different fillings. Wontons can be fried and served as snacks, or poached in soup. Wonton wrappers are available in Chinese stores.

XANTHAN GUM, CORN SUGAR GUM
An additive used as a thickener, stabilizer and emulsifier in dairy products and for salad dressings.

YAK A member of the cattle family bred in Tibet, yak are used for their milk and meat. Tibetans stir-fry small pieces of yak, and boil larger pieces as they only kill the animals when they are old and therefore rather tough.

YAKITORI Japanese kebabs with chicken and vegetables such as mushrooms, onions and bell peppers.

They are marinated in sake, miri, ginger and soy sauce before being broiled (grilled).

YAM The large edible, starchy root of several species of tropical and subtropical plants. It is peeled and boiled like potatoes, made into purées, used in curries or fried like French fries (chips).

YASSA A Senegalese broiled (grilled) mixture of fish, lamb and chicken marinated in lime juice and chili powder.

Y

YEAST A group of minute fungi that ferment sugar solutions to produce carbon dioxide and alcohol.

A yeast plant consists of a single round or oval cell. The individual cells are microscopic, their diameter varying between 1/2,500 to 1/4,000 of 1 in/2.5cm. Under the microscope the plant can be seen to consist of a transparent double-walled cell, inside which there is an aqueous solution called protoplasm. In the protoplasm there are dark spaces known as 'vacuoles' which contain a small dark point termed the nucleus. Yeast contains 12.67 percent protein.

There are wild yeasts and cultivated yeasts, some of which are used for bread-making and beer-brewing while many others are used for the fermentation of wine.

A yeast plant multiplies by budding when cultivated in a suitable medium. Yeast reproduces best at between 75-80°F (24-27°C). Yeast produces the enzyme zymase. *See also Bread.*

YOGURT A fermented milk product that is made by adding a culture containing the bacteria *Lactobacillus bulgaricus* and *Streptococcus thermophilus*, or ready-prepared live yogurt, to warmed milk, then letting it stand in a warm place until set.

Yogurt can be made into a creamy frozen dessert by adding 45-50 percent sugar dissolved in a little fruit syrup or fruit purée.

YOLK Egg yolk contains lecithin, which is a powerful emulsifier so yolks are used to make mayonnaise and hollandaise sauce.

Egg yolks are are also used for custard, sabayon and ice cream as well as mornay and Allemande sauces.

A green ring around the yolk of hard-cooked (hard-boiled) eggs is due to the reaction between sulphide released from the protein in the egg white and iron in the yolk. It can be prevented by boiling for the shortest possible time and cooling the eggs quickly in cold water. *See also Eggs.*

YORK HAM A well-known English ham that is particularly delicious baked in hard apple cider, glazed with spiced honey and served with baked apples stuffed with seedless raisins.

YORKSHIRE PUDDING A batter baked either in a baking dish or roasting pan (tin), or in muffin pans. It is traditionally served with roast beef.

Bread (strong) flour and not self-rising (self-raising) flour must be used so that the batter rises.

ZABAGLIONE A rich Italian dessert made of egg yolks beaten with Marsala wine and sugar until very thick.

ZAKUSKI The older Russian version of hors d'oeuvres, which are usually accompanied by vodka. Zakuski may be modest or a grand spread for a party. There may be eggs, fish, shellfish, salads, kebabs, cold cooked vegetables, small pies, tarts and blinis.

ZAMPONE A traditional north Italian delicacy. It is a boned pig's foot which is filled with ground (minced) pork and seasoning, then simmered for about 2 hours. It is served cut into thick slices.

ZARZUELA A delicious Catalan mixed fish and shellfish stew.

ZEPHYR A quenelle or soufflé lightened with additional egg whites.

ZEST The outer skin of citrus fruits. It is used to flavor sauces and cocktails.

ZHUG A hot condiment or seasoning from the Yemen and also made in other parts of the Middle East. Typical ingredients are chili peppers, garlic, coriander, cardamom and caraway, which are ground or pounded to a paste with lemon juice.

ZINGARA A rich tomato and meat sauce seasoned with paprika and chili pepper and garnished with strips of ham, tongue, gherkin, egg white and truffles. It is said that the chef, Alexis Soyer, took his inspiration from this sauce to create sauce reform.

ZUCCHINI (COURGETTE) A summer squash that is favored for making ratatouille.

ZUNGENWÜRST A German black pudding with the addition of diced tongue; it sometimes also contains liver

Zungenwürst is eaten on bread or as part of an hors d'oeuvre.

ZUPPA INGLESE Although the name means literally 'English soup', this is an Italian dessert. There are many variations but most are similar to the excellent Victorian trifle with very

Z

light sponge soaked in a liqueur and covered with egg custard or confectioners' custard. There may then be a topping of Italian meringue browned briefly in a hot oven, like baked Alaska.

ZYMASE A mixture of enzymes in yeast that are responsible for fermentation. They act on sugar, producing alcohol and carbon dioxide.

SUGAR TEMPERATURES AND STAGES

Temperature Range	Stage	Uses
223-234°F/106-112°C	Thread. Forms a lose, thin thread	For sugar syrups
240°F/116°C	Soft ball. Forms a soft, sticky ball	For buttercreams, fudge and fondant
250°F/123°C	Hard ball. Forms a sticky, firm but pliable ball	For Italian meringue
270- 290°F/132-143°C	Soft crack. Separates into strands that are firm	Soft nougat, some caramels and taffy (toffee)
300-310°F/148-150°C	Hard crack. Separates into brittle threads that shatter easily	For blown, spun and pulled sugar
320-360°F/160-182°C	Caramel. Becomes transparent and changes from light golden to copper color	For caramels and coating molds

Temperature Equivalents

FAHRENHEIT	CELSIUS
32°	0°
41°	5°
50°	10°
59°	15°
68°	20°
77°	25°
86°	30°
95°	35°
104°	40°
113°	45°
122°	50°
131°	55°
140°	60°
149°	65°
158°	70°
167°	75°
176°	80°
185°	85°
194°	90°
203°	95°
212°	100°

RECIPE MEASUREMENT

Metric measurement is the most accurate way of making sure the ingredients are in the correct proportions.

In this book American, British and Metric measures are given. Use one system at a time do **not** mix them.

Spoons
(level) unless indicated

1.25 ml	¼ tsp
2.5ml	½ tsp
5 ml	1 tsp
15 ml	1 tbsp
30 ml	2 tbsp
3 tsp	1 tbsp

Linear Measure

Metric	Imperial
3 mm	⅛ in
5 mm	¼ in
1.2 cm	½ in
2.5 cm	1 in
4 cm	1½ in
5 cm	2 in
6.5 cm	2½ in
7.5 cm	3 in
10 cm	4 in
12.5 cm	5 in
15 cm	6 in
17.5 cm	7 in
20 cm	8 in
22.5 cm	9 in
25 cm	10 in
30 cm	12 in
35 cm	14 in
37.5 cm	15 in
45 cm	18 in
60 cm	24 in
90cm	36 in

EQUIVALENTS OF MAIN INGREDIENTS

Food item	Weight	Metric	Equivalent in cups
almonds, ground	4 oz	100 g	1 cup
breadcrumbs, fresh	2 oz	50 g	1 cup
bulghur	4 oz	100 g	1 cup
butter	8 oz	225 g	1 cup
cashew nuts, ground	4 oz	100 g	1 cup
cheese, grated	4 oz	100 g	1 cup
chocolate, chopped	6 oz	175 g	1 cup
cocoa	4 oz	100 g	1 cup
cornmeal	5 oz	150 g	1 cup
cornstarch	5 oz	150 g	1 cup
couscous	5 oz	150 g	1 cup
cream	8 oz	325 g	1 cup
whole eggs	8 oz	225 g	1 cup
egg whites	8 oz	225 g	1 cup
egg yolks	8 oz	225 g	1 cup
flour wholewheat	5.5 oz	150 g	1 cup
all-purpose flour	4 oz	100 g	1 cup
hazelnuts, ground	4 oz	100 g	1 cup
lentils	6 oz	175 g	1 cup
milk, liquid	8 oz	225 g	1 cup
oil	8 oz	225 g	1 cup
peanuts, whole	6 oz	175 g	1 cup
peas, dry, split	6 oz	175 g	1 cup
potato, powder	6 oz	175 g	1 cup
rice	7 oz	200 g	1 cup
semolina	6 oz	175 g	1 cup
sugar, confectioners'	8 oz	180 g	1 cup
sugar, caster	8 oz	225 g	1 cup
sugar, granulated	8 oz	225 g	1¼ cup
walnuts, ground	7 oz	225 g	1 cup
water	4 oz	100 g	1 cup
yogurt	8 oz	225 g	1 cup (control)
			1 cup

NOTES

NOTES

NOTES

NOTES

NOTES

NOTES

NOTES

NOTES

NOTES

NOTES

NOTES

NOTES

NOTES